LOCAL STATES IN AN IMPERIAL WORLD

The Royal Asiatic Society was founded in 1823 'for the investigation of subjects connected with, and for the encouragement of science, literature and the arts in relation to Asia'. Informed by these goals, the policy of the Society's Editorial Board is to make available in appropriate formats the results of original research in the humanities and social sciences having to do with Asia, defined in the broadest geographical and cultural sense and up to the present day.

The Monograph Board

Professor Francis Robinson CBE, Royal Holloway, University of London (Chair)
Professor Tim Barrett, SOAS, University of London
Dr Evrim Binbaş, Royal Holloway, University of London
Professor Anna Contadini, SOAS, University of London
Professor Michael Feener, National University of Singapore
Dr Gordon Johnson, University of Cambridge
Professor David Morgan, University of Wisconsin-Madison
Professor Rosalind O'Hanlon, University of Oxford
Dr Alison Ohta, Director, Royal Asiatic Society

For a full list of publications by the Royal Asiatic Society see www.royalasiaticsociety.org

LOCAL STATES IN AN IMPERIAL WORLD

IDENTITY, SOCIETY AND POLITICS IN THE
EARLY MODERN DECCAN

∽

Roy S. Fischel

EDINBURGH
University Press

In memory of Tova (1926–2010) and Joseph Antler (1923–2017)

Edinburgh University Press is one of the leading university presses in the UK. We publish academic books and journals in our selected subject areas across the humanities and social sciences, combining cutting-edge scholarship with high editorial and production values to produce academic works of lasting importance. For more information visit our website: edinburghuniversitypress.com

© Roy S. Fischel, 2020, 2022

Edinburgh University Press Ltd
The Tun – Holyrood Road
12 (2f) Jackson's Entry
Edinburgh EH8 8PJ

First published in hardback by Edinburgh University Press 2020

Typeset in 11/13 JaghbUni Regular by
Servis Filmsetting Ltd, Stockport, Cheshire

A CIP record for this book is available from the British Library

ISBN 978 1 4744 3607 6 (hardback)
ISBN 978 1 4744 3608 3 (paperback)
ISBN 978 1 4744 3609 0 (webready PDF)
ISBN 978 1 4744 3610 6 (epub)

The right of Roy S. Fischel to be identified as author of this work has been asserted in accordance with the Copyright, Designs and Patents Act 1988 and the Copyright and Related Rights Regulations 2003 (SI No. 2498).

Contents

List of Illustrations and Tables		vi
Note on Transliteration		vii
Acknowledgements		viii
	Introduction	1
1	Mapping the Deccan	26
2	The Sultanates and the Deccan	66
3	Foreigners, Locals and the World	106
4	Locality, Vernacular and Political Language	149
5	Limitations of the Deccani System	192
6	Conclusion: Hoopoes and Falcons	236
Bibliography		261
Index		293

Illustrations and Tables

Map 1.1 The Deccan	27
Map 5.1 The eastern Deccan	193
Map 5.2 The western Deccan	203
Figure 1.1 Firishta's Deccan	30
Figure 1.2 Subdivisions of the Deccan	54
Figure 3.1 Shah Tahir's family	121
Figure 4.1 Political and cultural centres in the Deccani regions	160
Table 2.1 Alliances in the Deccan, 1542–74	84
Table 2.2 Campaigns in the Deccan, 1542–74: summary	85

Note on Transliteration

Throughout the book, proper names and works are used without diacritics for the sake of simplicity. I have, however, used full transliteration for specific terms and phrases from the sources. The transliteration largely follows the scheme presented in John T. Platts, *A Dictionary of Urdu, Classical Hindi and English*, with minor amendments for the sake of clarity and to reduce confusion. The scheme is detailed in the following table.

ʾ	ء		zh	ژ		q	ق	
ṭ	ٹ	ट	sh	ش		l̤		ळ
th	ٹھ		ś		श	ṇ		ण
ch	ج		ṣ		ष	ñ		ञ
c		च	ṣ	ص		ṅ		ङ
ch		छ	ẓ	ض		w	و	
ḥ	ح		ṭ	ط		r̤		ऋ
ḍ	ڈ		ẓ	ظ		m̥		
dh	ذ		ʿ	ع				
ṛ	ڑ		gh	غ				

Acknowledgements

This book has been in the making for more than a decade, from a modest paper early in my PhD programme at the University of Chicago to its current form. Its completion would not have been possible without the assistance and advice of many along the way. I would first like to express my gratitude to my PhD supervisor, Muzaffar Alam, and to the members of my dissertation committee: John E. Woods at the University of Chicago, Yigal Bronner, currently at the Hebrew University of Jerusalem, and Richard M. Eaton at the University of Arizona. I owe a special debt of gratitude to Philip Engblom for many insightful and delightful hours of reading Marathi texts and for inspiring conversations, and to Thibaut d'Hubert for his support with the mysterious ways of Dakhani. I also thank Elena Bashir, Orit Bashkin, the late Steven Collins, Cornell Fleischer, Jason Grunebaum, Mark Lycett, Velcheru Narayana Rao and Gary Tubb, as well as André Wink at the University of Wisconsin-Madison for guidance and many suggestions. Of the many friends from PhD days at Chicago, special thanks are due to Nick Abbott, Whitney Cox, Ferenc Csirkés, Abhishek Kaicker, Rajeev Kinra, Elizabeth Lhost and Hasan Siddiqui. I wish to express my indebtedness to Yohanan Friedmann, my first teacher of anything South Asian, and to David Shulman, who ignited my interest in India and encouraged me to pursue this direction.

My research in India and the United Kingdom has been made possible with the support of Elise Auerbach of the American Institute of Indian Studies and Tarini Bedi at the Committee of South Asian Studies at the University of Chicago. In Hyderabad, I wish to thank Dr Madam S. A. Kausar of the Salar Jung Museum, Dr T. Purandhar of the (then) Andhra Pradesh State Archives and Research Institute, and Madam Rafat Rizwana of the Andhra Pradesh (currently Telangana) Oriental Manuscript and Research Institute. Gurram Seeta Ramulu extended his help and friendship during my stay in Hyderabad. I wish to also thank Dr S. M. Bhave of Bharat Itihas Samshodhak Mandal in Pune, the staff of the Asian and African Studies Reading Room at the British Library in London, and Jim

Acknowledgements

Nye of the Regenstein Library at the University of Chicago. I also wish to thank Hannah Archambault, Mark Brand, Jeevan Deol and Carl Ernst for helping me to obtain certain manuscripts.

Since joining the History Department at SOAS University of London in 2012, I have had the pleasure of enjoying the intriguing academic environment and the benefit of working with remarkable colleagues and students. Several colleagues and friends at SOAS and elsewhere have been of great help in the long process of turning my PhD dissertation into a book by supporting, commenting and encouraging along the way: Crispin Branfoot, Sara Collins, Jorge Flores, Jan-Peter Hartung, Andrea Janku, Ceyda Karamursel, Jon Keune, David Lunn, Vayu Naidu, Eleanor Newbigin, John Parker, Amrita Shodhan, Pushkar Sohoni, Shabnum Tejani and Phillip Wagoner. Katherine Butler Schofield, Gijs Kruijtzer, Derek Mancini-Lander, Rosalind O'Hanlon, Francesca Orsini and Richard David Williams were of particular help in formulating parts of my research and ideas, for which I am grateful. At the Royal Asiatic Society, I wish to thank Evrim Binbaş, Alison Ohta, Peter Robb, Francis Robinson, Nilanjan Sarkar, and members of the Monograph Board for their confidence and encouragement.

Finally, I would like to thank my mother Ruthi and my sister Zohar for their endless care and support from another country. To Ilanit Loewy Shacham, an immense source of not only moral and intellectual support but also true friendship for over a decade, I am eternally grateful. Last, but not least, I am truly indebted to Ibai Madariaga Vergara for unlimited attention, patience, endurance and care, without which all this would not have happened.

Introduction

Travelling across the Deccan Plateau of India, one encounters a somewhat confusing environment. On entering the region, say crossing the steep Sahyadri Mountains on the Mumbai–Pune Expressway, the landscape changes only slowly and gradually. Even if not as monotonous as the great Gangetic Plains of north India, the terrain remains relatively uniform for long distances. Yet, within this vast plateau, cultural markers change sharply and rapidly. For one, the region hosts some of India's shiniest IT centres, most notably in Hyderabad and Pune, alongside of some of India's most impoverished rural communities.[1] Beyond this cliché of India's economic disparities, the cultural and linguistic diversity of the region is easily noticeable. When crossing almost invisible state borders, which do not usually follow natural features, the script on the road signs changes immediately and one enters a visibly different linguistic domain. However, these seemingly uninterrupted linguistic spaces are not as even as they look. The region is dotted with towns where the dominant signage is in a language (and script) other than that of the state. In certain places, Urdu in Nastaliq and Hindi in Devanagari are predominant. Even these are not simply islands in the wider space. On the contrary, spaces are shared between all linguistic markers. They are occupied and visualised by scripts that link them to separate traditions. Even the Char Minar, the most recognisable landmark of the Muslim history of Hyderabad, shares its space with the Sri Bhagyalaksmi Temple, decorated by saffron flags and with signage in English, Devanagari and Telugu but (strategically) not in Nastaliq.

Linguistic diversity not only marks separated places, but also indicates connections. In certain settlements around the Deccan, for example, in sites in Aurangabad (Maharashtra), Hyderabad (Telangana) or Gulbarga (Karnataka), one is likely to see signs in Nastaliq, creating visual links between those places. Another level of cross-border linguistic connectivity is created by the use of English, and to some degree Hindi, both visible everywhere even if not spoken by all. If we tried to map the Deccan according to language use, then each language would demonstrate a distinct geography. Marathi, Telugu and Kannada would correspond with the states of Maharashtra, Telangana and Karnataka, respectively, although communities of speakers of each language can be found in all neighbouring states and beyond. Urdu links localities and communities all over the Deccan, with centres in north India and across the border in Pakistan. The domain of Hindi is, of course, all-Indian, even if it never stopped being contested. English brings the locality into global networks. Unity and diversity, marked spatially and connected to significantly different geographies, are an important cultural marker of life in the contemporary Deccan. Each creates visual and cultural space of its own, which corresponds and overlaps only in part with the others.

The cultural and linguistic diversity cutting through today's Deccan is not a new issue that has emerged with the creation of language-based states in independent India. Cultural and linguistic diversity is the culmination of centuries-long processes that brought together social and cultural elements to the very same territory. The existence (and coexistence) of parallel social groups in a shared space, each with its distinct cultural, linguistic and religious identity, has been a basic feature of life in the Deccan for many centuries. Similarly complex was the relations between cultural spaces, often marked by language, in the early modern period.

In the sixteenth and seventeenth centuries, the Deccan was politically, socially and culturally divided along lines not dissimilar to those of the early twenty-first century. A central characteristic of the political system of the time was the emergence of five contemporaneous dynasties in the region: the Nizam Shahs of Ahmadnagar; the ʿImad Shahs of Berar; the Baridis of Bidar; the ʿAdil Shahs of Bijapur; and the Qutb Shahs of Golkonda. Of these, only Ahmadnagar, Bijapur and Golkonda survived as viable states to the late sixteenth century. The sultanates did not create homogeneous spaces, but hosted diverse society with members of various elite groups sharing stakes in the political system. Nor did the political boundaries create discrete spaces. Rather, certain groups resided and worked across boundaries, sharing cultural identity and political aspirations with their peers elsewhere. These groups varied significantly from one another in belief, language, origins and identity. These distinctions were clearly pronounced and became central in shaping political action and symbols. Within the relatively weak political system in the early modern Deccan, groups were powerful enough to promote their own agenda; no one gained long-term advantage or monopolised the space. Subsequently, not only could various groups assert their own identities, but these identities were widely acknowledged and incorporated into the history and political idiom of the region.

Introduction

The Deccan sultanates present an interesting case study within the early modern world. Emerging from the collapse of the erstwhile Bahmani sultanate in the closing decades of the fifteenth century, they all inherited a pre-existing socio-political structure that consisted of loosely defined identity-based parties, often at odds with one another. These groups can be clustered around Iranian migrants (Foreigners) and local Muslims (Deccanis, usually associated with Ethiopian military slaves), each representing an opposite pole: the Foreigners operated within trans-regional Persian-speaking networks, whereas the Deccanis were looking inwardly, into the Deccan. Their sense of locality was expressed by, among other things, the increasing use of Dakhani, a language that originated in north India but soon struck roots and became the vernacular widely used by the local Muslim population.

The issue of Deccanis and Foreigners represents only part of the picture as Muslims remained a small minority in the Deccan. The sultanates, as the Bahmani sultanate before them, did not uproot pre-existing elites. On the contrary, local, non-Muslim elites were increasingly integrated into the political system. One reason was necessity: administrative positions and taxation were well established, and removing this expertise would be inefficient. Moreover, the competition among the Deccan sultanates and between them and their ambitious neighbours, most notably Vijayanagara, Gujarat and the Mughal Empire, required the maximisation of resources. Indeed, non-Muslim elites were integrated into state service in increasing numbers. These groups included, among others, landed magnates such as Marathas, post-Vijayanagara potentates (*nāyaka*s) and Telugu hereditary landed elites (*nāyakwaṛīs*), as well as service elites such as Marathi- and Telugu-speaking Brahmins. These elite groups brought with them expertise, but also introduced linguistic and cultural sensitivities, which were shaped by centuries-long cultural processes in the region. Certain local elites articulated their identities in terms of language, historical memory and territory. However, not all of them worked on the same terms, and great variety can be observed in the treatment of space and language. The parallel processes created the Deccan as a political system built upon a complex web of spatial sensitivities, only partially overlapping, and not always corresponding with the political map of the time. This multi-layered analysis stands at the heart of this study.

Scholarship of the Deccan

The historiography of the Deccan sultanates thus far remains limited and lags behind that on the rest of the subcontinent. This, in part, is due to the motivations behind the writing of history in modern times. In South Asia, as much as elsewhere, colonial and post-colonial histories are preferred over the pre-colonial period as they are central to the understanding of the contemporary.[2] Furthermore, sources are relatively abundant, and, no less important, many sources are in English. Within the relatively limited writing on the pre-colonial, in particular, the Muslim-ruled parts of the subcontinent, the metropolitan north, especially the Mughal Empire, enjoyed more attention than the south. This was aided by the fact that the Mughals eventually took over almost the entirety of the subcontinent, even if they failed to hold it for long.[3] At the other end of the subcontinent, Vijayanagara and its successor Nayaka states attracted much attention. For many, this derived from its perception as 'the last Hindu kingdom'; for others, their position close to the southern coast and consequent links to international trade and European endeavour in south India brought them to scholarly attention.[4]

Located in between, the Deccan sultanates did not enjoy much attention and remained to a large degree understudied. The sources for the study of this region are relatively scarce. More significant is that within the cultural and political climate of India since independence, and even more so in recent years, the sultanates became orphaned so to speak, with no one claiming to possess their legacy. Since the 1950s, south India has been divided into a state based on vernacular lines: Maharashtra for Marathi, Karnataka for Kannada and Telugu for Andhra Pradesh (which included Telangana until its separation from Andhra in 2014). Accordingly, the study of vernacular sources and the non-Muslim past gained precedence over Persian, Dakhani and Muslim dynasties, including the Deccan sultanates. A good example is the scholarship on Maharashtra. From the nineteenth century, indigenous as well as Western scholarship focused on the Maratha Empire that first emerged in the mid-seventeenth century and became a significant power in the eighteenth century. With this focus, the sultanates of Ahmadnagar and Bijapur, in whose service the Marathas began their career, were examined mostly within their role in early Maratha history.[5]

Disregarding the immediate vernacular past, the Deccan sultanates were linked to the framework of communalism. These narratives painted the sultanates in broad brush, labelling them as Muslim states, and positioning them in the frontline of the war against Hindu-ruled Vijayanagara.

Introduction

This image is heavily distorted and based on selective readings of the sources. These selections were used to express a concept of society defined by communal hostility, rather than nuanced historical process.[6] Certain post-independence historians aspired to negate this understanding by applying close and careful reading of the sources, but even they did not always escape such sentiments.[7] The most substantial attempt to integrate the past of the Muslim-ruled states into the present was made in Andhra Pradesh, where the government sponsored the publication of the *History of Medieval Deccan, 1295–1724*. The chapters of these two hefty, oft-quoted, volumes discuss various dynasties in addition to their cultural products (language, literature, architecture), and are still one of the most exhaustive sources for many aspects of regional history.[8] Additional studies from the decades after independence linked the Telugu language to the Qutb Shahi sultans of Golkonda.[9] These efforts were integrated into the wider attempt to build the Telugu identity in a historically divided region. Furthermore, Hyderabad, the state capital, had, and still has, significant Muslim populations, whose belonging to the new state was crucial.

The result of these considerations and limited interest was the creation of a handful of monographs in the 1960s and 1970s, each discussing one sultanate in isolation. The main focus of these works remained limited to traditional themes such as political, military and dynastic histories. The narratives present a chronological summary of events and are heavily based on Persian chronicles. Radhey Shyam composed three monographs on the history of Maharashtra, covering the Kingdom of Ahmadnagar, neighbouring Khandesh and Malik Ambar, who led the Nizam Shahi sultanate in the early seventeenth century.[10] The Sultanate of Golkonda was the subject of two monographs, one by Abdul Majid Siddiqui, first published in Urdu and later in English translation, and another by Haroon Khan Sherwani. Focusing on a chronological political history of the Qutb Shahi dynasty, Sherwani employs a wide array of sources that go beyond the limited corpus of Persian chronicles, making this rich monograph one of the best of its kind.[11] The city of Hyderabad attracted scholarly interest due to its continuous importance since Qutb Shahi times, much in contrast to the marginal position of Ahmadnagar, Bidar, Bijapur and Ellichpur. These works mostly provide lists of buildings and personalities, as well as photographic albums and popular histories of the city.[12]

The Sultanate of Bijapur, too, was the centre of a handful of monographs. Two books by D. C. Verma deal first with the political and diplomatic history of the sultanate, and second with social, economic and cultural issues; however, it lacks the depth of Sherwani's work. M. A. Nayeem's monograph discusses the diplomatic relations of Bijapur. A clear summary of Bijapur's political history can be found in Richard Eaton's *Sufis of Bijapur*; however, the main interest lies not in the political history of the city, but with religious-social life.[13] Social issues were also discussed in the works of Sadiq Naqvi, one on the Foreigners in Bijapur and Golkonda, the other on the religious institutions of Golkonda; both are more descriptive than analytical.[14] In addition, several works present individual biographies, typically of people whose lives attract the attention of politically minded readers of the twentieth century. Most notable of these are the warrior and military slave Malik Ambar, who successfully resisted the Mughals; Chand Bibi, a queen and warrior, who stood against the Mughals; the romantic character of the sultan-poet Muhammad Quli Qutb Shah, founder of Hyderabad; and Madanna, a Brahmin who became prime minister and the most powerful figure in the late Qutb Shahi kingdom.[15] Like many of the monographs mentioned above, these works remain highly descriptive.

In recent decades, new interest in the Deccan sultanates, its social and political history and its cultural legacy has emerged, leading to significant new research on the region. These recent writings introduce new questions to the study of the Deccan. No less significantly, they re-examine the social and cultural boundaries between religious communities and states. In 1985, Catherine B. Asher challenged the easiness and clear-cut distinction between the categories 'Hindu' and 'Muslim'. Analysing the famous structure in Vijayanagara known as the Elephant Stables, she suggests that using these categories 'provides sectarian connotations that likely misrepresent the artisan's, designer's and patron's original conception'.[16] Additional studies on the visual arts of the Deccan question old assertions and offer a richer understanding of the region and its composite, rather than antagonistic, culture. Several PhD dissertations, books and articles have conducted in-depth analysis of styles and content throughout the Deccan, and the arts of the Deccan was the focus of an exhibition at the Metropolitan Museum of Art in New York in 2015.[17]

No less important were recent developments in the introduction of a wider, more flexible social approach to the historiography of the Deccan. Phillip Wagoner and Richard Eaton demonstrate in various studies, separately and together, that the boundaries between what was considered to be the 'Muslim' and 'Hindu' realm were permeable to goods, people and technologies, as well as symbols and idioms. Their studies not only challenged the relations between the so-called 'Hindu' and 'Muslim' states of the peninsula on the opposite banks of the Krishna River, but enabled the integration of the pre-Muslim past into the history of the sultanates, creating bridges over the temporal gap in the historiography.[18] The very catego-

Introduction

ries of 'Hindu' and 'Muslim' as the sole, or even dominant, determinants in social and political issues have been further questioned. Cynthia Talbot demonstrates the importance of ethnic and other identity markers.[19] Eaton famously disputes the seemingly religious actions of temple desecration, presenting it as politically motivated.[20] Finally, Gijs Kruijtzer discusses identities in seventeenth-century south India, suggesting social divisions that go beyond inter-communal ones.[21] These recent studies open new analytical frameworks and questions for further research. Yet certain issues remain unchallenged. Studies of the economic and administrative structures of the Deccan, abundant in the Mughal case, are yet to be conducted in the Deccan.[22] Another lacuna is with regard to the overview of the Deccan as a region. The various works look either at the Deccan as a clearly defined region or at each sultanate separately. However, they do not consider the particular characteristic of each sultanate in relation to one another in a comparative way.[23]

Place, Space and the Deccan

With these lacunae in mind, this study aims at examining the history of the Deccan sultanates within the wider social and political structure of the region and its connections both to the world around it and to the histories of the region itself. Taking the region as an analytical unit, I reject the latent preconception that, maybe paradoxically, assumes great similarities among the sultanates and, at the same time, treats each sultanate in isolation. Instead, I suggest taking the particularities and idiosyncrasies of each sultanate into consideration, while placing it against the background of their shared histories and the space in which they were operating not only in its physical sense, but also in the meaning it carries. This requires some elaboration.

Until fairly recently, scholars of the Deccan have had limited use of the physical space as a factor in their analysis of Deccani history. Often opening their narratives with a description of topographical, geological and climatic characteristics, these were not integrated into the research beyond the immediate impact they may have had.[24] The limited place given to the physical environment in historical analyses is not unique to the Deccan. The geographer Edward Soja lamented the disregard of space in the social sciences altogether.[25] More specifically, Alan Baker notices a 'restricted view of geography either as the physical stage upon which the drama of history is enacted or as a framework of physical frontiers and political boundaries within which history is to some extent contained'.[26]

Place and space, however, are more than only a physical stage. They also carry meaning. Defining place as an object to which value is attached and space as the geometric arrangement of places, Yi-Fu Tuan suggests that the understanding of place and space derives from sensual perception. With the human ability to perceive realities beyond immediate perception, he continues, space as a meaningful category expanded as the individual can identify with, and emotionally attach themselves to, complex spaces. This attachment allows humans to build group identities based on spatial distinction, linking 'us' to 'here' and 'them' to 'there', that go far beyond the immediate environment.[27] John Agnew complicates the link between space and people. He suggests that the sense of place (geographical or social 'structure of feeling' to everyday places) does not remain a closed unit, but is projected to wider scales, regional or national. The locale (that is, 'the setting in which social relations are constituted') is embedded in the place, but is shaped by social and economic processes on a wider scale, widening the sense of place itself. Place, he continues:

> involves a conception of 'topological' space in which diverse scales are brought together through networks of 'internal' and 'external' ties in defining geographical variation in social phenomena ... Geography, therefore, is implicated *in* social processes rather than being a 'backdrop' or a 'board' *upon* which social processes are inscribed.[28]

To complicate the picture, place and space are not only synchronic, but are also part of a diachronic process. Doreen Massey argues that places are always hybrid and 'constructed out of articulations of social relations ... which are not only internal to that locale but which link them to elsewhere'. This interconnectedness, she continues, has also existed in the past, adding temporal aspect to the understanding of place. Places, then, stretch through time; they comprise the combination of 'particular articulation of social relations' and the way they read their own pasts. Identifying a place, then, is:

> always inevitably an intervention not only into geography but also, at least implicitly, into the (re)telling of the historical constitution of the present. It is another move in the continuing struggle over the delineation and characterisation of space-time.[29]

This addition of the temporal to the understanding of time emphasises place as a process that involves multiple dimensions and trajectories.[30]

Space, Massey suggests elsewhere, is the product of inter-relations and interactions on different scales (in line with Agnew's definition). As such, it is 'the sphere of the possibility of the existence of multiplicity in the sense of contemporaneous plurality', therefore, it is heterogeneous and contains parallel distinct trajectories. Space is therefore never finished

Introduction

or complete, but is constantly changing, 'always in the process of being made'.[31] While analysing space with a certain part of contemporary politics in mind, these assertions can be of much use in the way we read the past, as recently demonstrated by Francesca Orsini. Rejecting the dominant view of world literature as emanating from a Western core and spread into what was perceived as the periphery (even if it accounts for most of the world and its literatures), she argues that in north India the multiplicity of languages and literary traditions, often with blurry and permeable boundaries, coexisted and constantly interacted. They further operated on distinct yet inter-related trajectories that at times brought them to mutual recognition, but other times excluded one another. Orsini concludes that:

> Thinking of space as 'the pluralities of stories and trajectories so far' helps us conceive of world literature as situated, plural, necessarily multilingual, always-in-the-making. It helps us hold *together* local and cosmopolitan perspectives, trust the local texts and genres.[32]

Orsini's convincing analysis can be extended to explain historical trajectories in the early modern Deccan. As we will see in the coming chapters, the social and political system of the sultanates was one of multiplicity. Comprising a host of groups, not only among the general population but also within the elites, the upper echelons of society were complex and changeable. Elite groups hailed from a variety of backgrounds and locations, and continued to develop and interact with their environs according to different trajectories, sometimes at odds with one another. Each group had its own idea of the space it was occupying and its meaning; each had its own pasts and memories thereof. All together they created a multi-layered and multidimensional map, making questions of territoriality and political identity particularly problematic. The picture was made ever more complex when we consider the place of the Deccan within the global system of the time and the historiography thereof.

The Deccan Sultanates and the Early Modern World

Situating the Deccan sultanates with their complex spatial setting in the world takes us to the context within which they operated. Considering the global perspective of the time, the Deccan sultanates were thriving in what became generally accepted in the historiography as the early modern period.[33] Twentieth-century historiography marks the beginning of this historical moment with the discovery of maritime routes between Europe and America (1492), and India (1498). These events not only mark new levels of global connectivity, but were also seen as the first steps in

European expansion. The rapid growth of European states, both maritime (first Spain and Portugal, later England, the Dutch Republic and France) and land-based (the Austrian Habsburgs and Russia) brought historians to identify the early modern period with a particular political formation, the empire. The new early modern empires and their expansion were linked linearly to nineteenth-century Western imperialism and colonialism.[34] Within this premise, several theories tried to explain the success of the early modern European state. One direction was the concept of 'military revolution', first introduced by Michael Roberts and further developed by Geoffrey Parker. This concept linked new technologies, in particular, gunpowder-based, and the increased size of armies to new military and financial institutions developed to support the armies and their training, encouraging the growth of a new and centralised kind of state.[35] The role of technological change in the emergence of the shifting global power balance in favour of Western Europe was further developed by William McNeil and Carlo Cipolla, emphasising the European military revolution as a major factor in the Rise of the West.[36] Marxist historians, most notably Immanuel Wallerstein, emphasised the development of the capitalist economy and the role of trade. Wallerstein links the sixteenth-century expansion to the success of the new capitalist endeavour in subjugating the rest of the world to a West-centred system that imposed a marginal position on non-European societies.[37]

In recent decades, historians began to think about the period as a whole, and the position of empires within it, in more complex ways. Not only technology and economy, but also geographical, sociological and ecological factors were introduced into the discussion.[38] In addition, ideology and imperial identity were brought to the foreground. These aspects were developed by Anthony Pagden. Diverging from the tradition that looks at the early modern as precursor of future Western imperialism, he looks at the period on its own terms. Examining what constituted an early modern empire, Pagden suggests that it consisted of diverse territories under a single legislative authority. The empire became increasingly identified with individual, authoritative rule under divine mandate. This ideology relies greatly on the interpretation of Roman ideology and the way it was perceived by early modern European thinkers, and was further pushed by intra-European competition.[39] To him, early modern empires were a solely European phenomenon that emphasise European exceptionalism.

However, it was not only Europe that saw the emergence of empire in the early modern period as similar trends can be traced in the Muslim world. Parallel to the rise of new states in Europe, the Muslim world, too, was

Introduction

an arena of expansionist empires. By the turn of the seventeenth century, most of the Muslim world fell under the dominion of strong, expansionist dynasties: the Ottomans in southeastern Europe, North Africa, the Levant and southern Russia; the Safavids in Iran; and the Mughals in north India. The three empires, sometimes with the inclusion of the Central Asian Shibanids, were often analysed collectively,[40] and their rise was treated as a singular historical phenomenon. Borrowing from European historiographical frameworks, technological and economic changes were put at the front. Notably, Marshall Hodgson followed reasoning similar to that of McNeill and Cipolla, promoting technological change as a major factor in the development of these 'Gunpowder Empires'.[41] Others followed Marxist frameworks to define the three empires as a single category, based on land taxation and state property within an Islamic legal system.[42]

The rejection of the technology-heavy theory, as well as the reliance on categories of land taxation in the 1980s and 1990s, led way to a more nuanced discussion in which intellectual and institutional factors were taken into account. Richard Bulliet links the new states of the sixteenth century to the process of re-centralisation of religious institutions after the Mongol crisis of the thirteenth century. The new institutional framework enabled Muslim polities to profess their control over the religious institutions, thus gaining a new path through which they could increase their authority over state and society.[43] This indicates not only similarity between the three empires, but also communication and mutual influence achieved by the circulation of texts and scholars.[44] Giancarlo Casale suggests that religious crystallisation was not the opening point but the end result of the political process of the period, part of the wider process of legalisation and bureaucratisation of the three empires.[45] This comparative framework that sees the three empires as an analytical unit comprising dynasties similar in their belief, connections to the Turco-Mongol past, and their reliance on Perso-Islamic traditions still produces interesting scholarship, with constant analysis of their links and influences.[46] Responding to European historiography, however, these works demonstrate an insular approach: the so-called Muslim empires are compared with one another, and reference to Europe remains as the remote model or in the context of European expansion.

From the 1990s, a new perspective tried to tie those two worlds together as one global phenomenon. New studies rejected Marxian and Weberian models that promoted European exceptionalism and turned Europe into the standard according to which all looked primitive in what David Ludden called 'Western master-narrative of global modernity'.[47]

Instead, a more balanced view emerged, employing the broader concept of 'multiple modernities'.[48] Accordingly, global histories no longer identify Europe as the sole model of early modern empire. In lieu of this, the early modern came to be interpreted as a global phenomenon shared by independent, yet strongly connected actors, none of which had a decisive advantage over the others.[49]

The early modern–empire nexus, then, became the general framework for the study of this period. To some, mostly Europeanists, Europe remained the main power behind the global process.[50] The narrative of the rise of the West was not completely abandoned; at times, the new Eurasian framework seemed almost lip service, while keeping Europe in the centre.[51] A more successfully decentralised view has emerged, marking the understanding of modernity towards what Sanjay Subrahmanyam describes as conjunctural global process.[52] In this process, worldwide interactions of unprecedented intensity and regularity brought an exchange on a global scale. Consequently, the focus shifts from a Eurocentric to a global, or at least Eurasian, model of empire.

Charles Parker characterises the early modern system in four forms of interaction: networks of commercial exchange; large-scale migration; biological exchanges; and transfers of knowledge, without any part of the system gaining dominance.[53] Within this system, empire emerged as the most significant political formation, almost synonymous with the period as a whole. An archetypical, non-region-specific empire can be characterised as an extensive geographical spread that embraced several cultural domains and ecologies, as well as a variety of ethnic groups. It required ideology as a motive to claim extensive or universal dominance, in itself a theme known from empires throughout history. Furthermore, an empire is defined by suzerainty, the overlordship over other polities allowed the emperor to declare himself 'king over kings'. This notion of hierarchy encompasses not only the sovereign and tributary kings, but also down to the bureaucratic structure, assisting in the creation of centralised and vertical structures of power. All these relied on the creation of a symbolic language. The crystallisation of imperial ideology reshaped thought and encouraged the transition to sovereign-mandated religious and cultural conservatism.[54] Derived from the hierarchical nature is also the ever-dynamic relations between centre and periphery, or 'insiders', 'outsiders' and various degrees in between, at times quite testing. Without fully absorbing the periphery, rulers had to create a reasonably acceptable ideology and sound policies to enable these relations between the sides. At the same time, their appeal could expand far beyond their actual political or military influence.[55]

Introduction

The new Eurasian framework became central to contemporary historiography of non-European empires. Most notably in the Ottoman case, recent scholarship takes this model as the framework within which they analyse a variety of issues, adding to our conceptualisation of what empire means. To use Kaya Şahin's words, 'the term *early modern Eurasia* provides a meaningful geographical and cultural space within which the histories of the new empires may be placed'. Eurasian polities, he continues, can be included in a shared time–space development as Europe. They shared parallel and roughly simultaneous developments, including territorial consolidation, the use of gunpowder, bureaucratisation, commercialisation, popular literature and vernacularisation; agricultural expansion; the creation of global networks that increased access to more resources; and the consolidation of legitimised central power attached to territory.[56] Other studies follow the same path, implicitly tying Asian empires to models of Eurasian early modern empire and further promoting the idea of connectivity.[57]

The similar framework of the imperial early modern period is prevalent in the historiography farther east. In a somewhat apologetic article, Rudi Matthee complains that even though it is considered to be one of the three 'Gunpowder Empires', the Safavids are hardly analysed in comparison with the Ottomans and Mughals. Using similar criteria to what we have seen before, he reintroduces the Safavids as an equivalent empire to the other two.[58] Similarly, Dirk Kolff analyses the short-lived state established by Sher Shah (d. 1545) in north India within the imperial framework, stressing his efforts to centralise administration, monopolise power, and to position the rulers in the centre of a vertical structure that came to replace pre-existing horizontal alliances.[59] Recent works on early modern South Asia are strongly located within this discourse. Most notable in that regard is the work of Sanjay Subrahmanyam, who links early modern India to a wider net of global historiography, both by means of comparison or within a comparative framework.[60] To this is often wedded the concept of cosmopolitanism as an intellectual framework with which to explore the world of communication and exchange that emerged in the world of the Indian Ocean in relation to the arrival of the Portuguese in the region.[61]

The Current Study

The discussion of the early modern world, then, emphasises empire as the main framework within which early modern polities are examined. This, however, does not leave much place for polities within this scheme that would be considered as mere prey in the hunting grounds of an empire, or, like Sher Shah, a failed attempt to become one. However, even in regions well integrated into the world system, empires cannot define all political formation; some of these non-imperial entities continued to exist even under increasing pressures.[62] Casale suggests that by identifying the early modern Muslim world with the Mughals, Safavids and Ottomans, 'we risk over-simplifying a story that is in fact a good deal more geographically extensive, culturally diverse and politically dynamic than might otherwise be imagined'. He nevertheless chooses to focus on these very three empires.[63]

In this study I argue that the Deccan sultanates are an example of non-imperial political organisations in the early modern world. The key features of these sultanates were multiplicity and negotiation rather than expansion and centralisation. The Deccan hosted many centres and dynasties: Ahmadnagar, Bijapur and Golkonda, alongside the weaker Bidar and Ellichpur. They all accepted the multiplicity and none tried to build an empire by taking over the region in its entirety. Internally, too, sultans had a weaker position in relation to their elites in comparison with the Mughal emperor or the Ottoman sultan. They were, therefore, less able to enforce their will and create coercive state mechanisms and a strict hierarchy in which all elements would participate as parts of one coherent whole. Instead, the ruling houses had a special role in maintaining a delicate equilibrium between various actors by taking into consideration each group both politically and symbolically. Each of these actors asserted their own position and operated within its own understanding of space; this space did not necessarily overlap with the other groups or with the sultans. The multiple trajectories operating in a complex space played a major role in shaping the political idiom of the sultanates in a unique way, marking it as distinct from the top-down system typical of, or aspired by, the contemporary empires. This created state systems which were highly functional – after all, the sultanates of Golkonda and Bijapur survived for two centuries in a highly competitive environment – yet profoundly different from early modern empires in terms of state mechanisms, socio-political structure and political idiom.

This is not to say that all these social, cultural and political trajectories were unique to the Deccan. Some similarities can be found with neighbouring empires, notably the Mughal Empire. Regional and elite identities could be naturally found everywhere. They were taken into consideration in the shaping of Mughal rule in the provinces.[64] Various cultural sensitivities were practised and promoted even within the imperial centres.[65] Furthermore, like the Deccan, north India was the arena for multiple linguistic and literary traditions.[66] Yet several points distinguish

Introduction

the Deccan from north India, and, accordingly, the political systems that developed in both places. The Deccan is marked by heterogeneity. Developed not around one historical core region of the kind marked by Romila Thapar as relatively homogeneous,[67] but rather within changing parallel centres that emerged relatively late, this plurality is inscribed into the history of the region. Regional identities and the politicisation of the vernacular has a longer history in the Deccan, and the nexus of political–linguistic–territorial identities was further developed in this very region. The nature of this multilingualism was also considerably different. Orsini suggests that in the north, Persian, 'the dominant High Language of literary and political discourse', circulated widely, resulting in the creation of less Sanskritised literary cultures.[68] In the south, the persistence of non-Muslim-ruled courts external to the sultanates, most importantly Vijayanagara and later *nāyaka* and Maratha courts, where Persian may have been influential but definitely not dominant, brought the development of vernacular literature in parallel with, and with less interaction with Dakhani and Persian, and more Sanskritised.[69] Consequently, southern vernaculars were predominantly, even if not solely, the domains of non-Muslims,[70] only adding to the sense of proliferation of parallel cultures.

The result of these processes was not only increased multiplicity, but also the persistence of horizontal identities and networks that were not confined to any geographical and political region. Combined with the weaker political authority in each centre, it resulted in more bargaining power to the elites, bringing competition of the kind that disappeared in north India by the mid-sixteenth century. As a result, the weaker states of the Deccan had to use a variety of strategies and methods to secure their precarious position, which were significantly different than the growing Mughal tendency to centralisation. Not only that, the multiplicity of political centres brought significant variations in strategies and structures between the sultanates.

My intention here is not to systematically map all trajectories and impacts of this complex and multi-layered political system, but rather to offer a general framework for the analysis of the non-imperial environment when the sultanates were at their prime. Opening with the foundation of the sultanates in the 1480s, most attention in this study will be given to the period following the collapse of Vijayanagara in 1565, which released the sultanates from the shadow of their most powerful neighbour and allowed them to act independently. This independence, however, was heavily curtailed by the Mughal campaign of the 1630s, which culminated in the annihilation of the Nizam Shahi dynasty of Ahmadnagar (1636), and more so from the late 1650s when Bijapur and Golkonda were facing existential crises.

A major challenge for this study is related to reconstructing the identities and relations of all those involved. There is an inherent bias within the archive. In the Deccan, the writing of self-aware history, or the conscious attempt to record events in a chronological fashion, was limited to Persian. The genre of the chronicle (*tārīkh*) was not transferred into other linguistic traditions. While this is not unique to the Deccan, the restriction it puts on regional historiography is more significant. In the Mughal Empire, Persian was fostered as the only language of empire. Consequently, both Muslims and non-Muslims, locals and Foreigners, supporters of the Mughal house and its opponents, participated in writing in that language.[71] In the Deccan sultanates, Persian remained the marker not of imperial culture but of a partisan identity, limiting writing in that language to the Foreigners alone. Therefore, all identified major court chronicles were associated with them, including Sayyid ʿAli Tabatabaʾi, Rafiʿ al-Din Shirazi, Nizam al-Din Ahmad Shirazi, Muhammad Qasim Firishta and Muhammad Hashim Fuzuni Astarabadi. Their writings created the predictable biases and lacunae. First, where political circumstances did not encourage the settlement of Foreigners, no chronicles were composed, most notably in the parts of Maharashtra that were not under Mughal rule in the seventeenth century. Second, chronicles present a pro-Foreigner, and more so anti-Deccani and anti-Ethiopian perspective, while mostly disregarding non-Muslims. Even the Persian sources themselves do not always converge to tell one decisive story, pointing at what Nilanjan Sarkar calls 'the impossibility of arriving at a conclusive history'.[72]

These issues leave us with serious lacunae regarding some of the elites in the Deccan, even if careful reading between the lines and a sensitive analysis of the actions described in the Persian sources provide some information, in particular, regarding points of contestation. Fortunately, an array of sources in other languages provides alternative perspectives, even if those are not always obvious and are rather limited in their perspective. Sources in Dakhani were usually produced in Sufi or courtly environments, but without much reference to the political circumstances in which they were created. Awaiting further in-depth study, they do provide glimpses into some sensitivities of the group. Maratha sources, including Marathi *bakhar*s and the Sanskrit *Sivabharat* date to the very last years of the Deccan sultanates and the following decades. Yet they contain valuable information on Maratha memory of the Nizam Shahi and ʿAdil Shahi realms, and the position of Shahji and Shivaji Bhonsle within their political system. Local histories developed in early modern South Asia, present-

Introduction

ing the historical memories of certain local classes, recorded in Marathi, Telugu and Tamil.[73] Some of these narratives were collected by the team of Colonel Colin Mackenzie in the early nineteenth century, however, these are limited to territories under British control at the time, all away from the core regions of the Deccan sultanates. Nevertheless, they provide an interesting idea of how the sultanates were remembered by local elites from their margins. Lastly, external sources written by Mughal historians, Safavid literati and European travellers add to our understanding of this period.

Chapter 1 provides the wider geopolitical and historical background of this study. The discussion first focuses on defining the Deccan, a term used widely but whose borders and content are difficult to pin down. Considering a variety of approaches and definitions, I argue that the Deccan as a concept is related to the historical trajectories that took part in shaping the social, political and cultural life of the region. Accordingly, the bulk of the chapter underlines some of these trajectories during the first half of the second millennium, with special attention given to the development of territorial, linguistic and cultural identities and their relations to wider society and political systems. An overview of this staggeringly long period, I suggest, offers a key to the complexity of circumstances with which the sultanates were dealing. It further helps understand the developments in the *longue durée*, across historical and political divisions created by the establishment of Muslim rule in the region.

The following chapters turn to examine various forms of identity and engagement among distinct elite groups within the Deccan, and demarcate their spatial/territorial sensitivities. Chapter 2 opens with the crystallisation of the Deccan sultanates in the closing decades of the fifteenth century. The chapter then turns to discuss those most associated with the core of the sultanates and their political system, namely, the Deccanis. Their perspective was largely responsible for the definition of the Deccan as a geopolitical unit, with clear ideas of belonging, peripheral and foreign. I argue that these ideas of belonging marked both international engagement, with close relations with peripheral Vijayanagara against hostility to the foreign Mughals, and internally, with a clearly marked hostility towards itinerant elites.

Those itinerants, self-styled Foreigners, stand in the centre of Chapter 3. Even though grouped together in early modern historiography, itself the domain of Foreigners, members of this group belonged to distinct lineages, identified by origin or genealogy that marks their activity within trans-regional networks. At the heart of state service, their presence had a significant impact on state formation. At the same time, they remained uncommitted to the Deccan and were open to moving on to a new place, sometimes working against their old patrons. This ambiguity in their attachment marked them as both constructive and disruptive of state formation.

The next two chapters focus on the non-Muslims in the state, the role their identities took in shaping the state, and their limitations. Chapter 4 examines the place that non-Muslim vernacular groups held in the political and social development of the sultanates. Looking at the cases of Golkonda and Bijapur, I argue that local elites held a central position in the functioning of the sultanates. The sultans acknowledged this role and worked to guarantee the continuous support of these elites. For that purpose, two distinct approaches emerged: Golkonda followed a vernacular-based identity that linked them firmly to Telangana, the Telugu language and the Kakatiya past. Bijapur, in contrast, chose a non-specific kind of localisation that communicated pre-Islamic imperial models, first, that of the Western Chalukyas, later Vijayanagara. This, in part, was due to the absence of any clear option of vernacular identity.

Chapter 5 examines the limitations of these models. Central to the chapter is the assumption that by choosing one direction, the sultanate gained on one front but lost on another. The regionalisation of Golkonda was effective in Telangana, but restricted its expansion only to Telugu-speaking lands. Even there, the Qutb Shahi sultans encountered competing ideological frameworks which they found difficult to win over. Bijapur's path was seemingly more supportive of expansion, but could not accommodate the needs of elites with regional, vernacular-based identities. Particularly challenging was the annexation of southern Maharashtra with its Maratha population. The problems both sultanates faced were of a different scale altogether: if Golkonda's expansion was curtailed, the rule of Bijapur at its heartlands was shaken. Accordingly, when crisis was looming in the mid-seventeenth century, Golkonda managed to recover, whereas Bijapur struggled.

The conclusive Chapter 6 revisits the question of early modern empires and examines how useful this framework is for our understanding of the Deccan sultanates. I argue that the sultanates do not fit into this model. Analysing their political language, I suggest that they did not fail to become empires, but present a different understanding of sovereignty, which was at the same time viable and distinct from that of empire. By that, I suggest that we should consider the possibility of a parallel, non-imperial model for the early modern state.

Introduction

Notes

1. According to India's National Crime Records Bureau, in 2015, the highest number of suicides among farmers were recorded in Maharashtra, followed by Telangana, see 'Maharashtra Tops List in Farmer Suicides, Telangana is Second', *Deccan Chronicle*, 9 September 2017, available at: https://www.deccanchronicle.com/nation/current-affairs/090917/maharashtra-tops-list-in-farmer-suicides-telangana-is-second.html, last accessed 18 September 2018.
2. Even there, Karen Leonard laments the marginalisation of the Princely states, including Hyderabad state, in the historiography of colonial South Asia. See: Leonard, 'Reassessing Indirect Rule'.
3. The rich historiography of the Mughal Empire is beyond the framework of this study. Good surveys include Subrahmanyam, 'The Mughal State: Structure or Process?'; Alam and Subrahmanyam, *The Mughal State*, pp. 1–71; Subrahmanyam, 'Making Sense of Indian Historiography'.
4. See, for example, Sewell, *Forgotten Empire*; Heras, *Aravidu Dynasty*; Venkataramanayya, *Further Sources*; Nilakanta Sastri, *A History of South India*; Rama Sharma, *Vijayanagar, the Last Phase*; Stein, *Peasant State*; Dallapiccola and Lallemant, *Vijayanagara – City and Empire*; Dirks, *The Hollow Crown*; Narayana Rao et al., *Symbols of Substance*; Rama Sarma, *Vijayanagar Empire*; Morrison, *Fields of Victory*; Verghese, *Religious Traditions*; Michell and Wagoner, *Vijayanagara*; Narayana Rao et al., *Textures of Time*; Bridges White, 'Beyond Empire'; Loewy Shacham, 'Krishnadevaraya's Amuktamalyada'; Stoker, *Polemics and Patronage*; Sarkar, *Heroic Saktism*.
5. Notable examples include Grant Duff, *Mahrattas*; Sardesai, *New History of the Marathas*; Sarkar, *House of Shivaji*; Deśmukh, *Śakakarte Śivarāy*; Wink, *Land and Sovereignty*; Gordon, *The Marathas*; Gordon, *Marathas, Marauders*; Kuḷkarṇī, *Śivakālīn Rājanītī*; Kulkarni, *Marathas*; Kulkarni, *Explorations*; Kulkarni, *Madhyayugīna Mahārāṣṭra*.
6. Gribble, *History of the Deccan*, vol. 1, pp. 186–97; Sewell, *Forgotten Empire*, pp. 196–213; Elliot and Dowson, *History of India, as Told by its Own Historians*; Venkataramanayya, *Further Sources*, pp. 190, 244–5, 257–8; Stein, *Vijayanagara*, pp. 2–8.
7. Joshi, 'Geopolitical and Cultural Relations'; Sherwani, *History of the Qutb Shahi*, 121, 138–9. Interestingly, a seminar held in Heidelberg in 1983 tried to incorporate Islam into Vijayanagara's story, and yet the organisers chose to dedicate a distinct and limited place to the 'Muslim' Deccan in the proceedings of the seminar, see Dallapiccola and Lallemant, *Vijayanagara – City and Empire*.
8. Sherwani and Joshi, *History of Medieval Deccan*.
9. Qadri Zore, *Qutb Shahi Sultans and Andhra Samskriti*.
10. Shyam *Ahmadnagar*; Shyam, *Malik Ambar*; Shyam, *Khandesh*.

11. Siddiqi, *Golcunda*; Sherwani, *History of the Qutb Shahi*.
12. Seshan, *Hyderabad-400*; Kumar and Reddy, *Hyderabad*; Luther, *Hyderabad: A Biography*; Nayeem, *Heritage of the Qutb Shahis*.
13. Verma, *Bijapur*; Verma, *Social, Economic and Cultural History*; Nayeem, *External Relations*; Eaton, *Sufis of Bijapur*.
14. Naqvi, *Muslim Religious Institutions*; Naqvi, *Iranian Afaquies*.
15. Chowdhuri, *Malik Ambar*; Qadri, *Chand Bibi*; Tamaskar, *Life and Work of Malik Ambar*; Ḥusayn, *Muḥammad Qulī Quṭb Shāh*; Sherwani, *Muhammad-Quli Qutb Shah*; Luther, *Prince, Poet*; Bhupala Rao, *Maadanna*.
16. Asher, 'Islamic Influence'.
17. The interest in the cultural legacy of the Deccan is not a new issue, and started very early on. Works include Taylor, *Architecture at Bijapur*; Cousens, *Notes on the Buildings*; Cousens, *Bijapur and its Architectural Remains*; Joshi, 'ᶜAli ᶜAdil Shah I'; Skelton, 'Farrokh Beg'; Merklinger, *Indian Islamic Architecture*; Zebrowski, *Deccani Painting*. Interest has increased in the last two decades with a large variety of works produced. Cross-sultanate surveys and edited volumes include Michell and Zebrowski, *Architecture and Art*; Husain, *Scent in the Islamic Garden*; Philon, *Silent Splendour*; Ali and Flatt, *Garden and Landscape Practices*; Haidar and Sardar, *Sultan of the South*; Haidar and Sardar, *Sultans of Deccan India*. Ahmadnagar was in the focus of Gadre, *Cultural Archeology*; Sohoni, 'Farah Bagh'; Sohoni, 'Local Idioms'; Sohoni, *Aurangabad*; Sohoni, *Architecture*. On Golkonda, see Sardar, 'Golconda through Time'; Simpkins 'Mysterious Milestones'; Simpkins, 'Road to Golconda'. Bijapur was discussed by Hutton, *Art of the Court of Bijapur*; Nayeem, *Heritage of the Adil Shahis*; Flatt, '*Nujum al-ulum*'; Overton, 'Collector and his Portrait'; Overton, 'Book Culture'.
18. Wagoner, 'Sultan among Hindu Kings'; Wagoner, 'Fortuitous Convergences'; Wagoner, 'Amin Khan'; Wagoner, 'Money Use in the Deccan'; Eaton, *Social History*; Eaton, 'Written Vernaculars'; Eaton and Wagoner, *Power, Memory, Architecture*.
19. Talbot, 'Inscribing the Other, Inscribing the Self'.
20. Eaton, 'Temple Desecration'.
21. Kruijtzer, *Xenophobia*.
22. Divekar, *Survey of Material*, laments over the dearth of scholarship regarding social or economic history of pre-Shivaji Maharashtra; in his important work, Hiroshi Fukazawa addresses some of these issue in the context of Maharashtra, yet this preliminary work only highlights the lacuna. See Fukazawa, *Medieval Deccan*.
23. Typical in that sense is Sherwani and Joshi, *History of Medieval Deccan*, in which each section deals with one sultanate/dynasty, but no overview or comparative work is offered.
24. For example, Sherwani, *Bahmanis*, pp. 3–11, discusses the physical features of the Deccan within South Asia. This description, however, remains only in the backdrop of the study. See further discussion in Chapter 1, below.

Introduction

25. Soja, *Postmodern Geographies*.
26. Baker, *Geography and History*, 16.
27. Tuan, *Space and Place*.
28. Agnew, 'Representing Space'. With the onset of globalisation, geographers began to think of the idea of scale more systematically, examining space both from the state down to the urban/local as a complex, multi-layered space, and up to the place and the state within the global. See, for example, Brenner et al., *State/Space*.
29. Massey, 'Places and Their Pasts'.
30. Eaton and Wagoner, *Power, Memory, Architecture*, seem to follow the same idea, even if not explicitly. Employing a diachronic approach to the study of archaeological sites in the early modern Deccan, they consider how places were remembered, reused and renegotiated by later generations.
31. Massey, *For Space*, p. 9.
32. Orsini, 'The Multilingual Local'.
33. Not all agree with this definition, see discussion in Goldstone, 'The Problem of the "Early Modern" World'.
34. Charles Verlinden creates an even broader connection, going back in time to the Crusades of the late eleventh century as a beginning of a millennium-long process, see Verlinden, *Beginnings of Modern Colonization*. A similar approach is presented by Michael Doyle, who opens his discussion of the general type of empire in Athens and Sparta as two models, continues by discussing Rome and then early modern empires, before finally reaching nineteenth-century European imperialism in Africa. Interestingly, he chose the Ottomans alongside the Spanish and English empires as a model, yet the Ottoman Empire serves as an exception to the models he has used, which is, of course, European. See Doyle, *Empires*.
35. Roberts, *The Military Revolution, 1560–1660*; G. Parker, 'The "Military Revolution", 1560–1660'; G. Parker, *The Military Revolution*.
36. McNeill, *Rise of the West*; McNeill, *The Pursuit of Power*; Cipolla, *Guns, Sails and Empires*.
37. Wallerstein, *The Modern World-System*. Aristide Zolberg points out that Wallerstein's emphasis on socio-economic processes brought him to ignore political structures (hence, empires) and their role in shaping the sixteenth century, see Zolberg, 'Origins of the Modern World System'.
38. A notable work that looked at the rise of the West as a deterministic, almost inevitable, process, is Jared Diamond's widely read *Guns, Germs, and Steel*. More recently, Ian Morris explains human history since the days of Homo habilis as following long-term trajectories of human history which will help to understand the future roles of East and West in the world system; see Morris, *Why the West Rules for Now*.
39. Pagden, *Lord of All the World*. The focus is on European maritime empires as an exceptional form of imperialism and on the rise of this state form only around 1500. A similar approach is also reflected rather explicitly at

the centre of Hart, *Comparing Empires*, as this work ignores non-European empires altogether.

40. Already sixteenth-century Portuguese historians had discussed them in terms of 'the collective myth of the omnivorous triumvirate of giants of south and south-west Asia, the Great Turk, the Great Sufi, and the Great Mughal', see Alam and Subrahmanyam, 'Deccan Frontier', p. 363.
41. Hodgson, *The Venture of Islam*, vol. 3, pp. 1–161.
42. Athar Ali, 'Political Structures'.
43. Bulliet, *Islam: The View from the Edge*, pp. 178–88. With this, analysis and generalisation cannot always be straightforward. Halil Berktay highlights the problem of historiography in all empires, in which the documentation exaggerates the position and power of the centre, where the documents were produced, vis-à-vis the provinces; the trajectory of integration of the margins, then, may well be misrepresented and less obviously parallel. See Berktay, 'Three Empires'.
44. Robinson, 'Ottomans–Safavids–Mughals'.
45. Casale, 'Islamic Empires', pp. 334–7.
46. Fleischer, 'The Lawgiver as Messiah'; Dale, *Muslim Empires*; Streusand, *Islamic Gunpowder Empires*; Blake, *Time in Early Modern Islam*; Anooshahr, 'Imperial Discourse'; Emiralioğlu, *Geographical Knowledge*, pp. 14–17. Mansura Haidar presents a wider history of India and its place within the world of Central and West Asia, however, without a comparison per se, see Haidar, *Indo-Central Asian Relations*.
47. Ludden, 'The Process of Empire', p. 132.
48. S. N. Eisenstadt rejects his own previous understanding of modernity as a purely European phenomenon dating back to the 1960s in favour of multiple modernities developing in parallel in different parts of the world, see Eisenstadt, 'Multiple Modernities'.
49. Richards, 'Early Modern India'; Ali, 'The Historiography of the Medieval'.
50. John F. Richards emphasises the role of Europe's 'expansive dynamism' in the development of 'the shared evolutionary progress in European organisation that has reached a critical threshold across Eurasia, if not the entire world', see Richards, *The Unending Frontier*, pp. 17–24. Julia Adams follows the same idea in her analysis of patriarchal and family structures and their role in the formation of the early modern Dutch Republic. Acknowledging that it is examined within 'European early modernity', she employs these models to examine the European impact on the colonies in the East and West Indies. Not challenging the Eurocentric framework, she simply rejects the hegemonic cases of France, England and Spain, see Adams, *The Familial State*.
51. John Darwin situates the early modern empires in west, central and east Eurasia on the same level, yet Europe remains his main focus of comparison. He further promotes European exceptionalism in the wider framework of the 'Rise of the West', and suggests that changes in Asian militaries were due to

Introduction

European expertise and imported technology, see Darwin, *After Tamerlane*. The hefty volume edited by Bartolomé Yun-Casalilla, Patrick K. O'Brien and Francisco Comín Comín tackles various strategies adopted by empires worldwide to tackle issues of expansion, globalisation, war and colonialism. While stressing that central to imperial success was the fiscal mechanism throughout Eurasia and emphasising their shift of perspective from Europe to a comparative decentralised view, only five of the seventeen chapters are dedicated to non-European powers (the Ottomans, China, Japan and India), and suggests that the trajectories of these empires 'further highlighting what happened in Europe', Yun-Casalilla et al., *The Rise of the Fiscal States*, p. 11.

52. Subrahmanyam, 'Connected Histories'.
53. C. Parker, *Global Interactions*. Similarly to Darwin, Parker suggests that the beginning of this global system was due to the Mongol–Timurid period that created a long-lasting impact over the entirety of Eurasia. However, Parker took this idea to develop a truly Eurasian understanding of empire, without Darwin's bias in favour of Europe.
54. Subrahmanyam, 'Written on Water'; Darwin, *After Tamerlane*, pp. 4–45; Burbank and Cooper, *Empires in World History*, pp. 1–22; Ludden, 'The Process of Empire', pp. 132–4; Casale, 'Islamic Empires', pp. 334–5. Peter Bang and Dariusz Kołodziejczyk suggest that universal claims were at their prime all over early modern Eurasia, from the universal claims of Western Europe (described by Pagden) to the Ottomans, Mughals and Ming dynasty. Their complex genealogies are not easy to trace, but reflect levels of continuity between traditions that were moving in all directions and throughout the millennia around Eurasia. Periods of unification such as that brought about by the Mongols were linked to pre-existing ideologies and created further models of rulership and universalism. See Bang and Kołodziejczyk, 'Elephant of India'.
55. Runciman, 'Empire as a Topic'; Ludden, 'The Process of Empire', pp. 134–6. Kołodziejczyk, 'What is Inside', demonstrates in the Ottoman case the variety of requirements from local rulers, which included tribute (e.g., Poland–Lithuania, Russia, Venice, or even the Habsburgs); tribute and military assistance (e.g., Moldavia, Wallachia, Transylvania); military assistance and Friday sermon (*khuṭba*) (Crimean khanate, Arab tribes, Kurdish principalities); or only sermon (Hejaz, Yemen, Aceh, Maldives, Kashgar; note that *khuṭba* requirements were imposed only on Muslim rulers). Instead of a binary system, one should consider the degree of sovereignty in given time and place and link it to the political and military ability to resist imperial demand, the economic and social links to the centre, and integration into imperial culture. Even beyond the boundaries, imperial appeal may have attracted local kings; Ottoman appeal has reached as far as Aceh and the Philippines, see Donoso, 'Ottoman Caliphate'; Santos Alves, 'From Istanbul with Love'.

56. Şahin, *Empire and Power*, pp. 6–12, 248–52. Interestingly, one manifestation of agricultural expansion and growing control was the state investment in projects for water management, including the construction of canals and drainage as can be seen in England's Fens, the Netherlands, China's southwest, and around Delhi in north India. See Ash, *Draining of the Fens*; Perdue, 'Official Goals'; Singh, 'Irrigating Haryana'.

57. For example, Sam White analyses the environmental crisis of late sixteenth- and early seventeenth-century Anatolia attributed to the changing climatic conditions during the Little Ice Age, and the significant social, economic and political impact it had, within the theories of the structure of early modern empires. He further suggests that the environmental conditions brought new challenges to imperial control on the margins, and the responses to it were shaped by and, in turn, had its own impact on the development of the empire, see White, *Climate of Rebellion*; see also Özel, *The Collapse of Rural Order*. In her study on the plague, Nükhet Varlık links the spread of epidemics with a certain structure of tributary empire in the early modern Ottoman Empire, questioning the connection between disease, globalisation and communications, see Varlık, *Plague and Empire*. Abdurrahman Atçıl marks the emergence of Ottoman bureaucracy, and the role of scholars within the process, as part of the augmentation of ever-growing territories and the necessary ideology to support this endeavour. He suggests that territorial expansion included 'the vigorous program of state formation and gradual development of a large civil-bureaucratic apparatus ... as the new rulers of the centuries-old imperial capital, Istanbul, the Ottomans began to fashion an imperial identity and articulate universalist claims'. He further promotes the idea of increasing hierarchisation of the system, see Atçıl, *Scholars and Sultans*, citation on p. 213. Heather Ferguson focuses on the creation of administrative and legalistic discourses in the Ottoman Empire in support of universalist claims and their dissemination throughout the empire, within what she calls 'the early modern mania of the state'. She further analyses 'how the production of specific records keeping genres and administrative discourses served to shape and augment imperial authority as the Ottoman Empire rapidly expanded in the fifteenth and sixteenth centuries ... This grammar of rule constituted a core administrative strategy comparable to other early modern empires ... Yet the particular legacies of the text ... led to a unique vision of Ottoman imperial order', see Ferguson, *The Proper Order of Things*, citations on pp. 10–12.

58. Matthee, 'Was Safavid Iran an Empire?' Oddly, Andrew Newman ignores the debates of early modernity and empire altogether. To him, the Safavid period simply 'stands between Iran's medieval and modern history', see Newman, *Safavid Iran*, p. 2.

59. Dirk Kolff appropriately titled the chapter dealing with Sher Shah 'A Warlord's Fresh Attempt at Empire', see Kolff, *Naukar, Rajput, and Sepoy*, pp. 32–70.

Introduction

60. See, for example, Subrahmanyam, *Explorations in Connected History*; Subrahmanyam, 'A Tale of Three Empires'; Subrahmanyam, *Three Ways to be Alien*; Subrahmanyam, *Courtly Encounters*.
61. See, for example, discussion in Biedermann and Strathern, *Sri Lanka at the Crossroads*, pp. 1–14. It goes beyond the scope of this work to further explore the issue of cosmopolitanism in full.
62. Reinhardt, *Empire and Encounters*.
63. Casale, 'Islamic Empires', pp. 323–4.
64. Philip Calkins notes the particularly central position of local landed elites during Mughal rule in Bengal, see Calkins, 'Ruling group in Bengal'; Kumkum Chatterjee demonstrates the complex relationship between Mughal imperial culture and various elite groups, including Hindu ones, in Bengal, see Chatterjee, *Cultures of History*; Farhat Hasan analyses Mughal rule in Gujarat and the role of local power-brokers and elites within the networks of imperial control, see Hasan, *State and Locality*.
65. See, for example, Allison Busch's work on Braj Bhasha in the Mughal context, see Busch, *Poetry of Kings*.
66. Orsini, 'How to do Multilingual Literary History?' p. 227.
67. Thapar, 'Significance of Regional History', p. 19.
68. Orsini, 'How to do Multilingual Literary History?' p. 238.
69. Consider, for example, the interesting case of extreme multilingualism in Maratha-ruled Tanjavur, see Viswanathan Peterson, 'Multilingual Dramas'.
70. That being said, the divisions are not always strict. For example, mystics, even if in retrospect are identified with one tradition, present intellectual, devotional and linguistic fluidity. See Deák, 'Making Sufism Popular'.
71. Thus, we have the writings of the India-born Abu al-Fazl and ᶜAbd al-Qadir Badauni in support and opposition to Akbar, respectively, or the writings of the Brahmin-minister Chandar Bhan, all in Persian.
72. Sarkar, 'Necro-Narratives', p. 279. I wish to thank Dr Sarkar for making this article available to me.
73. See discussion in Narayana Rao et al., *Textures of Time*, pp. 93–139.

1

Mapping the Deccan

In her essay on the importance of regional historiography, Romila Thapar writes that the definition of a region is not a simple matter. It derives not only from its natural location, but also from its content and the way it has been understood. The region is further projected back into the past. Often, she continues, the search for identity by people who are, at present, relating it to the region makes them examine their pasts. The region is thus redefined according to one's perspective, from the centre or within the region itself. These perspectives reshape our understanding of both the region and the centre.[1] Thapar sees the region, and the understanding thereof, as dynamic and negotiable, and, no less important, as subject to the perspective of the spectator. Following Massey's ideas of space and place, we can push the perception that any region, with the multiplicity it contains, is the site of a variety of definitions. This provides a good opening point for our discussion of the Deccan. Following on the understanding of the Deccan as a region, we will ask what this region entails, and what political, social and cultural trajectories led to the creation of a socio-political system under the rule of the sultanates.

What is the Deccan?

At first blush, the answer seems straightforward: the Deccan is the upland plateau in peninsular India, one of the four main macro-regions of South Asia.[2] This is a rather generic definition; however, a more accurate one is not easy to find. The name of the region derived from the Sanskrit *dakṣiṇa*, meaning south (or right-hand, when aligned to the rising sun, similar to *yamīn* in Arabic and Hebrew). Early reference to *dakṣiṇāpadā*, 'with southward foot', appears in the *Ṛg Veda*, but the region lies beyond the interest of Vedic writings. More direct references appear in later texts: in the *Mahabharata*, Sahadeva, having defeated the Pandya king, leaves a clear geographical trail on his way to the south. Greek literature, too, suggests some familiarity with certain political formation in the south.[3] In

Mapping the Deccan

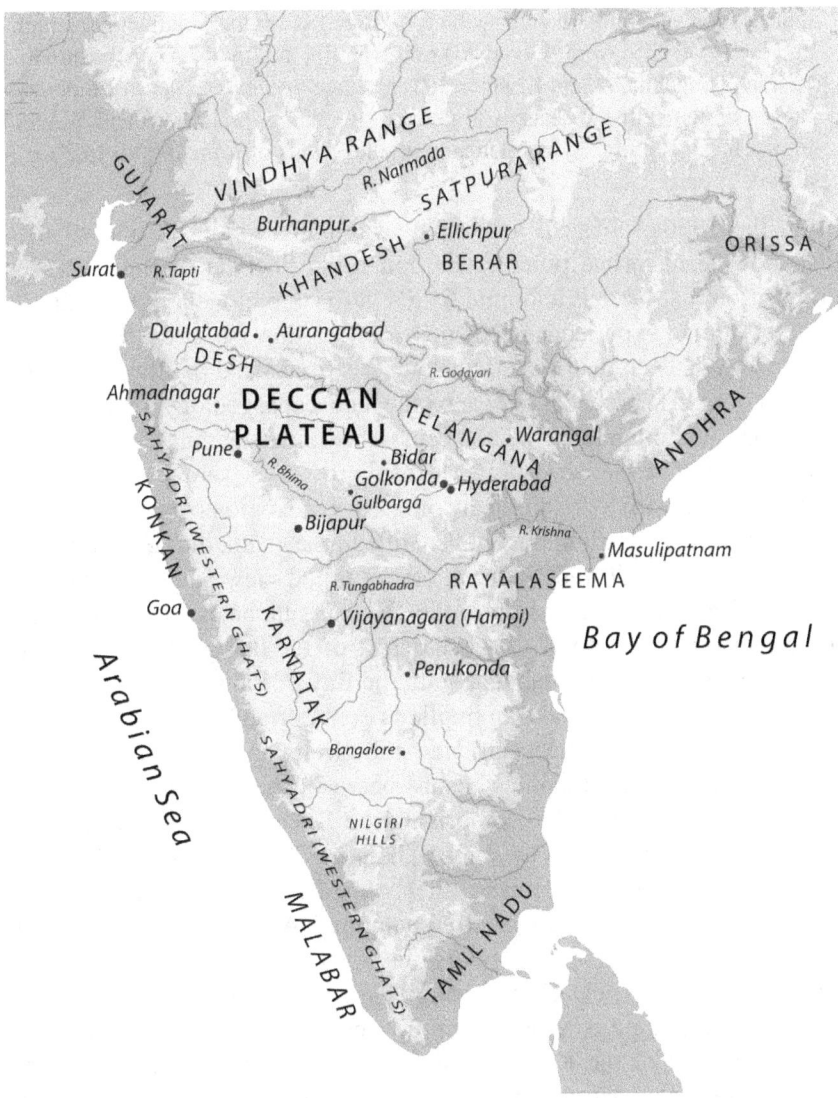

Map 1.1 The Deccan

these vague references, the term Deccan, in itself external to the region, might include the entirety of the peninsula, with the occasional exclusion of Tamil Nadu.[4]

Modern historians have sought to find a clearer geographical definition, even if the content associated with the region remains unexplored. The colonial historian J. D. B. Gribble defines the region in purely topographical terms, suggesting that the Deccan is that portion of Southern India which is bounded by the Vindhya Mountains and the River Godavery (Godavari) to the North, and by the Tungabadhra and Kistna (Tungabhadra and Krishna) Rivers to the South; the Ghats or mountain ranges which skirt the seacoast on either side being the Eastern and Western limits. It . . . is a high-lying plateau with elevations of from 1000 ft to 2000 ft above the sea.[5]

From the 1950s, physical geography was increasingly introduced as a factor in the historical process. Haroon Khan Sherwani writes that 'the proposition that there is an immediate relationship of Geography with the story of human experience needs no proof . . . this aspect of the question has, however, been overlooked by some historians and political scientists of great note.' He proceeds to discuss the landscape, geology, morphology, hydrology and climate of the Deccan.[6] This understanding led to further attempts to define the Deccan. P. M. Joshi provides several possible directions. A conservative definition encompasses the region from the Vindhya Mountains in the north to the Nilgiri Hills in the south, thus excluding the Malabar coast and Tamil Nadu. A more limited view equals the Deccan with the Bahmani domains, later the Deccan sultanates, spreading from the Narmada in the north to the Krishna or the Tungabhadra rivers in the south, and from the Arabian Sea to the Bay of Bengal.[7]

Sherwani and Joshi make an implied yet important distinction between 'the real geographical Deccan' and the 'Bahmani Deccan'. The first strictly refers to the 'Lavaic Plateau' between the Ajanta Range in the north and the Nilgiri Hills, comprising the Deccan Plateau north of the river and the Karnatak to its south. The second is historical rather than physical, identified according to the boundaries of the Bahmani state, even though those were constantly changing.[8] A similar use of the term Deccan (*daquem*) as a region distinct from Vijayanagara appears in Portuguese sources, clearly referring to the 'Bahmani Deccan'.[9] In this understanding, there is a distinction between the territory of the Deccan proper and that of the Karnatak, south of the Krishna. This distinction persisted in local writings in the mid-seventeenth century, for example, during Bijapur's campaign in the 1640s to conquer the Karnatak and Malabar further south.[10]

While modern scholars strive to define the Deccan, this question was not usually explicitly discussed by early modern writers. Yet the use of the term suggests that, for the most part, 'Deccan' was a political rather than a geographical entity. At the heart of this political identity was the collective action of Muslim rulers within a certain political genealogy. Sayyid ʿAli Tabatabaʾi, who was employed first in Golkonda and later in Ahmadnagar, writes that the sultans were 'all of the same royal house',[11] notwithstanding their varied ethnic origins. The anonymous chronicler of Golkonda provided a clearer political genealogy, mentioning that 'all the sultans of the Deccan' were 'of Bahmani descent' (*bahmanī-nizhād*).[12] Considering the vastly different origins of the dynasties, this reference emphasises political lineage, returning to the Bahmani sultans, still remembered in the mid-seventeenth century as 'kings of the Deccan' (*shahryār-i dakkan*).[13] The political sense of the Deccan was carried into the eighteenth century, after the Mughal conquest of the region. The Mughal chronicler Khafi Khan states that the troubles facing the Deccan sultanate when dealing with Vijayanagara derived from the division of the erstwhile Bahmani sultanate, thus adhering to the idea that the post-Bahmani Deccan was a political unit.[14] Within this system, the association with the Deccan varied according to context. For example, Sayyid Murtaza was an Iranian military commander, who left Ahmadnagar's service in 1585. He then joined the Mughals and was attached to the first imperial campaign against Ahmadnagar. The socio-political identity of Sayyid Murtaza and his men changed accordingly. When still in Ahmadnagar, they were considered 'Foreigners', who, as we shall see later, were contrasted with the Deccanis. Once in Mughal service, they became 'commanders of the Deccan (*umarā-i dakkan*)',[15] suggesting two different uses of the term: association with a certain elite group internally; or connection to the political system of the Deccan as a whole when observed from the outside.

A rather unusual treatment of the Deccan as a concept appears in the writing of Muhammad Qasim Firishta. The definition he suggested, later employed by Richard Eaton as the definitive framework of his work, centres around a genealogical allegory. Firishta asserts that Hind (namely, India), styled as the patriarch, fathered four sons, one of whom was Dakkan (Deccan). Dakkan had three sons: Marhat, Kanhar and Tilang (i.e., Marathi-, Kannada- and Telugu-speaking lands, respectively). The three divided the land of the Deccan among themselves. Firishta concluded that 'today, these three nations are found in the Deccan'.[16] The genealogical allegory provides an additional element to our understanding of the Deccan: not only geographical and political, but also a linguistic-cultural unit, inherently divided. Notwithstanding the familiar connections attributed to the three brothers, Firishta does not suggest concrete links between the linguistic regions, nor does he provide a general and cohesive idea of the Deccan. Furthermore, his linguistic-cultural explanation does not correspond with any of the definitions of the Deccan we have seen before. Thus, the 'Lavaic Plateau' leaves much of the Telugu-speaking lands out of the picture, maybe in similarity with the geographical-cum-cultural definition

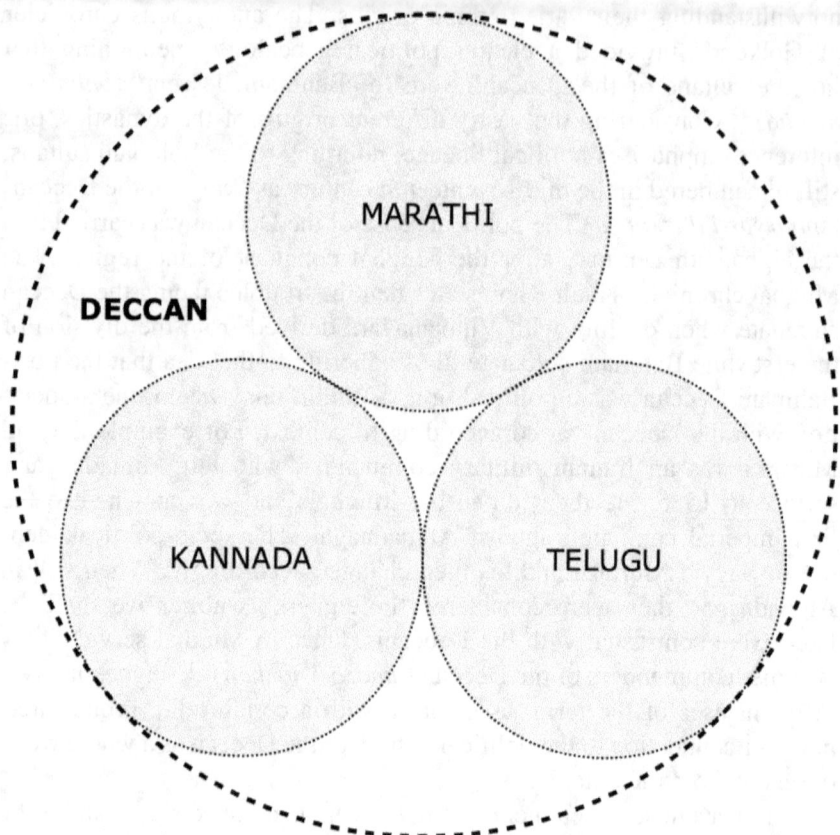

Figure 1.1 Firishta's Deccan

of the *Gazetteer*; the 'Political Deccan' does not contain the Kannada- and Telugu-speaking regions south of the Krishna–Tungabhadra, and the 'Linguistic Deccan' goes beyond the Deccan sultanates to include most of Vijayanagara territories, historically separate of the 'Political Deccan'.

In accordance with the multi-layered definitions of the Deccan, marking its boundaries, be they political, geographical, cultural or social, is not straightforward. No early modern source provides a systematic description of the borders of the Deccan, nor can we find a graphic depiction of the region. Systematic mapping was introduced into the region only by the Surveyor-General of India, Colonel Colin Mackenzie, in the early nineteenth century; the first local lithograph was produced by Kavali Venkata Ramaswami in 1827.[17] The idea of a border, however, does appear in early modern sources, primarily as a political concept.

Mapping the Deccan

Dariusz Kołodziejczyk argues that the early modern Ottoman Empire clearly demarcated its borders, at least in populated regions, even if less so in sparsely populated territories, demonstrating an awareness of geographical limitations.[18] Similar demarcation can be traced in the Deccan. Eaton and Wagoner point at the possibility of mapping political boundaries among the Deccan sultanates and between the sultanates and Vijayanagara. They assert that some borders were stable, whereas certain regions served as contested frontiers.[19] Early modern sources elaborately refer to borders (Persian: *sar-ḥadd*), typically within political contexts. For example, Rafiᶜ al-Din Shirazi states that Ibrahim ᶜAdil Shah I of Bijapur took care of the affairs of the land (*wilāyat*, in the sense of a sovereign territory) and protected its borders.[20] Borders themselves are marked as the place where one sovereignty ends and another begins, appearing when describing a particular location, or as part of a narrative of travel or military campaigns. For example, land assignment (*iqṭāᶜ*) of one Jahangir Khan Habshi in Ahmadnagar in the 1560s was located 'on the border of Berar, in the vicinity of the province of Khandesh'.[21] The newly built ᶜAdil Shahi fort of Dharur was perceived by the Nizam Shah of Ahmadnagar as a menace as it was located 'on the border of his territory', and therefore could be used for future invasions.[22] In tense times, rulers demanded control of territories on their borders.[23] Borders appeared in narratives of travel, too. Returning to Golkonda from his exile in 1550, Ibrahim Qutb Shah arrived in Pangal, 'which is the border of the kingdom (*mamlakat*) of Vijayanagara';[24] and the itinerary of Safavid envoys brought them in 1635 'to the border of the well-protected domains (i.e. Golkonda)'.[25] The word *sar-ḥadd* is sometimes attached to the name of locations,[26] likely to indicate their proximity to the limits of the sovereign's domains.

In rare instances, references are given not to a point, but to a line that allows us to draw a clear, continuous boundary, particularly where the border corresponds with a river.[27] For example, the peace signed in 1636 between the Mughals and Bijapur, the events around which will be discussed in detail in Chapter 5, included the partition of the domain of the, by then extinct, Sultanate of Ahmadnagar. The early nineteenth-century historian Muhammad Ibrahim al-Zubayri states that:

> Finally, a peace between Shah Jahan and the warrior king [Muhammad ᶜAdil Shah] was concluded in this manner: the domains of the Nizam Shah from that side of the Krishna will be annexed to Shah Jahan, whereas [the domains of the Nizam Shah] on this side will be considered the possession of ᶜAdil Shah. When the negotiations between the sides were concluded, Shah Jahan ordered to inscribe the charter of peace on a golden tablet.[28]

The passage above reflects a clear idea of a border between two political units, with a manifested distinction between 'this side' (*īn ṭaraf*), meaning 'ours', and 'that side' (*ān ṭaraf*), meaning 'theirs'.[29] A similar type of boundary is evident in earlier sources. The anonymous chronicler of Golkonda narrates the story of an imposter who posed as Shah Sahib, the late son of Ibrahim Qutb Shah. To claim his sovereignty over Golkonda, the imposter collected vagabonds and cavalry and marched towards 'the border of the well-protected domains'. Then, 'on the bank of the Krishna, he raised the parasol of sultanate and the banner of [royal] pomp'. The physical barrier here is clearly conceived as a political border. Using royal symbols (parasol), the self-proclaimed prince declared his plans in a location seen as the border of the territory he claimed.[30] The instances, then, suggest that for people in the early modern Deccan there was a clear perception of political borders, marking the limits of sovereignty and control of a sovereign.[31]

If some borders are easier to mark than others, there is one direction where the border remains clear and stable throughout: the north. The border between north and south India is considered to be the region of the Vindhya and Satpura ridges and the Narmada River.[32] Time and again, this region appears as the ultimate boundary for the actions of the Deccani polities. This is not a new phenomenon: meagre attempts to expand beyond this border region to nearby Malwa were rare and overall unsuccessful.[33] Around the turn of the second millennium, the Western Chalukyas saw the very same region as their northern frontiers.[34] Similarly, the Yadavas of Devgiri raided beyond this region when fighting against Malwa and Gujarat, but never established a permanent presence.[35] Even after the expansion of the Delhi sultanates into the Deccan in the fourteenth century, which linked the region with the north, none of the southern states (Bahmanis, Vijayanagara or Deccan sultanates) attempted expansion beyond the Narmada. Only the Marathas changed this pattern in the eighteenth century.[36] A dramatic symbol of this border was presented by Prataparudra, the last king of the Kakatiyas of Warangal in the eastern Deccan. Defeated by Delhi's commander Malik Kafur in 1323, he lost his kingdom. According to one account, when he was carried to Delhi as prisoner of war, he chose to commit suicide on the banks of the Narmada.[37]

The main challenge to defining the Deccan stems from the three distinct meanings of the region discussed above: the geographical, the political-historical and the linguistic-cultural. The different senses were used simultaneously throughout the centuries, down to modern historiography. Each meaning contains its own set of borders, rigid or changeable, and its own contents and coherence. Based on these separate layers of meaning, it may be better to imagine the Deccan not as a clearly defined and discrete space, but rather as a series of partially overlapping spaces, each with its own boundaries and internal logic. This flexible concept of the Deccan brought its own challenges to politics and society in the region.

The blurry definitions seem rather unique in late medieval and early modern South Asia. Elsewhere, an emergent local consciousness among elite groups and local rulers encouraged the development of certain forms of spatial recognition. In Bengal, regional identity that carried a strong linguistic component emerged under the local sultanate (1342–1576), and was part of the process of regional crystallisation. Rulers actively fostered the Bengali language and encouraged the creation of a localised artistic idiom as part of their efforts to tie together different segments of a diverse society. Bengal continued to function as a unit, administered as a Mughal province (ṣūba), and, finally, as an independent polity under the local rulers (nawwāb). Reflecting this sense of unity, Bengal demonstrated strong resistance to a colonial scheme to divide the province in 1905, a decision that was reversed.[38] Gujarat followed a similar trajectory. Samira Sheikh argues that from the early centuries of the second millennium, Gujarat began to crystallise as a region, combining diverse territories that gradually came together. Under the local sultanate (1407–1573), she suggests, 'new literary languages such as Gujarati ... represented the codification of the laity's language into written form, and texts in these languages now circulated for education and edification. This was a region self-consciously thinking about itself as a region.'[39] In both Bengal and Gujarat, political unity, settlement patterns, and linguistic and cultural identities developed in parallel, amplifying and encouraging one another, and eventually coming together to create viable and long-lasting, even if not uncontested, regional identities.[40]

The Deccan followed a different trajectory. The region was too diverse politically and culturally to allow these various processes to come together. Compared with Bengal and Gujarat, where various trajectories converged in the creation of regional identities, the nature of the Deccan's diversity worked against such processes. Some of the social-cultural divisions within the region had geographical links and historical associations that pushed them away from the Deccan. Even though the term Deccan was used extensively in early modern sources and continues to be in use today, it does not fully reflect the socio-linguistic make-up of the entire region: Muslims and non-Muslims, locals and Foreigners, speakers of Persian, Dakhani, Marathi, Telugu or Kannada, all had different ideas in mind. With such diversity, there is no clear definition upon which the idea of Deccan and Deccani identity could have been built. That is not to say that there has not been such identity, at least conceptually. However, its contents have been constantly contested, leading to contradiction and tension that played an important role in the history of the region.

Formation of the Political Deccan: Empires and Regional Kingdoms

The elusive borders of the Deccan did not emerge *ex nihilo* in the early modern period. Rather, it was the result of centuries-long, parallel, and at times contradictory historical processes that came together to create a multi-layered region. In order to understand the various trajectories, then, a look into the history of the region is necessary. Naturally, it will be beyond the point here to cover the entirety of south India from the beginning of the historical record. A more reasonable approach would be to focus on the regions north of the Krishna River, which were the core of the Deccan sultanates, with the occasional digression for the sake of contextualisation.

Setting the timeframe is less obvious when discussing long-term processes. Any choice will be at least somewhat arbitrary.[41] A common opening point for the discussion of the sultanates is Delhi's invasion around 1300, separating the 'ancient' (or, more controversially, 'Hindu') Deccan from the 'medieval' (or 'Muslim') period.[42] Starting at that point has its merits: Delhi's incursions to the Deccan a century later created new states and institutions that differed from their predecessors in structure, administration, military, as well as religious and cultural identities. Nevertheless, this division raises significant historiographical problems. It assumes much of a clean-cut from the past, disconnects the locality from its own history, and downplays, if not disregards, elements of continuity. Furthermore, such division implies the alienation of the new regime from the locality, marking it as foreign. However, the introduction of a new political order did not eliminate the past. New rulers required local expertise and manpower to secure their holdings. Accordingly, they found various ways to fold people, institutions, symbols and memories into their own systems. These seemingly contradictory processes of continuation and change had a major role in shaping state and society in the Deccan. To follow Eaton and Wagoner, it would be prudent to say that the roots of some social and political frames go back to the centuries before 1300.[43]

A possible point of departure can be the beginning of the second millennium, a period that marks the opening of several far-reaching processes in the Deccan. At that time, we find much of peninsular India divided between two major powers. Dominant in the north were the Western Chalukyas, who rose to prominence in the 970s after the collapse of the

Rastrakutas. Further south, most prominent were the Cholas, with their core in the Tamil coastal plains. At early stages, their border probably followed the Krishna–Tungabhadra rivers, with control over the fertile Raichur *doāb*[44] continuously contested. Later in the eleventh century, the borders changed considerably. In 1070, the minor dynasty of the Eastern Chalukyas of Vengi in Andhra was integrated into the Chola Empire. This gave the southern empire a significant stronghold along the eastern seaboard north of the Krishna, and also introduced a far-reaching transformation of the nature of kingship in the empire. In parallel, the Western Chalukyas advanced into the Karnatak, south of the Tungabhadra, while fortifying their control over Telangana in the eastern Deccan Plateau as well as in parts of Rayalaseema, south of the Krishna. This added an east–west element to the unstable borders. Late in the twelfth century, imperial authority began to shatter in both empires. The Western Chalukyas were facing political and military exhaustion, and domestic turmoil shook the foundations of their empire. Segments of society increasingly resisted the rigid hierarchy of the state and its elites, leading to the spread of reform movements, notably Virasaivism. The empire could not sustain the pressures from within and without, and by the late twelfth century, imperial authority collapsed. The elites, however, did not disappear, but found ways to survive; some were transformed into local chiefs and landlords, maintaining their historical memory. By the early thirteenth century, the Cholas, too, had disappeared.[45]

The decline of imperial authority gave rise to a system of regional kingdoms, most notably those under the Yadavas of Devgiri in the northwest, the Kakatiyas of Warangal in the northeast, the Hoysalas of Dwarasamudra (modern-day Halebidu) in the southwest, and the Pandyas of Madurai in the southeast. These dynasties typically began their careers as tributary chieftains, who took advantage of imperial weakness to better their position. The Yadavas were first reliably recorded as military nobility under the Western Chalukyas, active from the very early days of the empire. Originally named Sevunas, they took the mythical title Yadava, supported by their claim to have migrated from Dvarka in Saurastra in modern-day Gujarat. Their origin, however, is more likely to have been in the Kannada-speaking Karnatak, much like their Chalukya overlords. While serving the empire, the Sevunas expanded within the Marathi-speaking part of the Deccan, with which they later came to be identified. With the significant power-base they construct there, they successfully challenged dwindling imperial authority in the late twelfth century, and soon took over most of the territories north of the Tungabhadra in the western Deccan.[46]

Similar to the Sevunas, the Hoysalas originated in the Karnatak and claimed Yadava origins, even if less convincingly. Unlike the Sevunas, however, they remained in their Kannada-speaking homelands. They first appeared as local chieftains, carving their own principality in the western Karnatak amidst struggles against other local dynasties such as the Gangas and Santaras, eventually turning the two dynasties into their tributaries. The Hoysalas associated themselves with the Western Chalukyas against the Cholas, perhaps with the idea that a distant overlord is better than a proximate one. While raising their own prestige and adding to their territories and resources, the Hoysalas were instrumental in Western Chalukya expansion in the Karnatak. Eventually, imperial weakness and growing Hoysala ambitions put the two dynasties at odds, and under Ballala II (r. 1173–1220) the Hoysalas became independent.[47]

The origins of the Kakatiyas are even less clear. Several sources suggest that they served the Eastern Chalukyas of Vengi, but no convincing evidence supports this assumption. More likely is that they began their career in the early eleventh century as tributaries of the Western Chalukyas. Based in Telangana in the eastern Deccan, the early Kakatiyas played an important role in the struggle between the Western Chalukyas and the Cholas, for which they were rewarded. In the early twelfth century, the Kakatiya chief Prola II (r. c. 1117–58) is recorded to have fought against tributary rulers, but it is not clear whether it was on behalf of the Chalukyas or on his own accord. Following the Chalukya defeat to the Cholas in 1135, Prola II began to promote his ambitions in the open, significantly increasing Kakatiya territories. The continuous decline of the Western Chalukyas pushed Rudradeva (r. c. 1158–95) to assert his sovereignty. He later expanded into Andhra with its rich agriculture and trade connections, gradually slipping away from imperial grasp.[48]

The fine details regarding the history of the regional dynasties go beyond the scope of this survey, but several issues should be kept in mind. First, the political history of the period consists of long narratives of inter- (and intra-)dynastic hostility, alliances and meddling in each other's affairs. For example, the Hoysalas aspired to advance into Pandya territory in the Tamil country, where they were at first successful, although the Pandyas later had the upper hand.[49] The Hoysalas fought against both Yadavas and Pandyas in the late 1190s;[50] the Yadavas and Kakatiyas struggled for the control over border territories around 1230 and again in the 1260s and 1290s;[51] the Pandyas fought against both the Yadavas and Kakatiyas.[52] Throughout the thirteenth century, the Yadavas, Hoysalas and Kakatiyas contested the Raichur *doāb*.[53] The frequent wars indicate that the borders between the dynasties were changeable, and the system as a whole was in a state of unstable equilibrium. With that, the core region of each kingdom with its capital remained firmly within the hold of the respective dynasty. In many respects, this system resembles the Deccan sultanates with their multiplicity of political centres, constant border clashes and stable core regions.

One of the major changes at the time was the transition of the economic and ecological base of the regional kingdoms from the river deltas along the coast into the semi-arid plateau inland. The process had started already under the Western Chalukyas, whose capital city, Kalyani, is located on the plateau, but gained momentum under the regional kingdoms. The new core regions remained primarily inland until colonial times. Burton Stein notes that the new core regions of the Hoysalas, Kakatiyas and later also the Vijayanagara, were of mixed economy, consisting of peasantry, animal husbandry, trade and plunder, and required the construction of water tanks. Local society was, accordingly, flexible, mobile and trained, resulting in the rise of a martial political order.[54] This point is well demonstrated in the case of the Kakatiyas, who, according to Cynthia Talbot, 'established a new geopolitical trend in the Andhra country by rising to power from a home base in the dry inland region and only subsequently extending their influence into the more densely populated and wealthy coastal territory'.[55]

Expansion was not only a matter of conquest and direct control, but required forging of suzerain links with local chiefs. With these links, rulers adopted the possibly fanciful title of 'king of kings'.[56] But this title has not been the end point of the political process. Magnates constantly negotiated their position, reflecting a continuation of the very same process that brought the rulers of the regional kingdoms to power. For example, the aforementioned Gangas and Santaras began as competing rulers to the Hoysalas, but the latter were successful, leaving the formers as their tributaries. The Yadavas mixed direct rule and acknowledged local magnates, among which were the Sindas of Belagutty who had previously served the Rastrakutas and Western Chalukyas.[57] Not all local families remained loyal to their masters, for example, the Silaharas or Kadambas under the Yadavas. Other chieftains navigated between the dynasties to secure better terms, for example, the Soyidevas between the Hoysalas and Yadavas.[58] The picture was similar in the case of the Kakatiyas. Their eastwards expansion encouraged the absorption of coastal families such as the Eastern Chalukyas of Vengi, who had first been independent, then tributaries of the Cholas, then independent again. Similarly, the Viriyalas and Natavadis of Telangana served the Rastrakutas, the Western Chalukyas and the Kakatiyas.[59]

In the second half of the thirteenth century the Kakatiyas chose to introduce another direction. From the rule of Rudrama Devi (r. c. 1261–89), the position of locally-based hereditary elements was eroded in favour of a new, state-manufactured class of officer-subordinates (*nāyaka*), possibly in response to the challenge presented by subordinate rulers. The *nāyakas* typically came from non-noble backgrounds, often of peasant-warrior origins, in association with the transition of the political centre to the semi-arid and mixed economy Telangana. The *nāyakas* were incorporated as individuals in high positions and were directly linked to the centre. This change was supported by the assignment of lands to *nāyakas* as reward for their service (*nāyankara*), with the intention of linking them firmly to central authority; it is, however, not clear what obligations the system entailed. Nevertheless, this dramatic change in the composition of Kakatiya elites did not bring the complete disappearance of the old nobility.[60]

Another issue emerging in the regional kingdoms relates to language. Fundamental to this study, we will dwell on this issue at some length. At the height of Western Chalukya power around the late eleventh and early twelfth century, the dynasty developed a growing sense of imperial identity, central to which was the notion of universal domination. Supported by a growing body of juristic literature and aided by textual production in Sanskrit, Chalukya authority relied on the emperor's role in consolidating territorial expansion and promoting the rule of *dharma*. The empire promoted strict social order, central to which was patronage to various religious institutions made by emperors and nobles.[61] This order was increasingly rejected by significant elements in the society, leading to growing resistance that greatly weakened the empire.

One of the most far-reaching aspects of the cultural and social change in twelfth- and thirteenth-century Deccan was the rise of the vernacular. In a series of highly influential articles, followed by the monumental monograph *The Language of the Gods in the World of Men*, Sheldon Pollock argues that the early second millennium saw a major linguistic, cultural and political change in India. Up to that point, Sanskrit enjoyed the status of a cosmopolitan, with monopolistic status in political, literary and religious discourse throughout the subcontinent and beyond. In the first centuries of the second millennium, vernaculars emerged in new forms. First employed in limited contexts of political and worldly affairs, these languages slowly expanded to take over the role of Sanskrit for political, literary and religious purposes, developing into what Pollock terms 'the cosmopolitan vernacular'. Sanskrit did not fall out of use, and the language continued to provide a model for rhetoric and contents, now reworked into the vernaculars. However, it lost its monopolistic position as the sole idiom of political authority. Whereas the process of vernacularisation progressed at different pace around the subcontinent, it was most clearly pronounced in south India. In the peninsula, communities comprising the speakers of Kannada and later Tamil, Telugu and eventually Marathi, became increasingly aware of their vernacular as standing independently of Sanskrit. This awareness encouraged the development of new literary traditions, but also created the identification of territory and vernacular, often politicised in creating new ideas of kingship and elite culture.[62] The regional kingdoms contributed to, and benefited from, the process of vernacularisation in the development of their political identity.

The relationship of the vernacular with the respective kingdom varied considerably.[63] Cynthia Talbot argues that under Kakatiya rule, the use of Telugu has expanded from Andhra, long associated with the Telugu language, to Telangana on the Deccan Plateau, hitherto the arena for competition between Telugu and Kannada. The linguistic change was parallel to the intensification of agricultural production and settlement in Telangana. Both processes highlight the rise in the significance of Telangana, homeland of the Kakatiyas, once a marginal region on the borderline between empires. Consequently, Telangana became identified as Telugu-speaking. Furthermore, the region became increasingly integrated with Andhra both culturally and politically. The Telugu language was an important focus of this process, and a sense of linguistic and regional identity within the newly unified territory contributed to connecting elite groups over the entire Telugu lands.[64] The vernacular change is also reflected in the proclaimed modest origin of the Kakatiyas as Shudras (lowest of the fourfold *varṇa* system of social classification), alongside the rise of the warrior-peasants heavily represented among the ranks of the *nāyaka*s. The origins and their vernacular connection stand in contrast to the higher Kshatriya origins of the Western Chalukya, a claim that worked in tandem with the role of Brahmanism and Sanskrit in the empire. The distance between the Kakatiyas and Chalukya imperial heritage is further reflected in the new character of state–religion relations as the Kakatiyas reformulated a new form of state cult under the protection of state-deity (*rāṣṭra-devatā*).[65]

Yet the politicisation of Telugu and the 'Teluguisation' of Telangana were not a complete process. While creating links between territory, language and borders, the newly recognised Telugu space remained contested. Kakatiya territory was topographically, ecologically and economically diverse, and the plateau continued to be identified as distinct from the coast. The regions had already become politically separated once again in the 1330s, and remained split.[66] Furthermore, the boundaries of this Telugu space were hard to define as Telangana is topographically indistinguishable from the neighbouring Marathi- and Kannada-speaking portions of the plateau. Similarly unclear is the Telugu–Tamil border on the southeastern coast. Velcheru Narayana Rao shows that in religious centres such as Tirupati and Srisailam (both in modern-day Andhra Pradesh), Telugu literature enjoyed great support, but not exclusively, as these locales were the sites of writing in other vernaculars: Tamil in Tirupati, and Kannada and Marathi in Srisailam. Furthermore, even though Kakatiya rulers were identified with Telugu, they did not give patronage to literature in that language,[67] highlighting a more complex relationship between language, politics and territory.

Other vernaculars present even bigger a challenge. Kannada is one of the earliest written vernaculars of the Deccan. Under the Hoysalas, the language developed significantly in various literary genres. An important factor in the development of the language was the rise of mystical and devotional movements around Virasaivism, whose need to communicate their ideas with wider audiences encouraged writing in a language that could be understood widely.[68] The language also had political use, as the Hoysalas defined their boundaries in a series of inscriptions in Kannada. These inscriptions indicate that the dynasty ruled over territories largely overlapping with the spread of the language, and not much beyond.[69] It was in the Hoysala court of the thirteenth century that Harihara, a court administrator, composed the *Ragalegalu*, a collection of hagiographies of Saiva saints of the yet-to-be-called Virasaivism; it is the earliest known example of narrative literature in that language.[70] These findings roughly correspond with Talbot's ideas regarding Kakatiya use of Telugu.

Marathi seems to have developed a regional identity later. The first philosophical treaties and commentaries appeared in the thirteenth century, alongside the devotional poetry of Namdev and others; they are, however, possibly of earlier origin. Evidence demonstrates major literary activity during the reign of the Yadavas, particularly by various religious and devotional movements. The first signs of spatial identity emerged within this corpus. The writings of the Mahanubhava sect suggest a clear concept of Maharashtra as the land where Marathi was spoken, and, no less importantly, Kannada and Telugu were not, creating an identity between territory and only one language.[71] However, the political use of the language remains unclear. Inscriptions in Marathi are scarce, and limited to the northern parts of the kingdom, alongside Sanskrit.[72] Nevertheless, the growing involvement of the Yadavas in their creation, even if they originated in the Kannada-speaking Karnatak, suggests that Marathi and Maharashtra of the thirteenth century began developing vernacular-territorial identity.

This understanding of language, identity, territory and politics, however, is not without its problems. For one, there is not always an easy link of this kind to be made. Eaton promotes a clear-cut, somewhat schematic link of each regional kingdom, territory and one vernacular: the Kakatiyas with Telugu, the Yadavas with Marathi, and the Hoysalas with Kannada.[73] Yet, we cannot assume a similar advance of vernacularisation and its political significance throughout. This model works best, if imperfectly, for the case of Telugu. The vernaculars of the western Deccan are less clear. Marathi fell mostly, if not completely, within the realm of the Yadavas, the space identified as the Kannada country was divided between two realms: Hoysalas in the south, ruling over most of the territory; and the Yadavas in the north. Accordingly, Kannada inscriptions were found in the Kannada-speaking regions in the southern Yadava kingdom; more Kannada than Marathi inscriptions were found in Yadava territories as a whole. Furthermore, there is evidence of writing literature in Kannada in the Yadava realm.[74] In other words, even at the height of the regional kingdoms, Kannada lands were politically divided.[75] A possible factor contributing to the blurry boundary between the two spaces is the cultural, religious and linguistic proximity between Marathi and Kannada, notwithstanding their separate linguistic classification, with Marathi being part of the Indo-European family whereas Kannada is classified as Dravidian. Pandit Awalikar suggests that as the division between Sanskrit and vernaculars was stricter than among vernaculars, Kannada and Marathi were close in their early stages, developing independently of one another only later. Their proximity is derived from socio-religious rather than linguistic factors. He marks as particularly important religious reform movements such as Virasaivism that operated in both languages.[76] Even if we do not accept this argument in its entirety, Awalikar points towards permeable lines separating literary, cultural, religious and political traditions between the two vernacular spaces, putting them aside from the better-defined Telugu.[77] This division between a distinct eastern (Telugu) Deccan and the fluid space of the western (Marathi/Kannada) Deccan remained a constant historical factor in the region in the following centuries.

We cannot assume unity among all speakers not only between vernaculars, but even within each vernacular. The aforementioned Mahanubhavas were pivotal in developing the link between Marathi and the geographical concept of Maharashtra. Yet this identification was not all-encompassing. Anne Feldhaus suggests that the 'regional consciousness' of the sect had no political significance, and probably has not been widely known outside the sect. It rather demonstrates geographical–linguistic significance within the sect's tradition.[78] In the following centuries, parallel forms of regional identities developed, engaging with the locality and the vernacular in various forms without formulating a systematic vernacular–territory link. The sixteenth-century Brahmin-poet Eknath translated works from Sanskrit into Marathi and composed in that language, and remained identified with Paithan in Maharashtra.[79] In parallel, Maharashtrian Brahmins settled in Varanasi in north India, where they partook in the burgeoning intellectual life of Sanskrit, without abandoning networks and affiliations with locales and sub-castes in Maharashtra.[80] The vision of Maharashtra, the role of the Marathi language, and the affiliation with the territory must have varied significantly between the non-resident Brahmins, Eknath and followers of the Mahanubhava sect.

The various forms of engagement highlight the problem of the vernacular as an all-encompassing category. An interesting case from the Tamil lands demonstrates this problem. Blake Wentworth argues that tenth-century literature suggests an identification of Tamil with a certain territory, but not with specific people. Later in the second millennium, a connection is created between Tamil, the political order and those who assert such order. A parallel body of literature indicates that, for some, land and language were connected, under Pandya patronage, to Saivite traditions. Those who write in Tamil but do not follow this particular tradition, notably Jains, may be Tamil-speakers but are not considered Tamils.[81] Similar to the case of the Mahanubhava, language was not a single determinant in the imagination of a community, but other factors such as religious affiliation had to be considered, implicitly in the case of the Mahanubhavas, and more explicitly in the case of the Tamil Saivites.

In addition to problems between and within vernacular, recent studies further complicate Pollock's model. On a general note, Francesca Orsini questions Pollock's distinction between cosmopolitan and vernacular. She suggests that it 'maps onto the classic distinction between High and low languages (diglossia)', with a clear division between a web of cosmopolitan, High culture and imperial aspiration, on the one hand, and vernacular, informal setting and locality, on the other hand, in some zero-sum game. This, however, ignores certain aspects of interaction between the languages and the possibility of the simultaneity of multiple languages.[82] Furthermore, the very idea that Sanskrit declined in the second millennium and was replaced by vernaculars has been challenged. Bhairabi Prasad Sahu argues that the Sanskrit-based, pan-India culture that was gradually emerging from the second half of the first millennium was not an imposition of unified ideas from above. Rather, it consisted of two opposing trajectories: the 'Sanskritisation' of the local, for example, by associating local deities with all-India gods; and the 'tribalisation' or localisation of Sanskrit, for example, by integrating local elements into pan-Indian Brahmanical practices, leading to local impact on Brahmanical practices.[83] This bi-directional interaction only intensified in the second millennium. Stressing that 'rumours of the death of Sanskrit after 1000 A.D. are greatly exaggerated', Yigal Bronner and David Shulman suggest that Sanskrit was not an unchangeable language that stayed aloof from regional sensitivities. On the contrary, writings in Sanskrit, widely practised in the second millennium, participated in the development of regional identities alongside the vernaculars. This, in turn, was expressed in regional linguistic, poetic and thematic patterns now entering Sanskrit, allowing the writers the liberty to choose a scope of their work, whether universal or local.[84]

All-India and regional identities continued to live alongside one another, influencing each other's development. In the case of Telugu, argues Narayana Rao, early writers were aware of the tension between the vernacular and Sanskrit. The special status of Sanskrit encouraged the development of highly Sanskritised forms of Telugu poetry that enjoyed the support of court and temple. The employment of Telugu poets was almost contingent on the poets' familiarity with Sanskrit. Less Sanskritised Telugu poetry was composed, but usually away from political and religious centres. Growing awareness of the separate, yet complementary, existence of Telugu and Sanskrit encouraged the linguistic and thematic interaction between the two, creating a poetic language different from earlier styles in both Sanskrit and Telugu.[85] This interplay is well demonstrated in the early sixteenth-century *Amuktamalyada*, composed by poet and king Krishnadevaraya of Vijayanagara (r. 1509–29). Ilanit Loewy Shacham demonstrates that the king-poet used a new register, simultaneously poetic and mundane, imagined and hyper-realistic, that draws on both Sanskrit and Telugu in terms of style, imagery and lexicography. Moving freely between the two languages, Krishnadevaraya made a sophisticated use of the possibilities the two languages offer to create a firm, inseparable bond between them, without preferring either.[86]

To conclude, the rise of vernacular and regional identities in the early centuries of the second millennium had a significant impact on the social, political, cultural and religious trajectories of the Deccan. This process, however, was not complete and all-encompassing, nor did it suppress Sanskrit with its universalist appeal and pan-Indian ideology. Under the regional kingdoms, vernaculars turned into an important vehicle for political mobilisation and territorial expression, yet not uniquely and not equally in all kingdoms. At times the boundaries between vernaculars remained blurry; vernaculars occasionally served as factors of discord rather than unity. In parallel, Sanskrit continued to produce a rich, fresh and evolving body of literature. Sanskrit and the vernaculars developed alongside one another, nourishing each other. Writers, aware of the meaning of language choice, used the possibilities newly opened to them to link the local with wider experiences, offered by the appropriation of Sanskrit. Such developments argue against the dichotomy between Sanskrit–pan-Indian and vernacular–regional in favour of a cautious approach that stresses parallel and interlinked developments. In the Deccan, such parallel developments meant that old identities, sensitivities and memories resurfaced time and again in a constantly changing political scene, to which we turn next.

New Order? Rise of Political Islam in the Deccan

The old order that was shaped by the regional kingdoms altered rapidly with the arrival of new armies from the north. Muslim communities had lived in the south, along the Konkan and Malabar coasts but also inland, for centuries.[87] But military and political intervention of Muslim-ruled polities began only around the turn of the fourteenth century. Early invasions were clearly motivated by a desire for a share in what Delhi imagined as the wealth of the south, but the sultans soon aspired to claim sovereignty over the entire subcontinent. The first campaign was likely improvised and mundane in its intentions. Around 1296, Gurhasp Malik (later ᶜAlaᵓ al-Din Khalji) raided the Yadava capital of Devgiri. Without permission from his uncle and father-in-law, Sultan Jalal al-Din Firoz Shah (r. 1290–6), Gurhasp may have used the profits to build his own power base for a future bid for the throne. As the main Yadava army was occupied elsewhere, Gurhasp defeated Yadava forces and coerced Ramachandra (r. 1271–1312) to surrender large tribute, the revenues of Berar and, according to several reports, also his daughter. Even this did not change the geopolitical picture in the region: Ramachandra retained his control over Yadava territories and continued with his war against the Hoysalas. However, Gurhasp's raid began the long process of incorporation of the Deccan into the imagination of Delhi's rulers and elites, ushering in the migration of Muslims from the north.[88]

ᶜAlaᵓ al-Din Khalji (r. 1296–1316) continued raiding. Following an abortive attempt to attack the Kakatiya capital of Warangal in 1302–3, and on the pretext that Ramachandra failed to pay tribute, he sent his slave-general Malik Kafur to the Deccan. In 1308, Malik Kafur defeated the Yadavas and reaffirmed Ramachandra's status as a tributary of Delhi. He then proceeded to Warangal, probably with Ramachandra's assistance. Such a development should not come as a surprise, considering the tense relationship between the dynasties. Delhi's army defeated Prataparudra (r. 1287–1323) in 1310, and collected a large tribute; at around the same time, the famous Delhi-based poet Amir Khusrau described the plentiful supply of gems captured in temples, likely in the south.[89] The following year, Malik Kafur arrived in the Hoysala capital of Dwarasamudra. The Hoysalas were at the time exhausted by their involvement in the War of Pandya Succession, in which Prataparudra was also involved as Delhi's tributary and to chastise his rebelling tributaries. Consequently, the Hoysala king Ballala III (r. 1291–1342) surrendered and paid large tribute, thereby guaranteeing the survival of his dynasty for a few more decades. From there, Malik Kafur continued to Pandya territories. Collecting substantial wealth from the country and its temples, he did not defeat the royal army or loot the capital, Madurai. After returning to the north, Malik Kafur raided the Deccan again in 1312–14 with similar success; this time, his forces annexed Devgiri.

With ʿAlaʾ al-Din's death in 1316, the rulers of the Deccan stopped paying tribute to Delhi. Therefore, in 1318, Sultan Qutb al-Din Mubarak Shah (r. 1316–20) initiated yet another campaign, captured Devgiri and annihilated the Yadava dynasty. As per the familiar dynamics in the region, several tributaries of the Yadavas took advantage of the new situation to claim semi-independent status. Not only tributaries; Delhi's first Khalji governor of Devgiri, Malik Yaklakhi, aspired to establish independent rule in Devgiri. Suppressing the opposition, the sultan sent forces to further plunder Warangal and continued to the lands to the east, down to the Bay of Bengal.[90] This period of two decades severely interrupted the existing political order, however, it did not create a new one to substitute it as of yet.

This changed in 1320 with the collapse of Khalji rule in Delhi. The founder of the new dynasty, Ghiyath al-Din Tughluq (r. 1320–5), embarked on fully-fledged imperial expansion. In 1321, his son Ulugh Khan (later Muhammad b. Tughluq) arrived in the Deccan. Within two years he had defeated Prataparudra, annexed Warangal and continued to conquer the Pandya capital of Madurai. The policies of Delhi were clearly intended to annex the south, but with limited success. Early in the reign of Muhammad b. Thughluq (r. 1325–51), a rebellion broke in Sagar, followed by uprisings in Andhra, Kampili, Bidar and Gulbarga. The rebellions spread among various groups, including local magnates who refused to accept Delhi's rule at all, others who had at first cooperated but changed their minds, and even Muslim commanders who arrived with Delhi's armies. Discontent on similar grounds generated anti-Tughluq actions not only in the Deccan, but throughout the empire.

In order to secure their rule, the Tughluqs tried a variety of methods. Eaton and Wagoner note that there was a fundamental difference between the opposite sides of the Krishna River. South of the river, Muhammad b. Tughluq recruited chieftains as tributary commanders (*amīr*s), using the system of suzerainty; no governors or settlers were established there, nor were imperial coins minted or circulated. In contrast, the Tughluqs ruled the northern Deccan directly, by posting Muslim governors from north India in urban centres, setting mints and settling Muslim immigrants-colonists as rural landholders. In parallel, Delhi tried to assimilate old elites, who previously served the Yadavas or Kakatiyas, as revenue assignment holders (*iqṭāʿdār*s), in a fashion similar to the policies south of the Krishna.[91] Muhammad b. Tughluq went one step further. In 1327, he pronounced the old Yadava capital of Devgiri, now renamed Daulatabad, the secondary capital of the sultanate; the choice of Devgiri/Daulatabad reflects the continuation of its political and symbolic significance. Moreover, in a controversial step, he forced nobles and civilians from Delhi to settle there. Others were encouraged by money or land grants. This endeavour mobilised many into the Deccan, including Sufis, ulama and other members of the Muslim intellectual and political elites.[92] Many returned to the north within a few years, but others remained in the Deccan and became the kernel of the Muslim Deccani society.

The early decades of the fourteenth century reflect a substantial reorientation of the Deccan that reshaped political, social, religious and cultural life in the region. This 'revolution', to use S. Krishnaswami Aiyangar's phrase,[93] was explained in various terms, from religious to cultural.[94] Nevertheless, continuity can be traced in the identity of subordinate chieftains, administrative practice and service elites, as well as historical memory throughout the generations and across dynastic divides.[95] This is evident in the indirectly ruled regions south of the Krishna, where old Hoysala elites were absorbed into the sultanate on their former territories, following local patterns.[96] North of the river, too, elements of continuity are evident. Previous non-Muslim landed gentry continued to hold their roles under Tughluq rule. For example, a self-styled scion of the Western Chalukya dynasty named Harpal served under Delhi's rule. Yadava family members continued as magnates under the Tughluqs. The fact that the province of Daulatabad continued to prosper after Khalji raids and the Tughluq conquest indicates that land tenure and administration was not significantly interrupted.[97] In other parts of the Deccan, Delhi's control remained weak. The eastern parts of Telangana in the eastern Deccan, a region that the Western Chalukyas failed to fully absorb, followed the

Mapping the Deccan

pattern of indirect rule similar to the south. Delhi lost control over the region a mere few years after the conquest of Warangal, and by the early 1340s, Telangana was under the control of *nāyaka*s in an example of continuity with pre-Khalji times.[98] Telangana continued to be contested in the following decades. Further north in Andhra, a dynasty claiming to descend from the Eastern Chalukyas of Vengi established practical control over the region of Visakhapatnam (Vizag). Members of the family remained important magnates in the region; at times independent, at other times accepting powerful patrons such as the Gajapatis of Orissa, and finally were absorbed into the Qutb Shahi system in the late sixteenth century.[99] These stories demonstrate the durability of local nobility long after Delhi's conquest.[100] In sum, while Delhi's rule altered important elements of political life in the Deccan, aspects of local administration, landed elites and the military reflect a large degree of continuity.

REBELLION AND DECCANI INDEPENDENCE

Tughluq attempts to consolidate their rule over the Deccan were not successful. In 1339, the Sangama brothers left their allegiance with Delhi and declared their sovereignty south of the Krishna. Establishing a new kingdom that came to be known as Vijayanagara, this development represents significant continuity from the pre-Delhi past.[101] In the following years, a series of rebellions shook Delhi's control over the northern Deccan and elsewhere. Muhammad b. Tughluq introduced oppressive measures, including the killing of commanders whose loyalty he suspected. This only pushed others to unite against Delhi.[102] By 1346, the most successful of the rebelling commanders, Zafar Khan, had defeated Tughluq forces and established independent rule. He took the name Hasan Bahman Shah (r. 1347–58), a name later used for his dynasty. Hasan's success, however, did not sweep the entire Deccan: Tughluq loyalists continued to support the old regime. Various tributaries who gained independence in the turmoil of the 1340s were not willing to submit easily. Others, who had previously been loyal to the Bahmanis, now established autonomous principalities, rejecting central authority of any kind. In 1350, Hasan moved his capital to Gulbarga (renamed Ahsanabad, today Kalaburagi). Located more centrally in the Deccan and farther away from Delhi's border, this move reflects both security concerns and Bahmani choice to create a new and independent identity.[103]

Having established the sultanate, it was from the reign of Hasan's son Muhammad I (r. 1358–75) that the Bahmani sultanate took a truly independent path. Muhammad I reorganised the administrative and military systems, but kept many of institutions and titles inherited from the Tughluqs. At the same time, suggests S. K. Sinha, the Bahmanis followed 'Hindu' (that is, pre-Khalji) land revenue systems,[104] suggesting the resilience of local practices, at least on a local level. Yet the sultanate was facing serious challenges. Neighbouring polities had competing territorial aspirations of their own, most notably Vijayanagara and the still independent *nāyaka*s of Telangana. Defensive effort and expansionist zeal required additional resources and the rationalisation of their use, and the expansion of state service was, therefore, a pressing matter. Muhammad I and his successors turned to the source of manpower most readily available to them, namely, local administrative and military groups. While the integration of local elites had been successful, it also increased their power vis-à-vis the sultans. Landed elites, and occasionally even provincial governors (*ṭarafdār*s), cemented their interests over their locality, and in rare cases even openly rebelled against Gulbarga.[105]

These preliminary changes in the state accelerated in the fifteenth century, taking the sultanate in two seemingly contradictory directions. The first was inward-looking, based on the continuous absorption of local elites into the sultanate. Firoz Shah (r. 1397–1422) recruited non-Muslims such as Brahmins and Telugu *nāyaka*s. Local non-Muslims had an increasing cultural influence on the sultanate, reflected in new architectural features.[106] Firoz Shah even married a daughter of Devaraya I of Vijayanagara (r. 1406–24),[107] demonstrating the growing place the Deccan played in Bahmani political vision. The marriages did not end their struggle over the Raichur *doāb*, yet indicate the integrative nature of Deccani politics. The second direction taken by the Bahmani sultans was opening the court to non-Indian elites. Firoz Shah encouraged migrants from West and Central Asia, chiefly Iran, to come to the Deccan by offering positions in the administrative and military systems. The elites among these migrants were absorbed into the ranks of local nobility, where they were recognised as Foreigners (*gharībān*), changing the composition of the court. Not only in military and administrative affairs, sultans gave patronage to Arabic- and Persian-speaking literati, who added to the composite nature of courtly culture. These policies were attested in a series of anecdotes regarding Firoz Shah's alleged command over Persian, Arabic, Turkish, Telugu, Kannada and Marathi, and in relation to the diversity in origins of the women in his harem. Firoz Shah is recorded as saying that a good ruler should surround himself with people of all nations in order to draw information and expertise. It would be wise to take such enlightened statements with a healthy dose of scepticism, but they may well reflect a political culture of diversity and an effort to generate an accommodating environment.[108]

Inclusive policies, however, could not respond to all challenges. Particularly significant were Sufis, who were fundamental in shaping Islamic life in India. The popularity they enjoyed among the masses gave Sufis significant social appeal, which rulers tried to harness to gain popular support.[109] With their own history as rebels, the Bahmanis had a particular necessity to legitimise their rule. As a result, from the early days of the sultanate, individuals and groups of Sufis secured significant influence in the Bahmani court. Three orders were of particular importance at the time. Two originated in north India, namely, the Chishtis, who were present in the Deccan even before the Tughluq conquest, and the Junaydis. The third order, the Qadiris, represents a trans-regional rather than a local line.[110]

From an early stage, the Bahmanis enjoyed Junaydi support. They further invested in recruiting Chishtis due to their widespread prestige and popularity. Most instrumental in their effort was Shaykh Muhammad Husayni, better known as Khwaja Banda Nawaz Gisu Daraz (1321–1422). Having narrowly escaped the attack on Delhi by the Central Asian conqueror Timur (Tamerlane) in 1398, Gisu Daraz travelled to the Deccan to visit the grave of his father, who had migrated there as part of Muhammad b. Tughluq's Daulatabad project. When in Daulatabad, Firoz Shah approached the saint and invited him to settle in Gulbarga. Gisu Daraz accepted the invitation and established a new spiritual line within Chishti tradition in the city. At first, the sultan and the shaykh enjoyed great proximity. This, however, did not last long as doctrinal and political differences drove the saint and the sultan apart. Gisu Daraz asserted an increasingly oppositional stand on a variety of issues, including royal succession. Whereas political influence was not uncommon among Chishtis, Gisu Daraz utilised his popularity to an unprecedented level of direct political action. His hospice (*khānqāh*) became an independent centre of political power from that of the sultan.[111] The conflict between Firoz Shah and Gisu Daraz brought the sultan to seek the support of other Sufis. He built a new city-palace, Firozabad, possibly to distance the court from Gulbarga and the spiritually uncomfortable situation in which the sultan found himself. In the new site, he sponsored the shrine of another Sufi, Khalifat al-Rahman, who was probably Qadiri.[112]

The tense political atmosphere in Gulbarga around the succession of Firoz Shah drove his brother and successor, Ahmad I (r. 1422–36), to take far-reaching steps. In 1424, he moved his capital to the provincial town of Bidar (renamed Muhammadabad). This choice is indicative of Bahmani political ideas: at the centre of the sultanate, the city is located where the three main vernaculars of the Deccan meet, and not far from the old Western Chalukya capital of Kalyani. Central to the transfer of the capital was the sultan's desire to abandon Gulbarga with its existing elites of local Muslims, Sufis and others, following the model set by his predecessor in Firozabad. Furthermore, similarly to the Tughluq effort in Daulatabad, Ahmad I aspired to engineer a new elite altogether. He invited Foreigners in ever-larger numbers to settle in the sultanate, increasingly relying on their services in the administrative and military systems. With their trans-regional networks, Foreigners became crucial to facilitating international trade in economically and militarily valuable commodities, most notably warhorses. The sultan also created the position of 'Prince of Traders' (*malik al-tujjār*), reflecting the strong link between state formation and trade.[113] Not only politics and trade, Foreigners were also instrumental in turning Bidar into a centre of Islamic learning, where literati, artists and ulama enjoyed significant patronage; these developments are reflected in the architecture still visible in the city. With that, literary production in the court was not limited to Arabic and Persian, as the first signs of Dakhani emerged.[114]

The changing trajectories of the Bahmani court is reflected, once again, in the sultan's choice to alter Sufi allegiance. Just like Firoz Shah's experimentation with changing Sufi patronage in Firozabad, Ahmad I shifted his attention from Chishtis to the Niʿmatullahi branch of the Qadiri order, hitherto not represented in the Deccan. The sultan aimed to attract central figures of the Niʿmatullahi family to join his court, but only secondary members, in terms of spiritual authority, arrived. Most notable of these was Shah Nurullah. Ahmad I initiated himself into the order and married his daughter to the saint, securing links between the royal and Sufi families. The sultan also bestowed the title 'Prince of Shaykhs' (Sufi saint; *malik al-mashāʾikh*) on Shah Nurullah. Shah Nurullah's son Shah Khalilullah maintained high position in the Bahmani court. According to Muhammad Suleman Siddiqi, not only the royal family but 'most of those alien residents of Bider maintained close ties with the members of the Niʿmatullahi family'.[115] In one case at least, a Niʿmatullahi saint received a royal land grant (*jāgīr*).[116] Shah Khalilullah's residence became a central locus of political life during the reign of Ahmad II (1436–58), linking together Foreigners, Sufis and the royal family. This link is well reflected in the tomb of Ahmad I where, argues Peyvand Firouzeh, most inscriptions refer to Shah Niʿmatullah Vali rather to the sultan himself; the tomb 'depicts how the royal and the mystic role are becoming intertwined, and how they depend on each other in the process of institutionalisation of the Sufi orders and legitimation of Islamic dynasties'.[117]

Mapping the Deccan

This Sufi–royal power nexus notwithstanding, most segments of society were not drawn to the Qadiri order, which remained associated with the Foreigners.[118]

With the power shifting in favour of the Foreigners, Deccanis grew resentful.[119] This marks the main social tension among the elites; throughout the period, no evidence suggests inter-religious conflict. Competing identities remained focused around the question of local–foreign; religious divisions played a minor role in the political life of the sultanate. The places where we do see anti-Hindu rhetoric is typically in the context of conflicts against Hindu-ruled kingdoms, which continued throughout the period. To the west, local chieftains asserted considerable independence along the Konkan, bringing the Bahmanis to campaign in the region in 1427. Seemingly successful, the autonomous position of Bahmani officers in the west and the need for additional campaigns against local chieftains in 1447 and 1469–71 suggest that Bahmani control beyond the Sahyadris had never been firm.[120] To the east, the Eastern Gangas of Orissa (not to be confused with the aforementioned Gangas of the Karnatak), previously in competition against the Kakatiyas over Andhra, survived Delhi's invasion but failed to annex significant territories from Telugu *nāyaka*s. By the 1420s, Andhra had become a battleground fought over by independent *nāyaka*s (notably Reddis and Vellamas), Vijayanagara and the emergent Gajapatis of Orissa. Kapileshwara (or Kapilendra, r. 1434–68) conquered the Reddi kingdoms in the 1450s, brought Gajapati control along the coast down to the Krishna River. This put the Bahmanis and Gajapatis in competition for the eastern regions. The Gajapati advance encouraged the Vellamas, by then tributaries of the Bahmanis, to rebel (1459–60). The troubles in the east were accompanied by internal instability in Bidar under the unpopular Humayun (r. 1458–61) and the minor Ahmad III (r. 1461–3), as well as war between the Bahmanis the Malwa sultanate.[121] The Gajapatis captured territories as far inland as Warangal and Devarkonda at the heart of Telangana, and temporarily proceeded into Vijayanagara. For the rest of the century, the Bahmanis, Gajapatis and Vijayanagara continued to struggle for control over the east, with each kingdom trying to intervene in each other's affairs. Thus, the death of Kapileshwara gave rise to a struggle for succession between his son Purushottama and his cousin Hamavira. The latter petitioned for Bahmani assistance. Muhammad III (r. 1463–82) was happy to comply. He sent Malik Hasan Bahri (who later founded the Nizam Shahi sultanate of Ahmadnagar). Supporting Hamavira, he also conquered the strategic Rajahmundry and Kondavidu. Hamavira was eventually defeated by Purushottama (r. 1468–97), who later re-took much of Andhra and Telangana.[122]

Whereas the Gajapatis presented a short-lived and geographically limited challenge to the Bahmanis, Vijayanagara has always been a much closer neighbour and foe. We will discuss the role of Vijayanagara in more detail in the coming chapters. For now, a few observations shall be made. The history of the Bahmani sultanate and Vijayanagara was entangled from their very early days. The two kingdoms emerged in tandem from the same circumstances created by the Tughluq conquest, and grew side-by-side, sharing much of their histories. Their proximity, and the line dividing them, symbolised for many the border between Islam and Hinduism. Vijayanagara was, accordingly, analysed as the last bastion of Hinduism against Islam, a geographical manifestation of the temporal watershed between 'Hindu' and 'Muslim' India. The relations between the two, however, were infinitely more complex, combining factors of amity and hostility. The ambitions of both empires put them in competition, which usually remained limited to border regions, particularly the Raichur *doāb*. Expeditions may have penetrated each other's territory, but the borderline did not alter significantly between the metropolitan regions of the kingdoms. More significant were advances in the marginal and contested regions of Andhra, Telangana and, to a lesser degree, also the Konkan.[123] At the same time, large-scale exchange continued in people, culture, currency, trade and military technologies.

Delhi's brief rule over the Deccan brought about profound changes to the region. These changes were pushed forward under the Bahmanis. Gradually developing their own independent sense of rule, the sultans relied heavily on Muslim elites, whose composition continued to evolve. The new trends led many to see the period as marking an era of change, in which new people and institutions replaced the old ones. This assumption, however, underplays a strong component of continuity. From the early second millennium, parallel trajectories of continuity and change dominated Deccani history. New ideas regarding language, locality and society emerged beside old ones. Pre-existing institutions, ideologies and people continued to exist alongside the newcomers, with great mutual impact. Similar historical process can be assumed to have continued after Delhi's conquest, and, even more so, under Bahmani rule. The new elites and institutions were built on top of old mechanisms, practices as well as elite groups, not replacing them. When the rulers required local expertise or manpower, they turned to those who were found in place. Indeed, from Tughluq days, and more so from the turn of the fifteenth century, Muslim rulers incorporated old elites, from Hoysala magnates to Brahmins and Telugu *nāyaka*s. These old elites mark an avenue of continuation in the Deccan that continued to the Deccan sultanates.

Mapping the Deccan

The Multiple Spaces of the Deccan

Having surveyed the main trends in the history of the Deccan in the first half of the second millennium, let us return to the question with which we opened this chapter: what is, then, the Deccan? The historical processes mapped in the chapter suggest a multiplicity of definitions and trajectories. Throughout the long period discussed here, we can mark a series of developments, sometimes complementary, otherwise contradictory, in operation on diverse land and society. The rise of vernacular identities manifested itself as a unifying force and political tool under one dynasty and in one language, but not so much in another. Inclusive imperial or all-Indic identities did not die out even under thriving vernacular identities. Above all, trends did not replace one another but existed simultaneously alongside one another, even if latently. Frames of reference and group identity were carried for long periods of time. Elite groups, by themselves flexible and changeable, continued to serve across dynastic divides, perpetuating identities and memories, which themselves turned into a political currency.

Resulting from these parallel processes were several dividing lines that surfaced time and again. First, and most commonly referred to in the historiography, is the division between the northern and southern Deccan, along the Krishna–Tungabhadra rivers, with the Raichur *doāb* between them constantly contested. A second set of breaks is along vernacular lines, between Telugu, Marathi and Kannada. Third, is the topographical–ecological division between the semi-arid, mixed-economy plateau and the more intensively farmed agricultural coastal region. The three sets of borders present new problems. Borders were far from fixed; during the lives of dynasties, borders changed and regions were contested, and even more so when the political setting changed. Vernacular-based divisions, too, were not always clear-cut, as reflected in the blurry region in between the Marathi and Kannada spaces. Moreover, the three sets of borders do not sit comfortably with one another. Telugu and Kannada spaces are located on both sides of the Krishna. Historical dynamics brought inherent tensions within each space, notably between the uplands and the coast. As a result, historical, linguistic and political trajectories were in operation simultaneously in opposite directions. These processes brought about the creation of subsets of micro-regions within peninsular India. Some units were recorded by name for centuries, even if it is not always possible to precisely map them.[124]

With this in mind, we can now mark the main units in the Deccan. The Marathi-speaking region historically comprises two sub-regions (with

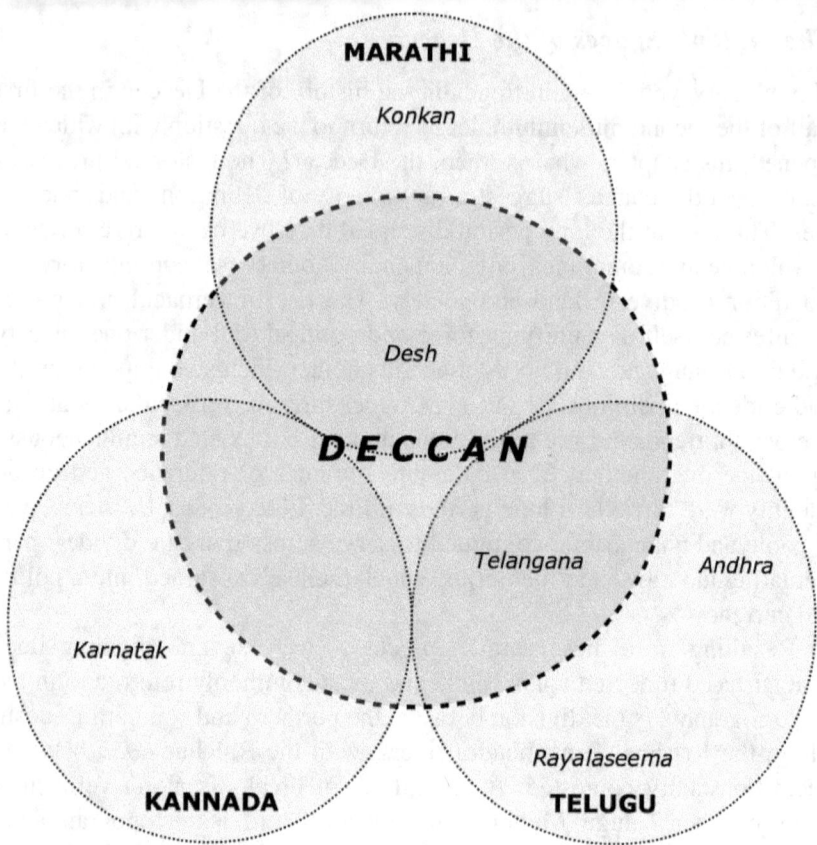

Figure 1.2 Subdivisions of the Deccan

further divisions also extant): the Desh (Marathi: *deś*, 'land, country'),[125] the Marathi-speaking part of the Deccan Plateau; and the Konkan, the coastal plain to the west, along the shores of the Arabian Sea. In between the regions stretches the steep Sahyadri Range (Western Ghats). The physical conditions dividing the regions do not facilitate easy communications in the best of conditions; in the heavy monsoon rains of western India, roads through the mountains became impassable. Notwithstanding the difficulties, trade links were well established between the regions, including foodstuff and resources, however, they remained secondary to trade within each sub-region.[126]

This geographical separation led to distinctive trajectories operating in each sub-region. The Konkan has historically been better connected to the world of the Arabian Sea and to trans-regional circuits of trade. This link attracted merchants and settlers; the Portuguese were by no means the first to have arrived this way. The Desh looked inwardly; we have seen that the region was historically linked to the Karnatak to its south, and at times also to Telangana to the east. Social divisions also existed, as language has not been an ultimate unifier. Among Marathi-speaking Brahmins, two groups are noted, Deshastha and Konkanastha. The identification is, clearly, geographical: the former are identified with the Desh, and the latter with the Konkan.[127] Even the alleged linguistic unity between the Desh and the Konkan is not straightforward, and regional variations continued to evolve. Already in the early seventeenth century, the Portuguese scholar Gaspar de S. Miguel noted that there was a linguistic difference between Konkani and Marathi inland; Marathi was used by some along the coast, too, but not understood by the masses.[128] This is not to suggest that there was no idea of Marathi-speaking lands. Yet, with the geographical conditions of the Desh and the Konkan, we cannot assume a smooth and uninterrupted Marathi space.

The other linguistic spaces of the Deccan demonstrate similar internal divisions. The Kannada-speaking lands spread on both sides of the Krishna in a historically contested region: its northern territories were included in political centres to either north (Kalyani) or south (Dwarasamudra, Vijayanagara). More often than not, the Kannada lands were politically divided; even in the period of regional kingdoms, the Hoysalas and the Yadavas struggled for the control over the northern half of the land. This contestation is reflected in nomenclature. Whereas the lands south of the Tungabhadra are widely referred to as the Karnatak, there is no clear term to include the northern Kannada lands notwithstanding their significance as home of the historical centres of Kalyani, Gulbarga, Bidar and Bijapur; none of these became associated with any vernacular in particular. More often than not, this region is simply called 'Deccan'.

The Telugu space, too, was divided to different sub-regions: Telangana, Rayalaseema and Andhra. Similar to the Kannada space, the Telugu lands have been more often divided than untied: Andhra was contested between its neighbours to the north and south; Rayalaseema was at times united with the Cholas and was part of the metropolitan regions of Vijayanagara; and Telangana often served as a frontier zone fought over by neighbours on all sides, to the west (Western Chalukyas, Bahmanis), east and northeast (Reddis, Velamas, Gajapatis) or south (Cholas, Vijayanagara).

With these divisions, it is clear that there is no one satisfactory definition of the Deccan; it depends on when and in whose opinion. A promising direction would be to understand the region as a space along the lines suggested by Doreen Massey: comprising a series of smaller units, each created by its own history and by its own people;

the connection between the sub-regions reflect specific historical circumstances and the memory thereof; the region did not remain fixed, but was constantly changing while hosting simultaneous contradictory trajectories.

This notion is rather different from Firishta's clear-cut idea of the Deccan as the sum of the three vernaculars. In the particular moment under discussion, the Deccan was a region in which a multiplicity of political centres were located: Daulatabad under Delhi; the Bahmani capitals of Gulbarga, Bidar and also the short-lived Firozabad; the political centres of all sultanates: Ahmadnagar, Bijapur, Ellichpur and Golkonda. This region cut across the three main vernacular spaces: Daulatabad, Ahmadnagar and Ellichpur in Marathi-speaking regions; Bidar, Gulbarga and Bijapur in Kannada (or, significantly, contested Kannada–Marathi) lands; Golkonda in Telugu-speaking Telangana; this was the core of the political system of the Bahmani and Deccan sultanates. However, parts of the three vernacular spaces were not included: the Karnatak and Rayalaseema, in the south; the Konkan in the west; and Andhra in the east. While these regions maintained obvious links to their respective vernacular, various forces pulled them away. Not completely foreign, then, I suggest seeing these regions as the periphery of the political system of the Bahmani and successor Deccan sultanates. This schematic definition focuses on the perspective of sultanates; a different view would emerge in the vernacular peripheries. Yet, for our discussion here, I argue that this geographical, political, historical and cultural understanding of the Deccan as comprising a set of subunits in varying relations provides a useful tool for the analysis of the region and the constraints within which the rulers were operating. First and foremost, was the need to keep it all together in a diverse and changeable environment, in which various forces operated against unity. For this, a stronger content to the Deccan proper was needed, to which we will turn in next.

Notes

1. Thapar, 'Significance of Regional History', pp. 19–20.
2. Fisher, *Mughal Empire*, pp. 36–7.
3. Raychaudhuri, 'Geography of the Deccan', pp. 3–4, 13–43; Joshi, 'Historical Geography of Medieval Deccan', vol. 1, pp. 3–4.
4. The external origins of the term and its lack of clear definition are similar to the vague-yet-broad medieval Islamic idea of *al-hind*, see Wink, *Al-Hind*, vol. 1, p. 5.
5. Gribble, *History of the Deccan* [n.p]. This is not the most geographi-

cally restricted definition: the *Imperial Gazetteer* xi, p. 205, suggests that the Deccan 'in the narrower sense ... has much the same meaning as Maharashtra, or the country where the Marathi language is spoken, if the below-Ghat (i.e.) coastal tract (i.e., the Konkan) be omitted'.
6. Sherwani, *Bahmanis*, pp. 1–11. A similar view is presented in Shyam, *Ahmadnagar*, pp. 1–3.
7. Joshi, 'Historical Geography of Medieval Deccan', vol. 1, pp. 3–4; see also Raychaudhuri, 'Geography of the Deccan', pp. 3–13. The two articles were published as the geographical introductions to edited volumes. They were part of an initiative to create a systematic and encompassing history of the Deccan from antiquity to modern times, along the lines of the *Cambridge History of India* (1922), with the support of the Government of Andhra Pradesh. See Yazdani, *Early History of the Deccan*, pp. v–viii.
8. Sherwani, *Bahmanis*, pp. 1–13.
9. Joshi, 'Historical Geography of Medieval Deccan', vol. 1, p. 4. A blurrier iteration of the same sense was introduced by the French traveller Jean de Thévenot, who claims that 'Decam was heretofore a most powerful Kingdom, if one may believe the Indians', but he includes in this definition 'all the Countries that are in that great Tongue of Land, which is betwixt the Gulfs of Cambaye (Arabian Sea) and Bengala', i.e., the entirety of peninsular India. He continues that the kingdom was unified under one king, 'but that Kingdom in process of time hath been often dismembered; and in the beginning of the last Age, (when the Portuguese made Conquests therein) it was divided into many Provinces'. This description seems to be based on a mix of geographical misunderstanding but more solid local historical memory which links the term Deccan with the political sense. See Thévenot, *Travels of Monsieur de Thévenot*, vol. 3, p. 87. See also discussion in Alam, 'Historic Deccan'.
10. *Futuhat-i ʿAdil Shahi*, p. 401r–v.
11. *Burhan-i Maʾathir*, p. 272.
12. *Tarikh-i Qutb Shah*, p. 146v. For a discussion of the complex narratives of origin of the Deccani dynasties, see Fischel, 'Origin Narratives'.
13. *Futuhat-i ʿAdil Shahi*, p. 25r. The Bahmani memory is also reflected in the continuous use of Bahmani (and Vijayanagara) coins in the region throughout the sixteenth century, see Sohoni, 'The Non-Issue of Coinage'; Wagoner, 'Money Use in the Deccan'.
14. *Muntakhab al-Lubab*, vol. 3, p. 332.
15. *Burhan-i Maʾathir*, pp. 547–8.
16. Eaton, *Social History*, pp. 1–2. In his description of the current situation of the Deccan, Firishta mentions the three *qaum*s of the region, referring to the speakers of the three vernaculars. The term *qaum* is not a straightforward one. Eaton chooses to translate it as a (language) community. This translation, however, seems to be somewhat limited, considering the nature of groups described here and their identity. In this context, *qaum* refers to

groups larger than any specific community as it includes all speakers of each of the three vernaculars, each comprising many communities varied in locality, class, religion and occupation. Therefore, a better translation here would be 'nation' as a larger, more loosely knit network of identity, notwithstanding the obvious problems raised by this term. Furthermore, it was not unusual in Islamicate historiography to locate groups (including non-Muslim) within familiar genealogies, typically biblical, thus folding them into familiar historiography. For example, Peter Golden suggests that the Khazar king Joseph called himself 'King of Togarmah', referring to the son of Japheth from whom the Turks derived according to medieval Jewish traditions; 'Khazar' is presented as one of Togarmah's ten sons. See Golden, 'Eternal Stones', pp. 20–1.

17. Mitchell, 'Knowing the Deccan', pp. 151–3.
18. Kołodziejczyk, 'Ottoman Frontiers', p. 212.
19. Eaton and Wagoner, *Power, Memory, Architecture*, pp. 331–49.
20. *Tadhkirat al-Muluk*, p. 37v.
21. *Tarikh-i Firishta*, vol. 2, p. 119. The term *iqṭāʿ* is generally equivalent in the South Asian context to the Persian *jāgīr*.
22. *Burhan al-Maʾathir*, p. 444.
23. For example, ʿAli ʿAdil Shah I of Bijapur demanded that Ibrahim Qutb Shah cede control of several forts and villages on his border. See *Futuhat-i ʿAdil Shahi*, p. 88v.
24. *Tarikh-i Qutb Shah*, p. 114v.
25. *Hadiqat al-Salatin*, p. 156.
26. For example, Sholapur, *Basatin al-Salatin*, p. 309; Murtazanagar, *Tarikh-i Qutb Shah*, p. 219r.
27. Anne Feldhaus demonstrates that rivers were, and still are, used as political or administrative boundaries and perceived as religious or ritualistic boundaries. See Feldhaus, *Connected Places*, pp. 38–42.
28. *Basatin al-Salatin*, p. 315.
29. The name of river in Zubayri's description is erroneous. The political centre of the Sultanate of Bijapur, including the capital and, in fact, all its early possessions prior to 1565, are located north of the Krishna, therefore this division does not make sense. The correct river is the Bhima, a major left-bank tributary of the Krishna. See Eaton, *Sufis of Bijapur*, map on p. xvi. *Bombay Gazetteer* xvii, p. 398 mentions 'the districts north of the Bhima' as the regions now under direct Mughal rule.
30. *Tarikh-i Qutb Shah*, pp. 219v–221v, quotation on p. 220v. This display, however, did not convince the royal army, and eventually the imposter's plan came to naught.
31. Whilst there is clear sense of boundary, it is not always easy to draw to borders due to the scarcity of data. Ziayuddin Shakeb was able to produce a convincing map of the Sultanate of Golkonda in the late seventeenth century, see Shakeb, 'Map of the Sultanate of Golconda'. Yet this cannot

Mapping the Deccan

be compared with the richness of sources regarding north India. Habib, *An Atlas of the Mughal Empire*, employs a series of land documents to construct a detailed map of the Mughal Empire. The maps of the Deccan as they appear in the atlas refer to the years after the Mughal conquest in the late 1680s. See also Habib, *Agrarian System of Mughal India*.

32. Thévenot says that this region, known as 'Balagate' (Balaghat), 'according to the Indian Geographers, divides India into the two parts of North and South'. See Thévenot, *Travels of Monsieur de Thévenot*, vol. 3, p. 80.
33. For example, the war between the Rastrakutas and Paramaras of Malwa around 972 did not create a lasting conquest of either side of the boundary, see Nilakanta Sastri, *A History of South India*, p. 171.
34. Ayyangar, 'Hindu States', p. 467. An interesting manifestation of the significance of the region, in particular the Vindhyas, can be found in the Telugu play *Satidānaśūramu*, attributed to the Maratha ruler Shahaji II (r. 1684–1712). In the play, one Brahmin is quoted as saying that 'People like us, who feed on good rice, fresh ghee, milk and curds have no hope of self-control any more than the Vindhya Mountains can float over the sea', suggesting that the Vindhya, and not the prominent Sahyadris (Western Ghats), were the symbol of stability and sturdiness. See Subrahmanyam, 'Hearing Voices', p. 86.
35. Ritti, *Seunas*, pp. 85–6, 113–16.
36. The expression 'the border of the Deccan' (*sar-ḥadd-i dakkan*) was attached to several places in the region, such as Handiya on the banks of the Narmada (on one of the main roads from the north into the Deccan). The region was known as 'the border of the Deccan and Malwa' or the 'High Ghats' (*bālā-i ghāt*), referring to the mountain ranges in the region, see *Tarikh-i Firishta*, vol. 2, pp. 119, 284; *Hadiqat al-Salatin*, p. 92; Khan, 'Roads to the Deccan', p. 243. Khandesh, the region and sixteenth-century sultanate, is located within the border region, and has a complex history associated with its position as the meeting point of the Deccan, Gujarat and Malwa. Khandesh was not part of the Bahmani sultanate, and therefore cannot be considered as part of the political Deccan. The sultanate was annexed by the Mughals in 1601. See Shyam, *Malik Ambar*; Shyam, *Khandesh*.
37. Devi, *After the Kakatiyas*, p. 25; Eaton, *Social History*, pp. 21–2.
38. Chatterjee, *Cultures of History*, pp. 35–45; Eaton, *Bengal Frontier*, pp. 56–70; Sarkar, *Swadeshi Movement*.
39. Sheikh, *Forging a Region*, citation on p. 218.
40. It is possible that other regions such as Orissa were amidst a similar process of developing linguistic-historical identities around the same time, however, this awaits further study; see Sahu, 'Brahminical Ideology', p. 12.
41. This issue is linked to the more general historical problem of periodisation, and its special challenges in the Indian context, where north India remains

the standard and the idiosyncrasies of the south are pushed aside. See Ali, 'The Historiography of the Medieval'.
42. Yazdani, *Early History of the Deccan*, ends his narrative with the decline of the Yadavas and Kakatiyas around 1300; Gribble opens his *History of the Deccan* with the rise of the Bahmanis. A clearer reference to the medieval appears in the highly influential, two-volume work by Sherwani and Joshi, *History of Medieval Deccan*. They define the beginning of the medieval in the Deccan with the Khalji invasions of the 1290s. Similarly, Sinha, *Mediaeval History of the Deccan*, refers to the Bahmanis as the first Deccani medieval dynasty, while his treatment of the pre-Bahmani past is very brief and focuses mostly on the Khaljis and Tughlaqs. In his *South India and Her Muhammadan Invaders*, S. Krishnaswami Aiyangar focuses on the invasion itself as a decisive event in the history of south India. This periodisation relies heavily on the importation of ideas that developed in the context of north India, with its division into 'Hindu' ('classical' or 'ancient') and 'Muslim' ('medieval') periods, popularised by James Mill in the early nineteenth century. See Mill, *British India*.
43. Eaton and Wagoner, *Power, Memory, Architecture*, pp. xxiii–xiv. And yet they chose to start their study in 1300.
44. *Doāb* (from Persian, *do āb*, two rivers) is a fertile tract between two rivers; compare with *panj āb* (Punjab), five rivers.
45. Nilakanta Sastri, 'The Chalukyas of Kalyani', vol. 1, pp. 315–468; Nilakanta Sastri and Venkataramanayya, 'The Eastern Chalukyas and the Chalukyas of Vemulavada', vol. 2, pp. 469–512; Eaton and Wagoner, *Power, Memory, Architecture*, pp. 3–15; Rama Rao, *Karnataka–Andhra Relations*, pp. 36–7; Cox, *Politics, Kingship, and Poetry*.
46. Ritti, *Seunas*, pp. 21–205; Murthy, *Sevunas*, pp. 22–143; Desai, Ritti and Gopal, *Karnataka*, pp. 225–50.
47. Derrett, *Hoysalas*; Krishnaswamiengar, 'Origin of Hoysalas', pp. 38–43; Desai, Ritti and Gopal, *Karnataka*, pp. 258–89.
48. Jha, *Kakatiyas*; Venkataramanayya and Sarma, 'The Kakatiyas of Warangal', vol. 2, pp. 575–713.
49. Edwin, 'The Hoysalas and the Tamil Kingdoms', pp. 66–70.
50. Derrett, *Hoysalas*, pp. 91–2.
51. Ritti, *Seunas*, pp. 127–8, 156–8, 172–4.
52. Nilakanta Sastri, *A History of South India*, pp. 207–8.
53. Eaton, 'Kiss my Foot', p. 292.
54. Stein, *Vijayanagara*, p. 21.
55. Talbot, 'Political Intermediaries', p. 262.
56. See discussion in Inden, *Imagining India*, pp. 213–62.
57. Murthy, *Sevunas*, pp. 226–9.
58. Murthy, *Sevunas*, pp. 150–7, suggests that 'generally, the defeated chief or his successors used to be appointed as feudatories. But in the absence of the members of the defeated family the imperial officers used to be appointed

as feudatories.' See also Ritti, *Seunas*, pp. 87–90, 94–5, 117–18, 159–160, 209–23.
59. The Kotas of Telangana, for example, present such need of reminders. See Ganapathi, *Subordinate Rulers*, pp. 10–11.
60. Talbot, 'Political Intermediaries'; Ganapathi, *Subordinate Rulers*, pp. 130–44; Nilakanta Sastri, *A History of South India*, pp. 212–13; Eaton, *Social History*, pp. 15–16.
61. Cox, 'Law, Literature', pp. 167–82; Eaton and Wagoner, *Power, Memory, Architecture*, pp. 4–15.
62. Pollock, 'Cosmopolitan and Vernacular', pp. 591–625; Pollock, *The Language of the Gods*, pp. 283–423.
63. The earliest known written inscriptions in Kannada can be traced to the sixth century, see Mugali, *Kannada Literature*, p. 2. Telugu inscriptions were issued before the eleventh century, but the greatest increase in their number is dated only to the mid-eleventh century and after, see Talbot, *Precolonial India*, pp. 18–37. Marathi is quite difficult to trace as it developed from Prakrit while the main literary language was still Sanskrit. The earliest inscription in Marathi is dated to 983 in Shravanbelgola near Mysore, Karnataka, far from the Marathi lands. It is likely that in Maharashtra it had been in use for centuries before. See Deshpande and Rajadhyaksha, *Marathi Literature*, pp. 4–6. However, considering the status of scholarship regarding the vernaculars in that period, conclusions remain highly tentative.
64. Talbot, *Precolonial India*, pp. 4–11, 25–47.
65. Eaton and Wagoner, *Power, Memory, Architecture*, pp. 15–18.
66. See discussion in Chapter 5.
67. Narayana Rao, 'Multiple Literary Cultures', pp. 384–5.
68. Pillai, *The Kannadas*, vol. 4, pp. 71–2; Desai, Ritti and Gopal, *Karnataka*, pp. 300–10.
69. Pollock, *The Language of the Gods*, pp. 381–3.
70. Ben-Herut, *Siva's Saints*.
71. Feldhaus, 'Maharashtra as a Holy Land', p. 535; Pollock, *The Language of the Gods*, pp. 417–19.
72. Murthy, *Sevunas*, pp. 28–9, 196–202; Ritti, *Seunas*, pp. 25–7, 199–200, 294–9; Altekar, 'The Yadavas of Seundesa', vol. 2, pp. 570–2; Deshpande and Rajadhyaksha, *Marathi Literature*, pp. 8–17.
73. Eaton, *Social History*, pp. 13–14.
74. Murthy, *Sevunas*, pp. 198–9.
75. Pillai, *The Kannadas*, vol. 4, pp. 92–3; Desai, Ritti and Gopal, *Karnataka*, pp. 252–4; Dikshit, *Medieval Karnataka*, pp. 12–13
76. Awalikar, *Marathi–Kannada Relationship*. Similar ideas of unclearly marked boundaries in the western Deccan of late medieval times appears also in Sharma, *Dvaita School of Vedānta*, pp. 342–3.
77. At the same time, Subrahmanian, 'Origin of the Hoysalas', p. 44, questions

the link between a linguistic and political border in the Tamil and Telugu regions (except for in Tirupati), suggesting that even the Telugu region may not have been as clearly defined as suggested.

78. Feldhaus, 'Maharashtra as a Holy Land', p. 546.
79. Keune, 'Eknath in Context'.
80. O'Hanlon, 'Letters Home', pp. 201–10.
81. Wentworth, 'Insiders, Outsiders'.
82. Orsini, 'The Multilingual Local', pp. 353–6.
83. Sahu, 'Brahminical Ideology', pp. 7–8.
84. Bronner and Shulman, 'A Cloud turned Goose'.
85. Narayana Rao, 'Coconut and Honey'; Narayana Rao and Shulman, *Srinatha*, p. 72. An example of the interplay between Telugu and Sanskrit is the writing of bi-textual or multi-textual texts (texts which carry simultaneous multiple meanings), which remained an active style almost exclusively in Sanskrit in the first half of the second millennium. The one exception is Telugu, in which bi-textuality began to appear in the fourteenth century and expanded significantly in the sixteenth century. Telugu authors appropriated the Sanskrit-based style, but continued to experiment in it. Thus, Telugu poets took Sanskritised works but relocated them in the Telugu environment with its unique themes and experiences. See Bronner, *Extreme Poetry*, pp. 132–9.
86. Loewy Shacham, 'Krsnadevaraya's Amuktamalyada', pp. 162–206.
87. The earliest Muslim communities in the Konkan are said to have originated from Basra, from whence they escaped the Umayyad governor Hajjaj b. Yusuf, settling in India in 699. More convincing evidence indicates that Muslim communities were well established in the region in the early tenth century, under the Rastrakutas, see Khalidi, 'Konkani Muslims', pp. 127–53. Derrett, *Hoysalas*, p. 71, suggests that Muslim mercenaries took part in the campaign of the Chalukyan emperor Jagadekamalla against the Hoysalas as early as the 1140s; it is clear that in the following centuries, significant numbers of Muslims served in Hoysala and Pandya armies. See also Jackson, *Delhi Sultanate*, pp. 193–4; Prange, *Monsoon Islam*; and discussion in Chapter 3.
88. Lal, *History of the Khaljis*, pp. 33–47; Joshi and Husain, 'Khaljis and Tughluqs', vol. 1, pp. 31–42; Jackson, *Delhi Sultanate*, pp. 100, 124, 146–7; Khan, 'Shaikh Burhanu'd-din Gharib', pp. 236–43; Ritti, *Seunas*, pp. 186–90; Murthy, *Sevunas*, pp. 129–32; Eaton, *Sufis of Bijapur*, pp. 19–39.
89. Dalrymple and Anand, *Koh-i-Noor*, ch. 1.
90. Lal, *History of the Khaljis*, pp. 226–61, 293–4, 301–4; Joshi and Husain, 'Khaljis and Tughluqs', vol. 1, pp. 42–52; Jackson, *Delhi Sultanate*, pp. 87, 158, 201–10; Derrett, *Hoysalas*, pp. 143–74; Jha, *Kakatiyas*, pp. 237–60; Eaton, *Social History*, pp. 16–19.
91. Eaton and Wagoner, *Power, Memory, Architecture*, pp. 27–8; Eaton, *Social History*, pp. 24–6, 37–43. Simon Digby marks the advance of Muslim (in

particular, Sufi) settlement, including in the northern Deccan, as part of a broader moment in the history of the subcontinent in the fourteenth century, one that included the emergence of new provincial centres mostly to the south and east of Delhi, and the spread of their literary cultures. See Digby, 'Before Timur Came'.

92. Joshi and Husain, 'Khaljis and Tughluqs', vol. 1, pp. 52–5; Jackson, *Delhi Sultanate*, pp. 164–5, 207–13, 232, 258–63; Eaton, *Social History*, pp. 34–43; Husain, *Tughluq Dynasty*, pp. 144–64.
93. Aiyangar, *South India and Her Muhammadan Invaders*, p. 74.
94. Eaton and Wagoner explain the change in terms of changing dominant cosmopolitan, from Sanskritic to Persianate. See Eaton and Wagoner, *Power, Memory, Architecture*, pp. 18–27.
95. Murthy, *Sevunas*, p. 144.
96. Fukazawa, *Medieval Deccan*, pp. 1–48; Eaton, *Social History*, pp. 24–6, 37–40; Guha, 'Serving the Barbarian', pp. 505–10.
97. Jackson, *Delhi Sultanate*, pp. 202–3, 210, 251.
98. Ranga, *Kakatiya Nayaks*, pp. 58–88; Devi, *After the Kakatiyas*, pp. 26–49.
99. Devi, *After the Kakatiyas*, pp. 230–8.
100. The Deccan was not an exception: the Delhi sultanate began to incorporate non-Muslim magnates in military and administrative capacities even in the heartlands of the sultanate as early as under Sultan Ghiyath al-Din Balban (r. 1266–87). See Khan, 'Attitude of the Delhi Sultans', pp. 45–51.
101. Carla Sinopoli presents various accounts of the foundation of the kingdom, many of which associate the founders to pre-Delhi formations, including the Hoysalas and the Kakatiyas, aimed at presenting the new kingdom favourably to various audiences, see Sinopoli, 'From the Lion Throne', pp. 371–2. Barbara Mears suggests that Vijayanagara coins used pre-Vijayanagara symbols, supporting the idea that continuity from pre-Vijayanagara times bore political significance within the empire, see Mears, 'Coins of the Vijayanagara Empire'.
102. During this period, Delhi lost control over the Deccan, Bengal and the Tamil lands, where the short-lived Sultanate of Maʿbar gained independence in Madurai, later to be conquered by Vijayanagara. Other rebellions broke out in Gujarat and even in the heart of the kingdom, however, they were quelled. Delhi's control over Gujarat lasted until 1411. See Jackson, *Delhi Sultanate*, pp. 162, 267–70; Husain, *Tughluq Dynasty*, pp. 195–57, 600–6.
103. Jackson, *Delhi Sultanate*, pp. 272–7; Sherwani, 'The Bahmanis', vol. 1, pp. 143–53; Sherwani, *Bahmanis*, pp. 27–52; Eaton, *Social History*, pp. 37–43.
104. Sinha, *Mediaeval History of the Deccan*, p. 131.
105. Sherwani, 'The Bahmanis', vol. 1, pp. 154–8; Sherwani, *Bahmanis*, pp. 53–96; Devi, *After the Kakatiyas*, pp. 65–7.

106. Sherwani, 'The Bahmanis', vol.1, pp. 76–7; Michell and Zebrowski, *Architecture and Art*, p. 115. A notable example is the use of motifs based on lotus and other plants in Bahmani architecture. Some sources even position the early Marathas in Bahmani service, see Krishna, *Shivaji the Great*, pp. 40–7. The sources, however, were composed later and suggest an attempt to legitimise the Maratha, in particular Bhonsle, position in retrospect.
107. Eaton, *Social History*, p. 74, also suggests that 'Firoz Shah also married his son to a woman who resided in a border region disputed by the Bahmani and Vijayanagara states, and whom the raja of Vijayanagara had *wished* to marry'.
108. Sherwani, 'The Bahmanis', vol.1, pp. 158–64; Sherwani, *Bahmanis*, pp. 97–120; Michell and Eaton, *Firuzabad*.
109. Digby, 'The Sufi Shaykh and the Sultan'; Ahmad, 'The Sufi and the Sultan'; Auer, 'Sufism and Power'. Needless to say, not all Sufis were keen on subjugating their charisma to secular authority.
110. Siddiqi, *Bahmani Sufis*, pp. 31–70, 95–116.
111. Eaton, *Social History*, pp. 47–58; Siddiqi, *Bahmani Sufis*, pp. 31–69, 119–9, 197–8. Siddiqi suggests that Deccani Chishtis were more involved in state affairs than their peers in north India, and many joined the sultanate's payroll.
112. Michell and Eaton, *Firuzabad*, pp. 15–16, 88; Siddiqi, *Bahmani Sufis*, pp. 75–7.
113. Subrahmanyam, 'Iranians Abroad'; Subrahmanyam, 'Of Imarat and Tijarat'.
114. Sherwani, 'The Bahmanis', vol. 1, pp. 164–70; Sherwani, *Bahmanis*, pp. 120–50; Yazdani, *Bidar*, pp. 3–9; Siddiqi, 'Ethnic Change', pp. 65–8; Michell and Zebrowski, *Architecture and Art*, pp. 29–35; Merklinger, 'The Madrasa of Mahmud Gawan'. In opposition to this, Mehrdad Shokoohy argues that the early Bahmanis used Sassanid royal emblems in their architecture, however, it fell out of fashion later in the fifteenth century, see Shokoohy, 'Sassanian Royal Emblems'.
115. Siddiqi, *Bahmani Sufis*, p. 162.
116. Siddiqi, 'Ethnic Change', p. 79.
117. Firouzeh, 'Sacred Kingship', p. 212.
118. Siddiqi, *Bahmani Sufis*, pp. 150–87.
119. Eaton, *Social History*, pp. 67–70. Siddiqi asserts that the Foreign–Deccani hostility originated in the reign of Ahmad II and his less delicately balanced policies regarding the elites. See Siddiqi, 'Ethnic Change', pp. 68–9.
120. Sherwani, *Bahmanis*, pp. 205–9, 240–3, 309–13.
121. Sherwani, 'The Council of Regency', pp. 47–53.
122. Narayana Rao, 'Coconut and Honey', pp. 26–40; Mukherjee, *Gajapati Kings*, pp. 23–71; Subrahmanyam, *Suryavamsa Gajapatis*, pp. 30–89; Sherwani, *Mahmud Gawan*, pp. 117–76; Eaton, *Social History*, pp. 84–7, 141–3.

123. Sherwani, *Bahmanis*, pp. 93–97, 119–23, 152–6, 159–64, 198–202, 231–3, 236–9, 315–18, 330–3.
124. For example, we can find early mentions of Karnatak, Andhra, Telangana or Maharashtra, see Raychaudhuri, 'Geography of the Deccan', pp. 22–43.
125. The Molesworth Marathi–English dictionary defines the word *deś* (4) as 'The middle country, the country bounded by the Sahyádri range, the Bálághát hills (i.e., the Satpuras), the Carnatic (usually refers to the portion of the plateau south of the Tungabhadra River) and the Godávarí river.' This region corresponds with the minimalist definition of the Deccan as the Marathi-speaking part of the plateau, down to the Krishna as described above; the Molesworth dictionary may well be the source of this definition in the *Imperial Gazetteer*.
126. Gordon, *The Marathas*, pp. 10–23, and see discussion on the historical importance of the mountain region with its social and political organisation in Guha, *Environment and Ethnicity*, pp. 62–82.
127. Feldhaus, *Connected Places*, pp. 2–3. Rosalind O'Hanlon and Christopher Minkowski suggest certain distinct characteristics that distinguished between the two amalgamations of Brahmins, arguing that 'unlike Maharahstra's Deccan uplands ... with their large and relatively homogeneous community of Deshastha or "country" Brahmins, the Konkan was home to many small competing communities of Brahmins, acutely conscious of their relative standing and prestige', see O'Hanlon and Minkowski, 'What Makes People Who they Are?', p. 384. Based on fieldwork in Pune District, Maharashtra, in the mid-1950s, Henry Orenstein suggests that the Konkanasthas and Desasthas were clearly marked (in that case spatially, as they resided in different villages), and while cooperation between the groups existed, they did not inter-marry with one another. See Orenstein, *Gaon*, pp. 120–4.
128. Pereira, *Konkani*, pp. 1–3; interestingly, the Portuguese sources also use Deccani for Marathi, pointing again at the difference between the plateau and the coast. The Portuguese presence in the Konkan by itself altered the way the language was used, and had an impact on its development, see, for example, Sardessai, 'The Portuguese Influence on Konkani'; Wherritt, 'Portuguese Loanwords in Konkani'. The linguistic issue remained a bone of contention between Maharashtra, Goa and the central government of India, with a struggle to recognise Konkani as an official language. This raised the problem of using the linguistic formula in regard to Goa due to the disconnected regions where Konkani was spoken, spreading between Maharashtra in the north to Kerala in the south. See Rubinoff, 'Goa's Attainment of Statehood'.

2

The Sultanates and the Deccan

The five Deccan sultanates, as their name suggests, were identified by the region within which they emerged. As successors to the erstwhile Bahmani sultanate, their centres of power were located on the plateau north of the Krishna. In their courts emerged a shared identity group that was most associated with, and committed to, their political system, even if they did not manage to monopolise political power. Furthermore, their perspective was largely responsible for the definition of the political landscape of the Deccan. In Persian historiography and in the modern historiography that followed, this group came to be known as Deccanis.

While central to the political, social and cultural life of the sultanates, the Deccanis were not a coherent group, nor is it simple to trace their genesis. Originating in a parallel process of migration, assimilation and conversion, the Deccanis emerged as a group defined first and foremost politically. But political identification is only one part of the picture; they also developed cultural and linguistic identities. Combined with territorial consciousness, the Deccanis came to mark their environment as a meaningful space along the familiar lines of the political language in south India. Of course, this identity did not uproot other identities in the region, which were related to other linguistic, social or religious groups. Rather, it joined them, adding yet another layer to the complex social and political setting of the region. This, in turn, complicated the spatial division of the Deccan, marking certain regions as central and others as peripheral.

In this chapter, I suggest that ideas of the local, peripheral and foreign were of great importance in determining social and political relations within the sultanates and their response to challenges from the outside. This process, however, requires some background. While not aiming at systematically discussing the five dynasties with the complicated relationship between them – elaborate accounts of the political history of the three main sultanates of Ahmadnagar, Bijapur and Golkonda are widely available – the main purpose here is to sketch an outline of their history to lay the ground for further investigation.

The Sultanates and the Deccan

The Political Setting: From Bahmanis to Deccan Sultanates

During the reign of Muhammad III (r. 1463–82), the Bahmani sultanate reached the height of its power. With the Foreigner Mahmud Gawan Gilani (d. 1481) as head of administration, internal stability was maintained and tensions between Deccanis and Foreigners were kept at bay. Mahmud Gawan's position allowed him to initiate far-reaching administrative reforms. He rationalised land administration, improved the military land grant (*jāgīr*) system, and curtailed the power of provincial governors (*tarafdār*) by bifurcating each province and appointing fort commanders (*qalᶜadār*) to represent central power in the provinces. He carefully balanced between the Deccanis and Foreigners, demonstrating the importance of thoughtful central government in maintaining internal stability. Although not inclined towards Foreigners, his measures raised opposition among Deccanis, who, according to the common version, conspired against him and brought about his execution.[1]

The vacuum created by Mahmud Gawan's execution and the death of Muhammad III soon after shook the foundations of the sultanate. With the severely weakened centre, political tensions resurfaced, ushering in centrifugal forces that tore the sultanate apart. First to succeed Gawan was the Deccani Malik Hasan Bahri Nizam al-Mulk (d. late 1480s). His success pushed the Foreigner Yusuf ᶜAdil Khan (d. 1510) to his possessions in Bijapur.[2] Deccanis, too, left, including Fathullah ᶜImad al-Mulk (d. 1510), who settled on his *jāgīr* in Berar.[3] In the late 1480s, the pendulum swung again towards the Foreigners, as Qasim Barid (d. 1504) took over Bidar. His ascendance alienated more Deccanis, notably Hasan Bahri's son Ahmad Nizam al-Mulk (d. 1510), at the time in his father's *jāgīr* in Maharashtra. Yet Qasim Barid failed to bring Foreigners back to the Bahmani side. He then resorted to a combination of force and diplomacy, trying to turn the autonomous commanders against one another, but insufficient funds and lack of interest foiled the plan. Bidar continued to haemorrhage territories and resources, bringing even the most loyal partisan, the Foreigner Sultan Quli Qutb al-Mulk (d. 1543), to push his own interests as *tarafdār* of Golkonda.

By the turn of the sixteenth century, four *de facto* independent dynasties had emerged in Ahmadnagar (Nizam Shah), Berar (ᶜImad Shah), Bijapur (ᶜAdil Shah) and Golkonda (Qutb Shah). In Bidar, the now autonomous Baridi rulers maintained the pretence of Bahmani rule.[4] In Maharashtra, Ahmad Nizam al-Mulk expanded his territories to the north and west,[5] and established a new capital city, Ahmadnagar, in 1494.[6] In Bijapur, Yusuf ᶜAdil Khan expanded his territories towards the Konkan, where

Bahmani control had been long contested, but lost Goa to the Portuguese in 1510.[7] Fathullah ᶜImad al-Mulk did not try to expand substantially, but strove to secure his position in his capital, Ellichpur.[8] Sultan Quli Qutb al-Mulk remained involved in court politics into the sixteenth century, while acting as an autonomous ruler, gradually increasing his possessions in Telangana.[9] In Bidar, Qasim Barid claimed to represent the Bahmani sultan to hold the empire together. In 1503, he tried to ally with Ahmad and Sultan Quli against Bijapur, but the campaign failed and Sultan Quli reached an agreement with Yusuf ᶜAdil Khan.[10]

Qasim Barid's death in 1504 marked the decline in Bidar's authority, losing any clout as the seat of the Bahmani sultanate and thus finalising the division of the Deccan. This had important outcomes not only within the Deccan: the struggle attracted neighbours to intervene. The powerful sultans of Gujarat, Mahmud Shah (r. 1458–1511) and Bahadur Shah (r. 1526–37), increased their influence in the north as part of their surge to take over Malwa, north of Maharashtra. They even managed to briefly force Burhan Nizam al-Mulk (r. 1510–53) and ᶜAlaᵓuddin ᶜImad al-Mulk of Berar (1510–30) to accept Gujarati suzerainty. To the south, under Krishnadevaraya (r. 1509–29) Vijayanagara's power increased significantly. The *rāya*'s expansionist zeal, however, focused on the Raichur *doāb* and Andhra, with some minor incursions into Telangana, but not against the core regions of the sultanates.

From 1530, Gujarat and Vijayanagara weakened substantially and turned their attention elsewhere, allowing the sultans to consolidate their rule. Sultan Quli strengthened his control over Telangana. Ismaᶜil ᶜAdil Khan of Bijapur (r. 1510–34) recaptured the Raichur *doāb*, and both Ahmadnagar and Berar shook off Gujarati suzerainty. The sultanates began to develop their own distinct identity, religious affiliation and courtly culture. With the death of Kalimulllah, the last Bahmani sultan (1538), the sultans proclaimed full sovereignty, expressed by adding *shāh* (king) to their titles.[11] With this newly acquired independence, the focus of all sultanates remained the Deccan Plateau. Yet no claim of Bahmani-style sovereignty over the entire Deccan was made, and each sultanate remained in its own territory. Conflicts were commonplace, but were contained in contested sites around the borders, while sultans continued to interfere in each other's court.[12] Their main goal was not to topple one another, but to create favourable conditions by means of war, diplomacy and political marriages.[13] Particularly sensitive were times when the sultan was weak, that is, a minor, ill or rumoured to be a madman. Not only attracting foreign interference at these junctions, the usually latent conflict between Deccanis and Foreigners also resurfaced, jeopardising the stability of the system.[14] The complex relations between the sultanates created a state of dynamic equilibrium, with contested boundaries but stable core regions; this resembles to a degree the balance of power between the regional kingdoms of the thirteenth century.

The middle decades of the sixteenth century saw renewed regional turmoil. In 1542, Rama Raya took over state affairs in Vijayanagara. Soon thereafter he embarked on an ambitious mission to reshape regional politics. Central to this effort was intervening in the politics of the Deccan sultanates. In 1543, he gave shelter to Prince Ibrahim of Golkonda (later Ibrahim Qutb Shah, r. 1550–80), and after seven years supported his bid to Golkonda's throne. More dramatically, for the next decades he operated a system of ever-changing military alliance, skilfully working the sultanates against one another. Between 1542 and 1565, at least fifteen campaigns were initiated. In most campaigns, Vijayanagara was allied with at least one sultanate. Notwithstanding the military activity, the map of the Deccan did not change dramatically beyond minor border shifts. After two decades of intervention, in 1564, four sultanates formed an alliance against Vijayanagara for the first time.[15]

The battle of Talikota in 1565 was a true game-changer in the history of the Deccan and India as a whole.[16] For the first time since the 1540s, a war ended decisively: Vijayanagara was defeated and its capital city was looted. The kingdom survived, but much weakened, gradually retreating to the east and south. Regional commanders (*nāyaka*s) asserted their autonomy, weakening the empire further. For the sultanates, this did not mean an immediate change. For a few more years, they continued wrangling, making sure that no sultanate profited too much as to break the delicate equilibrium between them. From the 1570s, however, new patterns emerged. Less entangled in each other's affairs, even if not completely conflict free, the sultanates began expanding away from one another.[17] This new direction was officially stated by an agreement between Murtaza Nizam Shah I (r. 1565–88) and ᶜAli ᶜAdil Shah I (r. 1558–80) to divide their spheres of expansion; accordingly, Ahmadnagar advanced to the northeast, taking over the weak ᶜImad Shahi sultanate in 1574.[18] Bijapur began decades of campaigns southwards into the Karnatak. In parallel, Golkonda attempted to expand east to Andhra and south to Rayalaseema. While conquest and control over the new territories were challenging, they marked the direction for the following century.

Not only military expansion occurred; the decades after Talikota brought great cultural and economic fluorescence in Bijapur and Golkonda. Ahmadnagar's fortunes were considerably grimmer. From the late 1580s, the sultanate descended into internal conflict that tore it apart. In the next decade, the Mughal Empire began to play an increasingly important role. Besieging Ahmadnagar in 1596, the Mughals were repelled by the defence put up by Murtaza I's sister, Chand Bibi (d. 1600), but returned to conquer the capital in 1600. The sultanate survived until 1636, but only in name. Actual government passed into the hands of commanders under titular Nizam Shahi sultans, most notably the Ethiopian Malik Ambar (d. 1626) and the Maratha Shahaji Bhonsle (d. 1664).[19] From the late 1620s, Mughal pressure on Bijapur and Golkonda mounted, and in the 1630s, both sultanates had to accept Mughal terms, increasingly introducing them into the orbit of Mughal imperial power.

Elite Society and Deccani Identity

The Deccan sultanates emerged in an environment shaped by centuries of parallel, and at times contradicting, historical processes. Elite society of the sultanates was accordingly diverse in terms of religion, language and history. With the notable exception of the Foreigners, most elite groups were identified with the territory where they resided. Among these, one group was most closely associated with the core region of the Deccan and with the political order that emerged under the Bahmanis. These were local Muslims, known as Deccanis. Dominant in all sultanates, the category 'Deccani' was not specific to any sultanate in particular, but could be found throughout the region.

The sources to trace the development of the Deccani community (or communities) are scant, yet enable us to draw the broader characteristics of the community.[20] It has been noted that the beginning of Muslim elite communities in the Deccan goes back to the Khalji excursions, if not earlier. The annexation of the region to Delhi by Muhammad b. Tughluq and the creation of a secondary capital in Daulatabad in 1327 encouraged significant migration of Muslims from north India, including military men, administrators, spiritual leaders and literati. By the time the Bahmani sultanate emerged two decades later, Muslim communities were well established in the region.[21] The relative stability of the Deccan in comparison with the north, particularly around Timur's invasion in 1398, encouraged others to migrate southwards. Most famous of these was the Chishti Sufi Khwaja Muhammad Banda Nawaz Gisu Daraz. Gisu Daraz may well have been the most influential saint, but was by no means to only one. Sufis continued to migrate to the Deccan for centuries.[22] Muslims from the lower strata of society, too, arrived in the Deccan; we will discuss an interesting case later in this chapter.

Migrants arrived not only from north India, but also from beyond the subcontinent, and integrated into local society, gradually shedding

The Sultanates and the Deccan

their previous links to trans-regional networks. The Sufi poet Miran Ji Shams al-ᶜUshshaq, for example, arrived in the Deccan in the fifteenth century, possibly from Mecca. He, his son, Burhan al-Din Janam, and his grandson Amin al-Din Aᶜla were important writers of Dakhani in ᶜAdil Shahi Bijapur.[23] Better documented are the founders of the Qutb Shahi and ᶜAdil Shahi dynasties themselves. Both dynasties remembered their origins in the lands to the northwest, and employed it for political purposes. For example, in a letter sent by ᶜAbdullah Qutb Shah (r. 1626–72) to the Safavid Shah ᶜAbbas I (r. 1588–1629) in 1039/1628–9, the sultan of Golkonda emphasised the friendship of his ancestral Qaraqoyunlu Turkmans with the early Safavids, stating that even though they were separated, strong bonds continued to unite the Qutb Shahis and Safavids.[24] Narratives produced in Bijapur in the early seventeenth century continued to mention the origins of the ᶜAdil Shahis as descendants of the Aqqoyunlu Turkmans or even the Ottomans.[25] Their background notwithstanding, both dynasties soon rose above partisan conflicts, or even occasionally preferred to side with the Deccanis.[26] Moreover, rulers of both dynasties were involved in local culture and in writing in Dakhani, suggesting a continuous process of assimilation. It is difficult to know how deep the process of assimilation ran beyond those particular elite actors.[27]

It is, however, likely that a significant part, if not the majority, of Deccanis were local converts or descendants thereof. Conversion stories of members of the elites tend to be dramatic and laden with symbolism, but may well reflect certain avenues of religious change. Two stories around the origin of the Nizam Shahi dynasty can highlight this point. Tabatabaʾi reports that at some time in the mid-fifteenth century, Bahmani troops conducted raids into 'the lands of the idol-worshipers' for collecting tribute and plundering. They captured 'a beautiful girl, a daughter of the kings of that realm' and sent her to the court. Her beauty and virtue attracted the attention of the sultan, and she became his favourite. She gave birth to Prince Ahmad. The sultan ordered an astrological map to be drawn for the prince, which predicted his future success. The sultan thought it would be prudent to keep Ahmad away from the court, and sent him to a loyal noble, Malik Naʾib (Malik Hasan Bahri), in Maharashtra. Malik Naʾib raised Ahmad and, after the sultan's death, the prince emerged as a worthy young man. This worried nobles in the court, who remembered the astrological prediction. Rejecting Ahmad's position, the (alleged) prince was pushed to foster his independence.[28] Firishta reports that Ahmad was in reality the son of Malik Naʾib, whose original name was Tima Bhat, son of Bhario. A Brahmin of Vijayanagara, he was imprisoned by Bahmani troops, joined the service as a military slave, and converted to Islam with the name Malik

Hasan Bahri (he received the title Malik Naʾib later). With his training prior to his imprisonment, he received further education in Persian.[29] The two stories seem contradictory, yet share a similar point: respectable genealogy (Bahmani or Brahmin), intensive education and local connection, demonstrating a process of 'conversion by patronage'.[30]

Considering the limited size of court circles, however, this kind of conversion probably was not widespread. More likely is that, similarly to elsewhere in India, conversion was a long and voluntary process of acculturation. An important avenue was Sufi centres, which became the loci of spiritual and social activities as well as cultural production, including the translation of texts for devotional purposes and proselytisation.[31] Their importance derived from the practice of both Muslims and non-Muslims to frequent such shrines.[32] A well-known story is that the Maratha Maloji Bhonsle had no sons until a visit to the shrine of the Sufi Shah Sharif. Following the visit, two sons were born, and were named Shahaji (Shivaji's father) and Sharafji, after the saint.[33] While this case did not end up in conversion, the story presents how conversion could have happened.

With their diverse origins, the category 'Deccani' seems far from reflecting any coherent ethnic group. Rather, it may well be a marker of political identity. This assertion is supported by the fact that Deccanis first appeared as a group in parallel to their main opponents (at least according to the Persian chronicles), namely, the Foreigners. The royal patronage and preferential treatment the Foreigners enjoyed created competition over resources and favours. These circumstances encouraged the crystallisation of the Deccanis as a political group. Richard Eaton suggests that the struggle not only had a political but also a social basis, making 'Deccani' a relational category. The Deccanis, he suggests, aimed to distinguish themselves from their north Indian ancestors and later from the Foreigners, who continued to view the Iranian world as their main point of reference. Deccanis and Foreigners represented not only competing political parties, but also different conceptions of state of society: land-based coloniser-settler Deccanis and culturally-based Foreign identity.[34]

The political-social nature of the category 'Deccani' is demonstrated by yet another group, the Ethiopians (*ḥabshī* or *ḥabashī*, lit. 'Abyssinian'), mostly active in Ahmadnagar and Bijapur. Unlike the diverse Deccanis, the Ethiopians had distinct origins as former military slaves. Best known of these was Malik Ambar (d. 1626), but he was by no means the only one.[35] The Ethiopians maintained their distinct identity as a group and constructed their political identity accordingly.[36] However, they chose for most part to cooperate with the Deccanis.[37] In the tense politics of the Deccan, this often meant an anti-Foreigner stand.[38] In the same vein, when

The Sultanates and the Deccan

Foreigners were not present, the former alliance collapsed with fights between Deccanis and Ethiopians and among each group common.[39]

The clear preference of the Ethiopians to work alongside the Deccanis rather than the Foreigners reflects an important aspect of their identity, deriving from their origins as slaves. Military slavery was, by definition, one-generational. This characteristic derives from the basic logic of this institution, which is to distance the slave from his kin and other social networks in order to make him loyal to the ruler alone. The sons of slaves, by contrast, were born Muslims, hence could not be enslaved. Furthermore, they were born already in the social setting where they were active, therefore not fit for purpose. The one-generational idea was at times only theoretical as slaves who became sultans promoted their descendants as successors.[40] Malik Ambar, too, groomed his son Fath Khan to succeed him as the *de facto* leader of Ahmadnagar.[41] More commonly, however, a slave's son could not maintain his father's position. Furthermore, he was no longer *ḥabshī* but received another title, *muwallad* (lit. of mixed origins), suggesting that he was no longer a slave. *Muwallads* were not pushed out of the elites, and some held important military roles.[42] In terms of society, they became immersed in the Deccani environment.[43] Their preference to remain in the Deccan and cooperate with the Deccanis suggests that their political identity did not lie in the past, but rather with the way a group saw their present and future; not from whence they came, but whereto they were going. The Ethiopians, as military slaves, did not have links to their ancestral lands in the way that Foreigners had. For better or worse, they remained in the Deccan and, therefore, saw their political destiny with the Deccanis.

Thus far we have considered Deccani identity as linked to political and social circumstances. However, with time, cultural elements were added to the mix. As suggested before, in the political-cultural climate of premodern south India, group identities were often marked not only by religion and territory but also by language. This may well have been the case for the Deccanis and the Dakhani language.[44] The language originated with the migration of Muslims from north India during Khalji and, more so, Tughluq, times. Stemming from the regions around Delhi, the language contains lexicographical and grammatical elements that link it with various dialects of the north, even if it is not always simple to draw direct lines to any one dialect in particular. Gradually, Dakhani emerged as a literary language. Dakhani compositions are attributed to early Sufis such as Gisu Daraz,[45] but this identification is problematic. The earliest work that can be dated with some confidence is the *mathnawī* (long rhyming narrative poem) *Kadam Rao Padam Rao*, which may have been written as early as the reign of Ahmad I (r. 1422–36).[46] In the following decades, the language became widespread, practised by various milieus from courts to Sufis; David Matthews states that Dakhani 'established itself as a lingua franca and was being used as a means of communication by the Muslims who were settled in the Deccan, and no doubt by other people in the area';[47] it was practised also by non-Muslim, even for religious purposes.[48]

Dakhani works of various genres began to be composed all over the Deccan. Towards the end of the sixteenth century, non-Sufi literature was freshly produced in courts and elite circles, reflecting a growing interest of the nobility in the spoken language; Sumit Guha suggests that Dakhani became 'an aspect of a dominant urban elite, and was perceived as such . . . expressive of a regional religious identity'.[49] Sultans themselves became important patrons of Dakhani literature, with several sultans composing significant works themselves, most notably Muhammad Quli Qutb Shah of Golkonda and Ibrahim ᶜAdil Shah II of Bijapur. The emergence of Dakhani in elite circles, maybe in similarity to Brajbhasha in north India around the same time,[50] was accompanied by the first signs of the standardisation of the language. Thematically, Dakhani compositions incorporated themes and structures from classical Persian. Compositions reflect elite sensitivity to local cultural tropes in its development of a localised cultural idiom.[51] While practised widely in the region, Dakhani did not enter the realm of administration, which remained the domain of Persian and the vernaculars.

In the context of the Deccan sultanates, then, the term 'Deccani' marks a very diverse group in terms of origin, identity and social standing.[52] At the same time, these diverse elites shared a political identity that relied on their locality and was clearly distinct from other groups, primarily the Foreigners. Ignoring the geopolitical circumstances, the Deccanis were not associated with any one of the sultanates in particular, but were rooted in the post-Bahmani system as a whole. Their diverse origins notwithstanding, they developed a shared cultural identity around the Dakhani language, in itself originating in the north. This new identity presents somewhat of a paradox: emotionally and politically attached to the Deccan and using the territory as a marker, the source of their legitimacy and prestige was external to the region; yet this new identity in itself became entirely local.[53] More so, the development of the Deccani identity reflects its constructed nature, highlighting the components perceived as being required for such political coherence at the time.

Insiders, Outsiders, and Social Boundaries

The complex identity of the Deccanis as a group was most clearly evident in their relations to the society in which they were active. Defined from the beginning by their relational position, it was through the prism of their often tense relations with the Foreigners that the Deccanis were defined. The permanence of the conflict suggests that it went beyond purely immediate political motivations. Rafi Ahmad Alavi suggests that racial difference between the groups increased the tension,[54] but the diverse origins of both Deccanis and Foreigners, and the painfully anachronistic nature of the term 'race' in that sense renders this explanation woefully unsatisfactory. More commonly, the hostility was explained by creed, associating Foreigners with Shiism and Deccanis with Sunni Islam.[55] This distinction is based on the imagination of clear boundaries marking primordial hostility between the creeds, stretching way beyond any historical context. Our sources, however, support neither a Foreigner/Shiite versus Deccani/Sunni nexus, nor incessant hostility between the groups. Some important examples demonstrate the ease of crossing the lines: the Foreigner Yusuf ʿAdil Khan is reported to have adopted Shiism, meaning that he was originally Sunni;[56] the Deccani Burhan Nizam Shah I, too, was happy to convert to Shiism.[57] Indeed, as Alavi notes, contemporary source material does not use religion as a general point of contestation except in limited cases. Furthermore, the diverse backgrounds of Foreigners work against any idea of creed unity;[58] we cannot assume unity among the no less diverse Deccanis.

A more compelling line of investigation, beyond the immediate political meaning, takes us back to the self-perception of each group vis-à-vis the place in which it was active. Such an idea is implied by the terms 'New-comers' (Foreigners) and 'Old-comers' (Deccanis), coined by H. K. Sherwani.[59] This division is not without its problems. For one, it ignores 'New-comers' such as the Ethiopians who were politically identified with the Deccanis. Nevertheless, the point of difference deriving from group's relations with their place suggests a promising direction. Focusing on the cultural element in the conflict, S. R. Sharma suggests that the Muslims in the Deccan 'were isolated from the outer Muslim world. Hence, they became more dependent upon and were more largely influenced by local conditions and people. They evolved a *modus vivendi* which soon differentiated them from foreign Muslims.' With this emergent local identity, the struggle against both Mughals and Foreigners were facets of the same cultural struggle.[60] While somewhat crude, Sharma's point on the cultural element is rather convincing.

A detailed examination of the events in Ahmadnagar points at a broad political element to the relations between local and foreign Muslim communities. The death of Murtaza Nizam Shah I (r. 1565–88) ushered in a period of complete disarray. Long torn by disputes between Foreigners, who complained of being mistreated by Murtaza the 'madman' (*diwāna*),[61] and Deccanis, the situation spiralled out of control.[62] In 1588, Murtaza's son Husayn II ascended the throne. Continuing his father's blatant preference of Deccanis, his actions encouraged further instability. The head of administration (*wakīl*) Mirza Khan took advantage of the sultan's disinterest in politics to promote his own agenda by playing the parties against one another. Finally choosing to rebuild the Foreigners, to which he originally belonged, Mirza Khan decided to move forward and assert this party's and his own complete control. But he still had one obstacle: Husayn II was allied with the Deccanis. To resolve this issue, Mirza Khan decided to depose the king in favour of his cousin, Isma'il, whom he picked as a puppet.[63] These intrigues naturally enraged the Deccanis and Ethiopians, who laid siege to Ahmadnagar Fort. The Foreigners escalated the situation by executing Husayn II, and, to make things worse, hurled his head over the wall into the crowd of Deccanis and Ethiopians.[64]

In response, the Deccanis attacked. Forcing their way inside the fort, they found foreign civilians (*sayyid*s, judges, scholars, doctors), whom Mirza Khan forced to cooperate as part of his effort to legitimise Isma'il's enthronement. The chronicler Sayyid 'Ali Tabataba'i, resident of Ahmadnagar at the time, describes the events that followed:

> [the intellectuals] crept into corners and hid themselves from the sight of the wicked rebellious people. Others ... ran in all directions. Attacked from all directions, this wretched group could not find an escape wherever they were looking. Helplessly, they stood firm in the court between the two gates of the citadel, and began to fight against the enemies. One group entered the citadel through Daulatabad Gate with the intention of killing and plunder. They ran in all directions, and severed the head of whomever they saw ... the broker of doom sold an old man of eighty and a child of eight for the same price, as the oppressive fire burnt together young and old, rich and poor.

The general massacre of Foreigners suggests hostility that went beyond politics to represent much deeper anti-Foreigner sentiment.

The story did not end here. After the Deccanis and Ethiopians took over the fort, they continued with their anti-Foreigner policy. Having enthroned the very same prince, Isma'il, the Deccani leaders gained royal consent for a 'general massacre of all Foreigners' (*qatl-i 'ām-i tamām-i gharībān*), affirming the status of the young sultan as a puppet. Subsequently, Deccanis and Ethiopians indulged themselves in continuous killing, plundering and the destruction of 'all houses, buildings, and gardens of the Foreigners'. Only the Ethiopian Farhad Khan, who opposed the massacre, could stop the slaughter.[65] The massacre of the intellectuals trapped in the fort does not seem coincidental, nor was it a collateral outcome of the war. Rather, it reflects a desire to exterminate all Foreigners from the city. Even religious figures, including *sayyids*, who maintained a particularly prestigious position in Islamic societies as descendants of the Prophet Muhammad were not spared. This was not a one-time occurrence; Annemarie Schimmel states that as early as the 1450s Deccanis attacked foreign *sayyids* in partisan disputes.[66]

Violence against Foreigners may have not been limited solely to the elites. Public opinion often remains obscure; the following story provides a rare glimpse into general sentiments. The anonymous chronicler of Golkonda reports that around 1608, 'a group of Mughal riffraff, who had come from the lands of Agra and Lahore to the capital of Hyderabad' (i.e., non-elite migrants from the north), when intoxicated, climbed the hill to Nobat Ghat Palace. Ignoring the warnings of the eunuchs and guards, they entered the palace in a clear breach of etiquette. The guards sent a petition to complain about this misconduct. Muhammad Quli Qutb Shah enquired about this matter. The city magistrate (*kotwāl*), ʿAli Aqa, reported back that 'many Mughal and Foreign riffraff have gathered in the capital [Hyderabad] at the same time that the Mughal army intended to conquer the Deccan'. The sultan then issued an order commanding the expulsion of all the Mughal and Foreign riffraff not in official employment or without commercial relations (*saudā-i muʿāmala*) in town.

The moderate solution suggested by the sultan turned in the hands of locals into a licence for mass violence. ʿAli Aqa took the liberty to send his infantry with the city's head watchmen to expel all Afghans (*patān*), Mughals and Foreigners, imprisoning all merchants and Foreigners they could catch, regardless of employment. The violence soon spread further with the rumour that the sultan permitted the murder of Foreigners. The chronicler continues:

> the fearless rebellious people of the Deccan, who were always upfront greedy, sent their oppressive hand and plundered the property of the merchants who set their stores in the market of the capital [Hyderabad] with various kinds of commodities. Looting turned into killing ... The helpless [Foreigners], wherever they turned, saw the world filled with the swords and daggers of their enemies.

Like the anti-Foreigner riots in Ahmadnagar two decades earlier, the general massacre in Hyderabad stopped only when a high official intervened. This time, it was the chief financial officer (*mīr jumla*), the Foreigner Mirza Muhammad Amin, who rushed into the royal palace, awoke the sultan, and informed him about these events. Muhammad Quli immediately sent an order to ʿAli Aqa to stop the attacks on the

Foreigners. Sending forces to the city, this response stopped the massacre. Finally, the sultan ordered the gruesome public execution of those responsible for the violence.[67]

The events in Hyderabad are different from those in Ahmadnagar. In this case, the violence broke out within a stable environment that was not accustomed to such behaviour. The sultan was at his prime and no one party had the monopoly over power at that moment, even though the sultan being asleep can be read as a metaphor to the damage caused by an absent or distracted ruler.[68] No plan can be seen behind the events, yet it appears that local potentates took advantage of a decree issued against minor misbehaviour. The target of the violent outbreak, however, was the same in both cases: all Foreigners indiscriminately, including petty merchants in the markets of Hyderabad, directly exempt from the sultan's decree. The instigators of violence, too, were not merely commanders, but violence seems to have spread to the general populace. The Deccanis as a whole rose against the Foreigners.

The chronicler goes on to provide insights into the motives behind the violence. Evidently, the Deccanis feared the Mughals, who were allegedly at the gates of the Deccan. This was not the immediate the reason, however, as after the Mughal conquest of Ahmadnagar in 1600, the border had been fairly static and the Mughals did not pose a direct threat. Moreover, no obvious link connected the Mughal 'riff raff' and the Foreigners in the city. Nor was this violence linked to an active political dispute between Deccani and Foreigner elites as the period was politically quiet, although M. Z. A. Shakeb suggests that the event was linked to court politics around the question of Qutb Shahi succession.[69] The political reasons seem to be only an excuse for hostility that ran deep in society, beyond the elites into the dwellers of Hyderabad. The commoners were ready to be activated by local leadership. Writing at the beginning of the seventeenth century in neighbouring Bijapur, Shirazi captured the vehement hostility between the Deccanis and the Foreigners, saying that 'the commanders and nobles of the Deccan are always opposing and hostile towards the Foreigners. They would rather not see even one Foreigner in that court, and always strive to bring destruction to the Foreigners.'[70] Such statements sound hyperbolic and we should not assume some all-encompassing hostility between Deccanis and Foreigners as the guiding force in the Deccan sultanates. However, we cannot discard such stories as mere rhetoric, but as representative of a certain element within elite society of the Deccan.

Within this contested environment, it may come as a surprise that the relations between Muslims and non-Muslims seem to have been calmer, as far as we can say based on the sources. Persian writing represents, for most, work within Persianate conventions, thus reflecting the position of Foreigners, not Muslims in general. Dakhani sources are usually not concerned with the political order. Within this, Persian sources typically employ strong anti-Hindu language, in which Muslims, represented by the sultans, are almost defined by their stand against the infidels. With this rhetoric, several scholars suggested that this indicates a general violent atmosphere. For example, S. B. Kodad argues that considering the language of the chroniclers, the Vijayanagara–Deccan wars of 1542–64 were motivated by religious conflict.[71] This example, as discussed below, correctly suggests that we cannot dismiss violent language as simply rhetoric; the authors chose to employ this language because it resonated with their audiences.

Nevertheless, the violent rhetoric worked within clear boundaries. We have no descriptions of violence against Hindus within the realm of the sultanates, bringing some to see this period as a golden age of Muslim–Hindu amity.[72] Even without accepting this statement, which may be political rather than historical, it seems that communal language was reserved for conflict against non-sultanate actors, or to the rebellion of non-Muslims within the sultanate.[73] The political nature of the rhetoric is reflected in ᶜAli Khan Lar's rebellion against Golkonda in the 1580s. The rebel turned to Vijayanagara for assistance, with some success. Muhammad Quli sent forces under the Muslims Rahm Dad and Tahir Muhammad Khan and the Hindu Bhali Rao, with whom the local magnate Ray Rao the Brahmin joined.[74] The language the chronicler employed in the description is indicative: ᶜAli Khan's choice to join Vijayanagara was 'with the delusions of Satan' (*taswīlāt-i shayṭān*); the army of Golkonda, comprising Muslims and non-Muslims, was described as the '*jihād* warriors of Islam' (*mujāhidān-i islām*), whereas ᶜAli Khan's forces were the 'army of infidels' (*lashkar-i kafara*). The categorisation of Muslims and Infidels here, then, indicates not the religious but the political affiliations of the commanders. Association with the sultans meant that their army related to Islam, regardless of the religion of those who served them. This maybe unusual reference suggests that politics were at the heart of these groupings; loyal 'infidels' were folded into the realm of Islam, suggesting less tense relations in comparison with the direct confrontation between Foreigners and Deccanis.[75]

This position of the non-Muslims within the social conflicts emphasises even more the borders of social conflict in the Deccan sultanates. The conflict started as a political competition between rival groups over resources and access to power, but grew ever further. Expanding beyond the confines of the elites, it turned into violent outbreaks that encompassed large segments of society. Violence was used against non-military groups from religious men to people in the marketplace, and included Foreigners as well as migrants from the north, but not Hindus within the realm of the sultanates. What marked these groups was not only their foreignness, but their perception as posing a menace to the political and social order. The challenge was clear in the case of north Indians, even if unfounded, due to the Mughal danger. The case of the Foreigners is more complex, and is suggestive more of conceptual differences between the groups and their commitments to the Deccan. The Deccanis, as well as local non-Muslims, were perceived as internal players; the Foreigners raised concerns because they continued to represent an element that was not rooted in the locality. The dividing lines and local sensitivities did not only demarcate social anxieties, but can also be used to understand Deccani policies towards states around them.

Friends, Foes, and the Boundaries of Foreign Relations

Thus far we have discussed the Deccan as an isolated region, comprising its own political units and diverse local communities, each with its own cultural, territorial and linguistic sensitivities. But the Deccan was far from being isolated. Located in the northern part of peninsular India, the region has always been the meeting point of north and south. Powerful neighbours were drawn to intervene for their direct interests or to pacify those who challenged their interests elsewhere. Similarly to social affairs, the relations of the sultanates with their neighbours varied significantly, offering yet another set of boundaries to mark social and political sensitivities. This, in turn, suggests proximity between the sensitivities of the Deccani elites to that of the sultanates as a whole. To examine this point, let us look at the main non-Deccani forces with which the sultanates were dealing, namely, Vijayanagara, the Sultanate of Gujarat, the Mughal Empire and the Portuguese. The purpose here is not to present a systematic analysis of their relations with the sultanates – each case deserves a full study of its own – but to outline some of the considerations that the sultanate had when dealing with these external forces.

Vijayanagara

For the young Deccan sultanates, the most influential neighbour was undoubtedly Vijayanagara, whose material and symbolic impact lasted well into the seventeenth century. This significance, combined with the religious difference, attracted much scholarly attention. Relations between the sultanates and Vijayanagara became emblematic of the communal question, with discussions that often reflect more on the ideology of the author than on the events discussed. For colonial historians, the relationship was marked by permanent violence. Vijayanagara was imagined as a Hindu state, struggling against jihadi-minded 'Mahomedan kings'. The conflict was, accordingly, one of a religious nature.[76] Anti-Muslim Indian historians, while distancing themselves from colonial views, maintained the anti-Muslim sentiment. S. Krishnaswami Aiyangar presented Vijayanagara as defenders of the *dharma* against Muslim invaders.[77] N. Venkataramanayya defined Muslim rulers as 'spread[ing] the gospel of Islam by means of the sword'. Cooperation between Hindu and Muslim individuals was only a disguise for intelligence-gathering for future wars.[78]

Post-independence historians drew an increasingly complex picture. While not abandoning religion as an analytical framework, some began to question the totality and productivity of such categories.[79] New studies challenge the line dividing 'Hindu' from 'Muslim' altogether and the meaning of each as a category. In the field of architecture, Catherine Asher suggests that these categories do not reflect the intentions behind buildings.[80] In their works separately and together, Eaton and Wagoner demonstrate that the boundaries dividing 'Muslim' and 'Hindu' states were permeable to goods, people and technologies, as well as symbols and idioms.[81] Cynthia Talbot argues that ethnic and other identity markers surpassed religion as the definitive category.[82] Gijs Kruijtzer adds that an even larger array of conflicting identities, based on ethnicity, social status, ritual and economic interests, shaped the history of early modern south India.[83] Finally, in a highly influential article, Eaton explains the motivation behind the seemingly religious desecration of Hindu temples by Muslim rulers in political terms.[84] Many of these writings stress that the line was porous, however, they continue to mark it as stricter than that dividing the sultanates and between them and other Muslim polities.

Many of these perceptions are reflected in the discussion around the Battle of Talikota in 1565. Fought between the sultanates of Ahmadnagar, Berar, Bijapur and Golkonda on one side, and Vijayanagara on the other side, the battle ended with the utter defeat of Vijayanagara and the collapse of its imperial order. Due to the identity of the two camps and its decisive outcomes, the battle came to be representative of the Deccani system as a whole. Furthermore, the events in the years prior to the battle were seen rather teleologically as 'the way to Talikota', assuming that such alliance was only inevitable.[85] The long-term developments, however, suggest a more complex issue. As successor states of the Bahmanis, the

Deccan sultanates inherited much of their predecessors' attitude towards Vijayanagara. Accordingly, in the early decades of the sixteenth century, hostility was mostly limited to contested border regions, most notably the Raichur *doāb* and Andhra, even as Vijayanagara strengthened significantly under Krishnadevaraya. This pattern reflects a geopolitical continuation that stretches back centuries before Delhi's invasion. Furthermore, the minor disputes did not interfere in fostering amicable contacts between the sides, and people and commodities continued to move throughout the region.[86]

From the 1540s, Vijayanagara's involvement north of the Krishna intensified. Pivotal in this endeavour was Rama Raya. As the *de facto* leader of Vijayanagara under the almost-nominal king Sadasiva (r. 1542–70), he embarked on an ambitious political project of imperial expansion. Eaton and Wagoner suggest that central to this was the rise in the symbolic importance of Kalyani, the former Western Chalukya capital, in Vijayanagara's political idiom. As Kalyani is located north of the Krishna, not far from Bidar, Rama Raya's endeavour resulted in increasing military intervention by Vijayanagara in the Deccan, leading to a series of campaigns from 1543. In 1549, Rama Raya convinced Burhan Nizam Shah I of Ahmadnagar to attack Kalyani, then in Bijapur's possession, quoting Bijapur's mistreat of Vijayanagara's ambassadors as a pretext. In 1558, Rama Raya entered an alliance with ʿAli ʿAdil Shah I of Bijapur against Husayn Nizam Shah I (r. 1553–65) of Ahmadnagar, conquering Kalyani in 1559. Continuing to Ahmadnagar, Rama Raya withdrew only after Husayn Nizam Shah submitted in person and delivered the key of Kalyani Fort. Three years later, Husayn Nizam Shah entered an alliance with Ibrahim Qutb Shah of Golkonda to recover Kalyani, but was defeated by the combined forces of Bijapur and Vijayanagara. Marching to Vijayanagara, Rama Raya plundered territories of both Bijapur and Golkonda, pushing them to unite against him in 1564–5.[87]

This description, however, remains rather limited in its treatment of the relations between the sultanates. Take, for example, the campaign of 1542–3. The war started as an alliance between Burhan Nizam Shah I and ʿAli Barid of Bidar (r. 1543–80) against Bijapur, taking advantage of the internal turmoil in that sultanate; Darya ʿImad Shah of Berar (r. 1530–61) joined in, even if reluctantly. To promote his position, Burhan I spread a rumour that Bijapur's minister Asad Khan invited the invasion, forcing the able minister to flee Bijapur. Then Ahmadnagar's army conquered Sholapur, a long-contested fort on the Ahmadnagar–Bijapur border. Ahmadnagar's forces also captured Belgaum, where Asad Khan's *jāgīr* was located, forcing Ibrahim ʿAdil Shah I (r. 1534–58) to flee to Gulbarga.

This success was short-lived, as Asad Khan returned to Bijapur's service and Darya ᶜImad Shah swapped sides, joining Bijapur. With the tide turning against Ahmadnagar, Burhan I pursued peace and returned the conquered territories to Bijapur. In the following year, Burhan tried to conquer Sholapur once again. This time he forged an alliance with Vijayanagara and Golkonda; Darya ᶜImad Shah distanced himself from Bijapur, even though he married his daughter to Ibrahim ᶜAdil Shah. The allies attacked Bijapur from all sides, forcing Ibrahim I to accept Ahmadnagar's terms, including the surrender of Sholapur to Ahmadnagar and paying tribute to Rama Raya. The agreement isolated Golkonda, simultaneously occupied in war against Bidar.[88] Events continued along these lines for the following couple of decades, as summarised in Table 2.1.[89]

The long list of alliances and wars was in itself remarkably similar to the regional system in the thirteenth century, suggesting a few conclusions. The system demonstrates a large degree of dynamism. None of the alliances was stable, nor did it continue for more than a mere few years at the time; the system continued to reformulate itself time and again. Within this dynamic system, Vijayanagara served as an integral part; Rama Raya had his own agenda and the means to promote it, but so did the sultans, who were active participants and not only passive puppets in Rama Raya's theatre. Moreover, none of the parties involved followed clear ideological or religious lines; great rivals cooperated with one another when it suited their immediate interests. Rama Raya fitted well into this system. He did not have to impose his presence on Deccani actors but, rather, was invited in. As the strongest actor on the stage of the Deccan, he knew how to use the system for his benefit. Eventually, he also overplayed his hand in 1562–3, pushing the sultans to form a unanimous opposition.

Examining the changing patterns of the alliances more closely reveals interesting details on the level of involvement of all participants, as detailed in Table 2.2. Until Talikota (inclusive), both Ahmadnagar and Bijapur were involved in practically all fifteen military affairs; the most persistent rivalry was between these two sultanates. They were followed by Vijayanagara (eleven), and only then Golkonda (seven). The weaker Bidar and Berar were involved even less, with five and six events, respectively, and Bidar withdrew from alliances after 1548. The decline in Vijayanagara's power following Talikota is evident in the drop in its involvement north of the Krishna; out of nine events listed, the defeated empire took part in only two. Golkonda seems to have been drawn closer to the affairs of their neighbours in these tense times, with six events, still lagging behind Ahmadnagar and Bijapur, with eight events each. Once again, Berar (three) and Bidar (two) were the least involved. The period

Table 2.1 Alliances in the Deccan, 1542–74

Year	Camp A	Camp B	Comments
1542	Ahmadnagar, Bidar	Bijapur, Berar	
1543	Ahmadnagar, Golkonda, Vijayanagara	Bijapur, Bidar	According to one version, Berar also joined Camp A
1545	Ahmadnagar, Bidar	Bijapur, Berar	
1546	Ahmadnagar, Vijayanagar	Bijapur	Bidar refuses to take part
1547–8	Ahmadnagar, Berar, Bijapur	Bidar, Golkonda, Vijayanagara	Golkonda temporarily; Vijayanagara inactive
	Ahmadnagar	Bijapur, Bidar	Bijapur changes sides
1548	Ahmadnagar, Golkonda	Bijapur	
1549	Ahmadnagar, Vijayanagara	Bijapur	
1552	Ahmadnagar, Vijayanagara	Bijapur	
1553	Ahmadnagar, Vijayanagara	Bijapur	
1554–5	Ahmadnagar	Bijapur, Vijayanagara	In support of a rebelling Nizam Shahi prince
1558–9	Ahmadnagar, Berar, Golkonda	Bijapur, Vijayanagara	
	Ahmadnagar, Berar	Bijapur, Vijayanagara, Golkonda	Ibrahim Qutb Shah switches alliance after attack over Golkonda
1562–3	Ahmadnagar, Golkonda	Bijapur, Vijayanagara	Including Vijayanagara's proxy rebellion against Golkonda
1564–5	Ahmadnagar, Berar, Bijapur, Golkonda	Vijayanagara	Battle of Talikota
1566–7	Ahmadnagar, Bijapur	Berar	
1568	Ahmadnagar, Berar, Golkonda	Bijapur	Golkonda retires amidst the war
1569	Ahmadnagar, Golkonda	Bijapur	
	Ahmadnagar, Bijapur	Golkonda	
1570	Ahmadnagar, Golkonda, Vijayanagara	Bijapur	Did not materialise
	Ahmadnagar	Bidar, Bijapur	Did not materialise
1572	Ahmadnagar	Bidar, Bijapur, Golkonda	Agreement on spheres of influence: Ahmadnagar in Berar; Bijapur in the Karnatak
1573	Bijapur	Golkonda, Vijayanagara	
1574	Ahmadnagar	Berar	Ahmadnagar annexes Berar

The Sultanates and the Deccan

Table 2.2 Campaigns in the Deccan, 1542–74: summary

	Ahmadnagar	Berar	Bidar	Bijapur	Golkonda	Vijayanagara
1542–65	15	6	5	15	7	11
1566–74	8	3	2	8	6	2
Total	23	9	7	23	13	13

ended with the conquest of Berar by Ahmadnagar in 1574 and the annihilation of the independent sultanate there.

The data suggests that until Talikota, the main battleground was the western Deccan, between Ahmadnagar, Bijapur and Vijayanagara. Golkonda in the east remained somewhat removed from the main events of the period. This pattern once again fits in the longer history of the region, with not only active north–south division, but also one between east and west. This, in turn, challenges even more the validity of the perceived strict lines dividing the Deccan sultanates from Vijayanagara. Naturally, with the collapse of Vijayanagara in 1565, things changed considerably, but not as dramatically as suggested before: Vijayanagara was still involved in Deccani politics; Ahmadnagar and Bijapur continued to be more rivals than allies; and Golkonda, even if more involved, maintained some of its standoffish position.

Vijayanagara, then, seems to have been regularly included in the political system of the Deccan. This was possible because it was not perceived by the Deccanis as foreign but as an integral part of the system. This inclusion was made possible due to the geographical location and historical connections of Vijayanagara. Centred in modern-day Hampi in central Karnataka, on the south bank of the Tungabhadra River, Vijayanagara's metropolitan region was just beyond the region we have defined as the core of the Deccan. Furthermore, located in the Kannada-speaking region and consisting of a strong Telugu element, Vijayanagara was not really foreign but rather an actor within the periphery of the Deccan, very familiar to the Deccan sultanates. As such, cooperation with the empire seems to have been perceived as natural. This is quite different from other foreign affairs, to which we turn next.

SULTANATE OF GUJARAT

The Sultanate of Gujarat was a significant power at the border of the Deccan before the rise of the sultanates. Not only the neighbour of Ahmadnagar, Gujarat strove to assert its influence in Khandesh, just to its north, as this strategic region is located on the roads linking the Deccan with north India. Gujarat's power reached its zenith in the early decades of the sixteenth century. To defend its northern boundary, Ahmadnagar tried to promote its own agenda in Khandesh, but with limited success.[90] In 1508–9, Mahmud Shah of Gujarat (r. 1458–1511) invaded Khandesh, conquered Thalner and Burhanpur (old and new capitals of the local sultanate, respectively), and installed his protégé, ᶜAdil Khan III Faruqi (r. 1509–20, not to be confused with Yusuf ᶜAdil Khan of Bijapur), arranging marriages between the families. The successful campaign cemented Gujarat's influence for the following decades.[91]

The rivalry intensified in the 1520s and spread from Khandesh into the Deccan proper, when Gujarat used the constant struggle between Ahmadnagar and Berar for its own purposes. When Berar's sultan ᶜAlaʾ al-Din ᶜImad al-Mulk (r. 1510–30) was defeated, he fled his kingdom and found shelter with his ally in Khandesh, Miran Muhammad Shah Faruqi (r. 1520–35).[92] In 1528, ᶜAlaʾ al-Din invited Bahadur Shah of Gujarat (r. 1526–37) to assist him against Ahmadnagar; this request suited Gujarat's expansionist zeal at the time. Claiming that 'The *amīr*s of the Deccan are oppressors, ᶜImad Shah is oppressed, and the duty of the pious king is to protect the oppressed',[93] he advanced to Daulatabad. Failing to conquer this important stronghold, he proceeded to Bidar. The march into the heart of the Deccan alarmed the sultanates. The ministers of Ahmadnagar, Bidar and Bijapur sent to Bahadur Shah, claiming that the real aggressor was ᶜAlaʾ al-Din; the other sultans' response was merely defensive. Bahadur Shah changed his mind, brokered peace and returned to Gujarat. His actions implied that he aspired to position himself as a distant suzerain rather than as an actual conqueror.[94]

The affair did not end there. In 1529, Berar complained again to Bahadur Shah that Burhan Nizam al-Mulk had broken the peace terms. In response, Bahadur Shah marched into the Deccan, reasserting his claims as suzerain.[95] Burhan asked for the assistance of the neighbouring sultans; Bijapur and Bidar complied.[96] Gujarat, aided by the armies of Khandesh and Berar, advanced swiftly and sacked Ahmadnagar before continuing to meet the Deccani armies.[97] Tabatabaʾi reports that the Deccani strategy was to divide Berar from Gujarat. ᶜAli Barid of Bidar sent to ᶜImad al-Mulk that his alliance with Gujarat was not prudent because if Ahmadnagar fell, Berar would be Gujarat's next target. ᶜImad al-Mulk agreed to retire from the alliance with Gujarat, but did not go all the way to change sides. He later wrote to Burhan Nizam al-Mulk that:

> The chains of love and friendship between Your Majesty and us have always been strong and solid. We agree to fight against the army of those who are

foreign (*bīgāna*) to this country, whose rulers are, in truth, all of the same royal house.[98]

Firishta's version is considerably different. He reports that Berar continued to support Gujarat; Ismaʿil ʿAdil Khan of Bijapur sent only 500 fresh cavalry to assist Ahmadnagar, with apologies that due to unrest on the Vijayanagara border, he could not contribute more. With the prolonging of the war and the Deccani forces not faring well, Ahmadnagar, Bidar and Berar pursued peace. ʿAlaʾ al-Din ʿImad al-Mulk explained his new policy to Bahadur Shah's minister:

> Our intention was that the Sultan [Bahadur Shah] would help us to restore Pathri and Mahur from the possession of Nizam Shah. [In return] we will carry the Friday sermon (*khuṭba*) in Berar and Ahmadnagar on his name and send him gifts and presents every year. But the situation is such that he desires to tear up this kingdom from our hands.

In both versions, ʿImad al-Mulk's withdrawal from his alliance with Gujarat was decisive. Bahadur Shah now agreed to end the war, and a peace was signed. As part of the agreement, Burhan Nizam al-Mulk was required to accept Gujarat's suzerainty as expressed in the *khuṭba*, an obligation which he reportedly fulfilled only once, but without instigating renewed hostilities.[99] Some attribute the peaceful conduct to the efforts of Burhan's envoy, Shah Tahir, whom we will discuss in detail in the next chapter.[100] More likely is that Bahadur Shah did not respond because from 1530 he was occupied in Malwa and Rajasthan, before being defeated by the Mughal emperor Humayun.[101] Following Bahadur's death in mysterious circumstances in 1537, a much weakened Gujarat could no longer impose its terms over the Deccan. The only political significance it kept, as per the perspective of the Deccan sultanates, was as a refuge place for Deccani nobles who fell afoul of their masters.[102]

Gujarat's short involvement in the Deccan was markedly different than Vijayanagara's position in the subsequent decades. Whereas Vijayanagara positioned itself at the heart of the Deccani system as a legitimate actor, enabling it to play the sultanates against one another, Gujarat's success was limited as it failed to make similar advances into the Deccan. For most sultans, the Gujaratis remained foreign (*bīgāna*),[103] and therefore illegitimate. Furthermore, if we follow Firishta, the threat they presented was perceived as existential. Accordingly, if cooperation with Vijayanagara did not require any particular justification, the Deccani response to Gujarat was almost unanimous, with the notable exception of Berar. Even in this case, Deccani sources suggest that ʿAlaʾ al-Din ʿImad Shah was reluctant to cooperate with Gujarat and acknowledged the problem such cooperation presented. This difference in response leads to the conclusion that while Vijayanagara was perceived as part of the system, Gujarat was not. This, at least, is the picture that emerges in sources composed after the Mughal conquest of Gujarat in 1572–3. It is well possible that while writing about cooperating with Gujarat, the sentiment of the chroniclers was in reality aimed towards the Mughals, to which we turn next.

THE MUGHALS

The Gujarati episode was only a dress rehearsal before the main challenge: the Mughal Empire. The conquest of Gujarat put the empire in direct contact with the Deccan, which became their next target.[104] The suppression of a rebellion in the early 1580s allowed Akbar (r. 1556–1605) to renew his expansionist spree.[105] In his discussion of Akbar's twenty-eighth regnal year (1583–4), his historian and ideologue Abu al-Fazl declared that the emperor 'would proceed to the Deccan, and take possession of that country which was longing for a just ruler'.[106] Similar ideas were expressed later by Abu al-Fazl's brother, the poet and diplomat Fayzi, who said that the Mughals were obliged to implement just rule on the Deccan,[107] an excuse similar to that employed by Bahadur Shah of Gujarat. A small-scale Mughal campaign in 1585–6 was a resounding failure.[108] Soon after, Akbar supported the bid of the exiled Prince Burhan (later Burhan Nizam Shah II, r. 1591–5) to the throne of Ahmadnagar, probably with the design of grooming him as his puppet. Burhan was probably aware of the problems in posing Mughal support explicitly, and eventually ascended the throne with the assistance of Ibrahim ʿAdil Shah II of Bijapur. During Burhan's short reign, he did not forge an alliance with the Mughals.[109]

The relationship between the Deccanis and the Mughals became increasingly tense in the following century, as will be discussed in the following chapters. In the coming paragraphs, I will analyse a handful of events that reflect responses in the Deccan to the advancing Mughals. For many, the Mughals presented a serious menace not only to their political independence, but also to the Deccani community. In an assertion regarding local identity, S. R. Sharma argues that the Deccani community 'had come into existence under conditions different from those of Northern India . . . Society and culture even among the Muslims of the Deccan were not identical with those of the North'.[110] This fostered resistance to the empire, placing the Mughals in line with Gujarat and not Vijayanagara. Abu al-Fazl recognised this sentiment and stated that 'if a foreign army entered their country (the Deccan) they united their forces and fought, notwithstanding their dissensions and quarrels they had among themselves'.[111] The Dutchman Pieter van den Broeke, who visited Maharashtra in 1617, noted that every year during the campaign season (autumn/winter), Golkonda sent 6,000 cavalry and foot soldiers and Bijapur sent additional 10,000 against the Mughals.[112] This cooperation was perceived as being so important that sultans were willing to take serious risks. The anonymous chronicler of Golkonda reports that in 1595–6, during the Mughal invasion, Muhammad Quli Qutb Shah sent numerous soldiers to support the Nizam Shah, leaving the court 'empty of army and soldiers', leading some to rebel against its rule.[113]

Deccani sources support the idea of unity against the Mughals that went beyond local quarrels. During the Mughal campaign of the early 1630s, a debate arose in the court of Muhammad ᶜAdil Shah. Zubayri reports that those in favour of resistance evoked past actions to support their position:

> Ibrahim ᶜAdil Shah [II] when he was the king, strived to assist and strengthen the Nizam Shahs, and invested in organising that dynasty. Nevertheless, many times they treated the ᶜAdil Shah with dishonesty . . . They always attacked ᶜAdil Shahi territories and brought misery. But that rock of patience (Ibrahim) ignored this . . . and forgave them. In the time of the difficulties that came upon them, he ordered to assist them, especially [against] the blows of the Mughals and the actions of the people of Delhi, because without support, the Mughals will find the opportunity [to eliminate] the Nizam Shahs.[114]

This passage stresses the value in aiding another sultanate, even if there is a need to overlook past discord; the need for unity superseded bitter memories.

The discussion in the court is interesting in another respect. Primarily guided by instincts of self-preservation, further motivations pertaining to the identity of the Deccanis and their independence of the north seem to have had a role in Bijapur's response. To many in the Deccan the Mughals were complete outsiders; combined with the danger they presented, one can understand the preference of the sultanates to cooperate with not always reliable, yet familiar, neighbours against a great menace. This anti-Mughal sentiment is further highlighted in the debate in Muhammad ᶜAdil Shah's court. Kruijtzer notes that two parties were at the heart of the debate, one supporting continuous war against the Mughals ('War Party'), which was led by the Ethiopian Khawwas Khan in league with the Brahmin Murari; the other pushed for peace with the empire ('Peace Party'), under the leadership of a Foreigner named Mustafa Khan.[115] Their respective positions fit the guidelines we have seen before: relations with the Mughals were dependent upon the sense of locality or the lack thereof. Ethiopians and Brahmins, alongside the Deccanis, were less likely to cooperate with the Mughals compared with the Foreigners, for whom the locality was not a central issue. Eventually, a peace agreement was signed between Bijapur and the Mughals in 1636, but this was not so much of a change of heart as it was a change of circumstances created by a decisive Mughal victory.

Needless to say, not everything was as clear-cut. With the significant military superiority of the Mughals, arrangements and tactical agreements were tried. Even the most local actors, from various Maratha clans to Malik Ambar, were willing at times to reach a settlement with the Mughals.[116] Marriage alliances, too, were promoted: in 1604, the daughter of Ibrahim ᶜAdil Shah II was married to Akbar's son, Prince Danyal. The prince, however, died soon after, therefore it is not very clear if and how this would have materialised.[117] Nevertheless, the tone that the sources maintained, at least until the 1630s, was that of opposition. No direct attempt to create a publicly manifested alliance between the Mughals and any of the Deccan sultanates was promoted in the way that was common among the sultanates as well as with Vijayanagara.

THE PORTUGUESE

Vijayanagara and Gujarat were familiar to the people of the Deccan for centuries, and could easily fit into frameworks of 'insiders' and 'outsiders'. The Mughals, too, represented continuity: even though newcomers themselves – Babur conquered Delhi only in 1526 – they worked within a familiar military and cultural framework. Furthermore, their elites included familiar elements such as Rajputs, Turks or Afghans.

The Portuguese, in contrast, presented a new entity altogether. Europeans visited India in the fifteenth century, but as individuals.[118] This changed with the arrival of Vasco da Gama to Calicut on the Malabar coast in 1498 and the establishment of the Estado da Índia in 1505, turning the European presence political and military. Assisted by their naval supremacy, the Portuguese took over key locations around the Indian Ocean. In 1510, they conquered Goa, previously in the possession of Bijapur. The city later became the centre of their Asian empire. The Portuguese further conquered Ahmadnagar's port of Chaul, where they built a fort in 1521. However, other than minor attempts to expand their coastal strongholds, no significant territories were conquered in India.[119]

In the following decades, the Portuguese used military, diplomatic and economic measures to secure their possessions. Ideologically, in the first decades the Portuguese were inclined towards Vijayanagara and its Christian-to-be Hindu rulers, as the hopeful Portuguese thought. On a declarative level, they continued to fight against the heresy of Islam, particularly in the spirit of the counter-reformation that emerged in the 1540s.[120] However, realpolitik often prevails and the Portuguese did not hesitate to manoeuvre between Bijapur and Vijayanagara, to trade in key military commodities with both or to conquer Vijayanagara ports.[121] Yet they were usually not interested in the internal politics of the sultanates. The most notable exception is the story of the ᶜAdil Shahi prince ᶜAli, allegedly the son of Yusuf ᶜAdil Khan. Taking refuge in Goa, he became the centrepiece of abortive political intrigues within Bijapur's court in the mid-1540s, to which Ahmadnagar, too, was drawn. The Portuguese and the prince acted again in 1555–6 with similar results. This affair can be understood within the wider strategy of the Portuguese in Asia to hold and use local princes.[122] Other than these minor political affairs, trade networks connected the sultanates with the Portuguese, intensifying after Talikota. Trade included commodities and raw materials necessary for the textile production centres along the coast.[123] Europeans travelled in the Deccan to gather knowledge, for example, Garcia da Orta, author of *Colloquies on the Simples and Drugs of India* (1563), a widely circulated scientific-cum-commercial treaties on *materia medica*.[124] Others found employment in the Deccan, for example, the physician Fernão Lopes, who, according to one report, failed to treat Ibrahim ᶜAdil Shah II of Bijapur, hastening his death.[125] Lastly, the Portuguese sent several missionaries to Deccani courts, in particular Bijapur, where a few Jesuits resided in the 1560s.[126]

With that, the links, in particular the military and political ones, remained intermittent, reflecting only marginal Portuguese interest in their immediate neighbours. Their main concern lay elsewhere, with the Mughal Empire, whose conquest of Gujarat put the two empires in direct contact. Much of their relations with the Deccan were shaped by Portuguese interest in the Mughals and their Deccan campaigns.[127] Portuguese interest in the Deccan sultanates, suggests Jorge Flores, was primarily intended to maintain Deccani autonomy as a buffer between Goa and the Mughals.[128] On the Deccani side, in contrast to the image that might emerge from Portuguese sources and the Western historiography that followed,[129] the sultanates do not seem to have been overly concerned about the Portuguese. The chronicles give them only a minute place. This may come as a surprise considering Portuguese aggression against ports and non-European traders. But to the Deccan sultanates, the impact of the Portuguese remained rather insignificant. For the entirety of the sixteenth century, the sides clashed only a handful of times: Bijapur fought against the Portuguese for control over small tract of mainland opposite Goa after the conquest of the port and again in 1535–6. The issue of Prince ᶜAli emerged in the mid-1540s and again in 1555–6, and more serious military engagement took place in the 1570s. On the wake of the Mughal advance into the Deccan, an anti-Mughal alliance was even discussed.[130] Ahmadnagar's relations with the Portuguese seem even less consequential, with only a handful of mentions in the sources; in addition to the alliance with Bijapur against the Portuguese in the 1570s, Burhan Nizam Shah II tried to build his own fort near Chaul in order to curtail their power.[131] These very few encounters only highlight that confrontation was the exception.

This minor place is clear when we examine the Persian sources. Other than a short description of the few hostilities, there are almost no references to the Portuguese even when discussing Goa. For example, in 1603–4, the Safavid Shah ᶜAbbas I (r. 1588–1629) sent his envoy Oghurlu Sultan to Golkonda. 'As he crossed the dark ocean and arrived in the port of Goa', states the anonymous chronicler, 'messengers brought the news of his arrival to the throne'. Muhammad Quli Qutb Shah sent his noble, the Iranian *sayyid* Ziya al-Din Nishapuri to ceremonially receive the envoy. Having met at the port, the two travelled together to Hyderabad.[132] Even though Goa was the centre of the *Estado*, the Portuguese are not mentioned in this account at all, not even as hostile lip service. Their control over the port did not, apparently, interrupt the free movement of people, even at an official capacity, presumably after the vessels paid the appropriate tolls. Similar disregard can be seen in the narratives left by Akbar's ambassadors to the Deccan. Muzaffar Alam and Sanjay Subrahmanyam note that the first ambassador, the poet Fayzi, did not pay much attention to the Portuguese, whom he characterises as 'minor irritants, and at worst arrogant troublemakers'. A similarly minor place is given to the Portuguese in the account of the ambassador Asad Beg Qazwini a few years later.[133] With the Portuguese presence deemed not worthy attention, we can reassess the chroniclers' disregard of the affair of the ᶜAdil Shahi prince ᶜAli. Subrahmanyam suggests that it was motivated by the desire to delete a competing prince from the record.[134] Whereas this reading makes sense for Bijapur's chronicles, it is less likely to be the case for sources from Ahmadnagar, notably Tabatabaʾi. It is possible that the affair was much more important to the Portuguese than it was to Bijapur, for whom, at best, it was related to those 'minor irritants'.

The best-known exception to this overall indifference can be found in the early sixteenth-century Arabic treatise *A Gift of the Fighters of the Holy War in Some of the Affairs of the Portuguese*. This work by Zayn al-Din b. ᶜAbd al-ᶜAziz al-Shafiᶜi narrates the history of Malabar coast (modern-day Kerala) from the rise of Islam to the arrival of the Portuguese. This work carries a negative image of the Portuguese, who are frequently referred to as Franks (*afranj*), a name that goes back to the time of the Crusades, marking the wars in religious hues.[135] Al-Shafi‘i's exceptional hostility towards the Portuguese is understandable, considering that the focus of his work was a region heavily exposed to direct Portuguese influence and, in local eyes, also damage. But it also highlights the lack of enthusiasm on the part of the Deccan sultanates. Located on the coast beyond the Sahyadri Mountains, campaigning against Portuguese strongholds required special investment. Furthermore, there does not seem to be strong motivation to conduct such campaigns. The Deccan sultanates remained focused on their core region on the plateau, to which the Portuguese posed no threat; rather, they remained in a region that we marked before as the periphery of the Deccan. Furthermore, the Portuguese did not block the circulation of people and commodities to the sultanates, even if for payment, thus not giving the sultanates reasons to resist them.

The relations with the Portuguese fit the wider framework within which the Deccan sultanates responded to the world surrounding them. On one side stands Vijayanagara, deeply involved in the Deccan. All sultanates found it appropriate at one point to cooperate with Vijayanagara, making the empire a legitimate regional player. On the other end of the spectrum, stand the Sultanate of Gujarat and the Mughal Empire. They were perceived as outsiders, and even more so, as truly dangerous to the Deccani system. Therefore, unlike Vijayanagara, the sultanates tended to unite against them. A third model is presented by the Portuguese. Complete outsiders, they remained focused on their littoral enclaves below the Sahyadri Mountains, therefore were not considered a significant threat to the core of the Deccan, and did not attract much of the sultans' attention. Two factors determining the policies of the sultanates emerge here: proximity and menace. Vijayanagara's proximity made it part of the system, therefore a legitimate participant in the system; it was only when it risked the equilibrium that the others united against it. Gujarat and the Mughals, in contrast, were both foreign and menacing, hence cooperation with them was marked as illegitimate. The Portuguese were foreign but not menacing, therefore did not deserve much attention. Interestingly, religious affiliation did not serve as a factor; alliances with Hindus were acceptable, but not with the Muslim Gujaratis or Mughals. This suggests that notwithstanding the divisive rhetoric in the Persian chronicles, ideas of locality and familiarity prevailed over religion and took the lead in shaping the political trajectory of the Deccani system.

* * *

The attitudes of the Deccan sultanates towards their neighbours reflect some of the sensitivities of the Deccanis within the local political system. More than any other group, the Deccanis were associated with the Deccan sultanates. Sharing one geopolitical unit, even if fragmented, these elites saw the core region of the Deccan as their home. From the fourteenth century onwards, the Deccanis gradually introduced social, cultural and political coherence to the region, which gave birth to, and was aided by, the rise of the Dakhani language. The further expansion of the language from a spoken and devotional idiom to a royal and literary one enabled the core of the Deccan to achieve unprecedented cultural unity. This unity encouraged the further crystallisation of the Deccanis, who were of diverse backgrounds, as a political and social group. This added to the complexity of the space identified as the Deccan. The region remained divided by political boundaries, even if they were not as clearly marked as that between the Deccan and north India. Furthermore, the space as perceived by the Deccanis was overlapping in part with other spaces, defined by the three vernaculars of Marathi, Kannada and Telugu, resulting in the creation of complex relations that may be interpreted as looking like core–periphery, at least from the perspective of the Deccanis.

The association of the Deccanis with the core of the Deccan became an important factor in shaping political and social life in the sultanates. Internally, the main dividing line rested neither on the borders between the five sultanates nor on religious lines, but primarily revolved around questions of locality. The hostility Deccanis demonstrated against the Foreigners, even if not all-encompassing and not always active, derived from this very notion of belonging. In foreign relations, too, local/foreign distinctions were an important guiding line. Those considered insiders, first and foremost Vijayanagara on the sultanates' periphery, were integrated into the Deccani system as legitimate collaborators. Those external to the system were perceived as a menace, in particular, when aiming at the core of the Deccan. In those cases, the sultanates forgot their differences and united against the invader, sometimes explicitly expressing the anxiety that the fall of one would be the end of them all. Unsurprisingly, this kind of policy was promoted by local actors, not only Deccanis but also Marathas, Brahmins and Ethiopians. This framing enables us to locate the Deccanis within their environment as the most dominant group when it comes to determining the direction of the sultanates. As dominant as they were, however, other elites continued to contribute greatly to the development of the sultanates. Among these were other local elites, primarily vernacular-speaking non-Muslims and, above all the Foreigners, whose dominant role will be discussed next.

Notes

1. Sherwani, 'The Council of Regency', pp. 48–50; Sherwani, *Mahmud Gawan*, pp. 59–77; Siddiqi, *Bahmani Sufis*, pp. 179–85; Eaton, *Social History*, pp. 70–7.
2. *Tarikh-i Firishta*, vol. 2, pp. 5–6; *Futuhat-i ᶜAdil Shahi*, pp. 25v–26r, 33v.
3. Firishta suggests that he officially broke away from Bidar in 1487, but this seems too early for such a move; see *Tarikh-i Firishta*, vol. 2, p. 343 and discussion below.
4. The first generation of autonomous leaders kept their original titles under the Bahmanis without taking the title *shāh*; i.e., Nizam al-Mulk, ᶜImad al-Mulk, ᶜAdil Khan and Qutb al-Mulk. Here, when referring to the characters, I follow the title they used in their lifetime; for the dynasty as a whole I use the later version with the title *shāh* for the sake of consistency.
5. *Burhan-i Maᵓathir*, pp. 150–4. An important destination was Daulatabad, the old Yadava capital, and then the Tughluq secondary capital remained one of the most important strategic as well as symbolic centres in the Deccan.
6. 'Ahmadnagar', *EI3*.
7. Nayeem, *External Relations*, pp. 214–15.
8. Shyam, 'ᶜImad Shahis', vol. 1, pp. 277–81.
9. These were the successful ones; many more tried. This makes sense when we consider Mahmud Gawan's step to split each *ṭaraf* into two, thus doubling the positions and opportunities, see Sherwani, *Bahmanis*, p. 225. Among these we can find Kamal Khan Dakkani in Sholapur; the Ethiopian Dastur Dinar in Gulbarga, who for some time positioned himself in between Bidar and Bijapur; and Shitab Khan in Warangal, see *Burhan-i Maᵓathir*, pp. 157–8; *Tarikh-i Firishta*, vol. 1, pp. 719–20, vol. 2, pp. 12–13, 16–17; *Futuhat-i ᶜAdil Shahi*, pp. 26r–30r, 37v–41r; Joshi, 'The Adil Shahis and the Baridis', vol. 1, pp. 292, 303–6; Eaton and Wagoner, *Power, Memory, Architecture*, pp. 165–202.
10. P. M. Joshi emphasises the religious side of the alliance, stating that the pretext for the war was Yusuf's reading of the Shiite Friday sermon (*khuṭba*), see Joshi, 'The Adil Shahis and the Baridis', vol. 1, pp. 298–9. Considering the position of creed in historiography, this could be yet another red herring; see discussion in Chapter 4.
11. The question of sovereignty is rather complicated. Rafiᶜ al-Din Shirazi suggests that in his last days, Mahmud III Bahmani (d. 1481) acknowledged the independent position of the rulers in their provinces, see *Tadhkirat al-Muluk*, pp. 31v–32r. Fuzuni adds that the ᶜAdil Shahis continued to carry the Bahmani ruling symbols of coinage (*sikka*) and *khuṭba*, see *Futuhat-i ᶜAdil Shahi*, pp. 25v–26r. Fuzuni's position seems more reasonable, as only after 1538 did the title *shāh* become widely circulated throughout, see Sherwani, 'The "Independence" of Bahmani Governors'. But the meaning

of this sovereignty was still restricted; even though coinage was such an important symbol, Bahmani coins, alongside those of Vijayanagara, continued to be in circulation until the 1580s, see Wagoner, 'Money Use in the Deccan'.

12. Eaton and Wagoner, 'Warfare on the Deccan Plateau'. See, for example, the multi-sultanate activity around the Nizam Shah's conquest of Pathri in 1520, discussed in Shyam, *Ahmadnagar*, pp. 60–1, or the affairs in 1530s, described by Fuzuni: 'against the will of the deceased king [Isma ͨil ͨAdil Shah], and with the complete attention of Asad Khan Lari and with the agreement of Darya ͨImad Shah and the consent of Amir Barid, changed the affairs of kingship with Prince Mallu Khan on the threshold', later took care of removing him and replacing him with Ibrahim ͨAdil Shah I, *Futuhat-i ͨAdil Shahi*, p. 59r–v. The Portuguese joined this game later.

13. Probably most famous of these was the double wedding between Ahmadnagar and Bijapur in 1564, leading to the alliance against Vijayanagara: Chand Bibi, daughter of Husayn Nizam Shah I, married ͨAli ͨAdil Shah I; Bibi Hadiya Sultan, ͨAli's sister, married Husayn's son, the future Murtaza Nizam Shah I. As part of the marriages, the long contested Sholapur was given as a dowry; this created serious problems further down the road, when Chand Bibi returned to Ahmadnagar after ͨAli's death, see *Tarikh-i Firishta*, vol. 2, p. 72; *Basatin al-Salatin*, pp. 94–5; *Muntakhab al-Lubab* vol. 3, pp. 163, 218; Nayeem, *External Relations*, p. 85. Shirazi mentions a similar case when Amir Barid of Bidar was married to a sister of ͨAli ͨAdil Shah I of Bijapur. They had no children, and upon her death, ͨAli I demanded the return of the precious jewellery given as her dowry, following the rules of succession. The sultan of Bidar agreed and sent the jewellery back to Bijapur, see *Tadhkirat al-Muluk*, pp. 149–50. On a more general note, the early eighteenth-century Mughal chronicler Khafi Khan commented sarcastically that 'it was a divine mystery that whenever the rulers of the Deccan gave one another a daughter [in marriage] for purposes of gaining peace and bringing accord, no girl was at ease in her husband's house, and [the relations] turned to an additional reason for conflict and discord', see *Muntakhab al-Lubab*, vol. 3, p. 219.

14. The conflict seems to have been active more in the western Deccan than in Telangana, reaching its most violent manifestation in Ahmadnagar in the closing decades of the sixteenth century; see Chapter 5.

15. The success of the war brought a debate over who was responsible for the formation of the alliance. The anonymous Golkonda chronicler attributed it to Ibrahim Qutb Shah, who sent his minister Mustafa Khan to Ahmadnagar and Bijapur in order to negotiate the details, see *Tarikh-i Qutb Shah*, pp. 145r–147r. Shirazi attributes the endeavour to Husayn Nizam Shah I of Ahmadnagar, stating that the idea reached Mustafa Khan's ears. The noble then convinced Ibrahim Qutb Shah to join in. Only then did Ibrahim appoint

Mustafa Khan as his representative to discuss the details with Ahmadnagar, see *Tadhkirat al-Muluk*, pp. 112–13.
16. The exact location of the battle has been debated by H. K. Sherwani, who came to the conclusion that it took place 'twelve miles south of the Krishna at Bannihaṭṭi on the sangam (confluence) of the Maski river and its southern tributary the Hukēri', see Sherwani, *History of the Qutb Shahi*, pp. 144–9. I choose to continue using the most common name, Talikota, out of historiographical consistency.
17. This is attested by the growing border stabilisation in the Deccan after Talikota, see Eaton and Wagoner 'Warfare on the Deccan Plateau', pp. 45–7.
18. The weak sultanate had long been deteriorating and was in practice under the control of the usurper Tufal Khan, see Shyam, 'ᶜImad Shahis', vol. 1, pp. 285–7. The agreement between Bijapur and Ahmadnagar is discussed in *Burhan-i Maʾathir*, pp. 457–61.
19. This period is discussed in detail in Chapter 5.
20. Persian chroniclers were uninterested in Deccanis, and, unlike prominent Foreigners (e.g., Afzal Khan in *Tadhkirat al-Muluk*, pp. 124–8, Fuzuni's own life in *Futuhat-i ᶜAdil Shahi*, pp. 3r–5r), do not provide many details. Dakhani sources, which still await further discussion, are often obscure in their details. Therefore, we are left with no details on lives of their writers, for example, ᶜAbdul Dihlawi, see *Ibrahimnama* or Wajhi, whose life circumstances are 'behind the veil of concealment', see Vashisht, *Mulla Vajhi*, p. 17. There are a few notable characters who are more widely discussed and allow us to draw some conclusions, including the founding fathers of the Nizam Shahi and ᶜImad Shahi dynasties, the Sufi Muhammad Khawaja Banda Nawaz Gisu Daraz and the Ethiopian commander Malik Ambar.
21. Sherwani, *Bahmanis*, pp. 12–33.
22. Green, *Indian Sufism*, pp. 7–23, Eaton, *Sufis of Bijapur*, table 2, pp. 73–4, and table 3, p. 126; Digby, 'Before Timur Came', pp. 325–30.
23. Matthews, 'Dakani Language and Literature', pp. 54–5; Siddīqī, 'Muqaddama', pp. 11–12.
24. *Hadiqat al-Salatin*, pp. 80–1.
25. *Tadhkirat al-Muluk*, pp. 26–32; *Tarikh-i Firishta*, vol. 2, pp. 1–3; Fischel, 'Origin Narratives'.
26. As late as the 1530s, suggests Fuzuni in a somewhat dubious passage, Ismaᶜil still resented the Deccanis and remained strongly identified with Foreigners. In contrast, it was claimed that Ibrahim ᶜAdil Shah II had only rudimentary Persian, and preferred to speak in Marathi. See further discussion in Chapter 4.
27. The trajectory and details of such a process of assimilation beyond the elites, however, is difficult to trace and requires a separate study. One possible avenue is to look at the way modern communities in the Deccan

28. *Burhan-i Maʾathir*, pp. 168–73.
29. *Tarikh-i Firishta*, vol. 2, p. 180. Tabatabaʾi acknowledges the existence of conflicting versions, and admits that he himself 'saw in the royal Nizam Shahi library a letter written by Burhan I (r. 1510–53), under the title Shaykh Burhan al-Din b. Malik Ahmad Nizam al-Mulk b. Malik Naʾib', yet the version he brings is supported by writings as well as stories 'he heard from news tellers', see *Burhan-i Maʾathir*, p. 168. Similar origins are attributed to Fathullah, founder of the ʿImad Shahi dynasty of Berar. He is said to have been a slave captured in Vijayanagara, who converted to Islam and was then introduced to the service of Sultan Ahmad I, see *Tarikh-i Firishta*, vol. 2, p. 343.
30. Eaton, *Bengal Frontier*, p. 116.
31. Qādrī, *Zabān-i urdū*, pp. 41–2, 67; Mohamed, *The Value of Dakhni*, pp. 44–59. Eaton points out the complexity and duration of the process of conversion, using the tomb of the Chishti Sufi Baba Farid al-Din Ganjshakar in the Punjab. It is likely that similar processes took place in Deccani shrines, see Eaton, 'Baba Farid'. He further suggests that certain Sufi compositions, for example, simple repetitive verses related to specific chores performed by women such as grinding or spinning the spinning wheel were one avenue of mediating Islam to the masses, see Eaton, *Sufis of Bijapur*, pp. 155–73. This, however, assumes that Dakhani, the language of these compositions, was understood by the masses; I am not convinced that such assumption can be made.
32. Eaton, 'Written Vernaculars', pp. 123–6.
33. Kincaid and Parasnis, *Maratha People*, p. 114. Another such story from Maharashtra links the Brahmin Ramesvara to the healing of a son of the early Nizam Shahi commander Zafar Malik; following this, 'the students, Zafar Malik, his *mlecchas* women, children, and the lowly all gained confidence in Ramesvara's power', see Benson, 'Samkarabhatta's Family Chronicle', 109.
34. Eaton, *Social History*, pp. 67–77.
35. Notable works on Malik Ambar include Chowdhuri, *Malik Ambar*; Shyam, *Malik Ambar*; Tamaskar, *Life and Work of Malik Ambar*; Eaton, *Social History*, pp. 105–28; Ali, *Malik Ambar*.
36. Not only by the Ethiopians themselves; in Maharashtra, they were usually not included in the category of *yavana*, which was widely used for other Muslims. See Laine, 'The *Dharma* of Islam', p. 315.
37. For example, Deccanis and Ethiopians are listed together in an expedition from Ahmadnagar to Bijapur in 1580, see: *Tarikh-i Qutb Shah*, p. 183v.
38. For example, according to *Burhan-i Maʾathir*, p. 569, Mirza Khan, the *wakīl* of Ahmadnagar appointed a few Foreigners to key roles in the state, including the position of *kotwāl* (head of civil affairs and magistrate) of

Ahmadnagar Fort, of which 'the Ethiopian and Deccani commanders became suspicious . . . and reached an accord to resist him', suggesting that rather than automatic alliance, Deccani–Ethiopian cooperation had to be constantly negotiated; we will return to growing rifts between Ethiopians and Deccanis throughout this study.

39. This was the case in Ahmadnagar after 1600, when Foreigners left the sultanates altogether, leaving Deccanis and Ethiopians in place.
40. Pipes, *Slave Soldiers*; Ayalon, 'Mamluk Military Aristocracy'.
41. In this case, the sovereign remained a puppet of the Nizam Shah; see discussion in Chapter 5.
42. *Burhan-i Maʾathir*, p. 299, mentions the sons of Khayrat Khan Habshi as holding important roles in the military; *Tarikh-i Firishta*, vol. 2, pp. 164–7, mentions the categories *muwallad* as well as *ḥabshī-zāda* (child of a *ḥabshī*), when discussing the career of Ikhlas Khan *muwallad* in 1590s Ahmadnagar.
43. That being said, certain groups maintained their ancestral identity as Africans for centuries after, see Obeng, 'Religion and Empire'.
44. Both Persian and Dakhani sources are often confusing. References to the name of the language include *dakhanī*, *dakanī* and *dakkhinī*, as well as *hindī*, *hindavī* (i.e., the language(s) the people(s) of India speak) and even *gujrī* or *gūjrī* (relates to the shared origin with the equivalent language that developed in Gujarat); see discussion in Matthews, 'Dakani Language and Literature', pp. 1–7, 35–42. *Tarikh-i Firishta*, vol. 2, p. 49, mentions *hindawī* as the new language of administration; Matthews suggests that in this context, the language should be understood as Marathi, not Dakhani, see Matthews, 'Dakani Language and Literature', p. 65. More vague a reference appears in *Burhan-i Maʾathir*, p. 278, where the author states that a message from Gujarat was delivered in the 'language of the land and time (*zabān-i zamīn-o zamān*)', which may refer to Dakhani, but can also be simply a poetic use. Similarly vague is the reference to *lisān-i ahl-i dakkan* in *Futuhat-i ʿAdil Shahi*, p. 25v; not referring to the political category of *dakkanīyān*, the phrase may mean Dakhani, Marathi or Kannada. This confusion is not only a matter of Persian, a vagueness of terms can be found in Dakhani sources as well. The poet Miran Ji, for example, uses the term *hindī* for the language he used, see *Irshadnama*, p. 135; ʿAbdul Dihlawi states that 'my language is *hindawī*, and I am from Delhi; I do not know (how to write) *mathnawī* in Arabic or Persian (*ʿarab hawr ʿajam mathnawī*)', this time this possibly refers to a north Indian language, see *Ibrahimnama*, v.99. The Dakhani poet Wajhi of Golkonda, too, uses the term *hindī* for his own language, see Matthews, 'Dakani Language and Literature', pp. 137–8. There are a few clearer references to language, such as the aforementioned statement of Firishta in which he acknowledges Marathi, Kannada and Telugu (but not Dakhani), or the Mughal ambassador to Bijapur, Asad Beg, identified the language spoken by Ibrahim ʿAdil

Local States in an Imperial World

Shah II as Marathi, see *Halat-i Asad Beg*, p. 168r. The clearest reference to what would be recognised today as the Dakhani language is by the early eighteenth-century chronicler Khafi Khan, who narrates that during the reign of ᶜAli ᶜAdil Shah II, 'Mulla Nusrati and other poets of Bijapur translated Mulla Jami's *Yūsuf and Zulaykhā* and [Kashifi's] *Rawẓa-i shuhadā*, and the story of Manohar and Madhumalati (known as *Gulshān-i ᶜishq*) ... into Dakhani (*be-zabān-i dakkanī*)', see *Muntakhab al-Lubab*, vol. 3, p. 360. A similar lack of clarity can be found in the reference to the variety of vernaculars in north India, referred to in generic terms such as *hindī*, *hindavī* or *bhakha* (lit. 'language'), see Orsini, 'How to do Multilingual Literary History?' pp. 228–9.

45. Qadri Zor, *Dakkani adab*, pp. 11–13.
46. Matthews, 'Dakani Language and Literature', pp. 15–34; Khan, 'Dakhni-Urdu', vol. 2, pp. 19–21; Qadri Zor, *Dakkani adab*, pp. 13–14; Digby, 'Before Timur Came', pp. 333–9.
47. Matthews, 'Dakani Language and Literature', p. 43. Sayed Mohamed surveyed the centres of production in Dakhani, suggesting that it was spoken 'from the Arabian Sea to the Bay of Bengal', but mentions centres of learning, all of which are on the plateau, including Gulbarga, Bidar, Gogi, Golkonda, Ahmednagar and Bijapur; other centres he mentions, including Bodhan, Chanpatan, Mysore, Cuddappa, Kurnool, Vellore and Madras, developed much later, see Mohamed, *Dakhni Language and Literature*, p. 9. Rather inaccurate in nature, Mohamed again maps the language into the core of the Deccan, in line with what we know.
48. Bawa, 'The Role of Sufis and Sants'.
49. Guha, 'Transitions and Translations', p. 25. Grahame Bailey defines, rather crudely, a transition from a 'religious' to a 'literary' period around 1590, see Bailey, *Urdu Literature*, pp. 14–30
50. See discussion in Orsini, 'The Multilingual Local'.
51. Eaton, *Sufis of Bijapur*, pp. 91–2; Sadiq, *Urdu Literature*, pp. 42–52; Saksena, *Urdu Literature*, pp. 32–44; Ahmad, *Intellectual History of Islam*, pp. 91–4. For a survey of poets and works, see Bukhārī, *Urdū wa Dakkani*; Matthews, 'Dakani Language and Literature', pp. 43–162; Qādrī, *Zāban-i Urdū*, pp. 34–92; Qadri Zor, *Dakkani adab*, pp. 25–81. This literary trajectory is supported by the development of Deccani art. Already under the Bahmani sultans, a local artistic idiom began to emerge, gradually setting the Deccan away from the visual language of the north. The local idiom transferred and continued to develop in the Deccan sultanates, see Sherwani, *Bahmanis*, pp. 123–4; Michell and Zebrowski, *Architecture and Art*. The unique character of Deccani architecture, shared by all courts, is easily visible in the royal mausolea in Bijapur and Golkonda. Similar to one another, they are markedly different to Mughal architecture in the Deccan, such as tomb of Aurangzeb's wife Rabiᶜa Durani in Aurangabad (Bibi ka Maqbara), that resembles mausolea from north India such as the Taj Mahal.

The Sultanates and the Deccan

52. Abdul Khader Fakhri suggests that in the early twentieth century, Deccani Muslims maintained their distinctive identity within the Muslim communities of Tamil Nadu, but even they were divided by creed, class and ideas of origin. Furthermore, they were identified by their language, Dakhani. See Fakhri, *Dravidian Sahibs*, pp. 30–41.
53. Interestingly, the Marathas, very much identified with Maharashtra, aspired to justify their positions as rulers and Kshatriyas by claiming to be descendants of Rajput immigrants from Rajasthan in the north, see Gordon, *The Marathas*, pp. 87–8; for a detailed discussion of their links to the Sisodia Rajputs, see Krishna, *Shivaji the Great*, pp. 35–50, 184–92.
54. Alavi, *Medieval Deccan*, p. 4.
55. For example, Eaton advocates creed as a sort of contestation in Bijapur, see Eaton, *Sufis of Bijapur*, pp. 62–70.
56. *Tarikh-i Firisha*, vol. 2, pp. 17–18, and see discussion in Joshi, 'The Adil Shahis and the Baridis', vol. 1, pp. 298–9.
57. *Burhan-i Ma'athir*, pp. 258–68.
58. Alavi, *Medieval Deccan*, pp. 6–7.
59. Sherwani, *Bahmanis*, pp. 131–4, 151–73.
60. Sharma, 'Cultural Background of Political Struggles in Medieval Deccan', p. 174. The text uses the term *Kulhr-Campf*, which I read as a garbled version of *Kultur Kampf*.
61. Shyam, *Ahmadnagar*, p. 151.
62. The maintenance of balance was central to successful leadership and depended heavily on the personality of the ruler. A strong sultan managed to keep the conflict at bay; a weak one enabled intensified struggle with each side trying to undermine its rival, damaging the sultanate as a whole. This kind of scenario is often used as an explanation for the collapse of the Bahmani sultanate, see Sherwani, *Bahmanis*, pp. 239–43.
63. We will see in the coming chapters that this was a common theme in the last half century of the Nizam Shahi dynasty.
64. *Burhan-i Ma'athir*, pp. 571–7; *Tarikh-i Firishta*, vol. 2, pp. 289–93; Shyam, *Ahmadnagar*, pp. 202–5.
65. *Burhan-i Ma'athir*, pp. 577–9.
66. Schimmel, *Islam in the Indian Subcontinent*, p. 54.
67. *Tarikh-i Qutb Shah*, pp. 241v–243r.
68. A visual manifestation can be found in the painting *Jahangir receives Prince Khurram on his return from the Deccan* by the Mughal painters Ramdas and Murar, painted *c.* 1640 and included in the Windsor *Padshahnama*. In the painting, Jahangir embraces his son Khurram (Shah Jahan), while the panel underneath the empty throne depicts scenes of thievery and corruption. Ebba Koch notes that this 'allegory of bad government' promotes the idea that Shah Jahan's accession brought to an end 'an era of corruption and religious decline', see Beach and Koch, *King of the World*, pp. 166–7. The absence of a righteous ruler, symbolised by the empty throne, vacated

absentmindedly by the ruler, like in Muhammad Quli's sleep, has resulted in oppression.
69. Shakeb, *Relations of Golkonda with Iran*, p. 66.
70. *Tadhkirat al-Muluk*, p. 35.
71. Kodad, *Deccani Wars*, pp. 3–6.
72. Sherwani suggests that since the Deccan ceased to be a frontier in the fifteenth century, inter-religious conflicts were reduced in intensity, and from the 1430s, inter-religious issues were political rather than communal. Similar relaxed relations can be seen in the case of Golkonda, in particular, under Ibrahim Qutb Shah. See Sherwani, *Bahmanis*, p. 153; Sherwani, *History of the Qutb Shahi*, pp. 179–91.
73. For example, Yusuf ᶜAdil Khan is reported to have been sent with 'the army of Islam' to subdue the 'infidels' of Telangana, *Tadhkirat al-Muluk*, p. 33.
74. *Tarikh-i Qutb Shah*, pp. 197v–200r; we will return to this interesting rebellion in Chapter 5.
75. Similar use of Islamic language when addressing Hindu loyalists can be found in correspondence between ᶜAli ᶜAdil Shah II of Bijapur and Shahaji Bhonsle's son Ekoji. James Laine interprets this language as if 'somehow, since Ekoji was a loyal ally, unlike his half-brother Śivājī, that meant that he shared in the Islamic mission, even though he was Hindu'. I suggest that rather than some grand Islamic mission, this language indicates the political inclusion of Ekoji within Bijapur's political circle at the time. See Laine, 'The *Dharma* of Islam', pp. 314–15.
76. Gribble, *History of the Deccan*, pp. 186–97; Sewell, *Forgotten Empire*, pp. 196–213.
77. Quoted in Stein, *Vijayanagara*, pp. 2–8.
78. Venkataramanayya, *Further Sources*, vol. 1, pp. 190, 244–5, 257–8.
79. Sherwani, for example, elaborates on Vijayanagara's abuse of Muslims in their campaign against Ahmadnagar in 1562–3, but as a whole promotes a view of communal harmony in Golkonda, see *History of the Qutb Shahi*, pp. 138–9. A volume of papers presented in a seminar on Vijayanagara, held in Heidelberg in 1983, included several papers on Islamic themes, yet the editors decided to mark them as a closed group, see Dallapiccola and Lallemant, *Vijayanagara – City and Empire*.
80. Asher, 'Islamic Influence'.
81. Wagoner 'Sultan among Hindu Kings'; Wagoner, 'Fortuitous Convergences'; Wagoner, 'Money Use in the Deccan'; Eaton, *Social History*; Eaton and Wagoner, *Power, Memory, Architecture*.
82. Talbot, 'Inscribing the Other, Inscribing the Self'.
83. Kruijtzer, *Xenophobia*.
84. Eaton, 'Temple Desecration'.
85. Sarkar, 'Necro-Narratives'; Sherwani, *History of the Qutb Shahi*, pp. 86–93, 121–42; Shyam, *Ahmadnagar*, pp. 103–23; Eaton, *Social History*, pp. 92–9; Eaton and Wagoner, *Power, Memory, Architecture*, pp. 77–124.

The Sultanates and the Deccan

86. For an analysis of this struggle, see Eaton, 'Kiss my Foot'. One of the most intriguing peaceful interactions is the visit of ᶜAli ᶜAdil Shah I early on his career in the court of Vijayanagara, see *Tadhkirat al-Muluk*, pp. 57–62.
87. Eaton, *Social History*, pp. 92–9; Eaton and Wagoner, *Power, Memory, Architecture*, pp. 77–124.
88. Shyam, *Ahmadnagar*, pp. 86–8; Nayeem, *External Relations*, pp. 80–1; Sherwani, *History of the Qutb Shahi*, pp. 86–93.
89. For a summary of the campaigns in these years, see Shyam, *Ahmadnagar*, pp. 86–162; Nayeem, *External Relations*, pp. 80–9, 98–101, 120–7; Sherwani, *History of the Qutb Shahi*, pp. 81–96, 120–42, 156–70; Joshi, 'The Adil Shahis and the Baridis', vol. 1, pp. 317–34.
90. *Burhan-i Maʾathir*, pp. 220–5, suggests that internal strife in Khandesh brought local factions to invite Mahmud Shah of Gujarat to intervene, pushing the local ruler Mahmud Shah to ask Ahmadnagar to interfere. Ahmad Nizam al-Mulk wanted to respond, but without notifying his minister Masnad-i ᶜAli Malik Nasir who had been employed before in Gujarat. Nevertheless, Masnad-i ᶜAli used his links in the court to prevent the Gujarati campaign and promoted a peaceful diplomatic solution, gaining Ahmadnagar significant influence in Burhanpur. P. Hardy suggests that this story comes 'to disguise the discomfiture of Ahmad Nizam Shah', but has no support in other sources, nor is Mahmud Shah recorded elsewhere. See 'Farukids', *EI2*.
91. *Zafar al-Walih*, pp. 54–8; *Miraʾat-i Ahmadi*, vol. 1, p. 60; Shyam, *Khandesh*, pp. 23–31.
92. *Burhan-i Maʾathir*, pp. 246–9; Shyam, 'ᶜImad Shahs', vol. 1, p. 282; Shyam, *Khandesh*, pp. 31–3.
93. *Miraʾat-i Sikandari*, p. 214.
94. *Miraʾat-i Sikandari*, pp. 215–16; Chaube, *Gujarat Kingdom*, p. 179.
95. *Miraʾa-i Sikandari*, pp. 216–17; Shyam, 'ᶜImad Shahis', vol. 1, p. 282.
96. *Tarikh-i Firishta*, vol. 2, p. 203.
97. *Miraʾa-i Sikandari*, pp. 217–18; *Miraʾat-i Ahmadi*, vol. 1, p. 73; Chaube, *Gujarat Kingdom*, pp. 184–91; Commissariat, *Gujarat*, vol. 1, pp. 321–3; Shyam, *Khandesh*, pp. 33–7.
98. *Burhan-i Maʾathir*, pp. 270–4, quotation on p. 272.
99. *Tarikh-i Firishta*, vol. 2, p. 207; *Muntakhab al-Lubab*, vol. 3, p. 169.
100. *Burhan-i Maʾathir*, pp. 274–81; Chaube, *Gujarat Kingdom*, pp. 192–3.
101. Chaube, *Gujarat Kingdom*, pp. 195–280; Commissariat, *Gujarat*, vol. 1, pp. 323–83.
102. See, for example, the conflict between Makhdum Khwaja Jahan, ruler of Paranda, approx. 115 km southeast of Ahmadnagar, and his escape (and return) from Gujarat around 1540, *Burhan-i Maʾathir*, pp. 296–301, 344–9.
103. Note that Tabatabaʾi employs the term *bīgāna* and not *gharīb*, which is kept for those Iranians from within the Deccani system.

104. Alam and Subrahmanyam, 'Deccan Frontier', p. 364.
105. Richards, *Mughal Empire*, pp. 40–1.
106. *Akbarnama*, vol. 3, pp. 616–17.
107. *Akbarnama*, vol. 3, p. 373.
108. *Burhan-i Maʾathir*, pp. 547–51.
109. Shyam, *Ahmadnagar*, p. 179; Alam and Subrahmanyam, 'Deccan Frontier', pp. 370–1.
110. Sharma, 'Cultural Background of Political Struggles in Medieval Deccan', p. 174.
111. Quoted in Sherwani, *History of the Qutb Shahi*, p. 450.
112. Quoted in Kruijtzer, *Xenophobia*, p. 92.
113. *Tarikh-i Qutb Shah*, p. 224v. This, of course, is possibly a literary hyperbole aimed at depicting the rebels in a bad light as well as to justifying the weakness of the central government.
114. *Basatin al-Salatin*, pp. 290–1.
115. Kruijtzer, *Xenophobia*, pp. 92–5.
116. Sarkar, *House of Shivaji*, pp. 18–23; Shyam, *Malik Ambar*, pp. 110–11, and see further discussion in Chapter 5.
117. Alam and Subrahmanyam, 'Deccan Frontier', pp. 380–5. A few decades later, Aurangzeb married his son Muhammad Sultan to the daughter of ʿAbdullah Qutb Shah of Golkonda, declaring their future son as heir apparent of Golkonda; this never happened. See Verma, *Bijapur*, pp. 195–7, and discussion in Chapter 5.
118. Most notable are the Venetian Nicolo de Conti and the Russian Afanasii Nikitin. See Oaten, *European Travellers in India*, pp. 26–47; Major, *India in the Fifteenth Century*.
119. Nayeem, *External Relations*, pp. 212–16; Subrahmanyam, *Portuguese Empire*, pp. 59–85; Subrahmanyam, *Three Ways to be Alien*, pp. 23–5; Subrahmanyam, *Written on Water*.
120. Anthony Pagden suggests that the European perception of empire, which was based on medieval and early modern interpretations of the Roman past, gave Christianity an important role within the framework of imperial expansion. In particular, Pagden states that 'those inside "the world" (i.e., Christians) could legitimately make war on those outside, particularly ... [those] who had wilfully persisted in their unbelief even after they had heard the Gospel'. Pagden, *Lords of All the World*, pp. 24–8, citation on p. 25; see also Subrahmanyam, *Portuguese Empire*, pp. 88–92.
121. Rubiés, *Travel and Ethnology*, pp. 191–5; Subrahmanyam, *Political Economy*, pp. 120–35; Subrahmanyam, *Explorations in Connected History*, pp. 82–3.
122. See discussion of this fascinating affair in Subrahmanyam, *Three Ways to be Alien*, pp 23–72. This was not the only case of this kind; around the succession of Husayn Nizam Shah I in Bijapur (1554), another claimant to the throne fled first to Berar and then to Bijapur, providing the neighbours

a pretext to intervene in Ahmadnagar's affairs, see Shyam, *Ahmadnagar*, pp. 104–5; Joshi, 'The Adil Shahis and the Baridis', vol. 1, pp. 323–4.
123. Subrahmanyam, *Political Economy*, pp. 79–85, 155–60; Joshi, 'Notes on the Textile Industry'.
124. A recent collection of essays summarises many of the issues surrounding this important work, see Da Costa, *Medicine, Trade and Empire*.
125. *Basatin al-Salatin*, p. 280.
126. Xavier and Županov, *Catholic Orientalism*, pp. 255–9; Rubiés, *Travel and Ethnology*, pp. 321–2.
127. Flores, *The Mughal Padshah*, pp. 3–21; Alam and Subrahmanyam, 'Deccan Frontier'.
128. Flores, *Unwanted Neighbours*, pp. 155–203.
129. Being the first Europeans to expand in India, the Portuguese attracted significant scholarly attention, assuming a much greater impact than they actually had. Take, for example, *The New Cambridge History of India*, of which the first volume is dedicated not to any South Asian polity but to the Portuguese, see Pearson, *The Portuguese in India*.
130. Nayeem, *External Relations*, pp. 216–20.
131. *Tarikh-i Firishta*, vol. 2, pp. 302–5; Alam and Subrahmanyam, 'Deccan Frontier', p. 367.
132. *Tarikh-i Qutb Shah*, pp. 236r–v.
133. Alam and Subrahmanyam, 'Deccan Frontier', pp. 376–86.
134. Subrahmanyam, *Three Ways to be Alien*, p. 71.
135. *Tuhfat al-Mujahidin*. The full title of the work (*Tuḥfat al-Mujāhidīn fī baʿẓī Aḥwāl al-Burtukaliyyīn*) suggests that the author was aware of the identity of the Portuguese within the framework of Europeans. Although he uses the term Portuguese, he still prefers to use the term Franks in the work. This suggests that he consciously used the term Franks in an effort to associate the Portuguese with the Crusaders, and by that, incite a war against them.

3
Foreigners, Locals and the World

On the opposite side from the Deccanis in terms of their association with the Deccan as a region and with the sultanates as its dominant political organisation, stand the self-styled Foreigners. In a sense, they represent a paradox in the region. On the one hand, they placed themselves at the very centre of political life in the local sultanates. On the other hand, working according to non-localised lines, they were the least related to the Deccan of all elite groups. While some settled permanently in the region and gradually became identified as Deccanis, others preferred to emphasise their foreign origin and orientations. Many continued to rely on their association with trans-regional networks that linked them to their ancestral lands rather than immersing themselves in local society. In that, the Foreigners represent an elite element that at the same time contributed to the sultanates where they settled and preferred to adhere to transient over settled life.

Albeit widely discussed in the scholarship, the analysis of these foreign elites remains limited. Previous historiography tended to treat them either as a group of loosely linked individuals, or as a united political agglomeration, overlooking their social complexity and inner workings. This partial understanding was carried further into the analysis of the Foreigners' position in the region, limiting their engagement only to either monolithic contradiction with the Deccanis or to individual contribution to the states. This chapter aims at analysing the Foreigners as a composite and diverse group, and, furthermore, to understand them within the political and social system of the Deccan. Examining their political structures, identities and sensitivities, the Foreigners will be introduced as a somewhat problematic political element, which not only contributed to the running of local institutions, but which was also disruptive, in action or in perception. As such, the chapter will highlight the duality they presented to the Deccan and their form of engagement that was different from that demonstrated by local actors.

Migration to India in Context

Migration from West Asia and the lands around the Indian Ocean into the Deccan was by no means a new phenomenon in early modern times. Possibly as early as Mauryan times (fourth–second centuries BCE) maritime links connected India to West Asia and East Africa. The discovery of the regularity of the monsoon, which enabled shorter, safer and cheaper routes across the ocean, further facilitated such links.[1] In the first millennium CE, merchants from Hadramaut (south Arabia) and elsewhere, were active in the Indian Ocean all the way to China. Settling around India's littoral, some merchants established new communities while often maintaining commercial and family links with their home country.[2] From the first centuries of the second millennium, India became ever more firmly linked to global commercial systems as a market for commodities, exporter of local products (textiles, black pepper), and as a link between the eastern and western Indian Ocean.[3] Particularly important was the Indian appetite for high-quality warhorses, usually imported from Iran and Arabia. The horse trade increased dramatically with the establishment of Muslim dynasties in India and the subsequent diffusion of new military technologies throughout the subcontinent.[4] Growing commercial connections encouraged the flow of customs, political models and cultural symbols between West and South Asia.[5] More significantly, people were increasingly moving between India and the surrounding countries, leaving their impact on all aspects of life.

Just like trade, migration into India predated Muslim rule in the subcontinent. Along the littoral of peninsular India, Muslim communities emerged with the settlement of West Asian merchants and their marriages into the local population.[6] These communities, however, remained relatively small and restricted to the coastal regions. Migration intensified significantly when India was drawn into the circle of Islamic politics more closely. With Mahmud of Ghazni's invasions from the northwest around the turn of the second millennium CE, and more so with the establishment of the Delhi sultanate two centuries later, India and the Muslim world reached new levels of integration. The Delhi sultanate became not only part of the Muslim world, but also of the Persianate cultural sphere. Persian language and Persianate culture, administrative practices and court etiquette were adopted by the Turkic and Afghan rulers of Delhi, gradually turning Persian into an overall language of state-making and political thought, shared by migrants and locals.[7] The transplantation of the Persianate-cum-Turco-Mongol state mechanism into the subcontinent transformed India from something of *terra incognita* in the eyes of

Muslims into an integral part of their world image. This was accompanied by intellectual changes that began as early as the eleventh century with Abu Rayhan Muhammad al-Biruni's (973–1048) curious enquiry of India.[8] Soon thereafter, the influential Sufi ʿAli b. ʿUthman al-Hujwiri (d. c. 1073), having travelled throughout the Muslim East, settled in Lahore in 1039, where he composed the first Sufi treatise in Persian, *Kashf al-mahjub*.[9] Others travelled in the subcontinent, leaving written accounts that helped to shape India's image to Persian readers and its growing integration in the eastern parts of the Muslim world.[10]

From the thirteenth century, movement to India grew significantly due to developments both in the India and in the Muslim East. In his analysis of Iranian migrants in the sixteenth century, Sanjay Subrahmanyam employs the categories of 'pull' and 'push' factors, which originated in migration theory, to explain spatial and temporal specificities.[11] Whereas he emphasises the temporality of migratory process, this model can be used more widely to discuss migration on general lines, combining the temporal with the *longue durée*. On the pull side, the establishment of the Delhi sultanate pushed the boundaries of Muslim-ruled territories and Muslim elite imagination well into the subcontinent. This new familiarity was based on the principles mentioned before: the establishment of a state system based on the familiar Persianate and Turco-Mongol principles; and the emergence of a Muslim community in India, whose values had much in common with that of elite communities in Iran and Central Asia. Culturally and ideologically, the new Indo-Islamic elites, even though remoulded and readapted to the new environment, remained closely linked to social and intellectual trends in the Persian-speaking lands of the Muslim East.[12]

On the push side, invasions from the steppe into Iran and beyond, culminating in the expansion of the Mongol Empire during the thirteenth century and Timur's empire in the late fourteenth century shattered confidence and stability in the Muslim East. Some chose to leave their homelands and find refuge elsewhere. Mostly spared Mongol aggression, India provided such a refuge, and, indeed, many sought shelter in the subcontinent.[13] In the following centuries, Iran and Central Asia, or parts thereof, continued to experience periods of instability. Consequent migration contributed some of India's most important dynasties. The turmoil in Upper Mesopotamia and western Iran around the collapse of the Black Sheep Confederacy (Qaraquyunlu) in 1467 brought the migration of Sultan Quli (d. 1543), founder of the Qutb Shahi dynasty of Golkonda.[14] The troubles faced by the White Sheep Confederacy (Aqquyunlu) in the following decades convinced Yusuf (d. 1510), founder of the ʿAdil Shahi dynasty of Bijapur, to take the same route.[15] The rise of the Uzbeks in Transoxiana and their invasions of Khurasan soon after brought fresh migration from these quarters, most notably Zahir al-Din Muhammad Babur (d. 1530), founder of the Mughal Empire.[16] The rise of the Safavids to power in Iran in 1501, the unsettled nature of their early rule, and the rapid political and social change they introduced brought many more to leave their home country. Further ideological, economic and political changes in the sixteenth and seventeenth centuries affected certain elements in Iranian society, who continued to migrate.[17] Whereas the circumstances that caused instability in the countries of origin changed with time, the reality of hardships prevailed for long periods between the thirteenth and seventeenth centuries. It would be an exaggeration to consider this half millennium as a period of continuous calamities in the Muslim East, but different groups experienced the troubles variably, resulting in continuous emigration of diverse and changing groups.

What caused people to go to India? India not merely represented a refuge, but also presented opportunity. When discussing the migration of Yusuf ᶜAdil Khan, the chronicler Rafiᶜ al-Din Shirazi reports that:

> When Yusuf arrived in Lar – lonely, distressed, and desperate – he stayed for a few days in the mosque of the righteous man of the time (*ṣādiq al-waqt*, probably Jaᶜfar al-Sadiq, the sixth Shiite Imam). One night, a saintly man (*pīr*) appeared in his dream, put a piece of warm bread (*nān*) in his hand, and said: 'You should go to the Deccan, where your bread is being baked.' When [Yusuf] woke up from his dream, he became happy and cheerful. Following the divine message, he travelled to the Harbour of Jarun (Bandar Abbas).[18]

The narrative suggests a divine command to go to the Deccan, perceived as a place where one could earn a living. Considering the difference in population size between India and Iran,[19] the need for an administration to arrange political issues there, and the extensive use of Persian practices and language, India offered numerous positions for Persian-educated elites. India's size also promised stability at least somewhere in the subcontinent: when north India was destabilised by Timur's invasion (1398), the Bahmani Deccan remained quite attractive. In addition, the rich courts of the subcontinent also offered patronage for intellectuals, religious men and artists.[20] All this created a perpetual movement of people for centuries, primarily into the subcontinent, but some moved the other direction or travelled back and forth.

Within India, the case of the Deccan is unique. Better connected to maritime trade systems, merchants from West Asia, particularly Arabs and Iranians, had long been active in port cities from Gujarat to Malabar.[21] In the Bay of Bengal, too, Persian-speaking merchants were centrally positioned.²² Delhi's conquest of the Deccan in the 1320s and the establishment of the Bahmani sultanate in 1347 created favourable conditions for intensification of migration, much like in Hindustan. Similarly to Hindustan, too, was the use of the Persian language and practices; a familiar political environment and increasing patronage. All these contributed to adding the Deccan to the mental world map of Persianate Muslim elites. The Bahmanis, on their side, were keen on fostering their connections with the Muslim East to secure supplies of warhorses. Furthermore, as a Perso-Islamic dynasty, they were interested in maintaining cultural links and enabling the movement of literati and religious figures, crucial for dynastic legitimacy. However, the relative isolation of the sultanate, which was disconnected from north India and from the land routes to Iran and Transoxiana, did not encourage migration. To bypass this difficulty, the Bahmanis used the well-trodden commercial networks, facilitated by their access to the coast. Instead of waiting for migrants to drift to the Deccan, the Bahmani sultans actively recruited skilled administrators, military personnel and intellectuals in Iran, and shipped them to the sultanate. A famous, yet dubious, story suggests that the Bahmanis tried to recruit the celebrated poet Hafiz (d. 1389 or 1390), but this did not materialise. Many others, however, did make it to the Deccan, and in significant numbers.

The migrants left an unmistakable mark on the Bahmani sultanate. They introduced new administrative and artistic models, and served as a major thread through which the links between the Deccan and the Persianate world were maintained.²³ The new elites, comprising those actively recruited and those who arrived of their own accord, began to hold central positions in the local courts. As we have seen in the previous chapter, these developments increased tensions with old elites, leading to occasional violence. The position of the migrants became strong enough that even after the Bahmanis stopped importing people from the late fifteenth century, migrants continued to arrive in the Deccan of their own accord and to hold high positions up to the last days of the Deccan sultanates. With this background, we will turn now to examining the characteristics as a group, if they were operating as such.

Who Were the Migrants?

NOMENCLATURE

Given the significance of the migrants to the history and historiography of the region (almost all identifiable chroniclers belonged to this group), it is not surprising that they attracted much scholarly attention as individuals or as a group, particularly within the context of their feud with the Deccanis. Yet their names and their place in society were much debated, as reflected in the terminology used both in early modern chronicles and in modern historiography. Colonial-era scholars tended to use the term Foreigners (typically in capital F).[24] Emma Flatt suggests that even though this use relied on terminology found in early modern sources, the categorisation of Foreigners/Locals reflects a 'binary modern understanding of national identities', rightly stressing the anachronistic ethnic and 'national' element in such identification.[25] Post-independence historians, averse to the divisive, anti-national sentiment that might be underlying such terminology, adopted the neutral term 'New-comers', as distinct from the Deccani 'Old-comers'.[26] This terminology implies that both Foreigners and Deccanis are the descendants of migrants (from north India or overseas), thus placing them on similar grounds. This category, however, inadvertently creates social division between the migrants and locals, the later comprising Hindus and local converts to Islam. This oversight echoes outdated theories of conversions to Islam in India which preferred to see Muslims as the descendants of migrants.[27] An even more obscure term, which began to be used in early post-independence historiography, was the somewhat romantic *āfāqīs* as interchangeable with New-comers. Deriving from the Arabic word *āfāq* (sg. *ufq*), 'horizons', the term means 'those who came from beyond the horizon'.[28] The purpose of using this term is clear: stylistically consider the migratory process while easing on potential divisive consequences. The term, albeit originating from Arabic or Persian, is a neologism; early modern sources use the term *āfāq* mostly in panegyrics when naming rulers as 'kings of the horizons/universe' (*salāṭīn al-āfāq, shahryār-i āfāq*).[29]

More recently, Eaton has introduced the new term 'Westerners' to the discussion, terminology that was later followed by Flatt, Victor Lieberman, Gijs Kruijtzer and others. Eaton argues that this term appeared in early modern sources in parallel to Foreigners, with each chronicler using his term of choice. Thus, Tabataba'i preferred 'Foreigners', whereas Firishta was inclined towards 'Westerners'.[30] Eaton himself employs the term Westerners, a choice that reflects the non-divisive terminology characteristic of his work.[31] This term, however, is likely to be based on a misreading of the text due to the nature of Persian orthography in early modern manuscripts from India. The combination of the letters *bā* (ب, with one diacritic dot underneath) and *yā* (ي, written in a similar manner but with two dots or a short dash underneath) is often identical to the reversed combination of *yā* followed by *bā*; in both cases, the combination creates a ligature that resembles the letter *pā* (پ, with three diacritic dots underneath).³² Consequently, in those cases, the words Foreigners (غریبان, *gharībān*) and Westerners (غربیان, *gharbīyān*) are written the same way, something like *غرپان, **gharpān*). This ambiguity does not apply to these words in their singular form, as the shape of the final *bā* (ب) in the word *gharīb* (غریب) is easily distinguishable from that of *yā* (ی) in the word *gharbī* (غربی).

These cases are not easy to find. Whereas terms to designate other groups such as *dakkanī* (Deccani) and *ḥabashī* (Ethiopian) are used abundantly as individual epithets, there is no such use of the term *gharīb/ gharbī*. Yet on the rare occasions that the term appears in singular form (usually as an adjective), it can be read solely as *gharīb*, Foreigner. For example, the anonymous chronicler of Golkonda refers to 'Turkman and foreign troops' (*jawānān-i gharīb wa turkmān*),³³ 'foreign and Turkman brave ones' (*dilāwarān-i gharīb wa turkmān*),³⁴ or 'foreign and Turkman commanders' (*silāḥ-dārān-i gharīb wa turkmān*).³⁵ Tabataba'i mentions a group of foreign troops (*jawānān-i gharīb*) operating in Ahmadnagar.³⁶ Shirazi states that the Deccanis in the court were hostile to the Foreigners, and 'would not see even one Foreigner staying in the court' (*na-mītawānand dīd ke yak gharīb darīn dawlat-khāna bāshad*).³⁷ More explicitly, the early eighteenth-century Mughal historian Khafi Khan, who relied heavily on Firishta, mentions 'the Foreign community' (*qawm-i gharīb*), meaning 'the communities of Arabic-speakers and Persian-speakers' (*qawm-i ᶜarab wa ᶜajam*).³⁸ Even Firishta, Eaton's source for the term Westerners, in reality prefers the term 'Foreigners'. During a campaign of the Bahmani sultan Muhammad Shah III, for example, the sultan dispatched 'many of the foreign commanders' (*umarā-i gharīb*). In another case, during the Ahmadnagar–Bijapur war in 1559 in which partisan politics played an important part, Firishta mentions that on one side were 'the Deccani and Ethiopian commanders' (*umarā-i ḥabashī wa dakkanī*), and on the other side, 'the foreign commanders' (*umarā-i gharīb*).³⁹ In short, all early modern sources prefer the term *gharīb*; I have not found a single instance in which the term *gharbī* was in use.⁴⁰

The terminology is not a simple matter of semantics, considering the hostility against the Foreigners. In a letter sent by the Prince of Merchants (*malik al-tujjār*), the Foreigner Khalaf Hasan Basri, then commander of Daulatabad, to sultan Ahmad II Bahmani in the late 1430s, the commander considered how to organise the army. He suggested that:

> Slaves have no option other than obedience or death. But to the people of the court it is clear that the [previous] defeat [of the Bahmanis] in Mahayim was

caused by the hypocrisy of the Deccani and Ethiopian *amīr*s. Due to envy, they refuse to loyally serve people of our kind (*abnā-i jins-i mā*), whom they call foreigners (*ishān-rā gharīb mī-gūyand*).[41]

Referring to the war of the Bahmanis against Gujarat over the island of Mahayim in modern-day Mumbai,[42] the letter captures the sensitivities of the time. In an instance of high partisan tension, a leading Foreign commander accused the Deccanis and Ethiopians of abandoning their duties by refusing to cooperate for the common interest of defending the sultanate. This factionalism is explained in the very foreignness of the Foreigners. The tone of this passage indicates that in Khalaf Hasan's opinion (or later Foreigners such as Firishta, who reproduced this letter) the term *gharīb* carries strong negative connotations. Having that in mind, and the self-styling of the Foreigners as such, this sense of hostility should be understood as part of the political reality of the Bahmani- and sultanates-era Deccan. Furthermore, this terminology reflects more complex (even if uncomfortable) realities, therefore, we should go back to colonial-era terminology and employ the emic term, 'Foreigners'.

FOREIGNERS AND IDENTITIES

Defining the migrants as 'Foreigners' does not give much place to heterogeneity within this group. Modern historiography discusses this collective as an almost monolithic entity, whose members formed a coherent and cohesive group, distinct from other groups in the Deccan. Considering the diverse background of the Foreigners, however, this assumption seems rather problematic, as an examination of their internal dynamics reveals.

Flatt argues that one of the unique characteristics of early modern courts in the Deccan was the organisation of courtiers within groups. This organisation was markedly different from earlier courts in the Deccan, where courtiers emphasised their role as individuals.[43] The way of organisation is reflected in the chronicles. Adding one or more epithet (*nisba*), chroniclers introduce a form of labelling individuals and their associations. We can assume that the choice of epithet reflects the chronicler's idea of the most recognisable characteristic in that particular context, thus creating a widely understood narrative. We have already encountered the extensive use of the terms Deccani, Ethiopian and, of course, Foreigners; these serve as Foreigners' classification of political organisation. Unlike the terms 'Deccani' and 'Ethiopian', which remained on this general level, for the Foreigners, epithets did not stop in these broad political categories. Whereas 'Deccani' and 'Ethiopian' were used for both individuals and the group in its entirety, the term 'Foreigners' was employed solely for the group; this explains the rarity of the term *gharīb* in the singular form. This distinction suggests that the chroniclers looked at their own group with much finer resolution.

This finer system of identification indicates several ways of categorisation. Common epithets are based on ethnic identities, in line with both Persian writings and South Asian practice.[44] These epithets appear typically in military contexts to mark warrior bands. Among these we can find Arabs, Circassians, Daylamis, Georgians, Kalmyks (*qalmāq*), Khurasanis, Kurds, Pathans, Turks and Turkmans.[45] Similar warrior bands were active as mercenaries throughout South Asia, including in Vijayanagara, where their commanders' tombs are still visible.[46] While marked with ethnic epithets, these did not necessarily designate their actual origin. Rather, ethnic identities could serve as political or occupational markers.[47] For these groups, the list of occupations remained limited; there is no evidence of social mobility among those identified with ethnic markers from military positions into the upper echelons of society.

The picture changes considerably when we examine the higher levels of state service. Among the high commanders, heads of administration (*wakīl*, *peshwa*), chief financial officers (*mīr jumla*) and other top positions, a different set of epithets was in use. We can divide these into two groups. The first designation, quite limited in use, refers to lineage. It pertains mostly to *sayyid*s, those who claim to be descendants of the Prophet Muhammad from his daughter Fatima and the Prophet's cousin ʿAli. Promoting such lineage suggests a choice of epithet according to what would be most identifiable or profitable; after all, an association as a *sayyid* had been rewarded politically, socially and economically.[48] For example, the influential Sayyid Shah Mir, who was a member of the close circle of Ibrahim Qutb Shah of Golkonda in the 1560s, is identified only by his lineage Tabatabaʾi, a family claiming to originate from ʿAli's son, Hasan. Another influential *sayyid* was Mir Muhammad Riza Razawi Mashhadi, whose name suggests his origins as descendant of the eighth Shiite Imam, ʿAli al-Riza. Lastly, the renowned scholar Shah Tahir, whom we will discuss in more detail later, was recognised by his *sayyid* lineage, al-Husayni.[49] Locality remained minor in this context. Mir Muhammad Riza is identified with Mashhad, location of ʿAli al-Riza's tomb, therefore, this identification may have worked to intensify the identification of the *sayyid* with the lineage. By contrast, Shah Tahir is identified as Husayni but also Dakkani, maybe a reflection of his position as a representative of Deccani sultans in international diplomacy.

A far more common form of identification linked individuals with the place from which they hailed. Among these we can find intellectuals and chroniclers (many of whom doubled in political, administrative, commercial or diplomatic roles) such as Muhammad b. Qasim Astarabadi (i.e., Firishta), Rafi˓ al-Din Shirazi, Mir Muhammad Hashim Fuzuni Astarabadi and Nizam al-Din Ahmad Shirazi. To these we can add the Sunni scholar Pir Muhammad Shirwani, the high commanders Mir Shah Mir Isfahani, Sayyid Murtaza Sabziwari, Maulana Husayn Tabrizi, or Muhammad Sa˓id Ardistani (Mir Jumla in Mughal sources; see Chapter 5). Others served in a large array of political, military and diplomatic roles, including the commander and *mīr jumla* Mirza Muhammad Amin Shahristani, the commander and *peshwa* Khwaja Mirak Dabir Isfahani (later Chingiz Khan), the Golkonda politician and strongman Salabat Khan Mazandarani, the *wazīr* ˓Ayn al-Mulk Nishapuri, the courtier Malik Ahmad Tabrizi, the commander and courtier I˓tibar Khan Yazdi, and the celebrated Khwaja Mahmud Gilani, better known as Mahmud Gawan.[50] It is very difficult, if at all possible, to find Foreigners in these ranks whose epithets indicate any kind of non-Indian origin other than urban, Iran-centric ones.

This kind of identification seems to reflect a lingering connection with people of the same place of origin or with the ancestral town. Locality-based networks played an important role in initiating new courtiers and establishing client–patron relations and promotions in the courts. Firishta, who was particularly sensitive to such cases, implies the importance of these networks. A notable case was that of Mahmud Gawan, who promoted certain Gilanis, although his entourage was not restricted to them. One of his clients was one Sa˓id Khan (or, according to an early manuscript, As˓ad Khan), whom Firishta describes in two different instances as belonging to Gawan's own community (*aqwām*, pl. of *qawm*).[51] The network remained alive even after Gawan's death. During these turbulent years, contestation over the control of the Bahmani possession was rife. Ahmad Bahri, stationed on the *jāgīr* of his father, Hasan Nizam al-Mulk, in Junnar in western Maharashtra, saw his possession as including the whole northwestern Deccan and the Konkan; however, this was not easily achieved. Firishta reports that in 1486, Ahmad wrote to his father that:

> During the reign of Muhammad Shah [III], the harbour of Goa was given as *iqtā˓* to Kishwar Khan, a slave of Khwaja Jahan Gawan. [Kishwar Khan] appointed Najm al-Din Gilani as his deputy to oversee his affairs in Goa. When Najm al-Din died, his servant (*naukar*) Bahadur Gilani abandoned his previous military obligations, and took over the aforementioned harbour along with Dabhol, Kolhapur, Kolhar, Panhala, Shirwal, and Belgaum.[52]

Local States in an Imperial World

This passage captures something of the network created by Mahmud Gawan. Gawan himself saw a great importance in controlling the western coastal plains for both political and commercial purposes, and initiated a major campaign to this region in 1469. Particularly important was Goa, a central harbour through which Foreigners travelled between Iran and India. Mahmud Gawan also had a personal interest, being a merchant with a strong independent commercial agenda.[53] With these combined political and personal interests, it is clear why Gawan chose to appoint his loyal servant as governor of Goa. Thereafter, other Gilanis continued to hold power, suggesting that in such sensitive cases, a locality-based group preferred to secure sensitive interests among their own kind.

Another instance of a locality-based network is that of another person named Kishwar Khan Lari, in Bijapur. As we will see later in this chapter, in 1580 he arranged the assassination of the influential commander Mustafa Khan Ardistani. This was only one of several unpopular moves, which led to increasing opposition to him in the capital. Eventually, Kishwar Khan was forced to flee the kingdom. He first tried his luck in Ahmadnagar, but was denied shelter there. Later he arrived in Golkonda, where 'one of the Ardistanis killed him with a strike of a dagger, avenging the blood of Mustafa Khan' (*intiqām-i khūn-i muṣṭafa khān*). The only detail the chronicle provides about the assassin is his origin,[54] implying the existence of network of Ardistanis in the Deccan. Those networks were not limited to India, but stretched back to the ancestral lands. Foreigners had the option to return to their place of origin once their employment terminated, their situation became unstable, or when their relationship with the patron turned sour. When Muhammad Quli Qutb Shah dismissed Mir Shah Mir, his father-in-law and *wakīl*, the latter was sent by royal order to his hometown of Isfahan.[55] Similarly, Qazi Beg Tehrani returned to his homeland, having lost the struggle for control over Ahmadnagar's administration.[56] Lastly, Allah Quli, uncle of Sultan Quli, founder of the Qutb Shahi dynasty of Golkonda, travelled back and forth between Iran and the Deccan.[57] In all these instances, the sources use the term *waṭan* (homeland) or *waṭan-i maʾlūf* (ancestral homeland) to designate the places from which these men travelled and to which they returned. Such narratives place them as belonging more to the Iranian side than to the Deccan. These links were not only nostalgic. At least some of these nobles, and even members of the royal families, retained family connections as well as landed interests in Iran.[58]

FOREIGNERS AS A GROUP

The use of the different sets of *nisba*s to refer to the Foreigners, whether they be ethnic-, genealogical- or location-based, not only demonstrates the position of the individuals within the large group, but also reveals a great deal of the characteristics of Foreigners as a group. The term Foreigners places its members as distinct from Deccanis and Ethiopians; similarly to the former, it was relational. It thus does not say much about the internal structure of the group. Internally, Foreigners did not act as a coherent group, but as a free association of individuals of diverse backgrounds, sharing social and political identity. Moreover, this identity held cultural significance, being mostly focused around, and identified with, Persianate culture.[59]

As a political marker, the term was not referring to any ethnic or racial identity. Religion, on the other hand, is a more complex issue. Several scholars identify the Foreigners with Shiism, adding a religious hue to the political struggle between Shiite Foreigners and Sunni Deccanis; state religion was determined by the dominant party.[60] We will return to this question in the next chapter. For now, it will suffice to suggest that this assertion was oversimplified. Consider, for example, the case of the Sunni-Hanafi scholar Pir Muhammad Shirwani. As a noble in the court of Ahmadnagar, he was the one who invited the celebrated Shiite scholar Shah Tahir to settle in Ahmadnagar in 1522, regardless of his pronounced Shiite inclination. The sultan, Burhan Nizam Shah I, still Sunni at the time, supported this invitation.[61] A few years later, we find in Bijapur Kamal Khan Dakkani, who was 'teacher of Ismaʿil [ʿAdil Shah], and of the Shiite creed' (*shīʿa madhhab*).[62] On a general note, Colin Mitchell points at the problem of identifying the Foreigners (and overall Iranian elites) in the early sixteenth century as Shiite, thus he questions their role in spreading political Shiism in the Deccan.[63]

Along these lines, Rafi Ahmad Alavi argues against the association of Foreigners with any religious identity. He suggests that the source material 'never uses religious connotations, except in the cases where religious instincts are apparent behind public transactions'. He further explains that as they 'belonged to various countries and were of various extractions, all of them could not be of the same faith'. Focusing on the history of Ahmadnagar, Alavi asserts that the Deccani–Foreigner conflict was neither racial nor sectarian, but one based on personal interests, even if sometimes taking religious lines, this was for non-ideological reasons.[64] Alavi's use of the term racial seems outdated and more than a little problematic. But he is right to argue that political motivation and loyalty by origin filled an important role in the factional rivalry of the Deccan, whereas religion remained only marginal to the story. Such assumption is supported in early modern sources, which mention one's confessional affiliations only rarely, most commonly in the case of Mahdawis and Brahmins (in itself not only a religious but also a social category), or in the rare case it was explicitly serving the plot, but hardly ever as simple epithet. The main form of identification remained the place of origin or political affiliation throughout.

The political nature of these links among Foreigners in their relative group, combined with the way in which early modern chroniclers chose to represent the identity of individuals of their own group, suggest that the coalition of Foreigners was mostly a loose-knit web of individuals or smaller-scale, locality- or linear-based networks. Flatt suggests that this social construct may have originated in the mobility of the Foreigners and their association with 'a communal web of reciprocity and obligation' even before they arrived in the Deccan. Furthermore, the collective actions of Foreigners, even though sometimes benefiting the group as a whole, were 'frequently understood and used as a means for an individual to gain benefit for himself and his immediate kin'.[65] It is, therefore, not surprising that bad blood occasionally appeared among the Foreigners. In the aforementioned story, Mustafa Khan Ardistani was in conflict with Kishwar Khan Lari, leading to the latter's assassination by an unnamed Ardistani. All actors in this story were Foreigners, whose political ambitions led them into conflict.

The lack of coherent identity among the Foreigners should not come as a surprise when we consider social structures in Iran at the time. Whereas a notion of Iran as a political-cultural space (*īrān-zamīn*), marked by its separateness of external identities (most notably, *tūrān*), has long been engrained in Iranian culture, Iranian society itself was divided according to various lines.[66] The distinction between tribal elements, operating in the Deccan as warrior bands, and the urban, educated individuals who were more likely to be employed in high positions reflects a similar division to that of Iranian elite society of the time, between Turks (occupational, nomadic category, not necessarily ethnic) and Tajiks (speakers and writers of Persian, identified with urban centres and settled life).[67] Just like the identity of Foreigners in the Deccan was relational and defined externally, so was that of the Tajiks, who were internally identified by place or region. Rudi Matthee argues that in Safavid Iran, local affiliation, identity and pride, accompanied by a sense of suspicion and hostility towards people from other locations, were central to social dynamics.[68] This is not to say that we can assume similarity of social, religious and political processes in the Deccan and Iran.[69] In particular, Tajiks were more dominant in the Deccan than in Iran, possibly as a result of their weakness in Iran that encouraged their migration,[70] or the demand for Persianate elites. However, the evidence from the Deccan suggests that migrants brought with them their old identities, affiliations and social structures. These identities, central to the migrants, continued to be a key component in the political and social life of the Deccan throughout the life of the sultanates.

Foreigners and Sultans

Our analysis has so far taken into consideration the background and actions of the Foreigners, and has largely looked at the dynamics within the group. However, their migration was beneficial not only for members of the group but also to the host courts. Sultans enjoyed the Foreigners' valuable military, administrative, cultural and artistic expertise, used to cement their rule in terms of both material assets and legitimacy. These benefits are reflected in the long list of positions held by Foreigners, supporting Subrahmanyam's understanding of the links between commerce and state formation in early modern India.

The picture, however, has not always been rosy. In addition to the conflict with local elites, the relationship of the Foreigners with the rulers themselves could, and often did, turn sour. The migration of the Foreigners to the Deccan did not necessarily change their social characteristics and behaviour once in India. On the contrary, it was not unusual for an individual to serve one ruler for a while, and then seek employment in another court. Nor did Foreigners abandon their identification with their lineage- and locality-based networks. This had the potential of creating a clash between loyalties. In the following case studies we will analyse the meaning of these tensions to the position of the Foreigners in the political system and their impact on the state.

FAMILY TIES

The collective of Foreigners did not only comprise individuals within locality- or lineage-based networks. Additional subsets of networks were in operation in parallel. A common form of association was the family. Families were an active form of political and social association. Family links were not limited solely to one sultanate at a time, but often crossed political boundaries. Nor were families, or individuals, limited to one occupation. In the early modern period, merchants became statesmen and bureaucrats maintained their interests in trade. This was the case for Mahmud Gawan in the second half of the fifteenth century, Muhammad

Saʿid Ardistani in the middle of the seventeenth century, and many others. The commercial connection required active communications with Iran as part of the trade networks, allowing the continuous mobility and, at times, the return to one's 'ancestral homeland'. All these created a network of family members who were involved in diverse occupations and spread over large territories and different political units.

The components of international and inter-occupational links are well attested in the family of Afzal Khan Shirazi, an important statesman in late sixteenth-century Bijapur. His father was a petty revenue collector in the province of Fars (*az jumla-i ʿāmilān-i wilāyat-i fārs*), where Shiraz is located. Afzal Khan's father had four brothers. Two of them were employed in financial roles, with one serving as *wazīr* and the other as auditor (*mustawfī*) in Ray in western Iran. The other two were involved in trade. Afzal Khan was orphaned at the age of seven, yet found his way to a madrasa, where he earned a reputation as a brilliant student. Later, he left Iran for India, and began to teach in Bijapur. Due to his connections with members of the elite, maybe other Shirazis, he was summoned to give advice to the royal council. He was gradually drawn into royal service, and became part of the political circle of Bijapur.[71] He was not the only member of the family to have migrated to India: his cousin (son of his father's youngest brother), the chronicler Rafiʿ al-Din Shirazi, arrived in Bijapur for trade. From the mid-1560s, Rafiʿ al-Din served in various administrative roles such as supervisor of the royal wardrobe and treasury. In parallel to his administrative roles, he composed the chronicle *Tadhkirat al-Muluk*, completed half a century later.[72] The family connection is further emphasised in the disproportionally large place that Afzal Khan's career occupies in the chronicle. Each of the ten parts (*faṣl*) that comprise this work is dedicated to one dynasty (the Bahmanis, Gujarat along with Ahmadnagar and Golkonda) or one ruler (sultans of the ʿAdil Shahi dynasty up to his patron, Ibrahim II; Akbar). The only exception is the seventh part, which is said to be dedicated to Afzal Khan (although in reality it mostly deals with the reign of ʿAli I). This case demonstrates, then, that members of the same family had administrative posts in different polities at the same time, while being involved in trans-regional trade. While on the move, they remained identified with a specific locality in Iran, as attested by a member of the family in his chronicle. The same family was involved in administration, politics, trade and scholarly pursuit. Even individuals were involved in different fields, showing the porous boundaries between occupations.

Trans-regional, trans-generational kinship networks were crucial not only for its members, but was perceived and reworked into the political

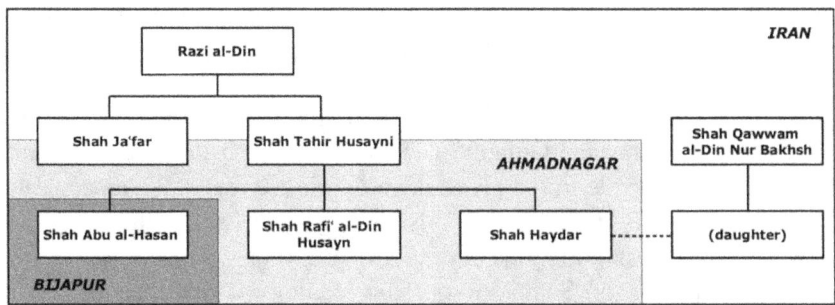

Figure 3.1 Shah Tahir's family

language both in form of employment and social status. Such a family network developed around Shah Tahir Husayni. He was born in Khund near Qazwin on an undisclosed date to a prominent family of the now extinct Muhammad-Shahi branch of the Nizari-Ismaʿilis, later to become their thirty-first imam. During the early years of Safavid rule, his fame and accomplishments earned him an invitation to the court of Shah Ismaʿil I (r. 1501–24). After a few years, however, a new line of Twelver (*ithnāʿasharī*) Shiism arose, leading to the adoption of a stricter, more formalistic, and self-assured Twelver Shiism in the court, with greater importance given to claims of genealogical connections to the line of the Twelve Imams.[73] The rise of Twelver Shiism challenged the position of Ismaʿilis and their separate lineage in the realm. Shah Ismaʿil began to suspect Shah Tahir's true leanings, even though Shah Tahir himself, like other Ismaʿilis (or more generally, Shiites, in certain periods), kept his actual creed a secret (*taqiyya*). Facing an increasingly uncomfortable situation, Shah Tahir left the court and settled in Kashan. He continued to teach until opposing Twelver *ulama* incited the authorities to arrest and execute him.[74] Shah Tahir narrowly escaped in what seems like yet another miraculous story of migration. He left Iran along with his family and travelled to India. In 1520, he arrived in Goa, following a familiar path. First, he approached Bijapur, a reasonable choice considering the high esteem in which Ismaʿil ʿAdil Khan held the Foreigners and Shiites.[75] But he was received there rather coldly, and considered leaving India for pilgrimage to the Holy cities of the Hijaz en route back to Iran. At that time, he met the Sunni scholar Pir Muhammad Shirwani, who was deeply impressed with Shah Tahir's learning. Upon his return to Ahmadnagar, Pir Muhammad talked greatly about this scholar and convinced Burhan Nizam Shah I to invite him. Shah Tahir arrived in Ahmadnagar in 1522 and was received with great honours.[76] In Ahmadnagar, he reached the height of his status and influence. Opening a Sufi hospice (*khānqāh*) and a madrasa, Burhan Nizam Shah I was drawn to his teachings. Soon, Shah Tahir became a close adviser and companion of the sultan. As his personal confidant, he was sent on diplomatic missions, including around the war between Ahmadnagar, Berar and Gujarat in 1528–30, and in Khandesh.[77] He also had an important role in the peace negotiation between Ahmadnagar and Bijapur in 1524–5, in the early 1530s, and again in 1542, with more thorough multilateral negotiations in the following year.[78]

After a period of Sunni, or possibly Mahdawi, dominance,[79] Shah Tahir increased Shiite presence in the court. With his personal links to the sultan, he is mentioned as the one who persuaded Burhan I to adopt Shiism in 1537, an affiliation that continued to the last days of the Nizam Shahi dynasty. Firishta states that the first inclination to adopt Shiism followed Shah Tahir's success in saving the life of the ill Prince ᶜAbd al-Qadir, when all others failed. Such a major shift did not go unchallenged by some at the court. However, the sultan followed his choice of creed, demonstrated by his allotment of villages as *waqf* to support Shah Tahir's madrasa and soup kitchen.[80] Burhan's conversion, however, was not to Shah Tahir's Ismaᶜili creed but rather to Twelver Shiism. This raises a question of why a prominent Ismaᶜili imam would convince a ruler to adopt another school of Shiism. Farhad Daftary suggests that even in Ahmadnagar, Shah Tahir's teachings and writings were explicitly inclined towards Twelver ideology, whereas his Ismaᶜili ideology was kept more secretly, in the disguise of Sufi writings, all suggesting his continued practice of *taqiyya*.[81] Considering the political meaning of an official conversion of a ruler in the sixteenth century, in particular, regarding his relationship with the Safavids, the motivation for conversion might have been in reality political. Nevertheless, Shah Tahir's impact on the development of the sultanate is undeniable. Being a prominent scholar himself, he was pivotal in turning Ahmadnagar into a centre of Shiite learning, attracting scholars from around the Muslim world.[82] Shah Tahir died sometime between 1544 and 1549. His remains were later buried in Karbala in Iraq, one of the holiest cities to Shiites.[83] This set a precedent to be followed by the Nizam Shahi sultans themselves, accounting for the lack of royal funerary architecture in Ahmadnagar, in contrast to Bidar, Bijapur and Golkonda.[84]

Several of Shah Tahir's relatives continued to hold high positions in the courts of the Deccan. His brother, Shah Jaᶜfar, is listed among Shiite scholars who settled in Ahmadnagar under the patronage of Burhan I, and later advised Husayn I.[85] Shah Tahir's son, Shah Rafiᶜ al-Din Husayn, served in the court of Ahmadnagar. He is first mentioned as Husayn's envoy to Berar, sent to forge an alliance with Darya ᶜImad Shah against

Bijapur in the mid-1550s. The diplomatic mission went awry due to Shah Rafiᶜ al-Din's misconduct, forcing him to return to Ahmadnagar. He is mentioned again only in 1566 as he served briefly as *wakīl*. He is last mentioned in the 1580s, when he was arrested along with other Foreigners in the partisan struggles in the last years of Murtaza I's reign.[86]

Another of Shah Tahir's son, Shah Abu al-Hasan, joined the service of ᶜAli ᶜAdil Shah I of Bijapur in the 1560s. In 1572, he was in command of the royal army in the Karnatak campaign. He played a pivotal role in the negotiations between Bijapur and Ahmadnagar that set the division of their respective spheres of influence in 1574. Yet ᶜAli I distrusted Shah Abu al-Hasan's skills and loyalty. Acknowledging the shah's faults, the sultan released him from his duties, and instead appointed the aforementioned Mustafa Khan Ardistani. When Ahmadnagar and Golkonda invaded Bijapur in the late 1570s, ᶜAli held Shah Abu al-Hasan personally responsible due to his family connections in Ahmadnagar; he therefore ordered his imprisonment. Later, the sultan used his imprisonment as a bargaining chip: Murtaza I of Ahmadnagar agreed to withdraw his forces from Bijapur in return for Shah Abu al-Hasan's release. Not admitting to his guilt, Murtaza I explained that he agreed to this deal out of respect to the memory of Shah Tahir. Shah Abu al-Hasan remained in Bijapur. After the assassination of ᶜAli in 1580, the queen dowager and sister of Murtaza I, Chand Bibi, appointed him *mīr jumla*; her choice may have relied on the long acquaintance between the two. Chand Bibi's decline to insignificance in the mid-1580s brought the fall and eventually the execution of Shah Abu al-Hasan.[87]

A third son, Shah Haydar, was the successor of Shah Tahir as leader of the Muhammad-Shahi branch of the Nizari-Ismaᶜilis.[88] He served as a diplomat under Burhan I, who sent him on a mission to the Safavid Shah Tahmasp (r. 1524–76).[89] Shah Haydar later became part of the intimate circle of Murtaza I, was involved in a war against Bijapur and Golkonda, and co-served as *wakīl* and *peshwa* while continuing his diplomatic service. After a few years in retirement, he returned to political life, but was arrested and exiled to Mecca in 1589 along with other Foreigners.[90] An interesting story involving Shah Haydar revolves around his marriages. As this issue is only seldom reported in the chronicles, this story provides a rare glimpse into the family life of those who did not marry into royal families.[91] According to Tabatabaᵓi, Shah Haydar married the daughter of Shah Qawwam al-Din Nur Bakhsh, who was 'among the most illustrious high-ranking *sayyids* of Khurasan and Iran)'. The lady, whose name remains obscure, had a respectable genealogy that linked her to the Prophet Muhammad himself, probably a good enough reason for Shah

Haydar to marry her. The story, however, is not one of importing a bride from Iran to India. Rather, it seems she continued to reside in Iran while being married to Shah Haydar, who remained in India; she visited India only occasionally. Sometime in the late 1560s, she arrived in Ahmadnagar. In accordance with her high social status, she hosted the sultan in her quarters, with the appropriate royal pomp. Shah Haydar was rather displeased with her openness, and the two fell into dispute. As they had not resolved the issue, she returned to Iran.[92] We cannot draw any conclusions from a single story, which opens more questions than it provides answers. It does, however, add to our understanding of Shah Tahir's family, who maintained links with Iran half a century after the patriarch fled the country. After Shah Haydar, the Muhammad-Shahi imams, descendants of Shah Haydar (maybe from the aforementioned Iranian lady?) continued to reside in the Deccan until the turn of the nineteenth century. The only exception was ᶜAtiyyatullah, who died in Badakhshan in 1663. This may not have been a coincidence, as Shah Tahir's father, Razi al-Din II (d. 1509), was active there, hinting at the possibility of family links also in that region. Those who remained in the Deccan relocated to the new urban centre, Aurangabad,[93] in accordance with the known settlement patterns of Foreigners elsewhere.

The story of Shah Tahir and his family demonstrates the viability of trans-regional kinship networks in the Deccan and beyond. Small-scale, kinship-based networks continued to play an important role in the careers of their members as a way to gain access to employment, as part of trans-regional trade networks or to bolster their prestige. Members of those networks, regardless of their family affiliation with any court in particular, maintained high mobility between different patrons, while not abandoning the advantages of their family affiliation. Using family networks as well as family prestige, they continued to roam when the circumstances changed. This issue of mobility, in itself, has been a key theme in the relationship of the Foreigners with their patrons. Let us now turn to examine some cases of such mobility among Foreigners in great detail.

SWAPPING PATRONS

The arrival of an individual to a certain court and a successful career there did not mean that he would stay there. Taking employment in one court for a few years, then moving to another court was a rather common occurrence. Such practice was almost to be expected among poets, scholars and artists, who depended on patronage. Take, for example, the literary circle of late sixteenth-century Ahmadnagar. A central figure in the circle was

Foreigners, Locals and the World

Mawlana Nur al-Din Muhammad Zuhuri (d. 1615), the most celebrated Persian poet of the Deccan. Born in the province of Turshiz in Khurasan, he lived in Yazd for a few years before arriving in Ahmadnagar in 1580. He enjoyed the patronage of Murtaza I, who appointed him poet-laureate (*malik al-shuʿarā*). In Ahmadnagar, he met other poets such as Mawlana Shakibi Isfahani and ʿAlama Mir Husayn. Later, the celebrated Mughal poet Abu al-Fayz (Fayzi), sent by Akbar as an ambassador to the Deccan, offered him to join the Mughal court but Zuhuri declined. Most important for Zuhuri's life, however, was Mawlana Malik Qummi, native of Qum who resided in Qazwin and enjoyed Safavid patronage, but later migrated to the Deccan. Zuhuri and Qummi grew closer as the former married the latter's daughter. In the turmoil of the late 1580s, Malik Qummi left Ahmadnagar along with Firishta and other Foreigners, finding a new patron in Bijapur. Zuhuri joined his father-in-law in 1595, after the death of Burhan Nizam Shah II. Possibly with Qummi's assistance, Zuhuri received the patronage of Ibrahim ʿAdil Shah II; the two poets cooperated in their work, and some even wrongly attribute *Kitab-i Nauras* to them (see Chapter 4). The family continued to serve the ʿAdil Shahi dynasty, as Zuhuri's son Zahur (who was, possibly, Malik Qummi's grandson), having served Muhammad ʿAdil Shah's administration, composed the chronicle *Muhammadnama* later in the seventeenth century.[94] Itineraries such as Qummi's (Qum–Qazwin–Ahmadnagar–Bijapur) and Zuhuri's (Turshiz–Yazd–Ahmadnagar–Bijapur, declining an offer to add an Agra leg) were the staple of what Flatt described as the peripatetic courtiers.[95] At the same time, members of other groups, too, followed such itineraries, for example, the Ethiopian eunuch Malik Sandal, who in 1603 migrated from Ahmadnagar to Bijapur, where he found employment in ʿAdil Shahi's service. He later became instrumental in construction projects, including the Ibrahim Rawza, resting place of Ibrahim II, his wife Taj Sultana and his daughter Zuhra.[96]

Mobility, however, was not limited to intellectuals. People from the heart of state apparatus migrated along similar lines. For example, Mirak Dabir was a leading noble in both Ahmadnagar and Bijapur. Following the death of Husayn Nizam Shah I in 1565, turbulence took over the sultanate of Ahmadnagar, as was 'the custom of the time' (*qānūn-i zamān*). Subsequently, 'most people of great wisdom, changed their leaning from that court (of Ahmadnagar) to the threshold of the refuge of the world (ʿAli ʿAdil Shah I of Bijapur), where good fortune nests. Among these was Mirak Dabir, known as Changiz Khan.' Mirak Dabir remained in Bijapur, where he took employment, achieved high rank and performed various tasks for the king. Eventually, 'the high-flying bird of felicity found its way back to the shadow-casting pinnacle of the Nizam Shahi castle, the great splendour of that old dynasty'. Acquiring an official leave from ᶜAli ᶜAdil Shah I, he left Bijapur and returned to Ahmadnagar, where he was reintroduced into the service of the sultan. In Ahmadnagar, too, he rose up the ranks rapidly, becoming 'the envy of all his peers'. Possibly because of his connections in both courts, Mirak Dabir strove to prevent an imminent war between Ahmadnagar and Bijapur in the early 1570s, serving as an envoy on the successful negotiations between the sides.[97] After this diplomatic success, he resumed his military position in Ahmadnagar's conquest of Berar in 1574.[98]

Similar to the poets, Mirak Dabir presents a successful movement between two courts and an ability to gain access to both. Sultans were, however, not always keen on letting their high officials move so freely in this way. On the contrary, quite often this practice was not viewed favourably. The story of Mustafa Khan Ardistani, whose assassination was mentioned above, presents such a conflicted transition between courts. He was born as Sayyid Kamal al-Din Husayn in the early sixteenth century in Ardistan, some 100 km northeast of Isfahan.[99] Facing economic hardships, or maybe looking for better opportunities, he travelled to the Deccan, eventually finding his way to Golkonda. He rose in prominence in the court in the troubled years of Jamshid Qutb Shah (r. 1543–50). During the brief reign of the infant Subhan Quli in 1550, Mustafa Khan became the strongest man in the court, along with Salabat Khan Mazandarani (not to be confused with the Circassian Salabat Khan whom we will encounter momentarily). Mustafa Khan and Salabat Khan had a crucial role in facilitating Ibrahim Qutb Shah's return from his exile in Vijayanagara and his subsequent ascent to the throne. Proving his loyalty to the new sultan, Mustafa Khan's position remained high, and Ibrahim appointed him to the high position of *mīr jumla*. By the late 1550s, he was acknowledged as the most powerful man in the sultanate, second only to the sultan himself. The sources remember him as being particularly skilled in diplomatic matters, a talent that proved to be crucial in the troubled politics of the mid-sixteenth century. Mustafa Khan was deeply involved in the negotiations that led to the Battle of Talikota; some even suggest that he convincing the sultan of the necessity of the alliance. His service was not limited to the diplomatic domain, but in the battle itself he served as a commander of Golkonda's forces.[100]

Following their decisive victory over Vijayanagara, the armies of the Deccan sultanates remained stationed in the vicinity of the conquered capital for a few more months. Taking advantage of their unprecedented success, the sultans thought to keep on increasing the fortunes that fell into their hands and to prevent Vijayanagara's recovery. As part of this lasting endeavour, the commanders of the three main armies, namely, Mustafa Khan (Golkonda), Kishwar Khan (Bijapur) and Mawlana ᶜInayat Allah (Ahmadnagar) were sent together to conquer the forts of Raichur and Mudgal in the centuries-long contested Raichur *doāb*.[101]

Considering Bijapur's long involvement in the *doāb*, it is not surprising that ᶜAli ᶜAdil Shah I thought he had the right to claim it for Bijapur. This claim, however, does not explain the surprising position that Mustafa Khan took. Even though he was a high official in Ibrahim Qutb Shah's service, he chose to deliver the keys of the forts of Raichur and Mudgal to Kishwar Khan, Bijapur's commander. Such action clearly went against Golkonda's interests as well as those of Ahmadnagar: not only did they lose potential income, Bijapur would add to its resources, putting the delicate equilibrium between the sultanates at risk. Enraged by Mustafa Khan's actions and facing increasing pressure on behalf of Husayn Nizam Shah I, Ibrahim Qutb Shah had to punish Mustafa Khan. Here the sources diverge in the details. According to the anonymous chronicler of Golkonda, Ibrahim Qutb Shah was respectful towards Mustafa Khan's *sayyid* status. Taking into account his nearly two decade-long service and his contribution to Golkonda's prosperity, the sultan did not imprison the disloyal noble. Instead, Mustafa Khan was banished from the realm. Claiming that he was continuing to Mecca, Mustafa Khan was able to rescue both his family and the immense property he had accumulated while in Golkonda, including household items (*buyūtāt*), workshops, treasuries, arsenal and armouries.[102] Thereafter, Mustafa Khan travelled directly to the Bijapur army camp, where he was received warmly.[103]

Shirazi tells a somewhat different version. In 1564, he suggests, Mustafa Khan became the leader of the allied forces aimed at campaigning against Vijayanagara. Even before the war, he informed Ibrahim Qutb Shah that after the completion of the campaign, he would ask the sultan's permission to leave the Deccan and visit Mecca, for which he received the sultan's blessing. After Talikota, Mustafa Khan asked the assistance of Kishwar Khan and Mawlana ᶜInayat Allah, and with the support of their respective sultans, ᶜAli ᶜAdil Shah I and Husayn Nizam Shah I, they convinced Ibrahim Qutb Shah to allow Mustafa Khan to leave Golkonda for Mecca and to send his property to a meeting point in Gulbarga. This signified his retirement from Golkonda's service.[104] The need for the intervention of the rulers of Bijapur and Ahmadnagar in favour of Mustafa Khan indicates that similarly to the version presented by the anonymous chronicler, the status of the noble was vulnerable at that point.[105]

Mustafa Khan was then admitted into the service of Bijapur. He served ᶜAli I for the next fifteen years, and in 1573–4 he was appointed *wakīl* and *peshwa* of the state. He played an important role in Bijapur's recovery of its territories lost to Ahmadnagar in previous years, and pushed the borders of the sultanate even further with campaigns in the southern Konkan. Following the agreement with Ahmadnagar on the partition of the spheres of influence between the two sultanates in 1572, Mustafa Khan accompanied ᶜAli I on his Karnatak campaigns, expanding into territories hitherto controlled by Vijayanagara. The campaign was successful, resulting in his appointment as governor over the newly conquered territories, basing himself in Bankapur, 250 km south of Bijapur. Nevertheless, his loyalty to Bijapur remained questionable. Correspondence with the Safavids from about the same time suggests that he remained loyal to the shahs of Iran and aspired to return there, however, ᶜAli I did not give him leave.[106] Staying in the Karnatak, he began to assert his autonomy in the region, leading to a contested relationship with the capital. Afzal Khan Shirazi intervened on behalf of the sultan to ensure the continuation of royal control over the region. With Mustafa Khan's return to the royal fold, he expected a reward as his nomination as *peshwa*, however, the position was offered to another noble, and Mustafa Khan remained in Bankapur. His name, however, is oddly absent from the reports of the campaign against the rebelling *nāyakwārī*s of the Karnatak in the closing years of the 1570s, suggesting that by then he was removed from the centre of political and military life of the sultanate.[107]

In the turbulent years following the assassination of ᶜAli I, Mustafa Khan kept his distance from the capital. This, however, was not possible, and he was drawn back into the politics of the court as Chand Bibi, the queen-dowager, summoned him back to duty. Kishwar Khan Lari, who took over state affairs in Bijapur, grew suspicious of the alliance of these two. He therefore sent an assassin, who stabbed Mustafa Khan to death. Due to Mustafa Khan's popularity, however, his death ignited a major backlash against Kishwar Khan. Along with Kishwar Khan's arrest and the imprisonment of Chand Bibi, general uproar arose against what was perceived by many as illegitimate actions. Facing opposition on the streets of the capital and the approaching of rivalling troops, Kishwar Khan saw no choice but to flee Bijapur, and was eventually assassinated in Golkonda by an unnamed Ardistani.[108]

The eventful career of Mustafa Khan Ardistani is somewhat confusing. For nearly two decades, he loyally served three sultans of Golkonda (Jamshid, Subhan Quli and Ibrahim). His successful service gave him access to power and he gathered immense wealth. This unquestionable success raises the question of what caused this man of such excellent standing in one court to leave his career behind and switch to the service of another sultanate, as foreign to him as Golkonda was when he first arrived in India? Unfortunately, the sources are silent regarding his motivations; we can only speculate. The sole source to deal with this issue was the Mughal historian Khafi Khan. Writing a century and a half after the deed, he blamed Ibrahim Qutb Shah's bad temper and Mustafa Khan's fear as his main reason for leaving Golkonda.[109] This explanation seems more anecdotal than convincing as no early source supports it. Furthermore, continuous mobility was a common practice among Foreigners as one of the ways to guarantee their personal interests in a challenging environment. Khafi Khan's explanation promotes a personal reason for this action. Even if not fear, other personal motives, perhaps Mustafa Khan's friendship with ʿAli ʿAdil Shah I, later leading to his appointment as *wakīl* and *peshwa* of Bijapur, contributed to his decision. Even more likely, Mustafa Khan's high ranking in Bijapur and his later appointment as governor of the Karnatak suggest that ʿAli I promised some form of promotion or personal gain which Mustafa Khan could not expect had he remained in Golkonda. Either way, what clearly arises from this case is that even though Mustafa Khan served under Golkonda successfully for a long time and established a family there (of which we hear only from the story of their rescue from thence), he considered himself to be mobile. In the same way that the prospects of finding employment drew him to Golkonda, a similar promise took him to Bijapur, turning Golkonda into a stop on the way rather than a final destination.

FLIRTING WITH DISASTER

Shifting loyalties between the Deccan sultanates may have been frowned upon, but was acceptable, maybe even predictable, in the shared space of the Deccan. But this mobility did not stop at the borders of the Deccan. Some Foreigners chose to leave the region altogether and join the Mughals. Such was the case of Mirza Muhammad Amin, who in 1618 left the Deccan for the Mughal court, having served as *mīr jumla* in Golkonda. This move was described in the Safavid chronicle *Tarikh-i ʿAlam-ara-i ʿAbbasi* in a very negative light, using the term 'defection' (*farār*).[110]

More dramatic is the case of Sayyid Murtaza Sabziwari (or Mir Murtaza in Mughal sources). He was a commander in Ahmadnagar's service in the early years of Murtaza I, and conspired alongside others against Khunzah Humayun, mother of Murtaza I and Chand Bibi, then the strong person of Ahmadnagar. When the plot was revealed, the conspirators, including Sayyid Murtaza and Mirak Dabir, fled the sultanate, finding shelter in Bijapur. In the early 1570s, Sayyid Murtaza took part in the peace negotiations between Bijapur and Ahmadnagar, leading to the non-intervention agreement of 1572. Other than this role, we do not know if he was employed in Bijapur. When Murtaza Nizam Shah I became free of his mother's influence, Sayyid Murtaza Sabziwari returned to Ahmadnagar, possibly at the sultan's invitation.[111]

He was then readmitted to royal service as a high-ranking commander (*sar-silāḥdār*) and filled important military and administrative posts.[112] Sayyid Murtaza is best known in the history of the region for his role in the war against Berar and thereafter. In the aftermath of Ahmadnagar's conquest of Berar in 1574, the region went through a period of military unrest. Sayyid Murtaza, fast rising in rank from *sar-nawbat* (commander of one of the military wing of the royal army) to high commander of Berar (*amīr al-umarā-i berār* or *sar-lashkar-i berār*). At his disposal stood the permanent forces of the region known as 'the army of Berar' (*sipāh-i berār*) or the 'commanders of Berar' (*umarā-i Berār*). With these loyal forces, Sayyid Murtaza played an important role in securing Ahmadnagar's control in the region: he subdued an uprising under the banner of an allegedly pretender ʿImad Shahi prince, participated in the war to repel the invading army of Khandesh and Gond forces, and led a joint force of Ahmadnagar and Khandesh to demonstrate their combined power to the Mughals, successfully dissuading Akbar from invading. While in Berar, Sayyid Murtaza remained deeply involved in court politics. He took part in defeating the claimant to the Nizam Shahi throne, Prince Burhan (the future Burhan II, r. 1591–5), brother of Murtaza I,[113] and may have taken part in the downfall of the *wakīl* and *peshwa* Qazi Beg Tehrani and the appointment of Circassian slave Salabat Khan. In the early 1580s, Sayyid Murtaza began to distance himself from the court due to the rising power of Salabat Khan. As Murtaza I withdrew from political life, his *wakīl* and *peshwa* came to hold full control over state affairs. His powerful position increased tensions with other ambitious commanders, including Sayyid Murtaza. Pushed away from influence, Sayyid Murtaza began to cement his autonomous power base in Berar, maybe similar to the actions of Mustafa Khan in the Karnatak. Now he could march against the capital with the purpose of taking over the high positions of the state for himself. The political struggle in the capital soon deteriorated to a fully-fledged war between a coalition of mostly, but not only, Foreigners, on the one hand, and, on the other hand, Salabat Khan with the capital's resources at his disposal.[114] In 1584, the opposition was defeated by the royal army, and Sayyid Murtaza was forced to flee the kingdom.[115]

He first travelled to Khandesh where he was attacked by the less than welcoming local army. He continued north, arriving at Akbar's court in

March 1585. Along with several other *amīr*s, he was admitted at Akbar's court with the appropriate favours, employment and *jāgīr*, and received a *manṣab* (rank) of 1,000.[116] His arrival at the court, suggests Tabatabaʾi, encouraged Akbar to invade the Deccan.[117] He appointed the governor (*walī*) of Malwa, his foster brother Mirza ʿAziz Koka, to lead an expedition to the Deccan, to which he attached Sayyid Murtaza and the other commanders who joined him ('*umarā-i dakkan*').[118]

The Mughal expedition against Ahmadnagar was a resounding failure. Facing fierce resistance, the imperial army retreated in early 1586. Under the direction of Sayyid Murtaza, the Mughals left Ahmadnagar city and marched to Ellichpur, capital of Berar. Writing in Ahmadnagar only a few years after the events, Tabatabaʾi describes how the Mughal forces:

> turned the brightest day for the people of Ellichpur to the darkest of nights. That day, people from the region gathered on the city streets and markets for purposes of commerce. The oppressors from Akbar's army encircled the city and laid siege, plundered, and ignited the fire of injustice in the country. In a blink of an eye, they razed to the ground a city that resembled Cairo and Damascus, burning down its dwellings. They plundered and took with them whatever they could find. They took as prisoners whomever fell into their hands, women and children, not distinguishing Muslim from Infidel.[119]

News of the brutal sack of Ellichpur arrived in Ahmadnagar, and the royal army marched against the Mughals, forcing them to flee, leaving their equipment behind.[120]

The sources are silent regarding the whereabouts of Sayyid Murtaza for another decade. His name resurfaces in 1595, when he was once again attached to a Mughal expedition against Ahmadnagar, this time under the command of Akbar's son Prince Murad.[121] Again, the Mughals faced significant resistance from the besieged Ahmadnagar under Chand Bibi's leadership. The Mughals withdrew to Berar in early 1596, ceded to them by the queen-dowager. Sayyid Murtaza was appointed to govern the region around Mehkar, approximately 150 km east of Daulatabad, and later set his headquarters back in Ellichpur. In 1600, he took part in Akbar's Khandesh campaign, and later returned with the Mughal army to besiege Ahmadnagar, this time conquering the fort. His service to the empire was acknowledged with the reward of a flag, a drum and a fertile *jāgīr*. In the following few years, his name arises time and again as he remained in Maharashtra as a Mughal noble, taking part in the futile efforts to oppose local commanders, including Raju Dakkani and Malik Ambar. In 1602, the last year for which we have a record of Sayyid Murtaza, his *manṣab* was raised to 2,000.[122]

Along with Mirak Dabir Chingiz Khan and Mustafa Khan Ardistani, Sayyid Murtaza Sabziwari represents highly mobile Foreign nobility. Unlike the other two, however, he demonstrates a much wider range of movement that covers not only the Deccan sultanates or only his ancestral Iran, but also the Mughal Empire, where he finally took employment. In the service of his new lords, Sayyid Murtaza took part in a campaign against his old ones, suggesting that he had no strong lingering ties in the Deccan in general, not even with Berar.

To understand his position, we should note the distinction between two kinds of military expeditions. The first, by far the more common in the Deccan, was the sacking and destruction of cities, villages and agricultural land in enemy territory. This was intended to fill the coffers of the invading armies and to deprive the enemy of resources; most invasions of the sultanates into each other's territories include descriptions of destruction. The second kind of expedition was the annexation of new territories to the domains of the invading sultanate. In this case, special efforts were made to reduce the damage to the land and its inhabitants. This ensured the fast flow of revenues from the new territory. This is clearly reflected in Ahmadnagar's conquest of the district of Pathri in 1572, part of what was then still independent Berar. When the army arrived in the district, its inhabitants left their houses out of fear, seeking shelter far away in the wilderness ('*jibāl wa bīsha-hā*', lit. mountains and forests). However, because 'the intention was subduing that province, not destruction and plunder', the commander of the invading army procured a written royal decree, pledging to the inhabitants that if they accepted Ahmadnagar's authority and paid their respects to the throne, they would enjoy royal favours and be able to return to their fields unharmed.[123]

The Mughal sack of Ellichpur in 1586 suggests that this expedition aimed to demonstrate imperial power or to save face after the defeat in Ahmadnagar, clearly not to annex the territories. Sayyid Murtaza may have been the one to encourage the Mughal army to advance to Berar and attack Ellichpur. It is quite possible that the choice to conduct the attack on a market day was not coincidental, but corresponds with the assumption that the purpose was maximising profit. As the previous governor of Ahmadnagar's Berar, Sayyid Murtaza was, most likely, aware of the day when the market was held, supporting the assumption that the purpose was pillage. Sayyid Murtaza was not connected to the region or to its inhabitants, although he had resided there for many years. However, he gained information that proved to be a valuable asset in his negotiations with the Mughals. After its demonstration in 1586, the choice to station him in Berar reflects the Mughal acknowledgement of his advantage and, furthermore, that they were not concerned with regard to his loyalty, once again indicating his detachment from the Deccan.

SHADOW OF DOUBT

The transient nature of the Foreigners was well known in their environment, and played an important role in the political life of the sultanates. Permanently considered foreign, they were often surrounded by a cloud of suspicion among local rulers, even around those who were at the very heart of the sultanates. Recall Mahmud Gawan's execution, allegedly due to such suspicion or Shah Abu al-Hasan's shaky position in Bijapur because of his family ties in Ahmadnagar. An even more explicit case is that of Mir Shah Mir Isfahani, a *sayyid* of the Tabataba°i lineage and a prominent figure in the court of Ibrahim Qutb Shah in Golkonda.[124] He served as *mīr jumla* for many years in addition to filling diplomatic roles as envoy to Ahmadnagar in the 1570s.[125] He achieved his greatest fame, however, on the battlefield. Mir Shah Mir led the expedition to suppress the tributary rulers of the lower Godavari River in Andhra in early 1579. Later that year, he was sent to join the forces besieging Bidar, and, after the assassination of °Ali °Adil Shah I, he was put in command of the royal forces of Golkonda in the failed invasion to Bijapur. In the crisis after Ibrahim Qutb Shah's death in 1580, Mir Shah Mir managed to sustain the stability of his army and to maintain his alliance with Ahmadnagar, then under Sayyid Murtaza Sabziwari, even as Bijapur attempted to draw Ahmadnagar on their side.[126] Mir Shah Mir's influence reached its zenith during the early reign of Ibrahim's son, Muhammad Quli Qutb Shah. The young king sent him on another expedition, this time to besiege Naldurg in southern Maharashtra, and the sultan later joined the general. The expedition did not deliver the anticipated results, and Muhammad Quli returned to Golkonda.[127] In early 1583, the sultan married Mir Shah Mir's daughter, demonstrating the particularly high position Mir Shah Mir enjoyed in the court.[128]

After these events, Mir Shah Mir fell from royal grace under circumstances that remain unclear. The anonymous chronicler is silent about these events and, moreover, does not mention Mir Shah Mir at all after the marriage of his daughter to the sultan. Khafi Khan refers to the changing fortunes of the noble briefly, saying that a rumour in the court accused Mir Shah Mir of an unspecified misdeed, leading to his imminent arrest and deportation to Isfahan.[129] Firishta's version is somewhat different. He states that the celebrated noble fell from grace due to bad advice he gave to Muhammad Quli, which led to poor results in the Bijapur campaign.[130]

This explanation is possible if we accept Firishta's version that the sultan's marriage took place prior to the Naldurg expedition. However, as both the authorities who had links to Golkonda, namely, the anonymous chronicler and Tabataba°i,[131] it is more likely that the marriage took place after the abortive mission to Naldurg; therefore, Firishta's version does not make sense.[132]

Tabataba°i provides another explanation behind Mir Shah Mir's downfall, which follows a *topos*; the same story is attributed to the execution of Mahmud Gawan. He reports that a group of commanders, who were envious of Mir Shah Mir's position, delivered a forged letter into the hands of Muhammad Quli. This letter was allegedly sent from Mir Shah Mir to the Foreign *amīr*s of the army of Bijapur. In the letter, Mir Shah Mir expressed the willingness of the Foreigners in Golkonda to cooperate with an invasion from Bijapur. Tabataba°i continues:

> Seeing that letter, the king's attitude towards Shah Mir, who was a great pillar of the state, has changed. He immediately ordered to imprison the incomparable *sayyid*, not even letting his natural inclination towards reconsideration and cautiousness into this issue ... The wise people of the past have prohibited the kings from impatience and haste especially when judging the accused, and ordered the appropriate measures of examination and inquiry.

As a result, the Foreigners in Golkonda's army were thrown into disarray, encouraging Bijapur to invade Golkonda. Tabataba°i reports that most warriors in the army of the Qutb Shah were Foreigners, who were offended by the imprisonment of Mir Shah Mir and did not make any effort to repel the attack. The army of Golkonda was routed without ever fighting back.[133] At the end of this affair, Mir Shah Mir was sent by royal order back to his hometown of Isfahan aboard a ship with the necessities for the journey. On his journey to Iran, he fell ill and died.[134]

Mir Shah Mir's story, even if its details seem too familiar, demonstrates the cloud of mistrust surrounding the Foreigners. After long years of loyal service under Ibrahim and Muhammad Quli Qutb Shah as an administrator and diplomat as well as on the battlefield, and even as he was tied through marriage to the royal house, his fortunes turned in a blink of an eye. Whereas the possible reason here might have been somehow within the personal realm, there seems to be a more general aura of disloyalty attached to the Foreigners, who, on their side, were not unlikely to change sides. Such behaviour was not hidden from outside observers such as the Venetian traveller, Niccolao Manucci. Commenting on Mughal elite society, he mentions that Iranians' loyalty was dubious; given their connections with Persia, they preferred their own people.[135] Combined with

Mir Shah Mir's return to Isfahan, we can once again see the resilience of the sense of *waṭan*, juxtaposed with the 'here and now' of the Deccan. Perhaps these intrinsic connections with locations in Iran, rather than with any locale in the Deccan, is what made Foreigners immediate suspects, illuminating the lingering detached nature of their presence in India.

Migration, Trans-regionalism and the Deccani Environment

The analysis of the lives and careers of the Foreigners in the Deccan sultanates reveal a complex, even somewhat confusing, reality: a successful community of migrants, who were implanted at the very heart of the political system of the host society, yet consciously chose to remain aloof from it, leading occasionally to grave consequences. Notwithstanding their attitude, their movement and high positions continued for centuries due to the persistence of a variety of push factors in Iran as well as the attractions of India. This ideal of shelter and prosperity aside, migration and settlement of Iranians in India was a movement of elite people, who enjoyed a relatively high status in their homeland in spite of the difficulties that drove them away. They had a set of skills and training, all of which were a marketable commodity in the new country, and which allowed them to maintain their high position in Indian polities. The migrants often enjoyed connections in the courts of the Deccan by way of relatives or compatriots, who provided a fast track in gaining patronage or employment. This might have been particularly easy in the Deccan, in comparison with north India. Jagadish Narayan Sarkar argues that 'in Hindustan ... Persians, while finding employment in the army and the civil government, could not hope easily to rise to the topmost rung of the ladder'.[136] Even though he admits there were exceptions, this statement seems to be an exaggeration; migrants held high positions in the Mughal system of the time.[137] Nevertheless, Sarkar is right that in no other place did Iranians have so much influence and unmitigated power as they had in the courts of the Deccan, enabled by the special circumstances of the region, and particularly shaped by local need.

In their new land, the migrants tended to keep much of their old affiliations. Accordingly, they had a rather complex relationship with their homeland, with other political and societal circles in the Deccan, and within their own groups. From the outside, Foreigners appeared as a cohesive group, particularly in their struggle against the Deccanis and the Ethiopians. However, internal dynamics reveal a diverse and fragmented group. Internal divisions were based on socio-ecological (and occupational) characteristics, separating settled-urban ('Tajik') and military-semi nomadic ('Turk') elements. Within the urbanite elites, additional divisions created subsets of groups based on lineage, place of origin or, on a smaller scale, also family.

The Foreigners' decision to maintain their former identities signified not only a framework within which they worked in the new environment, but symbolised its rejection altogether. No evidence suggests that those migrants were likely to be immersed in the new society or locality. Instead, many continued to follow their transient trajectory, as reflected in their change of patrons, switching alliance, return to Iran or even joining the Mughals. The distance that many Foreigners kept from the local scene is reflected in their name; after all, they chose to employ the term *gharībān* for themselves, a term that contributed to the perpetuation of their position as outsiders. Their insistence on maintaining this position is even more noteworthy when we compare them with another new-coming group, that of the Ethiopians. Whereas both groups came from beyond the ocean, the Ethiopians became politically associated with their new environment as is evidenced by their constant cooperation with Deccanis and their resistance to the Mughals.

This choice of the Foreigners led to their rejection by locally identified actors. This rejection, however, was a two-way street. Quoting the early twentieth-century literary scholar Shibli Nuᶜmani, E. G. Browne suggested that 'most of the Persian poets who went to India to seek a fortune, or at least a livelihood, had ... nothing but evil to say of the country',[138] a perception that resonates with the much-quoted unfavourable view of Babur on India.[139] A similar attitude is attributed to Ismaᶜil ᶜAdil Shah (r. 1510–34). Fuzuni demonstrates that while in the Deccan, the early ᶜAdil Shahi sultans maintained connections with family members as well as with the cultural realm of Iran; we will return to this story in the next chapter.[140] This is not to say that the history of the Deccan comprised a series of xenophobia-infused conflicts; the rule seems to have been peaceful conduct. However, we cannot ignore this element of separation that remained constant throughout the period.

How can we explain this insular attitude of the Foreigners? One direction that we might follow is the concept of diaspora, first popularised by Fernand Braudel. Philip Curtin defines a diaspora as a community dispersed in different localities while maintaining social bonds, varying from a mere sense of ethnic, religious or linguistic solidarity to complex internal institutional or political systems. The diaspora, continues Curtin, is clearly distinct from the host society in each of the locations, at times leading to resentment towards this group. At the same time, the diaspora was limited to one occupation, typically trade, and thus remained separated from the economically diverse host society and outside the circles of politics in the host country.[141] Some of these assertions seem to correspond with what we know about the Foreigners: they maintained social bonds and identity, remained distinct from the host society, and, at times, their interactions with local elites were less then friendly.

The diaspora model, however, is limited in some crucial points. Sanjay Subrahmanyam convincingly argues that in the Indian Ocean world in the early modern period, trade and state-building were not separate or contradictory realms but rather closely interdependent. Within this environment, Iranian migrants were deeply involved not only in trade, but also in politics and statecraft. As such, he continues, they were not isolated but rather major actors in the state.[142] As we have seen, along the lines of Subrahmanyam's critique, Foreigners indeed were crucial in Deccani politics of the time, filling some of the central roles of the state and contributing much to state-building. Moreover, we have seen the cross-over of individuals (in person or within kinship networks) between occupations. But this analysis does not explain their perpetual mobility nor their being shy of mixing with local elites. A concept that might come to our help here is that of 'circulation societies', which Sebouh Aslanian adapted to describe the early modern network of Armenian merchants, and which Derek Mancini-Lander proposes applying to the community of Foreigners in the Deccan. According to this model, a trade network or circuit comprises a nodal centre and dispersed nodes, each settled temporarily or for long periods by people from the centre. The nodes are linked to the centre and to each other. Within the circuit there is a circulation of information, priests and women (all crucial for the maintenance of identity within the network), as well as freer flow of merchants, credit and goods.[143] Mancini-Lander suggests that similarly to the Armenians, the Foreigners, many of whom belonged to the educated elite groups, circulated between courts, while maintaining their links to different places both in their home countries and in India. The limit of their circulation was the cosmopolitan world of Persian, where they were crucial not only for the efficient running of administration, but also in supporting the legitimacy of rulers, who relied heavily on Persian and Turco-Mongol tropes and identities.[144]

Both Subrahmanyam's and Mancini-Lander's analyses explain much of the logic in the circulation and activity of the Foreigners. Foreigners were politically and socially separated from their environment in the Deccan, a separation that was often marked by mutual antagonism. At the same time, they took part in the political system, to which they contributed greatly in terms of cultural and intellectual development, as well as the establishment of administrative and legitimacy practices. While doing so, the Foreigners maintained their links to other Foreigners and to their ancestral lands through ethnic, locality, kinship and cultural networks. These networks associated them more firmly, in some respects, with Iran than with the Deccan. Their continuous transient nature emphasises the weakness of their vertical connections to the locality and to the political structure that identified with the locality. Rather, when tensions arose, the Foreigners preferred the horizontal networks that linked them to a larger cultural space, as reflected in their ability to change loyalties and serve competing courts. In a way, administrators, bureaucrats and military men among the Foreigners performed what we assume was accepted for poets or traders. This is not surprising, considering that they all belonged to the same networks, families or, sometimes, were the same people. Just like court poets, they were providers of services in high demand in the courts.

The association of Foreigners with employment and trade, on the one hand, and weak connection with the locality, on the other hand, resulted in their dependency on the political durability of the host courts and on the protection of the ruler.[145] One such condition was the continuation of trade, however, this does not seem to be a major problem in early modern Asia. Notwithstanding European activity, 'little damage' was done to Asian (including Iranian) maritime trade as late as the seventeenth century.[146] More problematic was the perpetuation of patronage. This is obvious in the case of court-sponsored artists. T. N. Devare, in his discussion of the poet Zuhuri, linked the poet's fortunes directly with the patron's will; when the sultan became displeased with the poet, the latter 'became utterly helpless and was not even free to quit Ahmednagar fearing greater disasters'.[147] Such association was the rule for all those in high positions; similar misfortunes befell the bureaucrat and commander Mir Shah Mir. On a less personal level, the changing nature of courts, in particular, their stability or the lack thereof, were a major factor in the activity of Foreigners. Not having prolonged connections with the locality, when the situation worsened, Foreigners left altogether. The most notable case of exodus was Ahmadnagar: unstable from the 1580s, many Foreigners (including Firishta and Malik Qummi) left for Bijapur and Golkonda. Whereas some Foreigners, scholars as well as traders, remained in the city thereafter,[148] a second wave of Foreigners left following the death of Burhan Nizam Shah II in 1595, including Zuhuri. With the Mughal conquest of Ahmadnagar in 1600, the rise of the Ethiopian Malik Ambar, the collapse of the city as a major political and cultural centre, and the rise of the Marathas, there is no evidence of Foreigners active in western Maharashtra for most of the seventeenth century.

These limitations demarcate the boundaries of the activity of the

Foreigners. They were mostly limited to stable, permanent employers, who appreciated their skills and training, mostly in courts where the administration was based, at least in part, on Persianate models and the Persian language. Elsewhere, we can find Foreigners as mercenaries (e.g., Vijayanagara) or merchants, but not as much at the centre of the political system. More than other elite groups, the Foreigners associated with important centres: capital cities, provincial capitals (Mustafa Khan Ardistani in Bankapur) or strategic points (the Gilanis in Goa); there is no evidence for their involvement beyond. In a sense, we can liken of the map of their residence to lacework, with thin threads connecting nodal points but thin air in between. This marks one of the main characteristics that distinguished the Foreigners from the Deccani environment. Operating in trans-regional, usually urban networks, Foreigners were connected beyond boundaries. Family- or locality-based networks held more sway over the actions of the Foreigners than their connections with, and loyalty to, any ruler in particular. These interactions, combined with their mobility, resulted in hostility and, quite often, destabilised the political system within which they were active, leading at times to their abandonment of such locality altogether. In this sense, the Foreigners presented a distinct way of involvement with the politics of the Deccan, contributing at the same time to the building and unravelling of the Deccan sultanates.

Notes

1. McPherson, *The Indian Ocean*, pp. 43–5; Thapar, 'Significance of Regional History', pp. 20–6; Prange, *Monsoon Islam*, pp. 2–19.
2. Khalidi, 'The Arabs of Hadramawt in Hyderabad', pp. 52–4; Sheikh, *Forging a Region*, pp. 43–7; George, 'Direct Sea Trade'.
3. Abu Lughod, *Before European Hegemony*; Wink, *Al-Hind*, vol. 1, pp. 25–65; Devare, *Persian Literature*, pp. 1–17.
4. Eaton and Wagoner, 'Warfare on the Deccan Plateau'. On the Indian Ocean trade system in the fifteenth century, see Bouchon and Lombard, 'The Indian Ocean in the Fifteenth Century'. Throughout the early modern period, the Indian economy maintained a large degree of openness to the world, enabling the continuation of commercial and other links, see Balachandran and Subrahmanyam, 'Globalization and India'.
5. Richard Eaton demonstrates that the Bahmanis were influenced by Timurid imperial grandeur, which they tried to imitate in their capital cities, see Eaton, *Social History*, pp. 64–5. Phillip Wagoner suggests that the growing integration of Vijayanagara in the global system changed the political idioms employed by the kings both internally and in their interactions with the outside world, see Wagoner, 'Sultan among Hindu Kings'.

6. Dale, *Islamic Society*, pp. 11–32; Miller, *Mappila Muslims*, pp. 39–71; Ricci, *Islam Translated*, pp. 5–11; Qureshi, *Muslim Community*, pp. 1–10; Prange, *Monsoon Islam*.
7. Nizami, *Religion and Politics*, pp. 89–123; Alam, 'The Culture and Politics of Persian'.
8. 'Al-Biruni', *EI2*.
9. Ernst, 'Foreword'. Hujwiri's shrine still serves as a spiritual and political centre in Pakistan, see Knysh, *Islamic Mysticism*, pp. 132–5.
10. For a full discussion on these travel accounts as a corpus in the wider context of the early modern Muslim East, see Alam and Subrahmanyam, *Indo-Persian Travels*.
11. Subrahmanyam, 'Iranians Abroad', pp. 350–1.
12. Jackson, *Delhi Sultanate*, pp. 61–85, 171–92; Alam, *The Languages of Political Islam*, pp. 115–40.
13. Morgan, *Mongols*, pp. 73–83; Kumar, *Emergence of the Delhi Sultanate*, pp. 222–4; Wink, *Al-Hind*, vol. 2, pp. 190–4. The Mongols and the Delhi sultanate had contested relationships throughout the thirteenth century with occasional warfare, however, this never materialised to a fully-fledged Mongol invasion beyond the Punjab, let alone conquest. Furthermore, the cross-boundary links between the sides, often described in binary terms, were in reality complex and flexible, with elites of both sides sharing ethnic background, practices and traditions. See Jackson, *Delhi Sultanate*, pp. 103–22; Kumar, 'Ignored Elites'.
14. Sherwani, *History of the Qutb Shahi*, pp. 1–3.
15. At least this is one of the versions around Yusuf's migration, as I have demonstrated elsewhere. This narrative reflects familiar realities to readers of Persian in the early seventeenth century; see Fischel, 'Origin Narratives', pp. 73–80.
16. Babur himself provided one of the most interesting narratives of migration to early modern Asia, see Dale, 'Steppe Humanism'.
17. Subrahmanyam, 'Iranians Abroad', pp. 350–5; Streusand, *Formation of the Mughal Empire*, pp. 44–5; Moin, *The Millennial Sovereign*, pp. 162–4.
18. *Tadhkirat al-Muluk*, p. 28.
19. Stephen Dale suggests that in the early seventeenth century, the population of Safavid Iran was no more than 8 million people, compared with somewhere between 60 and 98 million in the Mughal Empire, to which we should add the Deccan and other regions not yet under their rule, see Dale, *Indian Merchants*, pp. 15–19. André Wink argues that the population of South Asia was even bigger, with the entirety of the subcontinent hosting some 155 million in 1571, about twenty times as many as in Iran and Transoxiana, see Wink, *Al-Hind*, vol. 2, pp. 162–8.
20. Alam, *The Languages of Political Islam*, pp. 115–28. For Golkonda, H. K. Sherwani argues that 'it was the patronage of learning on the part of the Court of Haidarabad which made poets of Persia throng into the city, and

Foreigners, Locals and the World

the capital became like a place of refuge for those who did not find Iran big enough to appreciate their talent', see Sherwani, *History of the Qutb Shahi*, p. 331.
21. Bouchon and Lombard, 'The Indian Ocean in the Fifteenth Century', pp. 57–62.
22. Hall, 'Ports-of-Trade', pp. 122–3.
23. Sherwani, *Bahmanis*, pp. 122–4; Devare, *Persian Literature*; ᶜAqīl, *Dakkan aur Īrān*; Siddiqi, 'Ethnic Change', pp. 33–51; Michell and Zebrowski, *Architecture and Art*, pp. 66–77; Eaton, *Social History*, pp. 60–2.
24. Haig, 'Kingdom of the Deccan', p. 403; Gribble, *History of the Deccan*, p. 100. These scholars followed the terminology in nineteenth-century histories, such as the Persian *Mukhtār al-Akhbār* from 1877, which contains a verbatim repetition of Firishta. See *Mukhtar al-Akhbar*, p. 144, and compare *Tarikh-i Firishta*, vol. 1, p. 689.
25. Flatt, 'Courtly Culture', pp. 90–1.
26. Sherwani, *Bahmanis*, pp. 131–4; Devare, *Persian Literature*, p. 809. Radhey Shyam uses the terms 'New Comers' and 'Foreigners' interchangeably, see Shyam, *Ahmadnagar*, p. 7.
27. For a concise summary of the prevailing theories on Islamisation in India, see Eaton, *Bengal Frontier*, pp. 113–19.
28. Sherwani, *Bahmanis*, pp. 152–3; Naqvi, *Iranian Afaquies*; Flatt, 'Courtly Culture', pp. 90–1. The Pakistani scholar Muᶜinuddin ᶜAqil prefers to use a neutral 'those who come from out of the country (*ghayr mamālik se āne vāle*)', or a simpler 'non-Deccanis', thus staying away from ideological statements. See ᶜAqīl, *Dakkan aur Īrān*, p. 11.
29. For example, *Futuhat-i ᶜAdil Shahi*, p. 103r; *Burhan-i Maʾathir*, p. 435.
30. Eaton, *Social History*, p. 68, n. 27.
31. This attitude is well reflected in Eaton, 'Temple Desecration'.
32. At the time the early copies of manuscripts were produced, the system of diacritics was still developing both in Iran and in India. The writing of the letter *pā* in its current shape (پ, with the three dots underneath) became universal only in the seventeenth or even eighteenth centuries, i.e., around or after the period under discussion; prior to that, writing was much more flexible. See Haravī, *Naqd va Taṣḥīḥ-i Mutūn*, pp. 140–50; Hashabeiky, *Persian Orthography*, pp. 73–87. This flexibility allowed the somewhat free agglomeration of diacritics that we can find in the word *gharībān* and elsewhere (e.g., *bayān* and even *bījānagar*, Persian for Vijayanagara, in which the diacritics of the letters ب *bā*, ي *yā* and ج *jīm* are agglomerated).
33. Asafiyya MS History 401, TGOML, 202. Another manuscript, *Tarikh-i Qutb Shah*, IO MS 179, 175v, drops the word *jawānān*; however, as this section was added in the margins, it is likely that there was a copying error.
34. *Tarikh-i Qutb Shah*, p. 176r. In the following line, the text mentions simply 'Foreigners and Turkmans' (*gharībān wa turkmānān*), demonstrating again that *gharīb* is the correct singular form of the widely used *gharībān*.

141

35. *Tarikh-i Qutb Shah*, p. 216v.
36. *Burhan-i Maʾathir*, p. 478.
37. *Tadhkirat al-Muluk*, p. 35.
38. *Muntakhab al-Lubab*, vol. 3, p. 211.
39. *Tarikh-i Firishta*, vol. 1, p. 689. In order to make sure that the term did not change in the 1830 lithograph, this reading was corroborated with an early manuscript of the same text, dated 1639. See BL Persian MS add.18,875, 440v. See also *Tarikh-i Firishta*, vol. 2, p. 164.
40. Interestingly, there is one occasion in which a word that can be translated as 'Westerner' appears, however this is a different word: *maghribīyān* rather than *gharbīyān*. The reference, however, is clearly to North Africa (the Maghreb), with special reference to the Ismaʿilis (i.e., Fatimids) in Egypt and Libya (*ifrīqīya*), followed by a Quranic verse on the setting sun. See *Tarikh-i Firishta*, vol. 2, p. 213.
41. *Tarikh-i Firishta*, vol. 1, p. 639, corroborated with BL Persian MS add.18,875, 411r.
42. Sherwani, *Bahmanis*, pp. 145, 152.
43. Flatt, 'Courtly Culture', p. 89.
44. For example, Talbot argues that in Telugu and Sanskrit epigraphical sources of the fourteenth to seventeenth centuries, religion was only secondary to ethnic and other forms of identification when referring to the Muslims as well as to Hindus, see Talbot, 'Inscribing the Other, Inscribing the Self'.
45. See, for example, *Tarikh-i Firishta*, vol. 1, p. 701, vol. 2, p. 89; *Burhan-i Maʾathir*, pp. 420, 455–7; *Tarikh-i Qutb Shah*, pp. 175v–177v, 207v–208r, 216v, 218v, 242r, 247v.
46. Wagoner, 'Fortuitous Convergences'. Notable Muslim tombs can be found around Vijayanagara city, outside the village of Kadirampuram and on the Nallur Road. See Sinopoli and Morrison, 'Metropolitan Region'.
47. Dirk Kolff demonstrates that in early modern Hindustan, the categories 'Afghan' and 'Rajput' were not ethnic or genealogical, but rather soldiers' (i.e., occupational) identities. In the context of the Deccan, Emma Flatt points at a similar ambiguous use of the term *turk* as a social/military rather than ethnic category. See Kolff, *Naukar, Rajput, and Sepoy*, pp. 54–70; Flatt, 'Courtly Culture', p. 90.
48. Already under the Bahmanis, several rulers such as Ahmad I had distributed money among *sayyid*s in holy cities and ordered the execution of those who insulted them. See Siddiqi, 'Ethnic Change', pp. 39–40. Recall, however, that this background did not guarantee protection in Ahmadnagar of the 1580s.
49. *Burhan-i Maʾathir*, pp. 451–2, 497; Schimmel, *Islamic Names*, p. 40. Note that the author of this chronicle, Sayyid ʿAli Tabatabaʾi, was identified as part of the same lineage as Mir Shah Mir, which might indicate the chronicler's choice of epithet.
50. For these characters, see *Tarikh-i Firishta*, vol. 2, pp. 79–80, 85, 217,

224, 271 and IO MS add.18,875, 431r; *Futuhat-i ᶜAdil Shahi*, p. 109r; *Muntakhab al-Lubab*, vol. 3, p. 377; *Burhan-i Maʾathir*, pp. 412, 433, 436, 440–52, 457, 456–61, 497, 506–7, 535–41, 544–50; *Tadhkirat al-Muluk*, pp. 103, 112–17, 123–4, 132–4; *Tarikh-i Qutb Shah*, pp. 145v–147r, 164v–169r, 182r, 192v–197v, 200r, 201r–204v, 216v, 220v–222r, 240v, 242v–243r.

51. *Tarikh-i Firishta*, vol. 1, pp. 692–3 and IO Persian MS add.18,875, 433r, 443r. See also Flatt, 'Courtly Culture', pp. 99–101.
52. *Tarikh-i Firishta*, vol. 1, p. 707; IO Persian MS add.18,875, 451r. There are small semantic differences between the lithograph and the manuscript, for instance, slave appears as *makhdūm* in the lithograph, and as *ghulām* in the 1639 manuscript. There is also a slight difference in the places listed in both sources.
53. Eaton, *Social History*, pp. 70–3; ᶜĀlamī, *Mulūk-i Bahmanī*, pp. 187, 195–6.
54. *Tarikh-i Firishta*, vol. 2, pp. 98–9.
55. *Tarikh-i Firishta*, vol. 2, p. 339; *Muntakhab al-Lubab*, vol. 3, p. 383.
56. *Burhan-i Maʾathir*, pp. 493–4; *Tarikh-i Firishta*, vol. 2, p. 276.
57. *Tarikh-i Qutb Shah*, pp. 31v–32r.
58. Subrahmanyam, 'Iranians Abroad', pp. 353–4. An interesting undated letter sent to Hajji Muhammad Shafiᶜ, the agent (*wakīl*) of Muhammad Saᶜid Mir Jumla (served between 1637 and 1653), who was in Iran asks the noble to take care of the property left by the sultan's aunt, who died in Iran, see *Golconda Letters*, pp. 33v–34r. Nile Green points out an interesting manifestation of the lingering links of people and places from Iran in the Indian environment in the way of commemorative spaces, created by many migratory communities in the subcontinent, see Green, *Making Space*, pp. xi–xvi.
59. Eaton, *Social History*, pp. 67–76.
60. Eaton, *Sufis of Bijapur*, pp. 67–70; Bredi et al., 'Shi'ism in the Deccan'.
61. *Tarikh-i Firishta*, vol. 2, pp. 215–18; *Muntakhab al-Lubab*, vol. 3, pp. 178–9.
62. *Tarikh-i Firishta*, vol. 2, p. 65.
63. Mitchell, 'Sister Shi'a States?' pp. 45–7.
64. Alavi, *Medieval Deccan*, pp. 6–10.
65. Flatt, 'Courtly Culture', pp. 89–90.
66. Amanat, 'Iranian Identity Boundaries'.
67. I would like to thank Derek Mancini-Lander for this comment.
68. Matthee, 'Was Safavid Iran an Empire?' p. 239.
69. Bredi et al., 'Shi'ism in the Deccan'.
70. Subrahmanyam, 'Iranians Abroad', pp. 353–5.
71. *Tadhkirat al-Muluk*, pp. 124–6.
72. *Tadhkirat al-Muluk*, pp. 161–3; *Basatin al-Salatin*, pp. 153–4; Carl W. Ernst, 'Notes on *Tazkirat al-muluk*', unpublished paper. I wish to thank Prof. Ernst for kindly sharing his notes and other valuable materials.
73. Glassen, 'Schah Ismāʿīl I'; Roemer, 'Safavid Period', pp. 197–200.

74. Daftary, *Ismaʿilis*, pp. 435–6, 453. The story follows *Tarikh-i Firishta*, vol. 2, pp. 212–15. Khafi Khan reports that Shah Tahir's opponents 'accused him' (*matʿūn wa muttahim sākhta*) of being Ismaʿili, forcing his escape to India, see *Muntakhab al-Lubab*, vol. 3, pp. 177–8. Tabatabaʾi does not mention Shah Tahir's Ismaʿili beliefs at all, but discusses him as a follower of Twelver Shiism. Accordingly, he reports that Shah Tahir's escape from Iran was due to jealousy and court intrigue which poisoned Shah Ismaʿil's mind against him. When the Shah realised that it was a conspiracy, he sent cavalry to bring him back to the court, but by then Shah Tahir had already departed for India, see *Burhan-i Maʾathir*, pp. 253–5. The disregard of Shah Tahir's Ismaʿili following supports Daftary's claim regarding the continuation of *taqiyya* even in India, however, chroniclers as early as Firishta in the early seventeenth century were aware of Shah Tahir's Ismaʿili leanings, lending Firishta the opportunity to discuss the history of the Ismaʿilis from Fatimid times onward. See also Shakeb, *Relations of Golkonda with Iran*, pp. 122–4.

75. Joshi, 'The Adil Shahis and the Baridis', vol. 1, p. 307. According to another version, he settled in Paranda in Maharashtra, see Mitchell, 'Sister Shi'a States?' p. 60.

76. *Tarikh-i Firishta*, vol. 2, pp. 215–18; *Muntakhab al-Lubab*, vol. 3, pp. 178–9; Hosain, 'Shah Tahir', pp. 150–1.

77. *Tarikh-i Firishta*, vol. 2, pp. 207–11, 557; *Muntakhab al-Lubab*, vol. 3, pp. 169–73, 447–8.

78. *Tarikh-i Firishta*, vol. 2, pp. 201, 227–9; *Muntakhab al-Lubab*, vol. 3, pp. 174–6, 304, 312, 371; Joshi, 'The Adil Shahis and the Baridis', vol. 1, pp. 317–20.

79. Khafi Khan suggests that many Hanafi Sunnis were secretly Mahdawis, see *Muntakhab al-Lubab*, vol. 3, p. 162; *Tarikh-i Firishta*, vol. 2, p. 218, implies the same. The obscure history of the Mahdawis found in a partial manuscript in Hyderabad claims that Burhan I himself was Mahdawi, and he promoted the sect in Ahmadnagar, establishing Mahdawi settlements (*dāʾira*s) around the capital and marrying his own daughter, Fatima Begam, to Sayyid Miran-ji, grandson of Mahdawi (probably Muhammad Jaunpuri, d. 1505). See *Tarikh-i Mahdawiyan*, pp. 16v–17r; I wish to thank Hannah Archambault to pointing this manuscript to me and her assistance in obtaining it. On the development and spread of the Mahdawi movement, see Rizvi, *Muslim Revivalist Movements*, pp. 68–134.

80. *Tarikh-i Firishta*, vol. 2, pp. 218–25; *Muntakhab al-Lubab*, vol. 3, pp. 176–83, 279.

81. Daftary, *Ismaāʿīlīs*, pp. 453–4.

82. *Tarikh-i Firishta*, vol. 2, pp. 225–8; *Muntakhab al-Lubab*, vol. 3, p. 293.

83. 'Shah Tahir', *EI2*; Cole, *Roots of North Indian Shi'ism*, p. 23; *Tarikh-i Firishta*, vol. 2, p. 230; *Muntakhab al-Lubab*, vol. 3, p. 186.

84. Michell and Zebrowski, *Architecture and Art*, p. 80; Sohoni, *Architecture*,

pp. 165–9. Sohoni suggests that Shah Tahir's body was buried in the enclosure around Ahmad Nizam Shah's tomb before it was transferred to Karbala.
85. Daftary, *Ismaᶜilis*, p. 454; *Tarikh-i Firishta*, vol. 2, p. 226; *Muntakhab al-Lubab*, vol. 3, p. 329.
86. *Burhan-i Maʾathir*, p. 433; Shyam, *Ahmadnagar*, pp. 106, 183; *Muntakhab al-Lubab*, vol. 3, pp. 188–9.
87. *Tarikh-i Firishta*, vol. 2, pp. 79–80; *Burhan-i Maʾathir*, pp. 448–9; Shyam, *Ahmadnagar*, pp. 156–81; *Muntakhab al-Lubab*, vol. 3, pp. 201, 350–2, 381.
88. According to Firishta, he was the eldest son, but Tabatabaʾi implies he was the younger brother of Shah Rafiᶜ al-Din Husayn.
89. Daftary, *Ismaᶜilis*, pp. 454–5; *Tarikh-i Firishta*, vol. 2, p. 228.
90. *Burhan-i Maʾathir*, pp. 452–8, 502–3; Shyam, *Ahmadnagar*, p. 208. Daftary suggests that Shah Haydar had already died by 1586, but the contemporary sources suggest the later date, see Daftary, *Ismaᶜilis*, p. 454.
91. With the exception of the royal and Sufi families, descriptions of marriages are extremely rare in the chronicles of the time. Thus, we have seen before such marriages among royal houses (e.g., Chand Bibi, daughter of Husayn Nizam Shah I, and ᶜAli ᶜAdil Shah I); between royalty and Sufis (e.g., Ahmad Bahmani I's daughter and the Niᶜmatullahi Shah Nurullah); and between royalty and leading nobles (e.g., Muhammad Quli Qutb Shah and Mir Shah Mir's daughter). In other cases, however, even when sources suggest that a certain person had a family, any information regarding the identity of the noble's wife remains obscure.
92. *Burhan-i Maʾathir*, pp. 453–4.
93. Daftary, *Ismaᶜilis*, pp. 451, 455.
94. *Khayr al-Bayan*, pp. 293v, 319v–322r; Devare, *Persian Literature*, pp. 67, 94–8, 186–236, 324–30; Browne, *Literary History of Persia*, vol. 4, pp. 110, 253.
95. For a thorough discussion of the peripatetic courtier, see Flatt, 'Courtly Culture', pp. 55–104.
96. Hutton, 'Carved in Stone', pp. 67–9.
97. *Futuhat-i ᶜAdil Shahi*, pp. 112v–113r.
98. *Tarikh-i Firishta*, vol. 2, pp. 265–8.
99. Later in his career, after excelling as a commander in a battle, he received the title Mustafa Khan. As the Deccani sources refer to him with this title, it will be the one used here.
100. *Tarikh-i Qutb Shah*, pp, 145v–147r; *Tadhkirat al-Muluk*, pp. 112–13; *Muntakhab al-Lubab*, vol. 3, pp. 376–81; *Basatin al-Salatin*, p. 133; Sherwani, *History of the Qutb Shahi*, pp. 98–103, 125–33; Subrahmanyam, *Courtly Encounters*, pp. 72–3.
101. *Tarikh-i Qutb Shah*, p. 151r. For the contestation over Raichur, which remained a contested issue in the politics of the region for centuries, see

Eaton, 'Kiss my Foot'; Eaton and Wagoner, *Power, Memory, Architecture*, pp. 241–53.
102. *Futuhat-i ᶜAdil Shahi*, p. 103r–v.
103. *Tarikh-i Qutb Shah*, pp. 151r–152r. The Asaf Jahi chronicler Qadir Khan Bidri repeats this version, but suggests that it was the sultan's idea to send Mustafa Khan to the Hijaz. See *Tarikh-i Qadiri*, pp. 409–12.
104. *Tadhkirat al-Muluk*, pp. 112–16.
105. Most sources imply foul play on behalf of Mustafa Khan, however, Fuzuni depicts his actions in a positive light, saying that the three sultans had agreed in advance to conquer the forts and deliver them to the hands of ᶜAli ᶜAdil Shah I, see *Futuhat-i ᶜAdil Shahi*, pp. 101v–102r.
106. Subrahmanyam, *Courtly Encounters*, pp. 59–60.
107. *Tadhkirat al-Muluk*, pp. 123–4; *Futuhat-i ᶜAdil Shahi*, pp. 117v–121v, 125v–136r.
108. *Tarikh-i Firishta*, vol. 2, pp. 80–5, 95–6; *Burhan-i Maᵓathir*, pp. 473–5; *Muntakhab al-Lubab*, vol. 3, pp. 339–46; Verma, *Bijapur*, pp. 22–3. Shirazi suggests a somewhat different version: Kishwar Khan sent five or six *amīr*s against Mustafa Khan, resulting in a battle in which Mustafa Khan was defeated. He then sought refuge in one of the forts of the *zamīndār*s (Fuzuni calls them Hindus; likely meaning *nāyakwāṛī*s), but 'no one opened the gate to Mustafa Khan'. The latter was eventually seized and imprisoned in Bankapur. Only then did Kishwar Khan begin to his abuse power, encouraging Chand Bibi to take action against him. See *Tadhkirat al-Muluk*, pp. 170–1; *Futuhat-i ᶜAdil Shahi*, p. 158r–v.
109. *Muntakhab al-Lubab*, vol. 3, p. 381.
110. Shakeb, *Relations of Golkonda with Iran*, p. 74; for full details, see *Tarikh-i ᶜAlam-ara-i ᶜAbbasi*, p. 883.
111. *Burhan-i Maᵓathir*, pp. 442–57. He may have been part of the campaign against Bijapur in the early 1580s, following the coronation of the infant Ibrahim ᶜAdil Shah II.
112. *Muntakhab al-Lubab*, vol. 3, pp. 202–3; *Maᵓathir al-Umarāᵓ*, vol. 3, pp. 290–1. Fuzuni refers to him in this instance as Mir Murtaza Mashhadi, which is, of course, erroneous, see *Futuhat-i ᶜAdil Shahi*, p. 155v.
113. Burhan Nizam Shah had been a claimant to the throne of Ahmadnagar for a few years. The authority of Murtaza Nizam Shah I, who was considered to be a madman, was constantly challenged by Burhan and others. After Burhan's failed rebellion, he found shelter in Akbar's court in Lahore, probably with the intention of obtaining Mughal assistance to take over the throne in Ahmadnagar; he later rejected such visible association with the Mughals. See Shyam, *Ahmadnagar*, pp. 169–80.
114. The alignment suggests that just like the Ethiopians, the Circassian slave chose to cooperate with the Deccanis.
115. *Burhan-i Maᵓathir*, pp. 471–94, 537–41, 544–9; *Tarikh-i Firishta*, vol. 2, pp. 270–81. Oddly, Firishta does not mention Sayyid Murtaza in the events

Foreigners, Locals and the World

following the rise of Salabat Khan; he further links the escape of Prince Burhan with the Mughal attack on Ahmadnagar.

116. *Akbarnama*, vol. 3, pp. 685–6; *Maʾathir al-Umaraʾ*, vol. 3, pp. 291–2; *Burhan-i Maʾathir*, pp. 547–9.
117. *Burhan-i Maʾathir*, p. 549.
118. *Burhan-i Maʾathir*, p. 549; Faruqui, *Princes of the Mughal Empire*, p. 74. Prince Burhan is not mentioned in relation to this campaign, suggesting that he had already tried to distance himself from over-enthusiastic Mughal support.
119. *Burhan-i Maʾathir*, p. 550.
120. *Burhan-i Maʾathir*, pp. 550–1. Needless to say, this version is promoted by Ahmadnagar's historian.
121. *Muntakhab al-Lubab*, vol. 3, p. 249.
122. *Akbarnama*, vol. 3, pp. 1050, 1148, 1157, 1166, 1180, 1189, 1199, 1209, 1212, 1236; *Maʾathir al-Umaraʾ*, vol. 3, p. 292.
123. *Burhan-i Maʾathir*, pp. 461–2.
124. He appears under a few names in the chronicles: Shah Taqi, Sayyid Shah Mir Tabatabaʾi and Shah Mirza Isfahani.
125. *Burhan-i Maʾathir*, pp. 476, 482; *Tarikh-i Firishta*, vol. 2, pp. 269–70.
126. *Tarikh-i Qutb Shah*, pp. 181v–188r; *Tarikh-i Firishta*, vol. 2, p. 338; *Burhan-i Maʾathir*, pp. 524–5, 528–9.
127. *Tarikh-i Qutb Shah*, pp. 192v–196v.
128. Both Tabatabaʾi and the anonymous Golkonda chronicler agree that the marriage between Muhammad Quli Qutb Shah and the daughter of Mir Shah Mir took place after the sultan's return from Naldurg, see *Tarikh-i Qutb Shah*, p. 200r; *Burhan-i Maʾathir*, p. 535. Firishta argues that the marriage took place immediately after Muhammad Quli's ascent to the throne, prior to his expedition to Naldurg, see *Tarikh-i Firishta*, vol. 2, p. 338.
129. *Muntakhab al-Lubab*, vol. 3, p. 383.
130. *Tarikh-i Firishta*, vol. 2, pp. 338–9.
131. Tabatabaʾi, before his discussion of these events, mentions briefly that he served Muhammad Quli Qutb Shah, and even accompanied the sultan during the siege of Naldurg, before moving to Ahmadnagar, see *Burhan-i Maʾathir*, p. 534. Tabatabaʾi was of the same *sayyid* lineage as Mir Shah Mir, thus likely to have had personal connections with Mir Shah Mir or his close circle.
132. Sherwani suggests another explanation: 'the king's (Muhammad Quli Qutb Shah's) character was loose, as is evident from his poem after poem in the *Kulliyat*, especially those dedicated to his paramours ... Even when he married Mir Shah Mir's daughter he was given to enjoyment of all kinds, and this might well have unnerved both the new queen and his (*sic*) father'. Sherwani does not provide any evidence that would support the assumption that either the queen or her father were upset, and even if they were, it is not likely that they would sever links to the royal family over such matters. This

interpretation seems to reflect more on the moral values and the conceptions of family and marriage in mid-twentieth-century Hyderabad than in late sixteenth-century Golkonda. See Sherwani, *History of the Qutb Shahi*, pp. 351–2, n. 10.
133. *Burhan-i Maʾathir*, p. 536.
134. *Tarikh-i Firishta*, vol. 2, p. 339; *Muntakhab al-Lubab*, vol. 3, p. 383.
135. Quoted in Wink, 'Islamic Society', p. 218. Manucci, however, was not always a reliable reporter, and his narratives are dotted with gross inaccuracies. See Butler Brown, 'Did Aurangzeb Ban Music?'.
136. Sarkar, *The Life of Mir Jumla*, p. 1.
137. Athar Ali, *Mughal Nobility under Aurangzeb*, pp. 16–21.
138. Browne, *Literary History of Persia*, vol. 4, p. 259.
139. *Baburnama*, pp. 333–4.
140. *Futuhat-i ʿAdil Shahi*, pp. 58v–59r.
141. Curtin, *Cross-Cultural Trade*, pp. 1–11.
142. Subrahmanyam, 'Iranians Abroad'; Subrahmanyam, 'Imarat and Tijarat'.
143. Aslanian, *From the Indian Ocean to the Mediterranean*, pp. 7–15.
144. Mancini-Lander, 'Tales Bent Backward'.
145. Shirazi captured this sense of dependence on the patron in these words: 'Day and night, with prayers to the perpetuation of his dynasty and addition of majesty of His Highness, Refuge of the World . . . to the protection and peace of his kingdom. May the shadow of mercy and compassion will remain firm and perpetual upon mankind to the edge of Resurrection, and may his shadow fall in particular on the likes of us, the *gharībān*, who without the light of the Refuge of the World, a woe and hundred thousand more woes would befall on us!' see *Tadhkirat al-Muluk*, p. 221.
146. Arasaratnam, 'India and the Indian Ocean', pp. 106–7.
147. Devare, *Persian Literature*, p. 217.
148. See Alam and Subrahmanyam, 'Deccan Frontier', p. 377.

4

Locality, Vernacular and Political Language

In the previous chapters we examined the Deccan as the stage on which a unique state system emerged, characterised by parallel contradictory trajectories and the relative weakness of the centre. Elite groups were struggling and reformulating themselves in relation to one another and to the locality, on the one hand, and, on the other hand, to international identities and trans-regional networks. The emphasis on these aspects of political and social life on the Deccan Plateau has clear limitations. First and foremost, the narrative is heavily linked to the Islamic identity of the sultanates, whereas non-Muslims are pushed to the margins. This emphasis is not merely the outcome of modern imagination. Persian and, to some degree, Dakhani sources only seldom discuss non-Muslims. The region as a whole was imagined as an Islamic space, even if carrying its own brand of Islam.

The Deccan, however, was not solely an imagined Islamic space. The political system of all sultanates did not erase centuries of history. From imperial formations with their all-Deccani ideas to vernacular kingdom and their local sensitivities, the establishment of Muslim dynasties did not wipe off all pasts to start from a clean slate. Not only history, locality and memory, but also people, including elites, remained in place. Non-Muslims continued to be the majority of the population, and many non-Muslim elite groups maintained power bases and privilege. In the competitive environment of the early modern Deccan, the sultans did not have any choice but to rely on local expertise and its agents to maintain their military and administrative systems and to successfully position themselves vis-à-vis predatory neighbours. Considering the power relations between relatively weak rulers and powerful ruled, the sultans could not simply force locals into their system. Rather, they had to gain elite cooperation, and to do so quickly, if they wished to keep afloat in the combative environment of the sixteenth century. The collapse of Vijayanagara in 1565 and the opportunities it provided the sultans beyond their core regions only intensified the need to appeal to increasingly diverse groups.

The result was an ever-growing effort on behalf of the ruling dynasties to incorporate ideas and forms of expression into their political language that would appeal to local elites. These elements did not come to replace Islamic reasoning and legitimacy. Yet local, non-Muslim voices had a growing impact on the image and direction the sultanates took.

The inclusion of elites and their identities, and the influence they had on the development of the political language of the Deccan sultanates are in the focus of this chapter. While acknowledged in modern historiography, the impact of the locality has been treated in a fragmented manner. No study has examined the sultanates as comparable yet separate entities. As a result, many generalisations were made, assuming that what can be traced in one sultanate must apply to all others. An examination of the sultanates side by side, however, offers a better understanding of the characteristics of each. Focusing on the Qutb Shahs of Golkonda and the ᶜAdil Shahs of Bijapur, I argue that similarities and differences appear in places least expected. In contrast to the narrative of united Golkonda against fragmented Bijapur, I argue that the early sultanates started from similar points in terms of internal cohesion and the gradual development of political language. At the same time, the sultanates differed significantly in the terms in which each dynasty associated itself with their environment. Even though both used local elements to attract non-Muslim elites, the models on which they relied were profoundly different: against Golkonda's vernacular identities, Bijapur followed non-vernacular, yet highly localised, language. By that, I suggest that a generalised idea of vernacularisation is insufficient to understand the development of the sultanates. Rather, we should consider the existence of two models of association operating in parallel.

The Qutb Shahs of Golkonda: Kings of Telangana

From early on, the sultans of Golkonda presented strong affiliations with the territory over which they ruled. In early modern Persian sources of the Deccan sultanates, sultanates were usually identified with either dynastic titles (e.g., Qutb Shah, ᶜAdil Shah) or with the capital city. Thus, rulers were presented as kings (*sulṭān*, *shāh* or *pādshāh*) of Golkonda (from 1591 also Hyderabad), Bijapur and so forth. This use continued in modern historiography, where sultanates are still identified by the name of the capital cities. However, in the case of Golkonda, another form emerges: Persian chronicles refer to the Qutb Shahs also as rulers of Telangana, the Telugu-speaking portion of the Deccan Plateau.[1] Firishta, for example, describes Ibrahim Qutb Shah as 'the sovereign of Telangana' (*farmān-farmā-i*

Locality, Vernacular and Political Language

tilang),[2] and his successor Muhammad Quli as the 'command-giver of Telangana' (*farmān-dih-i tilang*).[3] Tabataba'i mentions that Muhammad Quli 'ascended the throne of rulership and kingship of all the provinces of Telangana',[4] and a similar reference to the 'rule over the kingdom of Telangana' is attributed to the sultan by the anonymous chronicler.[5] The new city of Hyderabad is described as the 'capital of Telangana'.[6] The close geographical association is unusual in other contexts in the early modern Deccan.[7]

The link between the Qutb Shahi rulers and Telangana is evident, but less clear is the meaning of this regional identification. Persian sources do not provide such clear definition, possibly as the region and its boundaries were familiar to the intended readership. In certain instances, however, there emerges a sense of what the region means. When discussing the security conditions under Ibrahim, the anonymous chronicler states that 'even an old woman could put a bowl full of gold on her head and walk from the capital to the extremities of Bengal, Ahmadnagar, and Bijapur ... even though the people of Telangana are excellent in the art of thievery'. The passage emphasises the political content of the term Telangana: the kingdom that lies between Ahmadnagar, Bijapur and (the Mughal province of) Bengal. Moreover, discussing the sordid nature of the people of Telangana, the chronicler adds a (nefarious) social element to understanding the region.[8]

Qutb Shahi association with Telangana was not simply political, but was translated into a series of engagements with the locality, and more so with local elites. We have seen that similarly to their peers in Bijapur and Ahmadnagar, the sultans of Golkonda operated within a framework that contained Foreigners and Deccanis. They accordingly employed both Persian and Dakhani languages and tropes in the production of their political language. The association of Qutb Shahi rule with Telangana and, no less important, its elites, introduced Telugu as an important component in Qutb Shahi political imagination. Eaton and Wagoner identify two important Telugu-speaking groups involved in state service. First were the *nāyakwaṛīs*, a class of military gentry. The *nāyakwaṛīs* operated within locality- and family-based networks, yet remained mobile throughout the eastern Deccan, from Berar in the north to Vijayanagara in the south. The second group comprised Niyogi Brahmins, who were employed in various positions of the administration, from village level to the royal court, in addition to diplomatic positions, as governors, and as advisers to the king.[9]

The association of the Telugu-speaking elites can be probably traced back to the first half of the sixteen century, although admittedly evidence is scarce. The ruler who pushed this process forward is Ibrahim Qutb

Shah (r. 1550–80). During the reign of his brother Jamshid (r. 1543–50), Ibrahim, fearing for his life, fled the sultanate. He sought refuge with Rama Raya in Vijayanagara, demonstrating once again that the neighbouring empire was considered part of the political world of the Deccan sultanates. Ibrahim is reported to have had a good knowledge of Telugu; it is not clear whether he spoke the language prior to his exile, knowledge that facilitated his choice, or became versed in that language during his time in Vijayanagara. In 1550, he returned to Telangana, and with the assistance of several *nāyakwaṟīs*, ascended the throne in Golkonda.[10]

The increasingly important role of local elites promoted the use of Telugu in state service. Royal patronage was extended to literary activity in Telugu. Velcheru Narayana Rao suggests that under the Qutb Shahi sultans, Telugu became a language of culture in the court, and poets in that language enjoyed direct patronage.[11] At least one work, *Tapati-Samvaranamu*, a Telugu adaptation of a scene from the Sanskrit epic of the *Mahabharata*, was directly commissioned by Ibrahim. Other poets enjoyed patronage, as manifested in an array of panegyric and, posthumously, eulogies for the sultan, emphasising his generosity.[12] This activity earned Ibrahim Qutb Shah the Telugu title *ibharāma ćakravartī* ('Great King Ibrahim'). Patronage was extended from the royal family to other members of the elites. Phillip Wagoner demonstrates that during Ibrahim's reign, a Muslim noble, Amin Khan, a scion of a long-standing Deccani Muslim family in Patancheru near Golkonda, gave his patronage to the Telugu poet Telaganarya. The connection between the two was made possible with the assistance of Amin Khan's personal secretary, Maringanti Appana, a member of a Niyogi family that was linked to Telugu literary circles. Amin Khan also established a tax-free village, an irrigation tank, and a grove for the benefit of local Brahmins.[13] His actions reflect a practice that stems from the twelfth century, according to which a man can have seven children: 'a son, a water tank, a poem, an endowment, a temple, a grove, and a Brahman settlement',[14] suggesting the continuation of local traditions and political idioms under Muslim patronage. Various forms of patronage continued under Ibrahim's son and successor, Muhammad Quli, otherwise associated primarily with production in Dakhani.[15]

The engagement with local sensitivities did not remain only in relation to the Telugu language, but ran more deeply. Telugu writings evoked certain historical memories in the Telugu lands. Particularly important was the memory of the Kakatiyas, the dynasty that greatly contributed to the spread of Telugu in Telangana and the first rulers to have extended their support to Telugu culture.[16] The continuation of Kakatiya memory

Locality, Vernacular and Political Language

in Telangana, particularly in and around their capital city of Warangal, is reflected in the production of texts dealing with the dynasty long after its collapse in 1323. One such text is *Prataparudra Caritramu* ('History of Prataparudra', the last Kakatiya ruler, although the text deals with the dynasty as a whole). Cynthia Talbot suggests that the text was composed in Telangana in the first half of the sixteenth century, when the region was contested by the 'Turkish Lord of the West' (that is, Bahmanis or Qutb Shahs), Vijayanagara and the Gajapatis of Orissa. Whereas the circumstances around the creation of the text are unclear, she argues that the most likely patron was one of the *nāyakwaṛī* lineages with past affiliations to the Kakatiyas. The text thus creates a link between the conditions around the time of the writing and a glorified memory of a former dynasty, the very same one that allowed the *nāyakwaṛī* to climb up the social ladder.[17]

Evoking Kakatiya memory gradually became part of the overall political language of early modern Telangana. Eaton and Wagoner demonstrate such persistence of historical memory in their analysis of Shitab Khan, local ruler of Warangal in the opening years of the sixteenth century, and the use he made of Kakatiya architecture in the historical capital.[18] We can speculate that the strong historical memory was made possible, at least in part, due to the continuous role of local administrators in the system such as those employed by Amin Khan. Furthermore, after the fall of the Kakatiyas, Telangana remained farther away from political centres. Delhi's secondary capital of Daulatabad or the Bahmani capitals of Gulbarga and Bidar are beyond the region's boundaries. Moreover, neither Delhi nor the Bahmanis could establish their firm control over the eastern Deccan.[19] Under these circumstances, it is likely that pre-Delhi memories remained vivid in Telangana until the Qutb Shahi conquest.

It seems, then, that the Kakatiya past found its way into the Qutb Shahi sultanate: *nāyakwaṛīs* continued to hold roles in the administration, and Qutb Shahi land policies followed, in part, Kakatiya precedence.[20] Golkonda fort itself may have been a Kakatiya or *nāyakwaṛī* settlement originally, integrated into the Bahmani sultanate in the 1360s. Kakatiya heritage is reflected in imagery of local affiliation appearing on buildings in Golkonda into late Qutb Shahi days.[21] Such symbolic continuity was most likely a conscious choice. Eaton and Wagoner argue that the Qutb Shahi sultans responded to Kakatiya heritage. Understanding the symbolic meaning and cosmological significance of Kakatiya-era Warangal, they chose to maintain its monuments.[22] Moreover, the same symbolism was drawn into the design of the new dynastic capital, Hyderabad, established by Muhammad Quli in 1591. Earlier historiography analysed Hyderabad as corresponding with trends in the Islamic world such as millenarian and messianic ideas in

Local States in an Imperial World

the sixteenth century in the construction of new capital cities.[23] Eaton and Wagoner, however, suggest that the plan of Hyderabad builds on the same Indic cosmology that can be found in Warangal. This plan was adapted to Islamic conventions by tilting its orientation from the cardinal direction to the direction of Mecca.[24] By that, Hyderabad symbolises the simultaneous trends of Qutb Shahi political language as containing both Indic and Islamic elements, relating at the same time to the local and the foreign.

The clear association of the rulers with both the Telugu language and the historical memory of Telangana created several limitations. First, the success of this political language appealed in Telangana alone. As we will discuss in more detail in the next chapter, Golkonda's attempts to expand beyond Telangana into other Telugu-speaking regions encountered significant resistance among local elites. Second, Telugu did not become the main secondary language of the state. In higher ranks of the administration, Marathi may have been the secondary language after Persian in official, state-level matters. This is suggested by the modest collection of Qutb Shahi *farmān*s (royal decrees), hosted at the Telangana (formerly Andhra Pradesh) State Archives. Among the fifty-nine documents in the collection, eleven are bilingual documents in Persian and Marathi, one solely in Marathi, and two trilingual documents in Persian, Marathi and Telugu. The rest are in Persian; none is solely in Telugu.[25] The number of documents does not allow a reliable statistical analysis, but the advantage of Marathi over Telugu is surprising, indicating the problem in classifying vernacular-speakers solely according to the territory with which they were identified. Elements within the administrative elites, such as certain groups of Brahmins, were not confined to vernacular spaces. Rather, as Narayana Rao suggests, some Brahmins were 'unusually mobile, in a sense uninterested in acquiring roots in any locality'.[26] Accordingly, Marathi-speaking Brahmins were active around the subcontinent.[27] The use of Marathi, however, does not seem to have spread in Golkonda beyond the very narrow role of central administration, hinting towards a diversification of language use for administrative purposes and not a challenge to vernacular-territorial identities as a whole.

In conclusion, throughout most of the sixteenth century and into the seventeenth century, the Qutb Shahi rulers demonstrated a continuous and multi-layered engagement with their immediate cultural and social environment. Self-styled rulers of Telangana, they positioned themselves at the heart of the region, whose historical legacy and memory, or parts thereof, they utilised in constructing their political language. Not only sultans, but also certain parts of the nobility, non-Muslims and Muslims alike, took part in this engagement. Central to this association was the Telugu language. The language did not monopolise administrative or political use, nor did it become dominant in political use. The sultanate remained diverse, multilingual, Islamicate and heavily Persianate, and even Marathi held roles that Telugu did not seem to have had. Nevertheless, the Telugu language, and not Marathi, was crucial in shaping the political idiom of the sultanate. The language was part of a wider Qutb Shahi engagement with the historical legacy of Telangana, in particular, with the memory of the Kakatiya past, manifested in patterns of patronage and public displays of state power. The rationale behind this engagement is clear, considering the important role that post-Kakatiya elites, in particular, *nāyakwaṛīs* and Niyogis, held within the state, and the need of the sultans to tie them to their endeavour. This strategy was deemed successful. While direct evidence is scant, it is clear that those elites remained by and large loyal to Golkonda, the history of which was less contested and disrupted than its neighbours to the west, to whom we will turn now.

The ᶜAdil Shahs of Bijapur: Kings of the Deccan

This pattern of sultanate-vernacular connection should not be assumed to have applied across the board. Compared with Golkonda's fairly straightforward narrative of vernacularisation, the development of Bijapur's political language is significantly more complicated and contested in many respects. Following the model devised by court chroniclers,[28] modern historiography is constructed with individual sultans as its main building blocks, each with his idiosyncrasies. One characteristic with which sultans were associated was their creed: the first two sultans, Yusuf ᶜAdil Khan (d. 1510) and Ismaᶜil (r. 1510–34) are identified as Shiite; Ibrahim ᶜAdil Shah I (r. 1535–58) was Sunni; ᶜAli I (r. 1558–80) was considered Shiite; and Ibrahim II (r. 1580–1627) again Sunni. The following reigns, those of Muhammad (r. 1627–56), ᶜAli II (r. 1656–72) and Sikandar (r. 1672–86), were more relaxed in terms of creed. Changing creed was combined with the grand-narrative of divided elite society we have discussed before; Shiism was associated with the Foreigners, Persian language and Persianate culture, and to some extent, with antipathy to Sufism and to Indic culture. The Sunni sultans were positioned as their mirror-image: they were linked to local elites, both Muslim and non-Muslim, vernaculars (Dakhani, Marathi, Kannada), and a sympathetic view of both Sufism and Indic culture.[29] The vision of Bijapur's history that followed, then, was profoundly different from Golkonda's. Instead of being continuous, inclusive, even harmonious, Bijapur's history was depicted as disrupted and fragmented, emphasising abrupt changes over gradual development. This narrative is problematic in several respects. It stresses the pivotal role of the sultan in setting the social, political and ideological direction of the state as a whole; somewhat of Great Man theory with a dash of Asiatic Despotism. It further implies that each group was monolithic in its views. But we can hardly assume cohesion within a group comprising such diverse elements as Sunni Muslims, Ethiopian slaves, Marathas and Kannada-speaking Brahmins; even the Foreigners were far from unified.

A more substantial problem emerges with regard to the relationship between the ʿAdil Shahi sultans and the vernaculars. If in Golkonda there was a clear candidate for the position of local vernacular, namely Telugu, in Bijapur the picture seems less clear-cut. On the administrative side, Marathi was used in state apparatus. Eaton suggests that from the days of Ibrahim I, lower levels of administration, including judicial and financial affairs, were run in Marathi, reflecting a growing reliance on local agents and, accordingly, increased integration of local communities.[30] This could explain the choice of Marathi over Dakhani, in itself a literary language with neither administrative tradition nor deep roots in rural communities. Following Hiroshi Fukazawa,[31] Eaton emphasises the use of Marathi, a reasonable feature as the cases he examines took place in Marathi-speaking regions in the northern part of the sultanate. It is, however, not clear whether Kannada was used in the administration of the southern regions. Furthermore, no evidence for literary patronage of either Marathi or Kannada by Bijapur's elites is noted.[32]

This lacuna, however, highlights a more substantial question: with which vernacular could Bijapur be associated? The sultanate's core region was divided between Marathi- and Kannada-speaking regions. Moreover, the historical and symbolic centres associated with either vernacular fell outside Bijapur's territory until well into the seventeenth century. The Yadava capital of Devgiri was an important political and military centre of Ahmadnagar, later to move to Mughal hands. The Hoysala centres, too, were far beyond Bijapur's reach. The Hoysala capital of Dwarasamudra (Halebidu) is located more than 350 km south to Bijapur, in Vijayanagara's territory. Furthermore, Hoysala historical memory became part of Vijayanagara's imperial foundations.[33] In short, while Golkonda–Telangana–Warangal–Telugu reflects historical continuity, no such vernacular connection was possible in the case of Bijapur regarding either Marathi and Kannada.

This complexity notwithstanding, the sultanate became immersed in the locality. Gradually and continuously, the ʿAdil Shahi sultans intensified their links with Indic culture, and incorporated local tropes and ideas into their political language. Based on the different circumstances, the

Locality, Vernacular and Political Language

shape this engagement took was profoundly different from neighbouring Golkonda. In the following section I examine the crystallisation of the political languages in Bijapur until the reign of Ibrahim ᶜAdil Shah II. This engagement will be analysed in relation to two major questions: first, that of continuity, and, second, is the issue of vernacularisation. I argue that unlike the Qutb Shahi sultanate of Golkonda, no argument of vernacularisation can be convincingly made for Bijapur. Instead, the ᶜAdil Shahi sultans turned to another avenue of Indic culture, which focused on transregional identities. Similarly to their contemporaries, such association was promoted by adopting pre-existing tropes, past and present: first, relating to the Western Chalukyas, whose ruined capital city of Kalyani fell within the territory of the sultanate and in a similarly vernacular-ambiguous region. After the Battle of Talikota, another line emerged, linking Bijapur directly to Vijayanagara, which itself used Chalukya memory in constructing its imperial identity. This imperial line adopted in Bijapur could further support its expansionist zeal in several directions.

THE FORMATION OF ᶜADIL SHAHI IDENTITY

Yusuf ᶜAdil Shah, founder of the dynasty, was a Turkic migrant from western Iran. Rising to power in the factional environment of the late Bahmani Sultanate, it is not surprising that he leaned towards the Foreigners. Elite society maintained its blend of locals and Foreigners, leading to occasional struggles and rapid changes from the beginning of Ismaᶜil's reign. For the most part the Foreigners had the upper hand.[34] An interesting, even if dubious, depiction of Ismaᶜil's inclination was presented by Fuzuni. The chronicler states that the sultan 'was born in the Deccan, and has never seen any other country. He had a good grasp of Persian, Turkish, and other languages, but was not at all inclined towards Indian Languages'.[35] He further attributes the following monologue to the sultan:

> When I was a little boy (*ṭifl*), my illustrious father sent Khwaja Sultan Muhammad Kashi to the town of Sava[36] to invite our relatives, and to propose my paternal aunt (*ᶜamma*), Malika Agha, to come to this country. Soon, she travelled to India with her household. She brought along many Georgian and Circassian slave boys and girls (*ghulām wa kanīz*); [consequently] Indian servants were excluded [from service]. She was put in charge of my education: when I turned six, I was sent to school. One Mulla taught [me] the Persian language; Turkish tutors (*ataka wa anaka*) – the reputable Turkish language. I was prevented from mixing with the people of India and from sharing their language to the degree that in my council (*majlis*), no one could use any

language other than Turkish or Persian. When my father passed away, state affairs were entrusted in the able hands of Muhammad Aqa, who knew the language of India (*zabān-i hindī*) well. He translated whatever he heard in that language into Turkish for me. Therefore, by nature, I am not inclined towards the company of Indians, nor am I content with their looks or their voices.[37]

The excerpt reflects past memory of the early dynasty: its origins and the sultan's education led, eventually, to his heavy reliance on one element in elite society and on one cultural strand. Written more than a century after the sultan's death, and with the absence of sources from Ismaᶜil's reign, this monologue should be read with a pinch of salt. Yet it may reflect a memory of contested times, in which the royal family had a clear preference.

This inclination clearly changed during the reign of Ismaᶜil's son, Ibrahim I. Often depicted as reversing his father's policies, Ibrahim I's reign is identified with the shifting of focus towards the Deccanis, while dismissing most Foreigners from his service except for a powerful few. This policy continued with the introduction of Brahmins in local administration and the changing of the language used for revenue and judicial records from Persian to vernaculars, namely, Marathi or Kannada.[38] On another note, Ibrahim finally expressed independent aspiration as he promoted his official title from the noble ᶜAdil Khan to the royal ᶜAdil Shah. This change is likely associated with the death of the last of the Bahmani sultans, Kalimullah, in 944/1537–8,[39] relieving the dynasty from the long shadow of their former sovereigns and allowing it to experiment more freely with its political idiom.

Some of the steps taken by Ibrahim I, however, were not without precedence. Brahmins and other non-Muslims had served the Bahmanis,[40] suggesting that Ibrahim's reforms followed a path already known in the Deccan. Yet the sultan may have taken all this a step forward. Similarly to what we have seen in Golkonda, in Bijapur, too, the increasing inclusion of local elites was accompanied by, and probably directly influenced, a growing interest in local traditions, historical memory and political language. This new interest was not merely a way to reorient the sultanate to be more inclusive of local elites. Rather, it served as part of a larger effort to find a political idiom for the sultanate as a whole. An interesting attempt along these lines was linking the sultanate with a broader Deccani idiom. Analysing the southern gateway to Bijapur's citadel (built 1538–44), Eaton and Wagoner suggest that the structure was meant to evoke the memory of the long defunct Western Chalukya Empire. The use of inscriptions referring to the best-known emperors of the dynasty, Someshvara II and Vikramaditya VI, as well as Chalukya-era columns reflects intentional manipulation at a highly visible (and symbolic) point, leading to the official seat of ʿAdil Shahi power. In this, Ibrahim recruited imperial idioms of the Deccani past to galvanise local credibility to his reign.[41]

The local idiom was not a quirk of an idiosyncratic ruler. Once introduced into the political idiom, it became a permanent, even if never the sole, component of the language of the sultanate, one that lived across reigns. Ibrahim's son and successor, ʿAli I, presents such change. His Shiite inclinations are believed to stand behind his father's reluctance to declare him his successor. The same ideology was attributed to ʿAli's preference to employ Foreigners.[42] In the historiography of the Deccan, such choice marked him as anti-Deccani, anti-Sufi and anti-Indic, if not outright anti-Hindu, along the lines presented in his grandfather's aforementioned monologue-in-retrospect. Such abrupt change, however, does not seem to have been the case.

During ʿAli's reign, state power expanded considerably, in particular, after the Battle of Talikota in 1565. With new resources and confidence, the sultan embarked on a major construction campaign in his capital, including building a new defensive wall around the city; waterworks, based on an underground system to store and distribute water; and a monumental congregational mosque.[43] Built and presented as a collective effort of the royal house and the nobles, the construction linked the elites to the state, shaping the city and its legacies of patronage as a joint endeavour.[44] Evidence suggests that the diversity of his nobility persisted throughout his reign. One inscription, found above a postern gate, states that it was built during the reign of ʿAli ʿAdil Shah by Pandit Nandji (or Baid Panditji) in 976/1568–9. Below the Persian inscription, a ritual gate from the Chalukya period was reinstated, resonating with the gateway constructed by Ibrahim I.[45] Another inscription found on one of the bastions reads as follows:

> No hero like ʿAli! No sword like Dhu al-Fiqar (*lā fata illā ʿalī; lā sayf illā dhū al-fiqār*)! The foundations of this fortification of the Refuge of the World (*jahān-panāh*) were laid during the reign of Shah ʿAli ʿAdil Shah. Constructed by Jagdi Rao, son of Jagdi Rao on 1 Muḥarram 969.[46]

While the builder of the bastion, Jagdi (Jagadeva?) Rao, was a Hindu, the inscription begins with a talismanic formula identified with Shiism, praising ʿAli, the namesake of the sultan, and his sword. This odd pairing may reflect the politicisation of Shiite idiom and its talismanic value, rather than any confessional preference. Furthermore, it should be noted that the language of the inscription is Persian; it is doubtful whether such a phrase would have appeared in Marathi.

Local States in an Imperial World

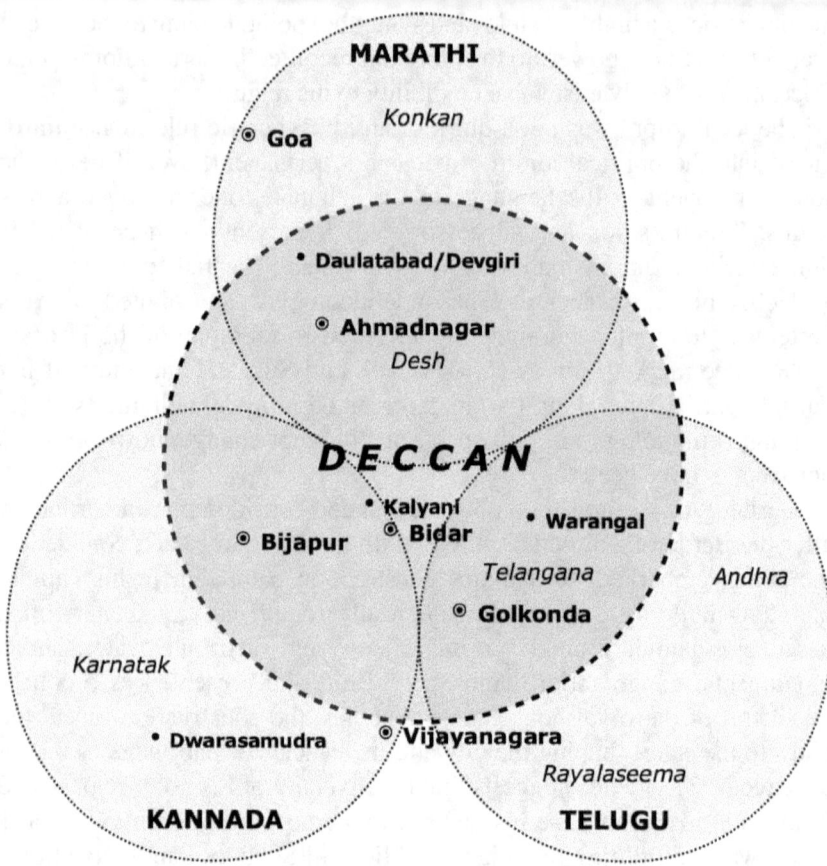

Figure 4.1 Political and cultural centres in the Deccani regions

Pandit Nandji and Jagdi Rao were not alone in their association with the realm. During the reign of ᶜAli I, other Hindus served in high positions. One was the general (*sar-i khayl*) and auditor-general (*majmūᶜ-i mamālik*) Daso Pandit, Brahmin by name. The personal library of the sultan, too, with which he was intimately engaged, was administered by a Brahmin named Sheh Waman, son of Anant Pandit.[47] This evidence is dated from late in ᶜAli's reign, suggesting that Brahmin officials were not simply inherited from his father's reign, but their position was conferred by ᶜAli – or maybe they were even appointed by him. Furthermore, there is no evidence of change in the linguistic trends set by Ibrahim, such as the return to Persian as the sole language of administration. We can therefore assume continuation in the engagement with local elites.

Ali's links with local elites were not solely utilitarian. A deeper engagement is expressed in a curious legacy from his reign, a work titled *Nujum al-ᶜUlum*. The exact date of this composition remains unknown, but it can be confidently associated with ᶜAli's reign, and no later than 1570. Recently, Emma Flatt has established that the author was likely to have been ᶜAli I himself.⁴⁸ The *Nujum* is an innovative astrological encyclopaedia that brings together knowledge from Islamic and Indic concepts, mystic and esoteric alongside mainstream ones. The numerous illustrations (the Chester Beatty Library manuscript contains some eight hundred) similarly combine stylistic elements of the various traditions: Indic, Hellenic, Central Asian, Persian and Islamic. Special attention in the work is given to ideas of kingship. The work identifies the sultan as universal ruler (*ćakravartin*, similar to the Telugu title given to Ibrahim Qutb Shah), emphasising the seven attributes and objects associated with the concept, for example, the seven-storeyed throne. The visual language of the *Nujum* is linked to both Islamic convention and Indic iconography. It presents an intercultural exchange of both form and content, reflecting the composite nature of the environment in which the text was created.⁴⁹ The text goes beyond presenting a simple image of a composite culture. Flatt suggests that ᶜAli I promoted another layer of claims of authority, linked to astrological association with certain geographies in the Deccan. This association allowed the sultan to promote his sovereignty over particular territories that at the time of the composition fell either north of his kingdom (in regions ruled by Berar or Ahmadnagar) or to its south (Vijayanagara).⁵⁰ This view may be a reflection of a nascent claim of authority over the entirety of the western Deccan – and also an admission of the geographical weakness of ᶜAdil Shahi regional claims. This assumption is reasonable considering ᶜAdil Shahi engagement with the Chalukya past, or, as we will see momentarily, with Vijayanagara. Eaton and Wagoner suggest a similar engagement under ᶜAli, when a Chalukya-era temple in newly conquered Bankapur was converted into a mosque, while maintaining its original form. This, they suggest, was intended to connect the current rulers with local pasts and memories.⁵¹ Links to the past may have been a wider phenomenon in ᶜAli's Bijapur. Katherine Butler Schofield suggests that Shangadeva's *Sangitaratnakara*, a major musical treatise composed in Sanskrit at the Yadava court in Devgiri, was translated into Dakhani around 1570.⁵²

ᶜAli's Shiism, then, did not curtail his desire to engage with Indic culture and Hindu elites. Another association that was questioned due to his creed was his link with Sufism. Modern historiography often emphasises the hostility between Shiites and Sufis. This notion is tied to the analysis of Ottoman–Safavid relations, the way in which each dynasty constructed its past and identity, the place of Sufis in that debate, and the growing hostility towards Sufis in the Safavid realm.[53] Deccani historiography often follows these lines of Shiite–Sufi antipathy. Eaton, for example, suggests that migration of Sufis into the Deccan almost ceased during what he calls Bijapur's 'Shia period' (1490–1583), only to resume early in the reign of the Sunni Ibrahim ᶜAdil Shah II.[54] While the evidence upon which he bases this assumption is solid, Eaton's interpretation that the ruler's creed in Bijapur determined Sufi migration to Bijapur is debatable. During the long reign of the Sunni Ibrahim I, no significant settlement of Sufis in Bijapur is noted.

Furthermore, the very idea of Shiite–Sufi hostility seems foreign to the Deccan, where Sufis were central to political life from the very beginning of Muslim rule.[55] Deborah Hutton notes that in a painting, titled *Dervish Receiving a Visitor*, produced late in the reign of Ibrahim II, a Sufi shrine is depicted with Shiite standards (*ᶜalam*) on its side.[56] Throughout the Deccan, funerary monuments of both Sunni and Shiite rulers were located by the side of Sufi tombs, following the Bahmani model.[57] The first two ᶜAdil Shahi sultans, the allegedly avid Shiite Yusuf and Ismaᶜil, as well as Ibrahim I, were buried in a funerary site in Gogi, near the resting place of the Sufi Shaykh Chanda Husayni (d. 1454).[58] In the unequivocally Shiite Golkonda, too, similar Shiite–Sufi association can be observed. Sufis were second only to the sultans in the prominent place given to their tombs in the necropolis near Golkonda Fort, and the tombs shared similar architecture. By this, the sultans aspired to turn themselves to focus worthy of veneration. Furthermore, marital connection existed between Qutb Shahi sultans and prominent Sufis.[59] It seems, then, that Shiite–Sufi links were profoundly different in the Deccan than in Safavid Iran, regardless of the creed of the ruler.[60] ᶜAli I himself worked within this frame of Shiite–Sufi amity. The sultan was interested in, and associated with, Sufis.[61] His mausoleum moved away from Gogi to Bijapur, yet reflects continuity as this modest building was modelled after Gogi's royal mausolea.[62] ᶜAli's mausoleum was built near, and in association with, the tombs of Qadiri Sufis.[63]

Considering the depth of this involvement with both Indic and Sufi ideas and elites, ᶜAli I's interest in the Deccani environment was beyond mere realpolitik. Operating in a setting that encouraged engagement with the local in various forms, inherited from his predecessor, ᶜAli defies the historiographical tradition regarding Shiite rulers in Bijapur. This engagement, however, was quite different from that presented by his contemporary, Ibrahim Qutb Shah of Golkonda. In contrast to the neighbouring sultanate, the vernacular and the geographical and historical memory accompanying it did not play any significant role in the development of this Indic-infused political language of Bijapur. Rather, ᶜAli I, much like Ibrahim I before him, preferred to engage with the non- (or even pre-) vernacular imperial past of the western Deccan, linking him to a general Indic line, or more particularly to the Western Chalukyas, instead of the vernacular-identified Yadavas or Hoysalas. This direction suggests that ᶜAli's reign should be seen as a stage in the development and crystallisation of Bijapur's political language as a force in the Deccan, a link in a chain that was carried from Ibrahim I, and not a reversal thereof.

Towards New Political Language: **Nauras** *and Vijayanagara's Memory*

The assassination of the childless ᶜAli I created a succession crisis in Bijapur. In order to keep the stability of the realm, a group of nobles decided to nominate ᶜAli's nephew, son of his brother Tahmasp. As Ibrahim ᶜAdil Shah II (r. 1580–1627) was a child at the time of his accession, the first decade of his reign saw a series of struggles between nobles, with the widow of ᶜAli I, Chand Bibi, serving as Ibrahim's guardian. Constant change of regents, mostly Deccani and Ethiopian, and discontent among Foreigners, prompted Ahmadnagar and Golkonda to invade, but with only limited success. By the second half of the 1580s, the situation had markedly improved, cemented by a series of marriage alliances: Ibrahim II married Chand Sultana, sister of Muhammad Quli Qutb Shah of Golkonda, and his sister, Khadija Sultana, married Husayn Nizam Shah II of Ahmadnagar. Around the same time, Chand Bibi returned to her ancestral Ahmadnagar, leaving him under the guardianship of his mother Makhduma-i Jahan until his coming of age.[64]

One of the first changes associated with the early reign of Ibrahim II was his choice to abandon his father's Shiite beliefs in favour of Sunni Islam. Similarly to the historiography discussing his ancestors, Ibrahim's new creed, too, brought scholars to assume a complete change of policies, including preference of Deccanis and the neglect of Foreigners, diminishing interest in the Persian language and Persianate culture in favour of Dakhani and Indic culture, growing localisation, and increased interest in Sufis.[65] This interest is reflected in a visit to the tomb of the Sufi Muhamad Husayni, Khwaja Banda Nawaz Gisu Daraz in Gulbarga, the most important Sufi shrine in the Deccan.[66] Under Ibrahim's reign, courtly culture demonstrated an interest in Deccani and Indic themes, styles and directions. For example, the original Sufi romance *Pem Nem* was composed during his reign. Hutton links paintings in this text's manuscript to the development of yogini paintings, indicating a courtly culture in which various cultural systems were at play. The language of mysticism, both Sufism and Bhaktism, was expressed in tandem: a few of Ibrahim's portraits link him to the world of Hindu devotionalism (four strands of *rudrākṣa*, dried berry beads around his neck) and Saivite traditions (castanets).[67] Affinities with local idioms can be seen also in his early architecture, for example, a seven-storeyed residential extension of the royal palace, known as Seven Storey Palace (*haft mahal* or *sāt manzil*), built in Bijapur's citadel sometime in the 1580s. Mark Brand suggests that the 'seven-storey palaces articulated levels of the heavenly realm in Indian tradition, suggesting royal divine blessing'.[68] We have seen similar symbolism in the seven-storeyed throne illustrated in the *Nujum al-ʿUlum*. The link between palaces and the seven heavens (*gagan sāt*) is made clear in ʿAbdul Dihlawi's description of a later palace from Ibrahim's reign.[69] All this reflects significant symbolic continuation from the reign of ʿAli I to Ibrahim II.

Ibrahim II, his ideology, cultural affinities, writing and musical association still await an in-depth investigation. Here I will focus on limited aspects of his actions and personality to highlight the general directions the political language of the state took during his reign. An important manifestation of Ibrahim's ideas is the appearance of the term *nauras*, a concept most associated with that sultan. A full analysis of its meaning is beyond the scope of the current study, however, as it reflects central issues in Ibrahim's reign and was used so widely to mark his ideology, it deserves some attention. The earliest mention of this term is on a seal inscribed *Ibrahim nauras* from 1586, bringing Keelan Overton to question the agency of the young sultan in introducing the concept.[70] Nevertheless, the term became synonymous with Ibrahim. Its meaning alludes to two cultural traditions in tandem. In Persian, *nauras* means 'newly arrived', reflecting the youth and innovation of the sultan and, in one story, also refers to fresh wine. In Sanskrit, *nauras* (or *nava rasa*), nine *rasa*s, refer to emotional essences. The nine *rasa*s are strongly associated with music and are experienced through the senses.[71] The term was attached to a variety of elements. Zubayri lists, among others, the standard (*ʿalam*) and seal (*nishān*); small coins, remembered until the composition time in the early nineteenth century as *fils-i nauras*; bands (*ṭawāʾif*) of storytellers and players. Literary works dedicated to the sultan were known by that name, including Zuhuri's *Dibacha-i Nauras* and Firishta's chronicle, one of whose names is *Naurasnama-i Firishta*. The poet ʿAbd al-Qadir took the pen-name Naurasi.[72] To this list we can add a bastion in Gulbarga Fort.[73] A particularly important use of this term is as the title of Ibrahim's own compilation, *Kitab-i Nauras*, attributed to the sultan himself. This Dakhani compilation is a musical composition, comprising fifty-nine songs and

Locality, Vernacular and Political Language

seventeen couplets. This work demonstrates the sultan's expertise in Indian music (in particular, the Hindustani Dhrupad), and reflects aesthetics and themes related to Indic poetry.[74] In accordance with the Sanskritic interpretation of this term, the number nine carried significant meaning, and was used widely: the gold currency *nauras hūn* was equal to nine *hūn*; a nine-sided palace was constructed in Nauraspur, as we will see momentarily; the king ascended the throne at the convenient age of nine, which may be a symbolic age (the exact date of birth is not indicated). Zuhuri attribute nine virtues to the sultan, referring to his: (1) religious character: divine knowledge (*ma'rifat*), a term often used in Sufi contexts; adherence to Shiite teachings, to which we will return later; (2) kingly nature: pomp; justice (*'adālat*), referring to the name of the dynasty; bravery; munificence; (3) his personal characteristics: beauty; good nature; and acquiring excellence.[75] Overall, the use of the term *nauras* reflects the systematic thinking of the message, values and images of the sultan, cleverly linking two traditions into one political idiom.

BIJAPUR, BIDYAPUR AND NAURASPUR

As part of his manifestation of political language, the sultan redesigned his seat of power. First, he changed the name of Bijapur ('City of Victory') to Bidyapur ('City of Knowledge').[76] Widely acknowledged in the scholarship, the explanation for this change remained limited to Ibrahim's ideas. However, other than an unconvincing attempt by Meadows Taylor, there was no serious effort to link this change to local tradition.[77] Similar changes of name had happened before, not in Bijapur but in Vijayanagara. K. A. Nilakanta Sastri states that with the establishment of their independent state in 1336, the Sangama brothers gave their capital two names, Vijayanagara and Vidyanagara (meaning 'City of Victory' and 'City of Knowledge', respectively), the latter to commemorate the role of the teacher and scholar Vidyaranya in its foundation.[78] Henry Heras rejects this link, arguing that the inscriptional references to Vidyanagara are dated to the sixteenth century.[79] If we accept Heras' opinion, the proximity of the appearance of the Vidyanagara tradition suggests the possibility that renaming Bijapur is associated with that of Vijayanagara.

Firmer links to the symbolic value of Vijayanagara arise from another endeavour initiated by Ibrahim II in his capital, namely, the construction of Nauraspur ('City of *nauras*'), a suburb of Bijapur. Started in 1599 under the supervision of the Iranian minister Shah Nawaz Khan, and populated a mere few years after, Nauraspur was designed to be larger than Bijapur itself; the wall, if completed, would have enclosed an area one and a half times the size of the old city.[80] Its size and importance notwithstanding, Nauraspur presents a frustrating challenge. Construction has never been completed. Buildings that had been completed were destroyed when the city was sacked by Ahmadnagar's general Malik Ambar in 1624.[81] Similarly to the physical evidence, textual records are scarce and far between. Court poems such as Zuhuri's *Khwan-i khalil* and ᶜAbdul's *Ibrahimnama* provide lofty and panegyric descriptions. While adding insights to our understanding of Ibrahim's cultural and political imagination and their projection, by themselves inscribed into city space, they do not provide much information regarding its actual structure and function of the suburb.[82]

Ibrahim's two court chroniclers provide more detailed evidence of the city. Firishta describes the construction of a palace (*qaṣr*) with open space in front (*peshgāh*), beside an octagonal (*muthamman*) structure, named *nauras-bihisht* ('Paradise-like *nauras*'). Additional grand buildings, a market and gardens are also mentioned.[83] The chronicler describes it as part of Bijapur rather than a separate suburb. The similarity between this description and the archaeological remains and his use of the name *nauras-bihisht*, however, suggest that Firishta indeed describes the beginnings of Nauraspur. As the section dealing with the ᶜAdil Shahi dynasty ends abruptly in 1601, Firishta provides no additional details.[84] This leaves only one contemporary account: Shirazi's *Tadhkirat al-Muluk*, completed in 'the sacred City of Nauras' in 1615.[85] Two later reports, Fuzuni's *Futuhat-i ᶜAdil Shahi* and Zubayri's *Basatin al-Salatin*, relied heavily on Shirazi's reports, but altered the text according to their own ideological programme; we will return to this point later.

The meagre sources, then, allow us only a limited understanding of Nauraspur. Yet, treading carefully, several conclusions can be drawn, even if somewhat speculatively. First, it is clear that Nauraspur was not intended to replace Bijapur, but to work in tandem with the capital. Hutton demonstrates that construction activity continued in Bijapur throughout the 1590s–1620s. She further suggests a differentiation of function between the two cities: Bijapur served as the formal political capital, whereas Nauraspur hosted artistic and ceremonial activities.[86] Shah Nawaz Khan and other nobles constructed mansions and gardens in both cities.[87] Bijapur and Nauraspur were linked by a commercial road, which became the central market of the growing urban agglomeration. Remains of this market were described by Henry Cousens in the late nineteenth century,[88] bearing witness to the accuracy of Shirazi's reports.

The details so far suggest nothing out of the ordinary in Nauraspur. Fuzuni explained its construction as a common practice:

Locality, Vernacular and Political Language

> Every sultan of my era built his own city. For example, Sher Shah Afghan [built] Shergarh (Purana Qila, Delhi); Akbar – Akbarabad, known as Agra; [The Safavid Shah] Tahmasp [built] Tehran . . . Shah ᶜAbbas [I] – Farahabad in Mazandaran; and Muhammad Quli Qutb Shah built Bagnagar (Hyderabad).
>
> [Couplet:] The kings, erecting their reign with crown, throne, and seal-ring// each built a country and set an abode where he dwells.[89]

The chronicler links Nauraspur to a common practice in the early modern Muslim East. While this practice was, indeed, commonplace, Nauraspur cannot be understood merely as an Islamic city. Similarly to Hyderabad, which was started only eight years earlier, Nauraspur was founded within a particular political and cultural setting and with a certain set of traditions in mind.

An intriguing innovation in Nauraspur is its water facilities. In the semi-arid environment of the Deccan Plateau, where most annual rain falls within only a few months, water infrastructure is crucial for the development of settlements.[90] A major improvement introduced by ᶜAli I was the expansion of storage and distribution systems, following the Iranian technology of underground canals (*qanāt*).[91] The remains from his reign, usually minor in scale, were built with the involvement of members of the royal family and other nobility, similarly to Bijapur's city wall.[92] Ibrahim upscaled his uncle's efforts. Shirazi reports that:

> For uninterrupted supplies, water pools were constructed; long, wide, and firm dams were built. On top of the dams, buildings were erected. Behind the dams, massive quantities of soil were dug out and [the reservoir] was deepened so that in the rainy season, it would be filled with water from the river. Below the dam, for about one *farsakh* (approx. 5 km), many built gardens. The construction of mosques was ordered; they were mostly completed (*wa akthar ba-itmām rasīda*). Big wells were dug. As the soil is rocky, [Nauraspur's] water is praiseworthy for its purity, sweetness and wholesomeness. A river flows near the sacred city of Nauras, called Dun(?). In the rainy season, it flows rapidly and forcefully. A royal order was issued to divert it to run through the City of Nauras in order to fill up the adjacent reservoir.[93]

The reservoir described is likely to be Ramling Tank, northwest of Bijapur, one of only two major tanks around the ᶜAdil Shahi capital.[94] This assumption is supported by Cousens' survey map, which shows that the Ramling Tank is, indeed, located downstream on a river that runs through Nauraspur.[95]

The construction of a major dam is undoubtedly related to the actual need to provide the expanding urban settlements with water for drinking and irrigation. Yet utilitarian understating does not reflect the entire picture. Julia Hegewald argues that a pleasure garden was laid around

Ramling Tank and water gardens were constructed behind the dam,[96] an analysis that agrees with Shirazi's description. Furthermore, the very choice of damming technology is intriguing. Analysing the waterworks in Bidar, Klaus Rötzer and Pushkar Sohoni establish a connection between water architecture, local history, social change and technical knowledge, linking migrants from Iran with types of waterworks new to the Deccan such as *qanāts*.[97] Elsewhere, Sohoni suggests an interplay between Indic and Persianate traditions in the creation of the sophisticated water system in Ahmadnagar.[98] A transition from *qanāt* to damming technology in Bijapur at that moment may be indicative of another source of inspiration.

Dams and reservoirs have long been part of the landscape in the Deccan. Burton Stein points out that the need to manage land and water supplies were important factors in the development of social and political systems.[99] Consequently, the construction of tanks was considered a meritorious religious act. This importance added an ideological and political dimension to construction activities, as demonstrated by Talbot in relation to Kakatiya kings and local chieftains in Telangana.[100] In Vijayanagara, the construction of dams and large tanks was widely practised, and their dominance in the landscape was noted by travellers who visited the city.[101] Kathleen Morrison and Carla Sinopoli note that reservoirs and other water facilities in the metropolitan region of Vijayanagara were built on a large scale, with rulers financing the larger projects, expected to yield hefty profits and economic expansion. The intensification of agriculture and settlement, alongside infrastructure such as reservoirs and canals, was conducted either directly by rulers or by way of endowments to temples, which served as centres of agricultural and economic development, political power and ritual.[102]

This link between dams and just kingship was noticed by Shirazi (albeit temples were left aside). Discussing Krishnadevaraya (r. 1509–29), the most iconic king of Vijayanagara, he writes that:

> He was a wise (*ᶜāqil*) and just (*ᶜādil*) king. Muslim commanders (*umarā*) who raised the suspicion of the Kings of Islam sought shelter with Krishna Raya, and enjoyed his promotion and patronage. As long as they ate salt (i.e., were his dependents) and remained under his protection, they did not diverge from his well-wishing and devotion. A river flows through his kingdom, passing between two hills. He built a firm dam there, nearly one *farsakh* (approx. 5 km) long, 60 *dirᶜa* (yard) wide, and 35 *dirᶜa* deep. [The dam] holds a large reservoir (*daryācha*), 30 *farsakh* long; there were seven hills in this reservoir, and twelve villages were sunk in its water. Until these days, the water in the reservoir is clear, pure, and sweet. There is vast land below [the dam], and a river that always flows (throughout the year); if one is to cultivate these lands,

Locality, Vernacular and Political Language

the region could yields lakhs (*lakūk*) [in revenue]. But the dam remained incomplete.[103]

For Shirazi, two issues characterise Krishnadevaraya as a just king. First, is sheltering Muslim commanders who were not treated well by their Muslims sovereigns. By that, the chronicler incorporates the king of Vijayanagara into values associated with Muslim kingship, using the titles *ᶜāqil* and *ᶜādil* and promoting notions of salt and shelter, similarly to the titles he employs to describe the rulers of Bijapur; after all, justice (*ᶜadālat*) was one of the nine virtues attributed to Ibrahim.[104] In addition, Shirazi's description of dams in Vijayanagara and Bijapur is remarkably similar. The author further links dams and prosperity when mentioning the completion of the same dam under Rama Raya.[105] Indeed, the first half of the sixteenth century saw a peak in the construction of dams in Vijayanagara.[106] Similar sentiment appears in an inscription on an impressive dam, 195 m long, built during the reign of Ibrahim II in 1022/1613–14 in Naldurg. Located in a region contested between Bijapur and Ahmadnagar,[107] the dam was constructed in the name of 'the king, refuge of religion' (*shāh-i dīn-panāh*), with a political message: 'by looking at it, the eyes of the friends brighten and the eyes of enemies are blinded'.[108] The evidence suggests that similarly, and possibly in direct relation to Vijayanagara, under Ibrahim II damming became associated with prosperity and kingship, a characteristic shared by the sultan and the *rāya*. Dams, then, promoted a political message in the language of the Deccan, understood in Bijapur and Vijayanagara alike.

ᶜID-I NAURAS

Nauraspur was used as a ceremonial space, where public festivals were held. Most important in that regard was ᶜId-i Nauras. Shirazi, our sole eyewitness, reports that :

> Friday that falls on the ninth day of the month is called ᶜĪd-i Nauras. Many celebrations take place on that day. An assembly (*majlis*) is held, to which the general public (*ᶜāmm*) are admitted. [Performers] sing, recite and orate to show their thanksgiving; in that country, the nobles (*khāṣṣ*) call them *ᶜaṭāʾī* ('gifted ones'), and the commoners (*ᶜāmm*) – *guṇījān* ('those full of virtue'). Nobles and commoners arrive, joining in rows. To acknowledge the honour of their service, they momentary stop playing *sāz*, song (*naghma*) and melody (*āhang*), sit down according to order (*be-tartīb*), then resume their chatter. Musk, saffron, and other perfumes are scattered in abundance. Trays upon trays of fruits of any kind are stacked upon one another for all to take as many as they can carry. Plenty of food is distributed in the *majlis*. Dignitaries, nobles,

military chiefs, ʿaṭāʾī, and dancers (kūn-jumbān), who are [Ibrahim's] distinguished disciples, sit in groups according to proximity and rank. When they finish eating, they arise [and leave], and another group come in. When all are satisfied, the [other] disciples, servants, and the poor take as much as they can. A palace was built, tall and magnificent; in its courtyard stands a pool. The palace is named Nauras Mahal, where the assembly is held. On the last day, many of His Majesty's people and disciples arrive. His agents, who were sent to the provinces, are asked to attend on that day. They are presented with robes of honour, and set to go [back]. Endless presents of money, articles, items inlaid with gold and jewellery (muraṣṣaʿ ālāt) and villages are gifted. The army of the Nauras recite, sing, and play their instruments.[109]

ʿId-i Nauras appears to be a public royal festival, aimed at confirming the sultan's axial role in the kingdom as a benevolent provider of nourishment, gifts and employment. Central to the festival is the affirmation of social and political hierarchies, expressed in terms of proximity, rank, order of attendance and eating, and etiquette. Of special political importance was the last day, when provincial office-holders attended the court to receive robes and gifts, demonstrating the sultan's control throughout his domains.

Certain elements are familiar from other early modern Muslim settings. The physical manifestation of order is similar to the Mughal court (darbār), most notably under Shah Jahan.[110] Distribution of food, robes of honour and precious presents, as well as the physical manifestation of obedience and hierarchy have also been practised widely.[111] Other elements, however, are less familiar in other Muslim courts. First, is the timing: the event took place on irregular occasions, when Friday falls on the ninth day of the month; which calendar is not designated. As the timing possibly links the Muslim sanctity of the Friday with the number nine, the symbolic element in Ibrahim's *nauras*, it is possible that the calendar is the Muslim Hijri one. Second, is the location: the festival was celebrated in the purpose-built Nauras Mahal in the epicentre of Nauraspur. The Nauras Mahal is enclosed in a courtyard with, again, nine equal sides (possibly can be identified with what Firishta described, probably erroneously, as an octagonal court). The building is identical to Gagan Mahal, ʿAli I's main audience hall in Bijapur's citadel.[112] Third, Shirazi does not provide exact details, but mentioning the last day, implies that the celebration was a multi-day affair. Four, while located in the royal part of town, the festival was open to the public, who could come to the centre of Nauraspur to see the ruler. This action may bear resemblance to the practice of *darśan* (the act of seeing the deity, integral to Hindu worship), known to carry political significance in the Mughal Empire.[113]

Locality, Vernacular and Political Language

Taken together, the components of ʿId-i Nauras suggest a peculiar festival, not familiar in other Muslim courts in India or elsewhere. While it is tempting to understand the festival as yet another one of Ibrahim's idiosyncrasies, such an extravagant public event is likely to be based on familiar idioms to render it significant in its particular political setting. Here again we can mark a potential link to Vijayanagara and the main public royal festival of the sixteenth-century Deccan: the Mahanavami (or Navaratri). This autumnal festival lasted nine days, followed by the Dasara. Its political significance derived from the link it provided between kingship and ritual. It combined, first, a public court (*darbār*), in which royal gifts were exchanged with members of the nobility; second, ritual elements, centred around *darśan* and *pūjā* (worship) of the royal deity; and, third, processions which included music and dance. Nine pavilions were erected for these events. The king presided over the celebrations from a raised decorated throne, which he sometimes shared with an image of the deity. This incorporative ritual, to use Stein's phrase, associated the king with Rama (the focus of Vijayanagara's Mahanavami), presenting the king as a warrior and as the source of riches under the god's protection. Bihani Sarkar further suggests that using ritual that was shared between king and subjects, the festival made royal/temporal power sacred.[114] Two loci were at the focus of the festival: the private Ramachandra Temple and the public Mahanavami Platform, a highly decorated structure that dominated the royal core of Vijayanagara city. An axial system and circumambulatory routes, suggest John Fritz et al., emphasised the centrality of the Ramacandra Temple. Alongside the platform, the temple was pivotal in turning the king into a manifestation of Rama.[115] The Mahanavami and Dasara festivals were continued in courts throughout south India, including Mysore, from the early seventeenth century (continuing under the Muslim Haydar ʿAli and Tipu Sultan in the late eighteenth century) and Ramnad in the late nineteenth century.[116] This continuation not only emphasises the political centrality of the festival, but also hints at the possibility of its reincarnation in post-Talikota Bijapur.

The similarity between certain aspects of ʿId-i Nauras and the Mahanavami is striking. Both festivals focused on the public and ritualistic affirmation of the supreme position of the sovereign in his kingdom, manifested by public audiences, reaffirmation of hierarchies, gifts and *darśan*. Music and dance were central elements in both Bijapur and Vijayanagara. The peculiar date chosen for ʿId-i Nauras may be related not only to the *nauras* but also to the element of nine (days, pavilions) in the Mahanavami. Lastly, while Vijayanagara and Nauraspur are different in their spatial organisation, the ritual was inscribed into their respective city space, with both Ramachandra Temple with the Mahanavami Platform nearby, and the Nauras Mahal in the physical and symbolic centre of the city.

The main difference arising from this comparison is within the spiritual and ritualistic realm. Naturally, under the Muslim ʿAdil Shah, no public worship of a deity was possible, nor would the identification of king and deity strike sympathetic chords among Muslim elites. Instead, ʿId-i Nauras incorporated its own spiritual contents, which were more appropriate to a Muslim ruler. Shirazi alludes to this possibility when attaching the adjective *muqaddas* (sacred) to Nauraspur. This use of the term is unique in the context of a place that lacks a concrete source of sanctity such as a Sufi shrine. Take, for example, the shrine of the Sufi saint Muhammad Gisu Daraz in Gulbarga. The site is mentioned in *farmān*s as the sacred garden (*rawza-i muqaddasa*) alongside adjectives such as illuminated (*munawwara*), pure (*muṭahhara*) or blessed (*mutabarraka*), a title extended to Gulbarga itself.[117] Shirazi attributes sanctity to only one other city, Mashhad in Khurasan, again a place with clear religious content: it is the resting place of the eighth Shiite imam, ʿAli al-Riza (d. 818).[118] Nauraspur had no religious buildings, shrines or tombs, other than a small mosque.[119] This absence is resounding not only in regard to Gulbarga or Mashhad, but also in comparison with Bijapur, with its many mosques and Sufi tombs. The oddity did not go unnoticed by historians in past generations. Relying heavily on Shirazi's report, Fuzuni whitewashed the narrative by dropping the term *muqaddas* altogether and adding to his description of the suburb's mosques (*jawāmiʿ wa masājid*), madrasas and Sufi hospices (*khawāniq*), none of which is known to have existed. The sanctity has similarly disappeared from Zubayri's narrative.

If the Muslim buildings were a later literary addition, what may be the content of Nauraspur's sanctity during the short time of the suburb's existence? Without any appropriate physical source, there is only one possibility: the sultan himself. Shirazi firmly situates the sultan as the centrepiece of the ceremony and of the city. The centrality is explained in terms of the sultan's field of expertise, namely, music. Shirazi continues:

> Since a young age, the Refuge of the World was deeply involved in the pursuit of musical knowledge. He achieved great understanding and advanced the science (*ʿilm*) of music. If Venus had the ability, she would have left her eternal abode in the Third House and come to the threshold of his court to tie the belt of servitude around her waist and become his disciple. All around India, whoever was skilful and accomplished in this science, had the desire that a melody or song from the Messiah of wisdom himself would come to his ear and give him a reason for eternal life. From long distances they would [come,] bow and kiss

the royal threshold. [By that] they attained their religious and worldly purposes and gained endless graces. At present, three or four thousand students are present, each considers him a hundred thousand times better than Pythagoras, the founder of this science. His followers (*ṭabaqa*) were divided into three. One part, [comprising those] who bestow complete comprehension, attend his presence; day and night, they are at his service. Whenever an idea worth spreading [appeared], they were brought into the court. His Majesty sang to this group an immensely fresh song. When it reached their bodies and ears, such great delight and joy overcame them that some became unconscious and uncontrollable. Thereafter, they recite [until] grasping the song. On account of the favours from the soul of that who is worthy to be called Caliph, they memorise [the song] with a group known as *darbārī* ('court attendants'), who are present outside the gate of the court day and night. The *darbārī*s are always occupied in orating and singing, both for their own benefit, and for instructing the crowd who are in the sacred city of Nauras and who came every day to the *darbārī*s as disciples. [The sultan] gives this group a monthly allowance of money out of the royal treasury; to some he allocates house rents in Shāhpūr, to others – revenues from the City of Nauras or the bazaars of Bidyapur. To a few, he gives chieftainship [and revenues from] villages and towns.[120]

This passage clearly aims at adding important elements to the sultan's image. It establishes a hierarchy of expertise, on top of which is Ibrahim himself. To affirm his position, the sultan is favourably compared with Pythagoras, widely considered the founder of music theory, and even above Venus, the celestial body that presides over musical performance. The position of all the rest under the ruler reaffirms this hierarchy. The followers are likewise categorised in a hierarchical manner into three layers. On top are those who possess sufficient knowledge to learn from the sultan himself. They recite until they gain full comprehension, without any additions of their own. They then deliver the composition to the second group, the *darbārī*s, who encamp by the gate of the court. At this point, the *darbārī*s communicate this knowledge further down to the people of Nauraspur. The flow of knowledge and inspiration is one-directional, from the sultan to the people, emphasising the pivotal position of the sultan. This position is reaffirmed again by royal income distributed to a selected few.

The role of the sultan was not simply that of spreading intellectual knowledge, but spiritual and moral guidance as well. Zuhuri states that the sultan's mission was:

to bear the pains of training his disciples . . . for the purpose of showing kindness and favour to both the people and the world, and to the talented ones, so that their intellectual capacity may not fall to decay, and they may be thoroughly benefited thereby.[121]

More generally, the hierarchies described resemble Sufi structures, at the heart of which stand master–disciple relations. This relationship is tied with the idea of learning and practising (by means of, among other things, music and recitation). Practice allows the disciple to advance on the mystical path, leading to greater proximity to the saint, through whom the disciple aspires to unity with the Divine.[122] The Sufi-inspired narrative is implied by those who become unconscious from this proximity to the Divine (here, the epiphany of Ibrahim's songs), and the order of progression of this divinely-mandated music expression: from the sultan downward (expressed in the three *ṭabaqa*s) and outward, beyond the court, to the entire sacred city space. The sultan himself is fashioned in religious terms, from Zuhuri's aforementioned virtue of possessing spiritual knowledge (*maʿrifa*) to 'worthy to be called Caliph' (*khalīfa-wār*) and 'the Messiah of wisdom' (*masīḥā-i fiṭra*). This idea is expressed in the title *jagat-guru* ('universal teacher'), widely attached to Ibrahim. This title is unusual in political contexts. In the epic *Ramayana* and in classical Sanskrit literature, it refers to gods: Shiva, Rama, Vishnu or the Father of the Worlds.[123] Later, the title was reserved to religious teachers, many of whom appear in inscriptions from Vijayanagara.[124] The title *jagat-guru* (or *viśva-guru*) designated influential community leaders: Basavanna, the main patron of Saiva devotees in Kalyani, the old Chalukya capital,[125] or Vidyaranya, active in late fourteenth-century Sringeri, later associated with the foundation of Vijayanagara.[126] Closer to Bijapur, Jain sources mention that, in 1584, Akbar conferred the title *jagat-guru* on Hiravijay Suri (1526–95), the chief of the Jain congregation in Gujarat. This title was linked to his intellectual activities, and in particular the part he took in religious debates and discussions with the emperor.[127] Associating the title *jagat-guru* with the sultan himself, then, turns him into a combination of political and intellectual-spiritual leader, providing content not only to Nauraspur's sanctity, but to the public ritual of ʿId-i Nauras as a whole.

The spiritual position of the sultan and his relations to music were manifested in yet another peculiar way. In a widely discussed painting, likely to have originally accompanied a manuscript of *Kitab-i Nauras* and now located in City Palace, Jaipur, Saraswati, the goddess of music and learning, is depicted on a golden throne. She holds her attributes, and at her feet stands a peacock, her vehicle (*vāhana*). Above the throne, a small image is hung, depicting two elephants and a rider, very similar to known images of Ibrahim by the same painter, Farrukh Beg. Inscribed above the throne is the verse 'Ibrahim, whose father is Guru Ganapati and his mother pious Saraswati' from *Kitab-i Nauras*. This image is based on the descriptions of Saraswati in the text itself.[128] While the theme is clearly

Locality, Vernacular and Political Language

Hindu, Overton argues that the imagery, created by an Iranian painter, represents 'the casting of Saraswati in Solomonic terms', linking the image of the goddess not only to general Islamicate traditions, but more specifically to imagery of kingship employed in creating Ibrahim's image more widely.[129] The inclusion of the painting in a royal manuscript meant that it was not available for the vast majority of people. However, there are other signs of the invocation of Saraswati beyond a restricted manuscript: Eaton and Wagoner show that several royal documents in Marathi from his reign began with an invocation to Saraswati. Furthermore, Sufi tradition promoted the story that an image of Saraswati was installed in the palace for Ibrahim's worship.[130]

The symbolism in using Saraswati's image, alongside Shirazi's construction of Ibrahim's image as *jagat-guru*, may well be what filled the role of the religious ritual in ᶜId-i Nauras, turning it even closer to the public language of the Mahanavami celebration. Like positioning the image of the deity on the royal throne in Vijayanagara that turned the king into the god, placing Saraswati on Ibrahim's throne and depicting him as a spiritual leader created another kind of identification of the royal and the spiritual, even if carrying a form unique to the composite language of Bijapur's court. Alongside the language that developed around ᶜId-i Nauras, the use of the name Bidyapur, and new types of water facilities in Nauraspur, we can suggest that in developing Bijapur's political language, Ibrahim ᶜAdil Shah II turned to Vijayanagara, an immediate source of royal imagery very much alive in regional memory.[131]

Ibrahim and the Perso-Islamic World

The political language of Ibrahim ᶜAdil Shah II, radical as it may appear, does not reflect a sharp break from other aspects of Bijapur's political culture as developed in the century prior to his ascendance to the throne. From Ibrahim I's use of Chalukya remains to the Indic tone in ᶜAli I's *Nujum al-ᶜUlum*, and with the continuous incorporation of Hindu elites to various roles in the state, Ibrahim II developed his ideas on firm intellectual, ideological and social infrastructure that he inherited from his ancestors. Likewise, Islamicate and Persianate legacies were not abandoned. Even though much of the modern historiography assumes a zero-sum game between the Deccanis–Foreigners, Indic–Persianate culture and Sunni–Shiite creeds, in reality seemingly contradictory trends coexisted comfortably. Ibrahim II was not only *jagat-guru* but also *khalīl* ('friend of God', a common reference to his prophetic namesake),[132] Kaᶜba and *qibla* (the direction to which Muslims turn at prayer),[133] and *ṣāḥib-qirān* ('Lord of the Auspicious Conjunctions'),[134] a title widely used in the central Asian and Iranian worlds.[135] Next to Seven-Storey Palace (*sāt manzil*) with its Indic symbolism, he built the Water Temple (*jal mandir*), a unique structure said to have hosted hairs of the Prophet Muhammad.[136]

The Islamic side in Ibrahim's reign was interpreted as following the Deccani path. This understanding is supported by a much-quoted report from the Mughal ambassador to his court, Asad Beg Qazwini. The ambassador, who visited Bijapur in the early seventeenth century, commented on the sultan's preference for Marathi and his 'broken' Persian.[137] This report should not be accepted uncritically. Asad Beg was sent from a Mughal court that strongly associated Persian with imperial culture and finesse.[138] Depicting Ibrahim, whose very sovereignty was contested by Akbar, as lacking in his knowledge of Persian could well be an imperial attempt to discredit the sultan. Furthermore, even if his Persian was limited, this does not mean that the sultan remained afar from Persianate culture. A careful examination of the evidence reveals quite the opposite. While Dakhani received a central position in the court, with the sultan himself taking part in literary production in that language, Persian continued to be held in high esteem. We have seen before that the poets Zuhuri, Qummi and others migrated from Ahmadnagar to Bijapur, where they found a new patron in Ibrahim II. In his introduction to *Kitab-i Nauras*, commissioned by the sultan, Zuhuri mentions that the sultan wanted to communicate his ideas to the Persian world, and therefore commanded that his work be translated to Persian, so as not to 'deprive the residents of 'Iraq and Khurasan of its flavour'. With his book, the sultan wished that the Persians (*ᶜajam*) 'may every day have a Nauruz (the Iranian New Year)'.[139]

Firishta, too, promotes the idea that Ibrahim II was personally interested in Persianate culture. He reports that in 998/1589–90, the Shiite intellectual Khwaja Saᶜd al-Din ᶜInayatullah of Shiraz, along with the poets Mulla Shakibi and ᶜInayatullah Ardistani, arrived in Bijapur, entered royal service and received a land grant (*suyūrghāl*). Khwaja Saᶜd al-Din grew closer to the sultan, until he became his councillor, under the title Shah Nawaz Khan, by which he gained his fame.[140] The association with Persian intellectuals was even wider. Overton demonstrates the variety of Persian artists who settled in Bijapur during Ibrahim's reign thanks to the 'welcoming climate for foreigners', naming poets, writers, painters and calligraphers. They were pivotal in creating the intellectual scene in Bijapur and had a major impact on aesthetics and courtly culture. The climate of openness towards the Islamic, and particularly Persianate, world is reflected in the holdings of Ibrahim's library and its role as a nodal point for the circulation of manuscripts of varied fields in Persian as well as Arabic. The holdings of Ibrahim's library, suggests Overton, contributed to the creation of Ibrahim's certain image as a Muslim sovereign.[141] Together with other Foreigners who filled high administrative and military positions, they linked the court to the Persianate world.[142]

The sultan himself was personally involved in production in Persian. Firishta reports that at a time when he had financial difficulties he attended a royal council (*majlis*). The sultan increased his rank (*manṣab*) and land grant (*iqṭāʿ*) in acknowledgement of his good service. Thereafter, the sultan put an exquisite copy of *Tārīkh-i rauẓa-i ṣafā*[143] in his hand and said:

> Until this auspicious time, no one has written a distinct history of the kings (*pādshāhān*) of Hindustan in one volume in a clear and elaborate way, except for [the Mughal] Nizam al-Din Ahmad Badakhshi.[144] However, it is very abbreviated, and does not provide an inquiry into the affairs of the sultans of the Deccan.

Ibrahim II then ordered Firishta to produce an 'honest' account of his reign. Firishta immediately began to write the chronicle, including recent events related to the sultan. These sections were first presented to Shah Nawaz Khan, who found them satisfactory.[145]

Personal commission was not unusual in Ibrahim's reign: the poet ʿAbdul reports that the sultan himself asked him to compose the *Ibrahimnama*.[146] But unlike ʿAbdul's work, Ibrahim's involvement with Persian and his familiarity with writing in that language seems surprising, unless we reject Asad Beg's testimony as indicative of Ibrahim's Persian. Firishta offers a contrary narrative. He suggests that Ibrahim recognised his need to know Persian in order to keep track of state affairs, and therefore made an effort to learn the language. With Shah Nawaz Khan's help, Ibrahim started from reading one or two lines of a report, gradually progressing to poetry and prose. Soon he became so versed in the language, that his teacher inscribed his seal ring with the sentence 'student of Ibrahim ʿAdil Shah, Shah Nawaz Khan'.[147] Hyperbolic as this last statement may be – and may reflect Firishta's acceptance of the Mughal view of the role of Persian as an imperial language – it is clear that Ibrahim considered it crucial to learn Persian or, at least, depict himself as one familiar with the Persianate culture in line with ideas of kingship in the Muslim East.

The linguistic and cultural aspects are only part of his engagement with a group usually thought to be shunned by the sultan. Several reports put Ibrahim in proximity to, or even directly linked with, the Shiite elements in his realm. Admittedly produced by Shiite writers, the sources were commissioned by the sultan, therefore, we can assume that they are at least indicative of a courtly environment less divisive than suggested. Such indications appear in literature, notably in Zuhuri's introduction to *Kitab-i Nauras*. Within a lengthy description of the qualities of the ruler, depicted as a gardener or as an ideal type according to astrological ideas (similarly to *Nujum al-ᶜUlum*), surfaces the following *rubāᶜī* (quatrain):

> He is the king of Apostles, the crown for the head of all;
> through whose favour the harp of Existence produces music.
> He alone within the four corners of this world can claim to be his offspring,
> who is conscious of the exalted position of the twelve Imams.[148]

This quatrain links Ibrahim to several realms in which he was active: the world of music, central to the *Kitab-i Nauras* (see below); Sunni Islam, as Muhammad ᶜAbduʾl Ghani links 'the four corners of this world' (*chār ḥadd*, lit. 'four borders') to the four righteous Caliphs of Sunni traditions; and Shiism, but even then as a musical reference: the term he is using is *dawāzda maqām*, meaning 'the twelve principal Persian tones of music', which ᶜAbduʾl Ghani links to the Twelve Imams of Shiite traditions. In *Gulzar-i Ibrahim*, Zuhuri mentions the sultan's 'good fortune of submissions to the illustrious Sharia of Mustafa (i.e. Muhammad), and the felicity of raising the banner of friendship for Murtaza (i.e. ᵓAli)', to which he adds that the state he established is 'a proof of his pure nature [and] his love of the pure Imams' (*aᵓimma-i aṭhār*).[149] This interpretation makes sense when we consider that Zuhuri counted adherence to Shiite teachings as one of Ibrahim's nine virtues.

Firishta provides direct evidence of the sultan's personal involvement with Shiism. Around the Karnatak campaign, in September 1595, the sultan decided to encamp and perform the Shiite rite of mourning over Imam Husayn. In the following year, the Shiite scholar Mir Muhammad Salih Hamadani arrived in India. Ibrahim II was thrilled and organised a royal reception for him. On the tenth day of Muharram 1005 (1596), the day of Imam Husayn's martyrdom, the sultan performed the mourning rites, 'in accordance with the custom of previous years'. He then invited Mir Muhammad to join him in Bijapur's citadel. When the caravan arrived, the sultan 'walked on foot a long way to receive him, and performed an adoration (*sijda*) of thanksgiving', showing particular reverence to the Shiite scholar.[150]

The evidence suggests that Ibrahim ᶜAdil Shah II was strongly associated with, and gave his support to, elements that, at first blush, seem to have been pushed aside. The place given to Foreigners, the Persian language and Persianate culture, and Shiism demonstrates that they were not only tolerated, but enjoyed direct and public support. Similar to the links that the Shiite ᶜAli I fostered with Hindus and Indic culture, Ibrahim II sustained links to the various elements of elite culture of this time. Believed to be Sunni, he demonstrates sympathy to Shiism and Shiite scholars. More comfortable with Dakhani and possibly Marathi, he made an effort to learn Persian and to engage with literary and artistic traditions associated therewith. In that, Ibrahim reflects the ᶜAdil Shahi line of his predecessor that emphasises continuation over change. This line, suggests Hutton, is evident in the architectural motifs in Bijapur: the monumental architecture in Ibrahim's reign reflects continuation and codification of the predecessors' visual language rather than the rejection thereof.[151] Furthermore, the activity of the sultans debunks notions of dichotomy between Deccani–Foreign with all that was associated, adding a large degree of stability and continuity in the development of the political language of the ᶜAdil Shahi sultanate.

Two Types of Localisation

In the second half of the sixteenth century and well into the seventeenth century, the Qutb Shahi sultans of Golkonda and the ᶜAdil Shahi sultans of Bijapur worked to build inroads into the locality. Hosting diverse elites, the rulers worked to accommodate local elites with their identities, historical memories and cultural sensitivities within the state. The basic challenges facing both dynasties were, on the face of it, comparable. Both started their careers as Foreigners under the Bahmanis. Both inherited similar social diversity and political tensions from their predecessors. Both were Shiite. However, the local circumstances varied significantly, leading to the development of a different political idiom in each sultanate.

Modern historiography does not account for these similarities and differences. Looking at the cases of Golkonda and Bijapur side by side reveals diversity not only in structures and solutions, but also in the historiographical frames in which the two sultanates were analysed. The historiography of Golkonda, heavily reliant on the seminal work of the prominent Hyderabad-based historian H. K. Sherwani, assumes a large degree of harmony and linearity. The unquestionable Shiite inclinations of the Qutb Shahi sultans and, accordingly, their association with the Persian language and Persianate culture, were not considered to be contradictory to the rise of Dakhani; after all, Muhammad Quli Qutb Shah was one of the first poets in that language. Nor was it seen as operating against the increasingly important role of Telugu in the state. The diversity was perceived as contained more-or-less harmoniously.

Bijapur has been approached in a markedly different way. Contrary to Golkonda's perceived harmony, in Bijapur profound social and cultural divisions were imagined. On the one side stood Deccanis, described as Sunni, attached to the locality, Hindu elites and Indic culture, and sympathetic to Sufism. On the other side were the Foreigners, who were Shiite, linked to the Persian language and Persianate culture. They were often presented as hostile to the locality, Hindus and Indic culture, and to Sufis. This division is believed to have run throughout elite society, including the sultans themselves. Consequently, the changing creed of the sultans assumed an abrupt turn for the sultanate as a whole. This view, however, misrepresents the history of the sultanate. While the creed may have changed, a large degree of continuity obliterates the stark differences between the two groups, at least in regard to political culture and patronage. Sunni rulers promoted Shiite scholars and ceremonies as well as Persianate culture; Shiite rulers were attracted to Indic ideas and Sufi veneration. Ideas and concepts persisted across reigns, suggesting greater continuity and cohesion than has been assumed before.

With this similarity, a major difference between the sultanates lies in the way in which they approached the locality and associated therewith. Central to Golkonda's identity was its association with a specific region, Telangana. The region, with its cultural heritage and historical memory, contributed to the promotion of the local vernacular, Telugu, within the state. Furthermore, it enabled the Qutb Shahi sultans and their elites to evoke the memory of the Kakatiya dynasty and their capital, Warangal. By that, the sultans sought to incorporate important elements of elite society, whose historical memory linked them to Kakatiya rule and the Telugu language. In contrast, no evidence suggests political association of the ᶜAdil Shahi sultans of Bijapur with Kannada, whereas links with Marathi seem to have been minimal and kept to the level of local administration. No clear geographical unit was marked as the main arena of that sultanate either. At the same time, the sultans expressed great interest in local culture: major patronage was extended to Dakhani, a language in which Ibrahim ᶜAdil Shah II composed his *Kitab-i Nauras*. Even without direct patronage to Marathi or Kannada, the sultans demonstrated keen interest in all-Deccani and even all-Indic ideas, but expressed them in Dakhani or even Persian (e.g., *Nujum al-ᶜUlum* or the visual language of Farrukh Beg). This association reflects royal aspiration to engage with local political language and historical memory, similarly to Golkonda. Unlike the Qutb Shahs, the ᶜAdil Shahs did not look at regional histories or vernacular-inspired dynasties. Instead, they followed the all-Deccani imperial past: first, the Western Chalukyas, and later Vijayanagara. This

Locality, Vernacular and Political Language

imperial language, remoulded to accommodate Islamic sensitivities, positioned the sultans of Bijapur as successors of their erstwhile formidable enemy. In short, if the Qutb Shahi sultans styled themselves as kings of Telangana, the ͨAdil Shahs became kings of the Deccan.[152]

The different process requires some explanation, even if a tentative one. We have seen that the eastern and western parts of the Deccan were not operating on the same grounds. Golkonda in the east was only reluctantly involved in the affairs of the western plateau. Bijapur was very much at the heart of the west, constantly struggling against Ahmadnagar and Vijayanagara for dominance. This struggle is demonstrated in the turbulent frontiers between the three polities. The difference between the sultanates is reflected in the political approach to the locality. Reclusive Golkonda remained inward-looking, fostering its Telugu-based concept as 'kings of Telangana'. Bijapur, in its competitive environment, required wider legitimacy and, furthermore, to appeal to wider elites. This need did not cease with Vijayanagara's defeat in Talikota, as the former empire remained an active player in the region and became the source of legitimacy to its successor Nayaka states.[153] In this competitive environment, then, Bijapur's need to attract post-Vijayanagara elites by using imperial language is clear.

Bijapur's all-Deccan inclinations, however, go one step further. In a sense, whereas Golkonda had an almost ready-made justification with territorial, linguistic and elite identities, Bijapur lacked all this. Its awkward geographical position in between linguistic regions and its mismatch with either vernacular space did not encourage the development of Golkonda-style vernacularisation. Not only was the core region of the sultanate divided between linguistic regions, but none of the capital cities of the old regional kingdoms was located within ͨAdil Shahi territory. In that case, vernacularisation was not a viable option, or at least not an easy one. With this lack, general Deccani identity had its appeal. Such association began with a relatively minor reference to the Western Chalukyas, whose capital city, Kalyani, was controlled by Bijapur (and was much desired by Vijayanagara's Rama Raya). This process gathered momentum after Talikota, and in particular under Ibrahim II, when the political language of the sultanate began to be remodelled after Vijayanagara, still fresh in Deccani memory. This new direction was reproduced in symbolic actions in the capital, including the renaming of Bijapur, the construction of Nauraspur with a large reservoir, and the celebration of 'Id-i Nauras. This association was further promoted in literary narratives composed both in Persian (the court historian Shirazi and the poet Zuhuri) and in Dakhani (the poets ͨAbdul and Ibrahim II himself), as well as in architecture and painting. Altogether, these actions suggest not a process of vernacularisation but rather non-particular localisation, which provides an alternate model to the one offered by Golkonda. The two models reflect another manifestation of the debate around vernacularisation as opposed to Sanskritic models with all-Indic sensitivities. The two directions taken, however, did not prevent the sultanates from encountering great challenges with the locality, to which we will turn next.

Notes

1. Early modern chroniclers employ two forms of the name Telangana, Persian 'Tilang' and Telugu 'Telangana'. Their choice seems to be related to the author's relations with the Qutb Shahi court. Chroniclers who worked in Golkonda, i.e., Nizam al-Din Ahmad and the anonymous author of *Tarikh-i Sultan Muhammad Qutb Shah*, tend to use the term Telangana. The term of choice for those who worked elsewhere, e.g., Muhammad Qasim Firishta (first working in Ahmadnagar, then in Bijapur) or Rafiᶜ al-Din Shirazi (Bijapur) is Tilang. Sayyid ᶜAli Tabatabaʾi, who wrote in Ahmadnagar, preferred to use Telangana, however, prior to his employment there, he had a long career in Golkonda. It is, therefore, safe to assume that in Golkonda itself, the Telugu version was the favourite term of reference.
2. *Tarikh-i Firishta*, vol. 2, p.100.
3. *Tarikh-i Firishta*, vol. 2, p. 338.
4. *Burhan-i Maʾathir*, p. 527.
5. *Tarikh-i Qutb Shah*, p. 192v.
6. *Tarikh-i Firishta*, vol. 2, p. 110.
7. Berar was named after the region rather than the capital city, Ellichpur. This sultanate, however, was short-lived, produced no known historiography, and received only little attention in contemporary sources, and therefore no conclusive comments can be made in that regard.
8. *Tarikh-i Qutb Shah*, p. 190v. The image of the people of Telangana as expert thieves seems to be widespread, as similar stories appear elsewhere. See, for example, *Burhan-i Maʾathir*, p. 528: 'the men of Telangana are excellent in the ways of thievery, [even] more than the robbers of our time. It is well known that they would take away the nose from between one's eyes.'
9. Eaton and Wagoner, *Power, Memory, Architecture*, pp. 208–14.
10. Sherwani, *History of the Qutb Shahi*, pp. 99–104.
11. Narayana Rao, 'Multiple Literary Cultures', p. 385.
12. Vasumati, 'Ibrahim Qutb Shah', pp. 28–42; Vasumati, *Telugu Literature*, pp. 54–65; Sherwani, *History of the Qutb Shahi*, pp. 85–6, 525–40. Wagoner provides a detailed list of seven literary works in Telugu written in, or in association with, the Qutb Shahi court under Ibrahim and Muhammad Quli, see Wagoner, 'Amin Khan', pp. 99–101.

Locality, Vernacular and Political Language

13. Wagoner, 'Amin Khan', pp. 90–8. The village still bears the name of Aminpuram, after Amin Khan.
14. Narayana Rao, 'Multiple Literary Cultures', p. 387, citing the mid-seventeenth-century poet Appakavi.
15. Eaton, 'Written Vernaculars', pp. 119–20; Farooqui, *Multicultural Dimensions*, p. 76. For a survey of Telugu poetry during the tenure of the dynasty, including valuable references to patronage, see Vasumati, *Telugu Literature*; Lakshmi Ranjanam, 'Telugu', vol. 2, pp. 145–72.
16. Narayana Rao, 'Multiple Literary Cultures', p. 385.
17. Talbot, 'Prataparudra', pp. 284–90; Talbot, *Precolonial India*, pp. 180–94. The *Prataparudra Caritramu* was not the only Telugu text discussing the Kakatiyas to have been composed around that time; another such text was the *Siddhesvara Caritramu*, see Wagoner, 'From Manuscript to Archive to Print', pp. 183–7.
18. Eaton and Wagoner, *Power, Memory, Architecture*, pp. 165–202.
19. The Qutb Shahi dynasty began its career from this weakness, as Sultan Quli Qutb al-Mulk, still a Bahmani officer, was sent to Telangana to establish Bahmani rule. See Sherwani, *History of the Qutb Shahi*, 7–9. See also discussion in Chapter 1.
20. Simpkins, 'Road to Golconda', pp. 352–3.
21. Sardar, 'Golconda through Time', pp. 21–65, 127–8, 132–3.
22. Eaton and Wagoner, *Power, Memory, Architecture*, pp. 214–20.
23. For a general discussion, see Babayan, *Mystics, Monarchs and Messiah*; Moin, *The Millennial Sovereign*. An example of such a link between messianism and city planning can be seen in the case of Isfahan, which became the Safavid capital under Shah ᶜAbbas I (r. 1588–1629). Sussan Babaie suggests that the messianic message of the political idiom of the dynasty is reflected in the design and architecture of the city, see Babaie, *Isfahan*.
24. Eaton and Wagoner, *Power, Memory, Architecture*, pp. 220–30. Compare this approach with the Huiziying Qingzhensi mosque in Beijing, built in the eighteenth century by the Qianlong emperor, which was oriented towards the throne instead of Mecca; this rendered it useless to the Muslim elites of Qing China. See Ben-Dor Benite, '*Hijra* and Exile'.
25. Qutb Shahi Documents, TSA. Out of the fifty-nine documents in the collection of Qutb Shahi *farmān*s, Nos 50 and 51 are trilingual; Nos 9, 11, 12, 14, 17, 28, 36, 37, 43, 44, 56 are in Persian and Marathi (Modi script); No. 59 is solely in Marathi.
26. Narayana Rao, 'Coconut and Honey', p. 26.
27. Gijs Kruijtzer suggests that the famous Brahmins who became the most prominent political figures in Golkonda during the 1670s, the brothers Madanna and Akkanna, were possibly Marathi-speakers, see Kruijtzer, *Xenophobia*, pp. 228–9. Beyond the Deccan, too, Brahmins created trans-regional networks, which linked the region with the all-India scene. Rosalind O'Hanlon discusses such networks around Maratha Brahmin

families who settled in Varanasi in the sixteenth and seventeenth centuries. While holding a high position in the intellectual life of the city and fostering connections to the Mughal court, while maintaining links to their ancestral lands in Maharashtra and even importing social tensions and disputes beyond the Deccan, see O'Hanlon, 'Letters Home',

28. Several early modern chronicles of the Deccan, including *Tarikh-i Firishta*, *Tadhkirat al-Muluk*, and the later *Basatin al-Salatin*, are divided into *faṣl* (section), *maqāla* (tale), or *bustān* (garden), typically describing one ruler each. The Mughal *Muntakhab al-Lubab* follows the same pattern.

29. See, for example, *Bombay Gazetteer*, p. xxiii; Joshi, 'The Adil Shahis and the Baridis', vol. 1, pp. 289–394; Eaton, *Sufis of Bijapur*; Verma, *Bijapur*, pp. 19–32. Eaton and Wagoner, *Power, Memory, Architecture*, pp. 128–34, follow the same narrative, but they admit that changes became less abrupt under Ibrahim ᶜAdil Shah II.

30. Eaton, 'Written Vernaculars'. Sumit Guha suggests that early state documents in Marathi, while written in Modi script, were comprised mostly of Persian vocabulary and even grammar, with only occasional terms and verbs taken from Marathi, see Guha, '*Mārgī, Deśī*, and *Yāvanī*', pp. 134–7.

31. Fukazawa, *Medieval Deccan*.

32. While I could not locate evidence for administrative use or cultural support, it may be related to the state of preservation of materials: for Marathi documents, the Bharat Itihas Sanshodhak Mandal in Pune strives to maintain documents from Bijapur (in Marathi as well as Persian), while Kannada documents from the ᶜAdil Shahi period do not seem to enjoy similar prestige. The question of vernacular, in particular Kannada, in the ᶜAdil Shahi realm awaits a study of its own.

33. See discussion in Kulke, 'Maharajas'.

34. Joshi, 'The Adil Shahis and the Baridis', vol. 1, pp. 303–7; *Bombay Gazetteer*, vol. xxiii, pp. 410–12.

35. *Futuhat-i ᶜAdil Shahi*, p. 58v. The term 'Indian language' (*zabān-i hindī*) is indistinct, and may refer to any Indian language, including Dakhani, Marathi and Kannada.

36. Sava (or Saveh) is a town in Iran, approx. 100 km southwest of Tehran, identified as the hometown of Yusuf ᶜAdil Khan.

37. *Futuhat-i ᶜAdil Shahi*, pp. 58v–59r.

38. Joshi, 'The Adil Shahis and the Baridis', vol. 1, p. 316; Eaton and Wagoner, *Power, Memory, Architecture*, pp. 127–8. With the absence of records from the earlier period, it is unclear whether the change was indeed profound or reflects more on a florid description in later sources. However, the persistence of the positions of Brahmins at the village level in various official roles suggests that, at least at village level, previous vernacular traditions persisted; see O'Hanlon and Minkowski, 'What Makes People Who they Are?', pp. 398–9.

39. H. K. Sherwani demonstrates that none of the rulers of the Deccan

claimed the title *shāh* until Kalimullah's death; Sultan Quli of Golkonda even kept the noble title Qutb al-Mulk until his own death in 1543. See Sherwani, 'The "Independence" of Bahmani Governors'.
40. Sherwani, *Bahmanis*, pp. 143–4.
41. Eaton and Wagoner, *Power, Memory, Architecture*, pp. 128–33.
42. *Tarikh-i Firishta*, vol. 2, pp. 64–5; Joshi, 'The Adil Shahis and the Baridis', vol. 1, p. 325; *Bombay Gazetteer*, vol. xxiii, p. 416.
43. The city and its monuments are thoroughly discussed in Cousens, *Notes on the Buildings*.
44. Hutton, *Art of the Court of Bijapur*, pp. 33–4. Collective effort tying the wider royal family and the nobility to networks of patronage is known from other contexts in early modern South Asia, most notably the Mughal Empire. See, for example, Kozlowski, 'Private Lives'.
45. *Bijapur Inscriptions*, No. 426, pp. 49–50; Eaton and Wagoner, *Power, Memory, Architecture*, pp. 137–8. The short inscription contains two dates: 969/1561–2 in words, followed by 976/1568–9 in digits. As the major construction project of the city had not begun until after Talikota, the later date is more reasonable.
46. *Bijapur Inscriptions*, No. 3312, p. 49. Once again, the date (1 Muḥarram 969/11 September 1561) seems too early. M. Nazim, who deciphered the inscription, admits that the inscription is worn down and the date is doubtful. Eaton and Wagoner mention only the name of the sovereign, but oddly ignore the Shiite slogan at the beginning of the inscription. See Eaton and Wagoner, *Power, Memory, Architecture*, p. 137.
47. Joshi, '῾Ali ῾Adil Shah I'. Sheh Waman's name appears on two documents, from 975/1567 and 983/1575. Daso Pandit and his family remained interlinked with the royal family of Bijapur into the reign of Ibrahim II, and two of his nephews are said to have been converted to Islam. See *Tadhkirat al-Muluk*, p. 189.
48. Flatt suggests that the text mentions the ῾Imad Shahis as rulers of Berar, therefore, it should be dated before 1568, which she marks as the end of the dynasty; see Flatt, '*Nujum al-ulum*'. However, a better estimate of the final conquest of Berar by Murtaza Nizam Shah I of Ahmadnagar should be 1574, a date that marks the actual end of that sultanate; therefore, the work could have been composed as late as 1570, the date of the earliest known colophon.
49. Hutton, *Art of the Court of Bijapur*, pp. 50–69.
50. Flatt, '*Nujum al-ulum*', pp. 225–9.
51. Eaton and Wagoner, *Power, Memory, Architecture*, pp. 134–46.
52. Butler Schofield, 'Music, Art and Power'.
53. See Kafadar, *Between Two Worlds*, pp. 60–117; Fleischer, *Bureaucrat and Intellectual*, pp. 253–72; Babayan, *Mystics, Monarchs and Messiah*, pp. 141–60.
54. Eaton, *Sufis of Bijapur*, pp. 62–70.

55. Ahmad 'The Sufi and the Sultan'; Siddiqi, *Bahmani Sufis*; Digby, 'The Sufi Shaykh and the Sultan'; Eaton, *Social History*, pp. 32–58; Auer, 'Sufism and Power'.
56. Hutton, *Art of the Court of Bijapur*, p. 177, n. 62; see also Zebrowski, *Deccani Painting*, pp. 78–81. Metal ᶜ*alam*s were produced in Golkonda, and their shape became a decorative motif, impressed in stucco. See Sardar, 'Golconda through Time', pp. 120–2; Safrani, 'Golconda Alums'.
57. The royal Bahmani mausolea outside Bidar are built some 600 m from the tomb of the Qadiri Shah Khalilullah (d. 1455), son of Shah Niᶜmatullah Kirmani (d. 1430); architecturally and stylistically, the tomb of Sultan Ahmad II (r. 1436–58) corresponds with that of the shaykh. See Yazdani, *Bidar*, pp. 141–6; Siddiqi, *Bahmani Sufis*, pp. 78–83.
58. Hutton, *Art of the Court of Bijapur*, pp. 45–6.
59. Sardar, 'Golconda through Time', pp. 105–9; Nayeem, *Heritage of the Qutb Shahis*, pp. 188–9.
60. This brings us back to the question of sudden Sufi migration to Bijapur in the 1580s. As the reason does not seem to be within Bijapur, a more promising line of investigation would be to look at the land of origin, namely, Iran. Indeed, under Shah ᶜAbbas I (r. 1588–1629), the Safavid state grew increasingly hostile towards certain Sufi orders, encouraging many to leave Iran for India. See Roemer, 'Safavid Period', pp. 346–7; Newman, *Safavid Iran*, pp. 51–5, 68–71.
61. In an oft-quoted passage, Shirazi discusses ᶜAli's fascination with Muslim and Hindu ascetics, and looked for their company. This inclination gained him a name of a madman among the neighbours, thus encouraging them to invade his territories. See *Tadhkirat al-Muluk*, pp. 56–7; translation in Eaton and Wagoner, *Power, Memory, Architecture*, p. 135. Hutton links the sultan with Shams al-Din in Miraj, a local Sufi whose shrine is located near Bijapur. See Hutton, *Art of the Court of Bijapur*, pp. 47–50.
62. Hutton, *Art of the Court of Bijapur*, pp. 42–7; *Epigraphia Indo-Moslemica* (1931/2), 5–9; Michell and Zebrowski, *Architecture and Art*, p. 88; Cousens, *Bijapur and its Architectural Remains*, pp. 54–5.
63. Hutton, *Art of the Court of Bijapur*, pp. 47–51.
64. *Tadhkirat al-Muluk*, pp. 151–74, 190–8; *Tarikh-i Firishta*, vol. 2, pp. 92–8; *Muntakhab al-Lubab*, vol. 3, pp. 344–7; *Basatin al-Salatin*, pp. 168–71.
65. Eaton and Wagoner, *Power, Memory, Architecture*, pp. 149–51; Eaton, *Sufis of Bijapur*, pp. 89–105. Ibrahim's choice of the Sunna creed is attributed to the influence of Shah Abu al-Hasan (d. 1635), a Qadiri Sufi who migrated from Bidar to Bijapur in 1580, see Eaton, *Social History*, pp. 107–12.
66. An inscription in Gulbarga indicates that Ibrahim visited the tomb in Muharram 989 (February 1581); his mother, Makhduma-i Jahan, ordered a well to be dug in the place. See *Epigraphia Indo-Moslemica* (1907/8), No. 13, p. 5.

67. Hutton, *Art of the Court of Bijapur*, pp. 73–107; Haidar, 'The *Kitab-i Nauras*', p. 26.
68. Brand, 'Bijapur', p. 74; see also Cousens, *Bijapur and its Architectural Remains*, pp. 63–4.
69. *Ibrahimnama*, p. 55. I am grateful to Dr Richard Williams for his assistance with the passages from this text.
70. Overton, 'Book Culture', p. 98.
71. *Nauras*, vol. 3, p. 311, tr. vol. 3, p. 340; Hutton, *Art of the Court of Bijapur*, pp. 110–11; Butler Schofield, 'Learning to Taste the Emotions', pp. 407–10; *Futuhat-i ᶜAdil shai*, pp. 215v–216r. The sensual aspect of *rasa* is nicely captured by ᶜAbdul, saying that the new Dakhani poets in his court were 'budding flowers of the Sultan's literary assemblies (*majālis*), on each of whom the Sultan's gaze would linger to savour the unique fragrance and *rasa*'; see *Ibrahimnama*, p. 64; translation of these verses in Husain, 'Courtly Gardens', p. 83.
72. *Basatin al-Salatin*, pp. 249–50.
73. *Epigraphia Indo-Moslemica* (1907/8), No. 18, p. 7.
74. *Kitab-i Nauras*, pp. 55–94; Matthews, 'Eighty Years of Dakani Scholarship', pp. 92–4; Haidar, '*Kitab-i Nauras*', p. 26. For the purpose of this study, I have used Ahmad's analysis and translation. With that, the work as a whole and, in particular, its great importance in the context of the history of Indian music, still awaits a thorough study.
75. *Gulzar-i Ibrahim*, vol. 3, pp. 347–62, tr. vol. 3, pp. 365–89.
76. *Tadhkirat al-Muluk*, p. 217.
77. Taylor, loyal to the dichotomies within colonial historiography, suggests that local memory relates the name to a Chalukya Hindu 'college' that was demolished by the Muslim invaders of the early fourteenth century. As evidence he points to the 'large stones of pillars, that are to be seen near the old Hindoo College, inside the second gateway of the citadel', most likely referring to the Chalukya remains installed there by Ibrahim ᶜAdil Shah I discussed above, see Taylor, *Architecture at Bijapur*, p. 58.
78. Nilakanta Sastri, *A History of South India*, pp. 229–30.
79. Kulke, 'Maharajas', pp. 120–4.
80. Cousens, *Bijapur and its Architectural Remains*, p. 83.
81. *Basatin al-Salatin*, pp. 273–4; Joshi, 'The Adil Shahis and the Baridis', vol. 1, pp. 350, 555. *Futuhat-i ᶜAdil Shahi*, pp. 216r–217r, describes the imposing remains he encountered when visiting the site in the 1640s.
82. *Khwan-i khalil*, vol. 3, pp. 401–7, tr. vol. 3, pp. 445–53; *Ibrahimnama*, pp. 55–9; Husain, *Scent in the Islamic Garden*, pp. 160–1.
83. *Tarikh-i Firishta*, vol. 2, pp. 156–8.
84. Hutton, *Art of the Court of Bijapur*, pp. 111–16, 187, n, 91; Brand, 'Bijapur', pp. 68–70. Firishta's description of the palace did not find its way to John Briggs' nineteenth-century translation into English, therefore, it has been overlooked in modern scholarship. This is a common issue with

historiography based on Firishta, see Truschke, *Culture of Encounters*, p. 309, n. 60.
85. The colophon provides the month of Jumada I 1024/May 1615 as the year of completion. See *Tadhkirat al-Muluk*, p. 414.
86. Hutton, *Art of the Court of Bijapur*, pp. 108, 117.
87. *Tadhkirat al-Muluk*, pp. 218–19; *Basatin al-Salatin*, pp. 247–8; Hutton, *Art of the Court of Bijapur*, p. 108; Brand, 'Bijapur', pp. 69–70.
88. *Tadhkirat al-Muluk*, p. 217; Cousens, *Bijapur and its Architectural Remains*, p. 84 and map on plate CXVIII.
89. *Futuhat-i ᶜAdil Shahi*, pp. 214r–215v.
90. Gadre, *Cultural Archaeology*, pp. 64–78; Nayeem, *Heritage of the Qutb Shahis*, pp. 125–6; Sohoni, 'Local Idioms', pp. 100–4.
91. Hutton, *Art of the Court of Bijapur*, pp. 35–7.
92. Royal women such as Fatima Sultana Bibi and Ibrahim II's mother Makhduma-i Jahan, and nobles such as Maliya and Malik Sandal (architect of Ibrahim's tomb), are among those who dedicated minor water structures. See *Bijapur Inscriptions*, Nos 477, 497, 3350, pp. 65–7, and No. 3350, p. 6; *Epigraphia Indo-Moslemica* (1907/8), p. 5; Cousens, *Bijapur and its Architectural Remains*, pp. 120–4.
93. *Tadhkirat al-Muluk*, pp. 217–18.
94. The other reservoir, Jahan Begum Tank, was built by Sultan Muhammad (r. 1627–56), and is located south of Nauraspur. See Imaratwale, 'Adil Shahi Gardens', p. 22. Hutton, following Zubayri, suggests that the Ramling Tank was built during the reign of ᶜAli I. The text, however, mentions briefly the construction of a large pool next to the citadel (*nazdīk-i qalᶜa ḥawẓ-i buzurg binā farmūda-and*), while not mentioning a dam and is quite inaccurate in its location. See Hutton, *Art of the Court of Bijapur*, p. 36; *Basatin al-Salatin*, pp. 112–13.
95. Cousens, *Bijapur and its Architectural Remains*, pp. 83–4 and map on plate CXVIII.
96. Hegewald, *Water Architecture*, pp. 87, 188, 209–10.
97. Rötzer and Sohoni, 'Nature, Dams, Wells, and Gardens', pp. 70–3.
98. Sohoni, 'Local Idioms', pp. 100–4; Sohoni, *Architecture*, p. 200.
99. Stein, *Peasant State*, pp. 24–9.
100. Tablot, *Precolonial India*, pp. 38–43.
101. Best-known reports are those of the Portuguese Domingo Paes and Fernão Nuniz, who visited Vijayanagara in 1520 and mid-1530s, respectively. See *The Vijayanagara Empire as seen by Domingo Paes and Fernao Nuniz*, pp. 26–7, 142–3.
102. Morrison and Sinopoli, 'Economic Diversity'; Morrison, 'Supplying the City'; Morrison, *Fields of Victory*.
103. *Tadhkirat al-Muluk*, pp. 48–9. The description is similar to the testimonies Paes and Nuniz.
104. At the beginning of the section on ᶜAli I, Shirazi writes that 'every place

Locality, Vernacular and Political Language

jahān panāh is mentioned in these papers, the meaning is Shah ᶜAli ᶜAdil Shah'; similar remarks appear at the beginning of the section discussing Ibrahim II, whom he calls ᶜālam panāh; both titles mean 'refuge/shelter of the world'. See *Tadhkirat al-Muluk*, pp. 54, 160. The idea of eating one's salt was widely used in the Muslim East to denote loyalty within a shared system of etiquette and conduct. See Gordon, *When Asia was the World*, pp. 137–56.

105. *Tadhkirat al-Muluk*, p. 51.
106. Morrison, *Fields of Victory*, p. 132.
107. See map in Eaton and Wagoner, *Power, Memory, Architecture*, p. 274.
108. *Epigraphia Indo-Moslemica* (1917/18), pp. 1–4; Rötzer and Sohoni, 'Nature, Dams, Wells, and Gardens', p. 57; Mate, *Water Management*, p. 65.
109. *Tadhkirat al-Muluk*, pp. 219–20. I wish to thank Dr Katherine Butler Schofield for her most valuable help in interpreting and translating this and the following passage.
110. Koch, 'Hierarchical Principles', pp. 130–43.
111. See, for example, Necipoğlu, *Architecture, Ceremonial, and Power*, pp. 15–75. On the act of bestowing royal symbols in the Deccan as part of a trans-Asian set of royal symbols, see Gordon, 'In the Aura of the King'.
112. Brand, 'Bijapur', pp. 68–70; Hutton, *Art of the Court of Bijapur*, pp. 111–16.
113. See Eck, *Darsan*, pp. 3–10; Asher, 'Mapping Hindu–Muslim Identities'.
114. Stein, 'Mahanavami'; Rao, *Re-figuring the Ramayana*, pp. 99–106; Sarkar, *Heroic Saktism*, pp. 210–12.
115. Fritz et al., *Where Kings and Gods Meet*, pp. 146–54; Stoker, *Polemics and Patronage*, pp. 37–8, 80–1; Dallapiccola, *The Great Platform*; Verghese, *Religious Traditions*, pp. 99–109.
116. Hayavadana Rao, *Dasara in Mysore*, pp. 133–49; Stein, 'Mahanavami', p. 84.
117. TSA, Khwaja Banda Nawaz Collection, ᶜAdil Shahi *farmān*s Nos 114, 121, 122, 124, 137.
118. *Tadhkirat al-Muluk*, pp. 291, 371; 'Mashhad', *EI2*.
119. Recall Shirazi's short reference to mosques which were 'mostly completed' near the reservoir, not in Nauraspur proper.
120. *Tadhkirat al-Muluk*, pp. 220–1. The idea of the rulers of Vijayanagara providing shelter to Deccani elites was not fanciful: recall Ibrahim Qutb Shah's exile in Vijayanagara between 1543 and 1550.
121. *Gulzar-i Ibrahim*, vol. 3, p. 349, tr. vol. 3, p. 386.
122. See Ernst, *Sufism*, pp. 81–146; Rahman, *Islam*, pp. 128–66.
123. See, for example, Shiva in Kalidasa's epic poem *Kumarasambhava* 6.15 (also 8.24); Father of the World in Kalidasa's *Raghuvamsa* 10.65; Vishnu in *Bhagavata Purana* 1.8.25, 2.5.12; and Rama in *Ramayana* 7.36.22. I wish to thank Dr Ilanit Loewy Shacham for her kind assistance in obtaining these references.

124. Stoker, *Polemics and Patronage*, p. 38.
125. Chandra Shobhi, 'Kalyana is Wrecked', p 91.
126. Kulke 'Maharajas', pp. 130–3.
127. Mehta, 'Akbar', p. 55.
128. Haidar, '*Kitab-i Nauras*', pp. 34–9. Saraswati is mentioned several places in the text. See *Kitab-i Nauras*, *dohra*s, pp. 1, 17 and songs 24, 25, 37, 39, 49.
129. Overton, 'Book Culture', pp. 117–23.
130. Eaton and Wagoner, *Power, Memory, Architecture*, p. 151.
131. Certain south Indian texts link Bijapur to Vijayanagara. In the late eighteenth-century *Sivadigvijaya*, a Marathi narrative of the rise of the Bhonsles, the sultanates of the Deccan, including Bijapur, are remembered as emerging out of Vijayanagara. The *Ramarayana bakhairu*, a text of unclear origin that can be dated to the late seventeenth century or later, presents 'the Adilshahi regime as the least illegitimate successor of Vijayanagara', see Guha, 'Frontiers of Memory', pp. 277, 284–7.
132. Hutton, *Art of the Court of Bijapur*, p. 98; Zebrowski, *Deccani Painting*, p. 73. Zuhuri recalls the story of the Prophet Ibrahim thrown into a fire that miraculously turned into a rose garden, and equates it with the *nauras*. See: '*Nauras*', vol. 3, p. 311, tr. vol. 3, p. 341; similar imagery appears in *Gulzar-i Ibrahim*, vol. 3, p. 362, tr. vol. 3, p. 365, or '*Khwan-i khalil*', vol. 3, p. 422, tr. vol. 3, p. 426. Similar reference, based on Quran 2:130, can be found on one of the royal seals. See Overton, 'Book Culture', pp. 101–3.
133. *Khwan-i khalil*, vol. 3, p. 422.
134. *Tarikh-i Firishta*, vol. 2, p. 163.
135. Balabanlilar, 'Lords of the Auspicious Conjunction'.
136. Brand, 'Bijapur', pp. 74–6.
137. Asad Beg reports that the sultan understood Persian well, but could speak the language only in a broken way (*be-qadr-i shikasta mī-guft*), see *Waqaʾiʿ-i Asad Beg*, p. 170r. See also, Eaton and Wagoner, *Power, Memory, Architecture*, p. 150.
138. Alam, 'The Pursuit of Persian'.
139. *Nauras*, vol. 3, p. 310, tr. vol. 3, pp. 341–2. Oddly, the Safavid chronicler Iskandar Munshi attributes the composition of *Kitab-i Nauras* to Zuhuri in cooperation with Qummi, who 'completed it in the name of ʿAdil Shah' (*be-nām-i ʿādil shāh tamām karda*), regardless of the fact that the text was written in Dakhani. See *Tarikh-i ʿAlam-ara-i ʿAbbasi*, p. 183.
140. *Tarikh-i Firishta*, vol. 2, p. 153, and recall his important role in the construction of Nauraspur.
141. Overton, 'A Collector and his Portrait', pp. 44–115; See also Bahl, 'Histories of Circulation', pp. 128–35.
142. Overton, 'Book Culture'; see also Haidar, '*Kitab-i Nauras*'.
143. *Rauẓat al-ṣafā* ('Garden of Purity') is a world history in seven volumes and epilogue. This influential history was written by Mirkhwand (d. 1498) in

the Timurid court of Herat, under the patronage of Mir ᶜAli-Shir Navaʾi, but was probably completed by Mirkhwand's grandson, Khwandamir. This history was important in the development of Safavid, and more generally, Persian historiographical traditions. See Maria Szuppe, 'Historiography, V: Timurid Period', *E.Ir*; Quinn, *Historical Writing*, pp. 13–14, 39–40.
144. Author of the Mughal chronicle *Tabaqat-i Akbari*.
145. *Tarikh-i Firishta*, vol. 2, pp. 153–4. This section was left out of Briggs' translation, and was therefore overlooked.
146. *Ibrahimnama*, p. 19.
147. *Tarikh-i Firishta*, vol. 2, p. 156.
148. *Nauras*, vol. 3, p. 319, tr. vol. 3, p. 326.
149. *Gulzar-i Ibrahim*, vol. 3, pp. 360–1, tr. vol. 3, pp. 368–70.
150. *Tarikh-i Firishta*, vol. 2, pp. 171–4.
151. Hutton, 'Carved in Stone', pp. 74–5.
152. The description of the ᶜAdil Shahs as kings of the Deccan was common, see, for example: *Nauras*, vol. 3, p. 311, tr. vol. 3, p. 339; *Epigraphia Indo-Moslemica* (1927/8), pp. 24–7.
153. See discussion in Narayana Rao et al., *Symbols of Substance*, pp. 23–56.

5
Limitations of the Deccani System

The engagement of the Deccan sultanates with the locality, be it as part of a state-acknowledged vernacularisation process or in the shape of non-particular localisation, achieved considerable success. The sultanates were able to gain the support of substantial elite groups, Muslim and non-Muslim alike, with whose backing they secured their rule for many years. Particularly in their core regions on the Deccan Plateau, the rule of the Qutb Shahi and ᶜAdil Shahi sultans remained unchallenged until the mid-seventeenth century. Even in shaky Ahmadnagar, where the Nizam Shahi rulers faced continuous internal instability and Mughal aggression, the dynasty maintained its monopolistic position of legitimacy.

The success of the sultanates, however, had evident limitations. In certain places, substantial gaps separated the sultans, the ideology they projected, and their ability to enforce it, on the one hand, and the willingness of local elites to accept their message, on the other hand. Regions not under firm sultanate rule, beyond the core region of a sultanate or under weakening authority, were particularly problematic. From the second quarter of the seventeenth century, more general upheaval put the system to the test. The events started with a historical coincidence. In 1626–7, a whole generation of rulers died. Sultan Muhammad Qutb Shah of Golkonda was succeeded by his son, ᶜAbdullah (r. 1626–72). Malik Ambar died the same year, throwing Nizam Shahi domains back into confusion. In 1627, Ibrahim ᶜAdil Shah II of Bijapur was succeeded by his son Muhammad (r. 1627–56). No less important was the death of the Mughal Emperor Jahangir in late 1627, to be succeeded by his son Shah Jahan (r. 1628–58). The combination of sweeping changes in leadership in the Deccan and the expansionist ambitions of the new Mughal emperor was bound to have a major effect on the region. The decade that followed was tense, not the least due to the Mughal invasion. A peace treaty in 1636 seemingly secured the northern border of the sultanates, allowing them to expand considerably. This expansion, however, brought the internal tensions and questions of control back to the surface, shaking the ruling

Limitations of the Deccani System

dynasties. With renewed Mughal aggression in the mid-1650s the situation seemed ever grimmer; the sultanates only barely survived the war.

This chapter examines cases in which sultanate authority was tested on the background of the distinct character of each sultanate. The sultanates varied significantly in terms of political idiom, ideology and relations to its locality; differences that became increasingly visible as pressure increased. A comparative analysis of the three sultanates reveals a great deal with regard to the place that political idiom and the imagination of space had in their political life. The first case discusses Golkonda's expansion in the late sixteenth and early seventeenth centuries into Andhra and Rayalaseema, placing its claims of Telugu kingship against local elites which were not yet integrated into the sultanate. The second case examines the situation in Maharashtra after the collapse of effective Nizam Shahi authority, focusing on the choice made by the Maratha Shahaji Bhonsle to continue official identification with the weakened dynasty. The last case is a comparative analysis of the fortunes of Bijapur and Golkonda

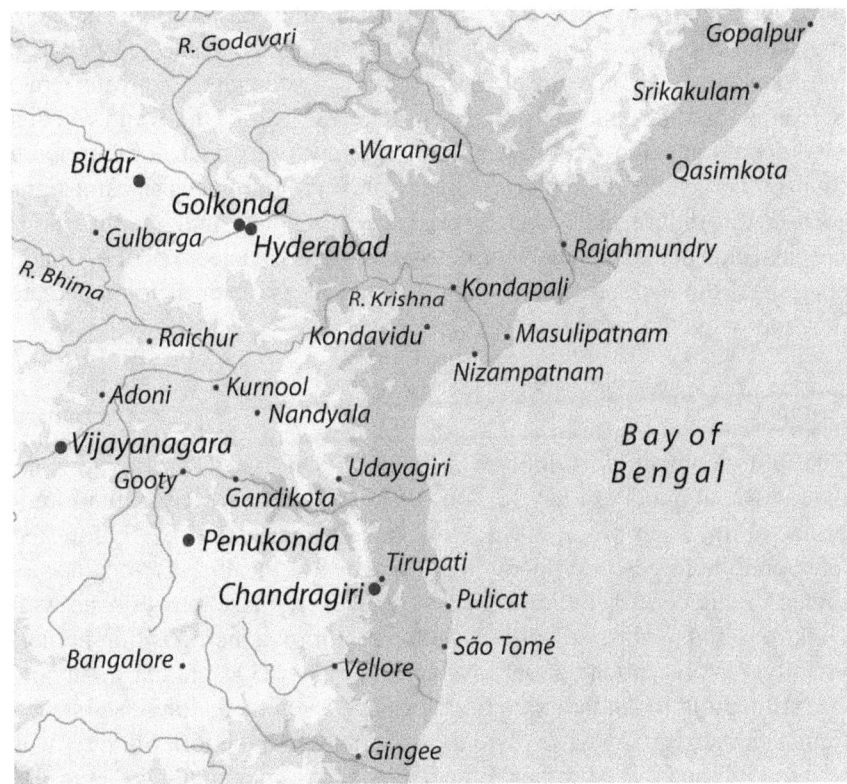

Map 5.1 The eastern Deccan

following the peace treaty of 1636. Both sultanates saw a period of rapid expansion, which raised new challenges to their rule not only in the new territories, but also in their core regions. In all cases, I argue, the challenges that the sultanates were facing, and their response, were closely linked to state ideology and structures, and the ability of the sultans to encourage elite cooperation.

Beyond Telangana: Qutb Shahi Expansion and Telugu Spaces

The case made by the Qutb Shahi sultans of Golkonda for associating with the Telugu language, the Telugu lands and the Kakatiya past seems to have been successful in their core regions. With the support of Telugu-speaking elites, the Qutb Shahs secured their rule over Telangana, where no significant rebellions were recorded after Talikota.[1] Beyond Telangana, however, things were not so simple. The Telugu lands lost political unity with the collapse of the Kakatiya kingdom in 1323. Within decades, Rayalaseema, the Telugu-speaking lands south of the Krishna, was integrated into Vijayanagara.[2] Andhra, the coastal region stretching along the Bay of Bengal in the east, remained contested between Vijayanagara, the Gajapatis of Orissa and local potentates. Vijayanagara's defeat in 1565 introduced the option of renewed Telugu unity and whetted Golkonda's appetite for new territories. A few years later, Ibrahim Qutb Shah embarked on an ambitious expansionist programme. The campaigns focused on Andhra and Rayalaseema, suggesting that, similar to their policies in Telangana, the sultans of Golkonda were engaged with the Telugu space and the Kakatiya past, while turning away from their immediate neighbours on the plateau.

ANDHRA

The first campaign was directed at Andhra (see Map 5.1). Having conquered Rajahmundry, a key fort on the lower Godavari River, the forces turned north. Their progress was slow and difficult in the heavily forested land, and the forces were facing the resistance of local *rāya*s, long accustomed to independence. Several *rāya*s, however, chose to cooperate with Golkonda and negotiated with the sultan to improve their position in their vicinity. Notable among these was Sarvaraj, ruler of Qasimkota, an important stronghold in Andhra's far northeast and a scion of a long-established family in the region.[3] After royal armies conquered the fort, Sarvaraj was sent to Golkonda. His brother, Bhaybalandar, was appointed group leader within the royal army. He was then sent against the province of Gopal,

Limitations of the Deccani System

which he had previously ruled.[4] In order to secure the loyalty of the newly integrated local magnates, a member of the family was continuously held hostage in the royal court in Golkonda.[5] Elsewhere in the northeast, Ibrahim implemented direct rule, assigning certain conquered territories as *jāgīr*s to his commanders,[6] suggesting that Golkonda introduced a mix of direct rule and incorporation of local magnates. By the mid-1570s, Ibrahim's armies had claim to take over the northeast to the Orissa border.

Nevertheless, the sketchy documentation indicates that with the notable exception of Masulipatnam, the major seaport of the sultanate,[7] Golkonda's control in Andhra did not last long. In 1580 Ibrahim died, and Bhaybalandar died soon after. Ibrahim's successor Muhammad Quli acknowledged Bhaybalandar's son, Mukandraj, as successor (*qāʾim-i maqām*) in Qasimkota. Diverging from his father's policy, Mukandraj rejected Golkonda's rule, stopped sending tribute, and imprisoned Golkonda's commander in the region. In response, the sultan sent his army against Qasimkota, to which he attached Sarvaraj, still hostage in the capital. Mukandraj gained the cooperation of several hereditary magnates ('*rāya*s of the country of infidels'). He even tried to convince Venkata (Venkatapati) II of Vijayanagara (r. 1585–1614), who was fostering renewed imperial ambitions, to attack Rajahmundry in order to deflect Golkonda's forces in that direction. Eventually, Vijayanagara did not join in, and Golkonda's army arrived in Qasimkota. Mukandraj was forced to flee to Srikakulam, 120 km to the northeast. Mukandraj then tried to raise Mughal support, but having failed in this endeavour, he continued to Bengal.[8]

Muhammad Quli's successful campaign, however, did not pacify the region, and rebellions broke out throughout his reign.[9] Telangana continued to face challenges in Andhra even long after the end of Qutb Shahi rule. After the Mughal conquest of Andhra (1687–91), Aurangzeb kept a similar pattern of mostly indirect rule, a policy markedly different than in Telangana. He appointed seven *faujdār*s (military commanders) in Telangana, but only two *faujdār*s were stationed in Andhra. Moreover, most of the Telangana *faujdār*s arriving from north India, indicating an attempt to fully incorporate the region into the empire; both *faujdār*s in Andhra had been previously employed by the Qutb Shahs, meaning that they had local roots. Similarly, 168 *jāgīr*s were allocated in Telangana compared with only 13 in Andhra. The Mughals further failed to integrate local magnates into their system and faced constant rebellions. These problems were carried further into the Nizam's state, established in 1724. From the War of Austrian Succession in the 1740s, Andhra became the target of the French and English companies. The Nizam first granted the right to collect revenue in the coastal region (known in colonial historiography as the Northern Circars, from *sarkār*, district). Local magnates as well as the Nizam's *faujdār* in Srikakulam refused to cooperate with the French, pushing the Nizam to use the unruly region as a bargaining chip vis-à-vis the two companies. By the mid-1760s, Robert Clive, then Governor of Bengal, obtained a patent (*sanad*) ceding the Northern Circars to the English.[10] It is striking that throughout the eighteenth century, the role of the Nizam remained marginal in Andhra.[11] More generally, from the campaigns of the 1570s to the English takeover two centuries later, Telangana's rule over Andhra had been indirect and unstable, maybe even only nominal.

RAYALASEEMA

In comparison to Andhra with its rugged terrain and contested history, Rayalaseema presents a different story. From the fourteenth century, the region was under Vijayanagara's firm grasp. The Battle of Talikota brought major shifts to the political setting. The capital city was sacked, even though the level of physical and economic destruction is debated; elites moved to new centres, and imperial authority was severely weakened.[12] Nevertheless, Vijayanagara persisted as a significant force in the region. Tirumala (r. 1565–72),[13] brother of Rama Raya, revived the empire under a new dynasty, Aravidu. Failing to restore the old capital, he moved to Penukonda in Rayalaseema, from whence he worked to rebuild his empire.[14] By this, Vijayanagara remained a viable, even if weak, actor in the arena of Deccani politics for several more decades.

In the first years following Talikota, Golkonda's relations with Vijayanagara improved as both dynasties shared their concerns over Bijapur's expansion: in 1576, ᶜAli ᶜAdil Shah invaded Vijayanagara, and reached Penukonda with the support of Hande Timma, a local *nāyaka*, but was forced to retreat. Ibrahim Qutb Shah was not involved in this campaign, but merely three years later, it was his turn to invade. Unlike the unapologetically expansionist attitude towards Andhra, the anonymous chronicler deemed it necessary to justify Ibrahim's policy change:

> In the days of the deceased king (Sultan Quli), Venkatadri, Kapuri Tamraj, and Narsing Rao used to send 200,000 *hūn*s annually as tribute to the royal treasury from the province of Kondavidu (in Rayalaseema). During the time of His Solomonic Highness (Ibrahim), too, they continued to follow in the submissive footsteps, until the gates of conflict (of Golkonda) with Nizam Shah and ᶜAdil Shah were opened . . . [the rebels] crossed the Krishna River to Kondapalli (in Qutb Shahi territory), oppressed its countryside, and brought misery upon the subjects of that land.[15]

Limitations of the Deccani System

The intervention in the south began as a punitive expedition against rebelling tributaries in the border region between Qutb Shahi and Vijayanagara territories, who not only failed to fulfil their financial obligations to Golkonda, but also harassed subjects of the sultan. This official narrative positions the campaign not as a whim of an expansionist ruler, but rather as the fulfilment of his royal duties to defend his subjects.

The campaign, however, soon expanded beyond the subduing of rebelling nobles. Several magnates sided with Golkonda, including the Hande family, indicating their rejection of Aravidu rule. Vijayanagara's fragmentation added to the agonies of the new king, Sriranga (r. 1572–85). By the end of the campaign, Golkonda had taken over most of Rayalaseema, as far as Udayagiri in the southeast, Adoni in the west and the vicinity of Penukonda.[16] With the lack of sufficient documentation, the nature of Golkonda's rule in that region remains unknown. It is, however, likely that older administrative patterns were kept as they were, as reflected by one *kayfiyat*. According to the *karaṇam*, in S. 1501 (1578–9 CE), 'Moguls' (i.e., Qutb Shahis) arrived, they defeated the 'King of Carnatic' Sriranga, and established a garrison in the hill forts. They further 'entered this village . . . and had continued authority for some years through the means of Dasayees (*desāīs*) and Dasapandeyas (*deśpaṇḍe*)', both hereditary village-level administrative positions.[17] Combined with the Andhra experience, then, it is likely that early Qutb Shahi administration in the regions beyond Telangana relied on local practice, much like in Telangana itself.

By the end of Ibrahim's reign, the Sultanate of Golkonda could claim control over almost the entirety of the Telugu-speaking lands, but none beyond.[18] This achievement, however, was short-lived as Muhammad Quli was facing problems in controlling the region from early on in his reign.[19] The resentment towards Golkonda's rule was shared by Muslim and Hindu magnates alike. One such rebellion, which we have briefly mentioned before, broke out in the 1580s, when the sultan sent one ᶜAli Khan Lar to guard the province of Kondavidu, now renamed Murtazanagar. The Qutb Shahi governor of the region, Ray Rao Brahmin, refused to grant ᶜAli Khan the land promised to him as *jāgīr* for an undisclosed reason. Tempted by 'the delusions of Satan', ᶜAli Khan, turned to Sriranga, with whose support he captured Kondavidu. In response, the sultan sent the generals Rahm Dad, who only a few years later would join the *nāyakwarī* named Bhali Rao in another rebellion against Golkonda,[20] and Tahir Muhammad Khan. Even with these reinforcements, quelling the rebellion was strenuous: several forts had to be conquered, at least in one of which the besieged were massacred. ᶜAli Khan escaped and continued to roam the country, plundering his way to Nizampatnam before being defeated.[21]

The duration of the rebellion and the repeated sieges required indicate that ᶜAli Khan enjoyed the support of at least a few local magnates, as suggested by the punitive element in the campaign.

Golkonda's problems in the region continued under Sriranga's successor, his brother Venkata II, who attempted to unify his reign and recapture Rayalaseema. Using direct warfare and political manoeuvring, he recovered significant territories in the east. His campaigns prompted Muhammad Quli to invade in the early 1590s. After conquering Nandyala from an Aravidu noble, the local *nāyaka*s and tax officers (*chaudhrī*s) 'hastened to the service [of Muhammad Quli] with the keys of [their] forts and great tribute, and turned the royal courts into [Muslim] places of worship'.[22] The Qutb Shahi army took over Gooty, Kurnool and Gandikota, then arriving in Penukonda. The details vary significantly between the sources in accordance with each side's political narrative. The anonymous chronicler reports that Venkata II convinced Muhammad Quli that he was willing to surrender, but during the negotiations re-equipped the fort. As the supplies of Golkonda's army were dwindling and the rainy season was approaching, Muhammad Quli had no choice but to withdraw to Telangana.[23] Vijayanagara sources depict a different chain of events, suggesting that Golkonda's army was defeated and forced to retreat as Venkata's allies in the region regrouped. Either way, the monsoon rains flooded the Krishna River and kept Golkonda's army in the north, allowing Venkata to recover most of Rayalaseema; Kondavidu remained the only Qutb Shahi stronghold south of the river. Venkata, on his side, was facing increasing instability in his realm: potentates who aided him against the Qutb Shah challenged his rule; major *nāyaka* rebellions broke out in Gingee (1595–1608) and Vellore (1603–4); Keladi and Mysore became increasingly independent after 1600, marking Vijayanagara's gradual disintegration.[24] Vijayanagara's weakness, however, was not translated into major gains for Golkonda. Some time in the 1630s, forces were sent from the capital to subdue rebellions around Kondavidu.[25] A few years after, ᶜAbdullah Qutb Shah sent Muhammad Saᶜid to recapture Nandyala, Udayagiri and Gandikota.[26]

Telangana, Andhra and Rayalaseema demonstrate significant variations. The Qutb Shahi sultans, supported by *nāyakwaṛī*s and other magnates, controlled Telangana firmly. Golkonda's rule over both Andhra and Rayalaseema was significantly weaker. While demonstrating military superiority at times, the support they drew from the locality remained intermittent and contested. The constant unrest indicates that local magnates did not fully accept, if not outright rejected, Qutb Shahi claims for sovereignty. This was not due to Golkonda's lack of effort. Ibrahim and

Limitations of the Deccani System

Muhammad Quli employed similar methods of incorporation in the newly conquered territories as in Telangana: incorporation of magnates on their patrimonial lands and in the centre alongside stationing agents from the centre as *jāgīr* holders. These attempts brought Sherwani to suggest that by 1579 'the whole of the Telugu-speaking country [was brought] under one aegis', linking Ibrahim's campaigns to the Telugu lands.[27] Sherwani's assumption of Telugu unity indeed relies on the geographical extent of the sultanate, largely following the vernacular backdrop. But more than historical reality, his view reflects on political sensitivities of mid-twentieth-century Hyderabad, with the raging debate on the relations between Andhra and Telangana.[28] Sherwani's stand is clear: he emphasises the all-Telugu nature of the Sultanate of Golkonda, which he names Tilang-Andhra.[29] This position, however, ignores the sultanate's emic identification with Telangana and its failures in Andhra and Rayalaseema.

HISTORICAL MEMORY AND COMPETING SOVEREIGNTIES

Golkonda's weak control beyond Telangana should not come as a surprise. We have seen that throughout the last millennium, each sub-region within the Telugu lands followed a distinct historical trajectory. The space as a whole was often divided; political unity was achieved only under the Kakatiyas, the Qutb Shahs, the Mughals and the Nizam, with the last three only briefly and intermittently. The region has been united again after two centuries in the state of Andhra Pradesh (1956–2014), recently bifurcated due to similar tensions. In all these cases, the political centre was located in Telangana, from which power was projected. Qutb Shahi expansion and its problems fit well in the long-standing pattern and the issues associated with regional control.

The problem of control has its physical reasons. Qasimkota is located approximately 500 km east of Golkonda as the crow flies, across the hilly and heavily forested Eastern Ghats, conditions that are not conducive to transportation. Seasonal conditions, too, add to the problems of mobility and communication; recall the flooding of the Krishna and its role in Muhammad Quli's failure to defeat Venkata II. With the limited resources available to the Qutb Shahs, these challenges were a significant barrier to Golkonda's expansion. Geographical considerations aside, ideological and historical factors, too, contributed to the chronic problem of control. Throughout Qutb Shahi rule, local magnates in Andhra and Rayalaseema continued to rely on previous sources of sovereignty, while usually not promoting themselves as sovereigns. A central source of this kind was Vijayanagara. While the relationship between Vijayanagara and its regional commanders, *nāyaka*s and other tributaries was complex, the empire nonetheless retained its power and prestige long after Talikota. Rulers in as far as Keladi-Ikkeri in western Karnataka and Madurai in Tamil Nadu emphasised their connections to Vijayanagara as an instrument to legitimise their rule for many years to come.[30] The political idiom of Vijayanagara itself had long afterlife.[31]

To the extent that we can trust local historical recollections recorded long after the events, Vijayanagara's memory may have been not only political but also ideological. According to the *karaṇam* of Kondavidu, the first local encounter with armies from the north was the invasion of unspecified 'Mongols' (Delhi sultanate or Bahmanis). The invaders encountered fierce resistance from a local minister, who not only drove them away, but 'preserved the Tellinga Country for some years'. Following that episode, the narrative provides more concrete details. In S. 1493 (1570–1), a commander named Murtaza Khan, with 'forces from the Mogul padshahs' (clearly Qutb Shahs), conquered Kondavidu, 'destroyed the Hindu temples and took the idols of them'. Tirumala expelled them and retook the lands south of the Krishna. His son, Sriranga, founded two temples in Kondavidu, for which he assigned several *agrahāram* villages. In S. 1501 (1578–9) 'Mulkey Vebhoo Ram' (Malik, or king, Ibrahim) appointed the Brahmin Ray Rao, whom we have encountered before, with major resources to conquer 'the Tellinga Country southward of the River Kristna (Krishna)'. The successful campaign ended with Ray Rao's conquest of Kondavidu. Upon his return to Golkonda three years later, security deteriorated, therefore Muhammad Quli appointed Amin al-Mulk to pacify the region. During his tenure (S. 1514–20/1591–8 CE), he 'prevented all the Charities or grants of the Hindoo Temples'. The iconoclastic theme continues when discussing the reigns of ᶜAbdullah (r. 1626–72) and Abu al-Hasan Qutb Shah (r. 1672–86; their reigns are fused together), when a tax collector named Ikhlas Khan destroyed a Ganesha temple near Kondavidu.[32]

The recollection of Qutb Shahi rule in Rayalaseema offers a different perspective to what we find in Persian chronicles. Muslim rulers create an indistinct body of foreign invaders, collectively titled 'Mongols' (Mughals), which included all Muslims from the Delhi sultanate to the Qutb Shahs. The narrative, which is quite accurate in the timeline presented, emphasises the iconoclastic dimension of their rule, including Golkonda's Muslim commanders Murtaza Khan and Ikhlas Khan; the Brahmin historian attaches no anti-Hindu actions to the Brahmin Ray Rao. As a mirror image of the Muslims stands Vijayanagara, whose rulers fulfil their obligation as Hindu kings: they build temples and assign villages for their maintenance. The line dividing the two domains is marked clearly:

the Krishna River. Yet the space as a whole is identified as 'Tellinga Country', in this case referring to the Telugu lands as a whole and not only Telangana. This narrative then suggests not only Golkonda's failure to project Telugu association in Rayalaseema, but Vijayanagara's success with the maintenance of their image as dharmic kings.

The durability of Vijayanagara's memory was not limited to Kondavidu. Imperial claims appeared throughout the region in inscriptions, plates and historical narratives. They were further promoted by the re-emergence of imperial authority, limited as it may have been, under Tirumala, Sriranga and particularly Venkata II. The combination of these factors brought several modern historians to attribute great power to post-Talikota Vijayanagara. Henry Heras argues that Sriranga 'was the Viceroy of the whole Telugu country'. Discussing Venkata II's reign, he includes both Rayalaseema and Andhra in his empire.[33] These statements seem exaggerated: the constant sieges of Penukonda and Venkata's reluctance to support Mukandraj in Qasimkota are sufficient to question Vijayanagara's power at the time.[34]

The decline in Vijayanagara's fortunes notwithstanding, the empire maintained a certain appeal and symbolic capital that relied on its glorious past and cultural heritage. Within this framework, imperial association with Telugu culture had an undeniable appeal to certain elites. We have seen the role of Telugu in cementing local support for the Qutb Shahs in Telangana. Vijayanagara was a more important centre of Telugu production and patronage than Golkonda has ever been. Pivotal to this was its iconic king, Krishnadevaraya (r. 1509–29). Narayana Rao notes that the king, not himself a Telugu but a Tuluva, understood the political benefit of using Telugu to engage local elites in the Telugu-speaking domains of his kingdom.[35] He accordingly extended his patronage to, and was closely associated with, the Telugu poet Allasani Peddana. Remembered as the 'Creator of Telugu Poetry', Peddana was a towering figure who changed Telugu literature at a moment remembered as Vijayanagara's golden age.[36] Not only patronage; Krishnadevaraya himself was an important poet, whose *prabandha*,[37] titled *Amuktamalyada* ('Giver of the Worn Garland'), reflects new levels of Vijayanagara's relations with Telugu.

The Vijayanagara–Telugu link extended beyond directly-ruled Rayalaseema into Andhra, far away from Vijayanagara's centres. From the late fifteenth century, Andhra was claimed by the Gajapatis of Orissa. The region was eventually conquered by Krishnadevaraya in his Kalinga campaign of 1513–19. Regional association with Vijayanagara was not merely political. Ilanit Loewy Shacham argues that the *Amuktamalyada* reveals a royal view of Vijayanagara which binds together the military and the theological. The story narrates simultaneously the military expansion of the empire, especially during the Kalinga campaign, and the sacred geography of the Srivaisnava community. Moving between mythic and historical events, people and places, the *Amuktamalyada* narrates the expansion of the Srivaisnava community into royal courts and further within the empire, in particular, into Andhra, creating a text in which kingship and theology are intertwined.[38] This link, furthermore, has a strong linguistic connection. The *Amuktamalyada* and its composition in Telugu are identified geographically with Andhra itself. In the temple of the local god Andhra Vishnu in Srikakulam (not the same Srikakulam we have encountered before), the god appeared in Krishnadevaraya's dream and instructed him to write the *Amuktamalyada* in Telugu.[39] Of only minor religious significance, Srikakulam is strongly associated with the Telugu identity of the empire and with its most celebrated ruler, and alludes to the lingering appeal of Vijayanagara's memory to local elites. Vijayanagara's claims were at least in part successful. The Kalinga campaign was followed by a spike in the production of Telugu inscriptions in Andhra acknowledging Vijayanagara. Talbot found that around three-quarters of all Telugu inscriptions in Andhra are dated to the period 1500–65, or roughly between the Kalinga campaign and Talikota. Mostly dedicated by local Telugu chiefs, their creation coincided with increasing royal patronage and endowments to religious institutions.[40] The process initiated by Krishnadevaraya, linking Andhra to Rayalaseema/Vijayanagara may have been in the background of Golkonda's problems in the region. Furthermore, this link can explain Mukandraj's request for assistance from Venkata II.

Golkonda's engagement with the Telugu language and the Kakatiya past had clear limitations. While it enabled the sultans to successfully associate themselves with Telangana and with its elites, their success was limited to Telangana. In Andhra and Rayalaseema, the sultanate's rule remained unstable and contested well after their initial conquest in the 1570s. The main challenge came from local elites who, unlike their peers in Telangana, did not accept Golkonda's views. In Rayalaseema, close to Vijayanagara's metropolitan region, and even in remote Andhra, the memory of the empire remained strong even when imperial power was waning. This memory was embedded in the political language of local magnates, and it was invoked as part of their resistance to Golkonda. Considering Vijayanagara's weak position and the independence of *nāyaka*s, we can assume that their actions were motivated by their desire to maintain their newly acquired independence rather than resurrecting Vijayanagara. But it also reflects the sultans' difficulties in appealing to these local rulers, showcasing the basic problem that the sultanate was facing beyond its core region.

Limitations of the Deccani System

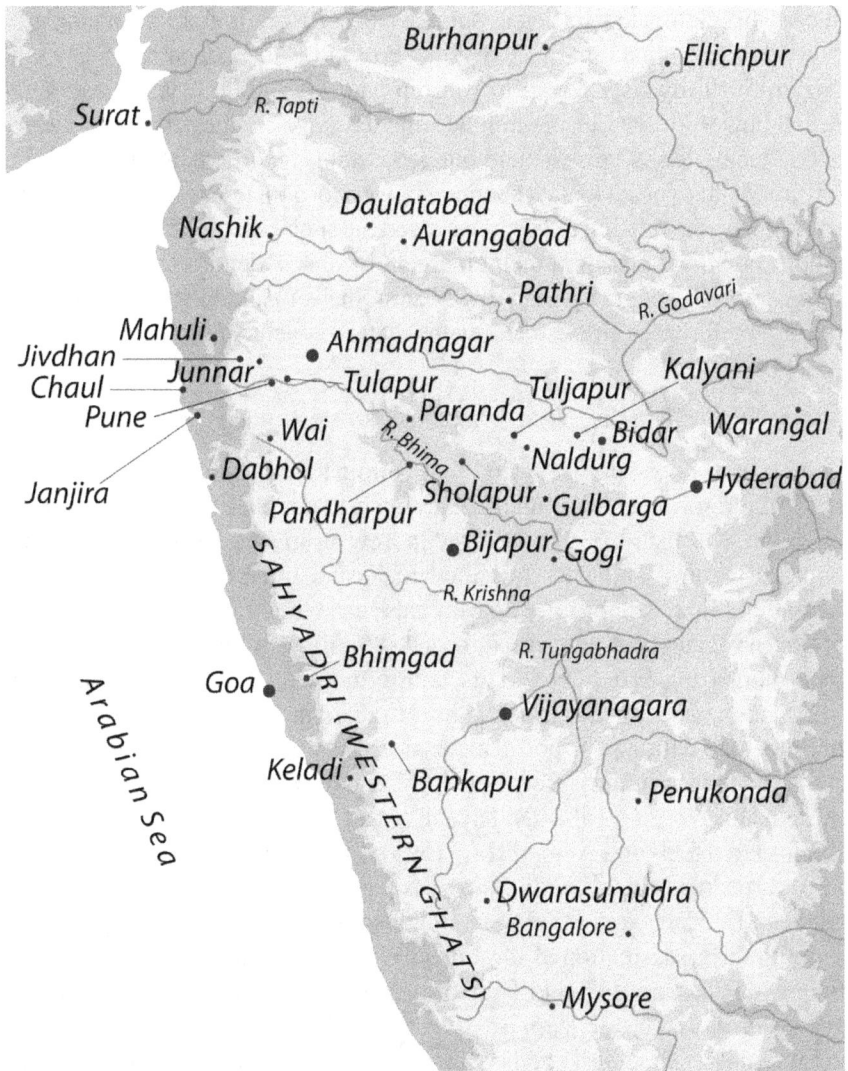

Map 5.2 The western Deccan

Marathas and the Memory of Nizam Shah

The contested relationship between past sovereignties and present circumstances was not only a matter for the sultanates' periphery. In the core regions of the Deccan, too, this question emerged time and again and became fundamental to the existence of the ruling dynasties. While the sultanates of Bijapur and Golkonda were able to create a stable political system that successfully attracted sufficient support at their core regions, Ahmadnagar presents a far more complicated story. From the late sixteenth century, the Nizam Shahi dynasty began to weaken, and after 1600 it lost most of its actual power. Instead, the region became the stage for the activity of generals, reducing the sultans to mere puppets. In this environment, in which the Nizam Shahi dynasty lost its coercive power, local magnates had to redefine their position in relation to the dynasty and the social and political system as a whole, taking into account their emergent localised identities. Nevertheless, I argue, throughout the period, the Nizam Shahs maintained their appeal in this region for large elite circles, even when their actual power was lost.

NIZAM SHAHI DECLINE, NOBLE ASCENDANCE

After a brief expansionist period that culminated in the conquest of Berar (1574), the fortunes of Ahmadnagar began to decline. In the late years of his reign, Murtaza I (r. 1565–88) withdrew from state affairs. The weakening of central authority reignited the usual internal strife, leading to overall political instability. The Mughals made their first appearance in the region with an abortive campaign in 1585–6 that achieved nothing other than plundering Ellichpur.[41] This failure did not improve the conditions in Ahmadnagar, nor did it deter the Mughals in the long run. Following the death of Murtaza I, political tensions increased, leading to the constant change of sultans. Between 1588 and 1595, five sultans sat on the throne: Husayn II (r. 1588–9), Isma'il (r. 1589–91), Burhan II (r. 1591–5), Ibrahim (r. 1595) and Ahmad II (r. 1595). Sultans were drawn ever deeper into partisan politics, leading to regicide.[42] Cracks appeared not only between Deccanis and Foreigners, but also within each party.

With the assassination of Ibrahim (1595), the sultanate was barely functional. At this point, Chand Bibi, widow of ʿAli ʿAdil Shah I of Bijapur and sister of Murtaza Nizam Shah I, stepped in. Acting as guardian of her great-nephew, Bahadur, she became the king-maker in Ahmadnagar. She was not alone in it as at least two more nobles found their own alleged Nizam Shahi princes (rejected by the others), but Chand Bibi prevailed. When the Mughals returned and laid siege to Ahmadnagar in the winter of 1595/6, most nobles as well as her nephew, Ibrahim ʿAdil Shah II, joined her cause. This was sufficient to convince the Mughals to ask for peace, for which Chand Bibi ceded Berar. The peace reignited internal conflicts, with certain nobles even requesting Mughal assistance. In early 1597, the Mughals renewed their campaign, but were repelled. Soon after, Akbar arrived in Khandesh and sent his son Danyal to Ahmadnagar. Chand Bibi saw no choice and agreed to surrender the fort in exchange for securing the safety of the garrison. Several commanders accused her of treason; she was assassinated in 1600.[43] These events mark the collapse of central authority and the beginning of a period characterised by competition between powerful nobles. Yet symbolic Nizam Shahi authority perpetuated in Maharashtra. Several nobles chose to join the Mughals, but no new claims of sovereignty were made as yet.

These trends continued for a few decades. In 1600–1, Murtaza II ascended the throne, but he was so insignificant that the sources disagree about his very identity.[44] The actual political struggle took place between generals, most importantly Raju Dakkani and the Ethiopian Malik Ambar, suggesting a growing rift between Deccanis and Ethiopians. In 1608, Malik Ambar emerged triumphant and became the *de facto* ruler of the sultanate.[45] With his proven military, political and administrative abilities, the sultanate thrived for two more decades. Throughout his rule, Malik Ambar kept a titular Nizam Shahi sultan as a legitimate head-figure.[46] However, he made sure that the sultan would not become overly independent. Around 1610, Murtaza II formed an alliance against Malik Ambar; in response, the general arranged his assassination. Thereafter, Malik Ambar found yet another prince, Burhan III (r. 1610–31), whose reluctance to become involved in politics assisted his longevity.[47] Malik Ambar remained the true leader of the sultanate: he was in charge of foreign relations and initiated a war against Bijapur, culminating in the sack of Nauraspur and the conquest of long-contested Sholapur.[48] He further tried to establish dynastic policies, marrying his son ʿAziz Malik (later Fath Khan) to the daughter of Yaqut Khan, a commander from the inner circle of Ibrahim ʿAdil Shah II. By that, he established a diplomatic network below the royal level but along similar lines; he also trained his son as successor, further demonstrating his sub-royal dynastic aspirations.[49]

The new political directions marked shifts in elite structure. Foreigners left the court in droves, and the Deccani–Ethiopian alliances collapsed, further fragmenting the elites. In parallel, the importance of Hindu rural gentry rose. Maratha warrior bands (*bargī*) had long been active in the armies of the western Deccan.[50] Their status rose under Malik Ambar: Marathas of the Bhonsle, Jadhav, Nimbalkar, Mane and Ghorpade clans, among others, entered state service in high positions, probably becoming the largest component of the army by Malik Ambar's death in 1626.[51]

Turmoil in Ahmadnagar, 1626–33

The late 1620s were turbulent all over the Deccan (see Map 5.2). In Ahmadnagar, Malik Ambar's death opened the door to yet another power struggle. Fath Khan, Malik Ambar's eldest son, inherited his father's position. The son, however, was neither as competent nor as charismatic as his father. Furthermore, the succession itself did not go uncontested. For example, the Ethiopian Hamid Khan tried to build his own power. Claiming to serve Burhan III, whom he held in captivity, and possibly with the silent consent of the Mughal commander Khan Jahan Lodi, he recovered significant Nizam Shahi territories. All this suggests that Malik Ambar may have secured his authority in his lifetime, but failed to establish a dynasty.

The ascendance of Shah Jahan to the Mughal throne ushered in a major change in the region. From the very first year of his reign, he sent expeditions against supporters of the Nizam Shah and even against Mughal officials in Maharashtra whose loyalty was dubious.[52] Fath Khan, albeit officially at peace with the Mughals, cooperated with local parties to block the roads in preparation for the Mughal invasion. He was defeated, allowing Hamid Khan to imprison him in Daulatabad. In the meantime, Shah Jahan grew suspicious of Khan Jahan Lodi's loyalty, and the latter sought refuge with Burhan III. In 1629, the emperor sent an army to the Deccan.[53] Facing food scarcity, he soon turned to diplomatic measures. In 1630, he incited Lakhoji Jadhav Rao, an important Maratha leader and tax agent (*kārkun*) in Nizam Shahi service, to join the Mughals in return for a considerably higher rank (*manṣab*) for him and members of his family.[54] This suggestion came as part of a broader Mughal programme to absorb Maharshtrian nobility, both Marathas and Deccanis, into their system.[55] In parallel, Khan Jahan left Burhan III's court, possibly after suffering a defeat at Mughal hands, escaped, but was caught and killed in 1631.[56] Significantly weakened, Burhan III ordered the murder of Lakhoji and others in his family. Consequently, another important Maratha leader in Nizam Shahi service, Shahaji Bhonsle, who was Lakhoji's son-in-law, felt that his position in the court was eroding. He rebelled against the Nizam Shah, plundered lands around Pune, left his family in the newly renovated fort of Bhimgad, and joined Mughal service with a high *manṣab*. Burhan III now sought support from the sympathetic 'War Party' in Bijapur. Nevertheless, by 1631, the Mughals had taken over significant Nizam Shahi territories; Bijapur advanced in southern Maharashtra.[57] Hard pressed, Burhan III released Fath Khan from prison and reappointed him to his father's previous position.[58] Fath Khan himself was suspicious towards the sultan and arranged his imprisonment and later assassination.[59] He later enthroned Burhan's ten-year-old son Husayn III (r. 1631–3). Combined with Fath Khan's overall unpopularity, more nobles deserted the court, turning to support either the Mughals or Bijapur. Fath Khan tried to recruit the

Limitations of the Deccani System

support of Bijapur and Golkonda, and finally surrendered to the Mughals. In return, he received some of Shahaji's *jāgīr*s, which, according to the Mughals, had originally been Fath Khan's possessions.[60] This, in turn, pushed Shahaji to turn against the Mughals. He plundered the environs of Pune once again, and gradually took over a vast territory, extending to Nasik in the north and the Konkan in the west. He further tried to recreate an alliance with Fath Khan, and, alongside other nobles, encouraged him not to surrender to Shah Jahan. Notwithstanding assistance from Bijapur, Fath Khan was forced to surrender Daulatabad Fort as well as Husayn III to the Mughals in late June 1633. Fath Khan was pardoned and received his previous *jāgīr*, but the young sultan was imprisoned in the Mughal fort of Gwalior.[61]

SHAHAJI AND THE END OF NIZAM SHAHI RULE, 1633–6

The imprisonment of Husayn III was supposed to achieve the annihilation of the Nizam Shahi dynasty, but not all were willing to accept the end of regional independence. Zubayri reports:

> When the kingdom of the Nizam Shah became kingless, and the stitches of good order (*intiẓām*) unravelled, the district-collectors, fort commanders and military leaders of the Nizam Shah remained in the place, fort or district in their possession ... they showed obedience to no one, but rather established themselves in their places [as rulers]. Sidi Rayhan in Sholapur, Shahaji in Pemgad, Sanwas Rao in Junnar, Sidi Saba Sayf Khan in Tal Konkan, Sidi Ambar in Jazira (Janjira?) Rajupri. Other magnates (*zamīndār*s) raised their heads in their respective places, and strived to collect armies and annex territories.[62]

Zubayri emphasises the practical independence of the various commanders, but there is no indication as to the symbols they employed to justify their actions, if any at all. Shahaji Bhonsle demonstrated one option. Fighting against the Mughals, he rejected their offers to join the empire with a considerable *manṣab*. Instead, he worked to resurrect the Nizam Shahi kingdom.[63] He sent to Khawwas Khan, *wakīl* of Bijapur and leader of the 'War Party', saying that:

> If one out of the eighty-four forts of the Nizam Shahi kingdom is gone, let it be so. Junnar, [worthy to be a] capital city, is in [our] hands. If you help this loyal servant (Shahaji) and organise your assistance, I will take upon myself to raise the banner of the Nizam Shahi sultanate.[64]

Khawwas Khan and Murari joined in, maybe hoping to keep a buffer zone with the Mughals.[65]

Shahaji did not act as a frontman for the ambitions of Bijapur, but established himself as the *de facto* ruler of the region. His ambition was demonstrated in public ceremonies, most notably the kingly ceremony of weighing of an elephant and the distribution of alms of an equal weight during the solar eclipse of 23 September 1633. The ceremony was performed near the confluence of the Bhima and the Indrayani rivers near Pune, alongside Murari.[66] While doing so, Shahaji did not style himself as a sovereign in the fashion of his son, Shivaji, four decades later. Instead, he continued the tactic employed by Malik Ambar and many others: he found a Nizam Shahi prince of ten or eleven years old, who was held in Jivdhan. With Murari's consent, Shahaji enthroned him as Murtaza III (r. 1633–6) in Pemgad, raised an entourage to serve and monitor him, and presented him to the army; the young sultan joined his campaigns.[67] Now Shahaji turned to crystallising his domains. Raising substantial forces and aided by diplomatic skills, he took over a significant portion of former Nizam Shahi territories, raising up to one-quarter of its revenues, according to one report.[68] While this expansion did not go unchallenged, the death of the Mughal commander Mahabat Khan undoubtedly assisted Shivaji's endeavour.[69]

This success threatened Mughal interests, eventually pushing Shah Jahan to respond. In 1636, he sent substantial forces while applying pressure on both Bijapur and Golkonda to abandon Shahaji.[70] Bijapur was forced to pay tribute to the Mughals and to acknowledge the nullification of the Nizam Shahi dynasty. The Nizam Shahi territories were divided between the Mughals (northern two-thirds) and Bijapur (southern third).[71] To complete the campaign, the Mughals conquered several forts, arriving at Mahuli, where Shahaji was fortified. Shahaji had no choice but to negotiate his way out, surrendering Mahuli and six other forts to the Mughals. He further had to turn over Murtaza III. In return, Shahaji was allowed to leave unharmed. He entered Bijapur's service with a substantial *jāgīr* near Pune. Murtaza III was imprisoned in Gwalior, just like Husayn III three years beforehand, bringing an end to the Nizam Shahi dynasty.[72]

THE NIZAM SHAH IN MARATHA MEMORY

In the decades leading to its annihilation in 1636, the survival of the Nizam Shahi dynasty depended upon the work of various commanders. For two decades, Malik Ambar managed to keep the sultanate afloat with the cooperation of several elite groups, particularly Ethiopians and Marathas. His death was a major setback for the dynasty. Without an authoritative figure to lead the way, elite loyalties scattered in all directions, each trying to secure his own interests. When Shahaji Bhonsle's relations with Malik Ambar soured around 1625, he did not hesitate to join Bijapur in order to secure his *jāgīr* near Pune,[73] possibly leaving Bijapur's service after Malik Ambar's death in 1626. Following the murder of Lakhoji Jadhav Rao and the desertion of his ally Khan Jahan Lodi, he once again felt a threat to his position and joined the Mughals.[74] When the Mughals promised to grant parts of his *jāgīr* to Fath Khan, he deserted Mughal service, again demonstrating that his *jāgīr* was his first priority. Loyalties were made on an individual level; families with a wide portfolio of possessions were often divided between various patrons.[75] This constant movement reflects atomisation to micro-local interests coming in lieu of the wider identity groups which had enabled grand coalitions of Marathas, Ethiopians and Deccanis against the Mughals.[76]

At the same time, no new forms of sovereignty had emerged. Similarly to the *rāya*s of Andhra, the memory of past sovereigns in Maharashtra was a powerful symbol. The Nizam Shah was the only widely accepted sovereign in the region until the very last days of the dynasty. A Brahmin informer of the Portuguese captured this sentiment, reporting in 1634 that '[i]n the other territories of Nizam Shah, petty rebel thanadars (*thānādār*, local guard) and havladars (*hawāladār*, local-level military officer, sent from the centre) hold sway, refusing to obey anybody except the Nizam Shah'.[77] The same idea of sovereignty – and the understanding that once the Mughals conquered the region, the local magnates would lose their bargaining power – may have guided Shahaji's last desperate attempt to re-establish regional unity around the symbolic figure of Murtaza III. The Mughals, too, understood that the Nizam Shahi name was a powerful symbol that worked against their control over the western Deccan. The Mughal historian ᶜInayat Khan notes that in order to 'win the hearts of the people of the place' Shahaji found a child 'of that clan' (*qabīla*, i.e., Nizam Shah) and put him on the throne.[78] Therefore, even when they were willing to negotiate the position of the resisting commanders Fath Khan (1633) and Shahaji (1636), the Mughals insisted on receiving Husayn III and Murtaza III, respectively, to their hands, and imprisoning them in Gwalior, away from the Deccan.

We can assume that Nizam Shahi association with Maharashtra facilitated Shahaji's policies. From a purely geographical perspective, the core region of the Nizam Shahi sultanate, including Ahmadnagar and Daulatabad, is located at the heart of Marathi-speaking lands. While the origins of the Nizam Shahi dynasty remain obscure, it has been widely acknowledged that they were of Hindu origin, placing them also as Deccanis in the Bahmani context.[79] Even without references to the past, their rise to power was associated with Maharashtra, where Malik Naᵓib was based and Ahmad Bahri was raised.[80] Some accounts mention Pathri in Maharashtra, 180 km east of Ahmadnagar, as their ancestral land.[81] Their control over Daulatabad (Devgiri), the Yadava capital, became a symbolic part of their reign; the Mughals identified this symbolic importance during their siege and conquest of the fort in 1633.[82]

Moreover, evidence suggests that the Nizam Shahi sultans were associated with significant elements in Hindu society, not only in terms of administration but also within the culture with which they were associated. From the very early years of the dynasty, the Nizam Shahs offered patronage to scholars of various Hindu traditions. The court supported Sanskrit learning. Rosalind O'Hanlon et al. demonstrate that already the early Nizam Shahs promoted Brahmins in their service; in return, at least two digests of *dharmasastra* were composed in their honour, one by Dalapati for Ahmad Nizam Shah, the other by Sambhaji Citnis (Pratap Rai) for Burhan I, a work that reflects 'concerns of conservative Brahman scholars perhaps less integrated into the syncretic culture of the Sultanate court'.[83] Another Brahmin scholar who enjoyed Nizam Shahi patronage was Ramesvara Bhatta, founder of the Bhatta lineage in Varanasi. According to his family history, his ability to cure the son of one of the Nizam Shah's Muslim commanders of leprosy earned him a royal request of audience, which he rejected; he nevertheless enjoyed material support of the Nizam Shahi elite.[84] Some evidence links the early sixteenth-century Sanskrit poet Bhanu Datta to royal patronage in Ahmadnagar, notwithstanding his north Indian lineage; this view was promoted by the early seventeenth-century commentator Ananta Pandit, who hailed from the vicinity of Ahmadnagar.[85]

The Nizam Shahi sultans not only linked themselves to Sanskrit traditions, but also to devotional traditions in Marathi.[86] Forms of Bhakti devotion had great significance in the religious landscape of medieval and early modern Maharashtra, mostly among Hindus, but with great influence on, and the participation of, Muslims as well.[87] This significance was due in part to the heavily localised idiom it offered; Bhakti literature was important in the articulation of the devotion to local deities. As such, it expresses evidence to attachment to the region, often in the vernacular.[88] One of the most significant figures in sixteenth-century Maharashtrian devotionalism was the Brahmin saint-poet Eknath, who was born in Paithan, some 90 km to the northeast of Ahmadnagar. Jon Keune argues that while no evidence links Eknath directly to the Nizam Shahi court or state service, some indirect connections are possible. Later works by Eknath, if indeed composed by him, reveal familiarity with the Persian language in its formal use. Furthermore, according to common traditions, Eknath became a disciple of a locally famous *swami*, Janardara, who was at the service of the Nizam

Shah (the traditions vary regarding his position, from fort commander in Daulatabad to administrator).[89] This very memory as appearing in later hagiographies reflects yet another avenue though which the Nizam Shahs were remembered as a positive, or at least benign, force in Maharashtra's history. With this evidence in mind, we can assume that the Nizam Shahs positioned themselves in Maharashtra along similar lines to the Qutb Shahi identity in Telangana.

Later Marathi writings support that the Nizam Shahi dynasty was indeed able to establish a convincing link with Maharashtra. These links were recognised by the Marathas, demonstrating the persistence of this identity for many generations. From the end of the seventeenth century, new kinds of writings discussed the beginning of Maratha power, aiming at integrating the near past of Shivaji's ancestry into the present in meaningful ways. One of the earliest *bakhar*s to discuss this period, *Sabhasad Bakhar* (1694), begins its narrative with Maloji, the vizier (*vajīra daulatā*) of the Nizam Shah and a devotee of Sri Sambhu Mahadev. Having built a tank for the pilgrims, the deity appeared in his dream and promised: 'I will give your lineage (*vaṃśa*) a descendant. He would protect Gods and Brahmins and destroy the barbarians (*mleccha*).[90] I will give [him] a kingdom in the Deccan (*dakṣaṇa*)'. But the new kingdom had to wait; after Maloji's death, his sons Shahaji and Sharafji remained in Nizam Shahi employment. Sabhasad continued that while they were in royal employment, 'the Nizam Shahi [kingdom] fell. Upon this, Shahaji became the vizier of [Muhammad] ᶜAdil Shah, who bestowed on him the title *mahārāja*, and put him in charge of ten or twelve thousand troops.'[91] The passage ignores Shahaji's political manoeuvring between the Nizam Shah, the ᶜAdil Shah and the Mughals. Yet it reveals important elements in the way the Bhonsles recollected their past. First, is the association with place, from the particular temple of Sri Sambhu Mahadev to the Deccan in general. Second, the ascendance of the dynasty had a prophetic mandate and a dharmic obligation to protect Gods and Brahmins and to fight the barbarians, likely referring to Muslims.[92] Third, notwithstanding the reference to the *mleccha*, the Bhonsles remained closely associated with the Nizam Shah as high officials. Only after the dynasty collapsed did Shivaji join ᶜAdil Shahi service.

These elements developed further in later *bakhar*s. The eighteenth-century *91 Kalami* starts the narrative of the marriage of Shahaji and Jijabai in a festive gathering on Holi, when Lakhoji Jadhav Rao saw his only daughter, Jijabai, playing with Shahaji. Without thinking of the consequences, he uttered that the two were suited together. These words reached the ears of the Bhonsles, who accepted them as Lakhoji's agreement to their betrothal. Marriages would serve the Bhonsle well: the Jadhavs claimed to descend from the Yadava kings of Devgiri/Daulatabad. But for the Jadhavs, it would downgrade their social status. Consequently, Lakhoji denied any agreement and discharged the Bhonsles from his service. Maloji and his brother Vithoji returned to Ellora and their ancestral administrative position as village heads (*pāṭīl*). After a few years, Bhavani appeared in their dream,[93] promising long-lasting kingship to their family. She instructed them where to dig to find gold and jewels. With both treasure and divine promise, the Bhonsles raised an army and set to action. First, they chose a surprising tactic: they threw dead pigs into a mosque, to which petitions were attached. This action, however, did not derive from religious motives but was meant, and understood, as an act of political defiance. This plan worked, oddly, bringing the Nizam Shah to inquire with Lakhoji. The sultan sided with the Bhonsles, and accordingly raised their position and titles, allowing Lakhoji to agree to the marriage.[94] Notwithstanding its fantastic elements, this *bakhar* continues with the themes mentioned before. First, is the geographical links to Maharashtra, in particular, to Devgiri/Daulatabad as the seat of power, both Nizam Shahi and in relation to the Yadavas and their Jadhav descendants. Second, the Bhonsles themselves were linked to Ellora, by then a pilgrimage site. This link was intensified by the construction of the Grishneshwara Temple by Maloji in 1606, with Hindu monuments in the Nizam Shahi style by its side, providing another link between the Bhonsles, sacred places in Maharashtra, and the Nizam Shahi dynasty.[95] Third, an important role was given to divine intervention and prophesy. Fourth, the Nizam Shahi sultanate is marked as central to the success of the Bhonsles, facilitating the link between them and the Yadavas.

Similar themes are repeated in the *Sivabharata*. This panegyric courtly poem (*mahākāvya*) in Sanskrit was composed by Kavindra Paramananda during Shivaji's time, probably at his instigation.[96] The beginning of this work discusses Maloji's time, linking him directly to Maharashtra and to dharmic kingship. His success took place under the Nizam Shah, who is described as the *yāvana* (foreigner, lit. Greek, here: Muslim) yet pious (*dharmātma*) ruler of Devgiri. Many other *rāja*s, including Lakhoji Jadhav Rao, served the Nizam Shah as well. When war broke with the ᶜAdil Shah, Maloji and Vithoji joined the service of the Nizam Shah, 'Lord of Devgiri' (*dhārāgirīśvaram*), where Maloji took residence.[97] Maloji was killed in the war, leaving his two sons, Shahaji and Sharifji, under the care of Vithoji. The three were summoned to the Lord of Devgiri, who 'conferred on them their father's wealth and rank'. The poet shifts his focus to Shahaji, described as a kingly character. His qualities attracted Lakhoji's attention, and the latter gave his daughter Jijabai to him.[98] The following

Limitations of the Deccani System

cantos describe in great detail the upheavals of the time. Not shy of political controversies usually ignored by Sabhasad, Paramananda explains the constantly changing alliances in detail. First, the relationship between the Bhonsles and Jadhav Rao deteriorated steadily into open war, blamed on Lakhoji's jealousy. At the same time, Jijabai, Lakhoji's daughter, is hailed for her great qualities.[99] Second, the Bhonsles increased their position as the greatest warriors of the time, who defeat the enemies of the king they serve; there is no claim to sovereignty of their own yet.[100] Third, throughout the story, the sovereignty of the Nizam Shah over Maharashtra is not challenged. Admittedly, Shahaji joins ʿAdil Shahi service, in which he excels. But the text works to explain it as a result of Malik Ambar's treachery that pushed Shahaji away. Paramananda states Shahaji's wish to continue serving the Nizam Shah, but the sultan is so 'influenced by evil advisers / and drunk with sensual pleasures' that he misjudged people and action.[101] This led to Lakhoji's murder and the subsequent flight of nobles. Without the Bhonsles, the kingdom fell into disarray, and famine and misery spread all over. This brought the downfall of the kingdom and the Mughal conquest of Daulatabad.[102]

Similarly to the *bakhar*s, this *mahākāvya* promotes the legitimacy of the Nizam Shah as the true king of Maharashtra, who worked in almost symbiotic relationship with the Bhonsles and enabled their rise. The sultan acknowledged Maloji's position, facilitated the links to the Jadhavs, and tied the Bhonsles to Devgiri. The Nizam Shahs themselves are presented within an interrupted historical continuum of legitimate rulers that go back to the Yadavas. Similar historical continuum is reflected in the *kayfiyat* of Ahmadnagar, recorded in Marathi on 28 December 1805, soon after the first British conquest in 1803,[103] and translated by Babu Rao on 27 November 1816. The genesis of the city was associated with the pilgrimage of a certain rishi and the establishment of a temple and a tank in remote times. The temple fell into disrepair but was rebuilt with the support of the 'Raja of Devgiri' (i.e., Yadavas). Following that the Muslims arrived but the site remained intact. Then, '320 years ago' (*c.* 1485), Ahmad Nizam Shah Bahri arrived to establish his garrison, to find a Sufi saint ('fakeer') in a garden. Ahmad was pleased and decided to build a fort nearby, but could not complete it due to the 'disruption of Ram Raja of Hampi and Virupaksha' (Rama Raya of Vijayanagara, in a clear confusion of dates). One day the king went hunting with his dog. Chasing a hare, the dog retreated, and the king decided to build his fort there. Approved by the Sufi, two palaces were built, and later Ahmadnagar was established, The document then continues to describe the history of the city during Nizam Shahi, Mughal, and Maratha times.[104]

This early nineteenth-century recollection, even if not directly linked to the question of Marathas and Bhonsles, reflects similar memory in which the Nizam Shah sits firmly within the historical continuum. The site of the capital city is linked to both Hindu and Muslim spirituality, and the arrival of Muslims is not marked as disruptive. An interesting addition is the story of the hare and the hound. Suchitra Balasubrahmanyan suggests that such stories were widespread and are linked to the establishment of new capital cities, including Vijayanagara and Ahmadabad (Gujarat), and of new dynasties. They represent the formation of a new political order under a legitimate ruler that is approved by an interpreter of the cosmos (astrologer or, in this case, a Sufi).[105] The *kayfiyat*, then, links the foundation of Ahmadnagar to wider traditions that presents the Nizam Shahis in a positive light, further cementing their memory as legitimate rulers of Maharashtra, accepted by all parties in the region, including the Marathas. In that, the Nizam Shahs seem to have followed a similar path to Golkonda in marking themselves as regional kings, accepted by vernacular-speaking elites. Even when severely weakened, no other power emerged in the region to try to claim their place, attesting to their great success in the region.

Expansion and Crisis: Bijapur and Golkonda, 1636–58

The models of interaction with the locality tried by the sultanates with varying degrees of success met their most significant test towards the middle of the seventeenth century. The 1636 treaty with the Mughals came at a price. ᶜAbdullah Qutb Shah had to submit to the Mughals and pay a hefty tribute. He was forced to accept Mughal sovereignty, expressed in the Sunni sermon (*khuṭba*), and conceded the sultanate's foreign policy to the empire, allowing Shah Jahan to regulate Golkonda's relationship with Bijapur and the Safavids. To add to his humiliation, ᶜAbdullah had to sign under the downgraded title Qutb al-Mulk, not used since the death of the last Bahmani sultan.[106] Muhammad ᶜAdil Shah was treated less harshly. Shah Jahan did not acknowledge his sovereignty, using the downgraded title ᶜAdil Khan. The sultan was required to assist the Mughals in conquering forts in Maharashtra and to send tribute and precious gifts to the Mughal court, both signs of tributary status. However, Bijapur gained much from this arrangement: the sultanate annexed the southern portion of the Nizam Shahi territories, long battled between the two sultanates.[107]

The treaties bruised the prestige of the two sultans and were burdensome on their treasuries, but also secured their northern borders for the first time in decades. Shah Jahan, maybe remembering the assistance he

Limitations of the Deccani System

received from Golkonda during his rebellion against his father in the early 1620s,[108] strictly kept his commitment and refrained from intervening in the region.[109] The peace was kept also by his appointed governor of the Mughal Deccan, Prince Aurangzeb, during his first tenure (1636–44). The prince settled in Malik Ambar's old capital of Khirki, now renamed Aurangabad.[110] With a quiet northern border, the sultanates looked to the south, where Vijayanagara's disintegration left a fragmented political landscape.[111] Muhammad ᶜAdil Shah and ᶜAbdullah Qutb Shah embarked on expansionist endeavours, the most significant since the post-Talikota decades, recapturing territories conquered in the 1570s and lost since then and expanding beyond.[112]

These favourable conditions did not last long. By the mid-seventeenth century, both Bijapur and Golkonda were engulfed in deep crises, aggravated by renewed Mughal pressure. The beginning of the crisis was similar in both sultanates: fast expansion brought ambitious nobles to assert autonomous positions in the newly conquered territories, bringing tensions between them and the court. The return of Prince Aurangzeb as governor of the Deccan in 1653 ushered in a new era of Mughal assertiveness, only partly mandated by the throne. The two processes combined pushed both sultanates to the verge of extinction within a few years.[113] Notwithstanding the similar challenge, the fortunes of the sultanates varied significantly. Golkonda successfully sustained the pressure, later to become the strongest sultanate in the Deccan. In contrast, Bijapur continued to weaken. Gradually losing control over territories and people, it remained a sultanate in name only. This difference seems surprising, considering that Golkonda suffered harsher treatment at the hands of the Mughals. However, it was the internal structure and ideology that deemed Golkonda durable and Bijapur vulnerable. To understand the different trajectories, let us turn now to the examine the crises in more detail.

EXPANSION, CRISIS AND RESPONSE

In 1642, ᶜAbdullah Qutb Shah appointed Muhammad Saᶜid (d. 1663) to lead military expeditions to the south and east. Born in the early 1590s in Ardestan, Muhammad Saᶜid arrived in the Deccan in the 1620s in the service of an Iranian merchant. In the 1630s, he entered royal service, first as *ḥawāladār* in the port city of Masulipatnam, where he fostered his own commercial links with the European companies, then in Mustafanagar (Telangana). In 1642, he was sent on the southern campaigns. Based on his success, in the next year he was appointed *mīr jumla*, the title by which he was remembered thereafter, and continued campaigning. Crossing the

Krishna River, he conquered Rayalaseema and beyond, reaching as far as Pulicat, Tirupati and São Tomé (Chennai). He recaptured territories that Muhammad Quli had claimed half a century earlier, bringing the entire Telugu-speaking lands under Qutb Shahi control. With no significant opposition, the campaign was a resounding success.[114] The rapid advance put Golkonda in competition with Bijapur, which advanced in parallel. ᶜAbdullah Qutb Shah and Muhammad ᶜAdil Shah acknowledged the danger, and agreed to divide their sphere of expansion and influence around 1640.[115] But a few years later, their forces clashed on several occasions. One point of contestation was Gingee (1648). Designated to be annexed by Golkonda, the town and its substantial spoils fell into Bijapur's hands with Muhammad Saᶜid's assistance. By 1652, the sultanates clashed directly, both petitioning Shah Jahan to intervene, in accordance with the terms of the peace of 1636.[116]

The main danger, however, came from Muhammad Saᶜid. After his military success, he established his control over the newly conquered territories and mustered significant power. The French traveller François Bernier reports that not only militarily, he also gained control over diamond mines 'under feigned names' and developed extensive commercial links. Using the profits, he kept a private army, which included European mercenaries.[117] ᶜAbdullah Qutb Shah grew worried about his noble's autonomy in that distant region. When he tried to force his sovereignty over Muhammad Saᶜid, the latter left Golkonda's service.[118] This choice was made possible with changes in the northern Deccan. In 1653, Prince Aurangzeb arrived in Aurangabad to start his second tenure as governor. In the first years he struggled to regulate the administration of the loss-inducing territories.[119] Muhammad Saᶜid and the rich territories under his control presented a great opportunity to the prince. In 1656, Aurangzeb convinced the emperor to offer Muhammad Saᶜid a high *manṣab* to join the Mughals.[120] Remembered by his Qutb Shahi job title, Mir Jumla (and also by the title Muᶜazzam Khan), Muhammad Saᶜid had a glorious career in Mughal service as Aurangzeb's partisan. He was appointed *wazīr* and joined Aurangzeb's Deccan campaign. Finally, he served as Governor of Bengal and commander of the Koch Bihar and Assam campaigns.[121]

Compared with Golkonda, the treaty of 1636 left Bijapur in a better position. Not only did the sultanate significantly increase its territories, but these lands were in the core region of the Deccan. However, the incorporation of these territories did not prove to be easy. Former Nizam Shahi nobles continued their resistance, for example, Fath Khan, who rebelled in 1052/1642–3 around the Konkan port of Chaul. Fuzuni reports that

Limitations of the Deccani System

once it became known that it was Fath Khan, son of Malik Ambar, many joined his cause, blocking the roads and engaging in banditry. It took a major campaign to subdue the rebel and annex his territories.[122] This was a sign of future problems: the refusal of some former Nizam Shahi elites to accept ᶜAdil Shahi sovereignty.

The troubles in the north remained minor at that point, and Bijapur could expand to the south, making significant gains. Soon after the treaty of 1636, Muhammad ᶜAdil Shah initiated a series of successful campaigns under Randaula Khan, bringing significant expansion. By 1644, Bijapur-affiliated forces had conquered Bangalore, and two years later, defeated the last ruler to carry the Vijayanagara name, Sriranga Rayal, in Vellore. This success, however, was curtailed by Muhammad ᶜAdil Shah's illness. As was often the case in the Deccan, the weakness of the sultan unleashed partisan politics in the capital. In the provinces, commanders took advantage of the odd combination of weak centre amidst military success. One of these was Shahaji Bhonsle, who joined Bijapur's service in 1636. He was attached to Randaula Khan's campaign in 1642–3, with the promise of additional allotments in the south.[123] Leaving his eldest son Shivaji on the family *jāgīr* in Maharashtra, Shahaji became central to Bijapur's campaign. He set up his headquarters in Bangalore, from which he fostered local alliances in the Karnatak to cement his position against Bijapur. Muhammad ᶜAdil Shah responded by ordering Shahaji's arrest in 1648.

Shahaji, however, had leverage against Bijapur: his son Shivaji. During Shahaji's campaign, Shivaji, aided by Dadoji Konddev (d. 1647), who likely to have been originally in ᶜAdil Shahi service, worked to increase the Bhonsle power base in Maharashtra when royal attention was focused on the Karnatak. Shivaji continuously increased his possessions, using various methods: from negotiation and alliances to threats and military confrontation. Shivaji further systematised his holdings, possibly in continuation of Nizam Shahi practice, and increased his military might.[124] With the newly accumulated forces, Shivaji could pressure the sultan to release his father. In the following years, father and son acted each in his own region to increase the family possessions in their respective strongholds on both sides of Bijapur.[125] The death of Muhammad ᶜAdil Shah and the ascendance of his young son, ᶜAli II (1656–72), made things even shakier.[126]

The crisis in the Deccan escalated during Aurangzeb's governorship. After a few years of quarrelling with the Qutb Shah over Mughal claims for overdue payment of tribute, he sent his son Muhammad Sultan against Golkonda in 1656, under the pretext of protecting Muhammad Saᶜid's *jāgīr*. The Mughals conquered Hyderabad and forced ᶜAbdullah Qutb Shah to seek shelter in Golkonda Fort.[127] In parallel, Aurangzeb tried to stir up a commotion in Bijapur, claiming that ᶜAli II was not Muhammad ᶜAdil Shah's son,[128] and convincing Shah Jahan to allow him to invade. Seizing strategic forts, including the symbolic Bidar and Kalyani, and assisted by Muhammad Saᶜid, Aurangzeb continued to Bijapur. At that point, Shah Jahan, possibly encouraged by his son Dara Shukoh, ordered Aurangzeb to suspend the aggression and instead start negotiating.[129] Eventually, both sultanates were forced to accept new terms: ceding strategic territories to the Mughals; in Golkonda, marrying Auragnzeb's son, Muhammad Sultan, to ᶜAbdullah Qutb Shah's daughter, declaring their future son heir apparent of Golkonda. In addition, heavy war indemnities were levied.[130] Fortunately for the sultanates, Shah Jahan fell ill soon after, and Aurangzeb rushed north to secure his position in the ensuing War of Succession. His accession to the Mughal throne in 1658 was ominous for the sultanates, but his involvement in other parts of the empire postponed their elimination for three more decades.

Notwithstanding the similarity in the events as they unfolded in Bijapur and Golkonda, the results of the lingering crises differed significantly. A few years after the Mughals withdrew their forces, Golkonda began to recover. The lands south of the Krishna, considered Muhammad Saᶜid's *jāgīr*, were first contested by his appointees, local magnates, and Europeans. But in 1662, ᶜAbdullah Qutb Shah sent his general Neknam Khan to the region; the general was successful in asserting Golkonda's control over these lands.[131] Furthermore, even amid the turmoil, there are no signs to indicate the decline of political stability in Telangana, the core region of the sultanate. The ᶜAdil Shahi sultanate, albeit not as harshly treated by the Mughals, never fully recovered. After the Mughals had left, ᶜAli II could not muster sufficient forces to impose his authority over his vast territories. Shivaji increasingly asserted his independent policies in the north. In parallel, Shahaji continued to cement his control over the Karnatak. In the centre, power struggles between Deccanis and Ethiopians, now drifting apart, and between them and the Foreigners, aggravated by the weak monarch, pushed nobles to promote their own agenda. Shivaji's growing independence and his often conflicted relations with the Mughals drew the empire to intervene in 1665–6, and both Aurangzeb and Shivaji increased their pressure on Bijapur.[132] By the 1670s, central authority had collapsed, and the sultanate relied on financial and military assistance from Golkonda.[133]

Golkonda's Success, Bijapur's Failure

Golkonda's success and Bijapur's failure are rather baffling. Until 1636, Bijapur had been the stronger sultanate in the Deccan, and sustained less

Limitations of the Deccani System

pressure from the Mughals in 1636 and 1656–7. Nevertheless, time and again, Golkonda showed an impressive ability to recover while Bijapur slid into chaos, hollowing the sultanate from authority and power. This difference, I argue, did not come from the very challenge to sultanate authority, but rather from the identity of those who presented the challenge.

The instigators of the crises belonged to different socio-political milieus. Muhammad Sa'id was a typical Foreigner the like of whom we have encountered before. He arrived in the Deccan as an adult, and had a successful career there, promoting his personal interests. When his position seemed at risk, he sought another patron, finally embarking on a similarly brilliant career under a new one. He then joined a military campaign against his previous patron, demonstrating the duality in the position of the Foreigners. This ambiguity indicates the limitation of the danger he posed to Golkonda. Foreigners did not usually operate as a collective, but worked as individuals or within small-scale networks. The change of patron was, accordingly, an individual choice. Even if this could be harmful (as it was in this case), the damage was neither systematic nor structural and could be relatively easily contained. Other Foreigners were not encouraged by this to leave en masse. In a way, their employment included a calculated risk, suggesting that advantages in their employment outweighed the danger. Employment of the Foreigners as a group was infringed only when networks of patronage collapsed altogether as was the case in Ahmadnagar after 1600. But this was not the case in Golkonda of the 1650s, where Muhammad Sa'id's choice did not facilitate an exodus of Foreigners.

Shahaji and Shivaji Bhonsle introduced a significantly more dangerous challenge. As mentioned before, when Shahaji joined Bijapur's Karnatak campaign, Shivaji remained behind to take care of the family *jāgīr*s in Maharashtra, considerably increasing territories and military power. The death of Muhammad 'Adil Shah and the ascendance of 'Ali II to the throne improved Shavaji's position in several ways; it not only weakened the court, but the presence of Bijapur's commanders in Maharashtra may have declined. Mulla Ahmad, a major *jāgīr* holder in the former Nizam Shahi territories, left his domain for the capital to improve his position there. In his absence, Shivaji seized even more lands and, against his prescribed *jāgīr*, also forts, gradually expanding towards the Western Ghats and the Konkan. At this point, he was already seen in Bijapur as a rebel. After Aurangzeb's withdrawal in 1657, the sultanate could turn against Shivaji. In 1659, Afzal Khan was sent with substantial forces. In the encounter between the commanders, Shivaji famously disembowelled Afzal Khan, the Maratha forces defeated Bijapur's army, and relations between the two sides reached a new low, bringing the alienation of additional *deśmukh*s (landed elites) from Bijapur.[134]

Shivaji's expansion marks the substantial difference between Muhammad Saʿid's actions and those of the Bhonsles. Shahaji joined Bijapur not as an individual, but as a local magnate, with followers and with *jāgīr* identified as hereditary (*waṭan*).[135] Accordingly, any action he, and later Shivaji, took had wider implications on his group as a whole. Bijapur's problem began with the refusal of the Bhonsles to accept the sultanates' sovereignty over their ancestral lands. Furthermore, Shivaji was gradually developing his own sense of independence within former Nizam Shahi territories. No less significantly, others chose to follow him. By the mid-1650, if we accept the narrative promoted in the *bakhar*s, many *deśmukh*s in Maharashtra had transferred their support to Shivaji.[136] His success placed him not as a petty rebel but as a symbol of his own. In the late 1660s, the Mughal historian Muhammad Bakhtawar Khan identified this support, reporting that:

> Shiva, son of Shahu Bhonsle – both nobles of Bijapur (*ʿādilkhāniya*) – control most of (the Nizam Shah's) forts and lands. Most of the *rāja*s and all the *rāya*s from all around Hindustan sent tribute (*peshkash*), showed obedience and submission, and bowed their wretched heads in front of him [in submission].[137]

The chronicler agrees with the Maratha version, marking significant support among the Marathas even prior to Shivaji's coronation in 1674.

Shivaji's success demonstrates Bijapur's inability to incorporate the Bhonsles and, more generally, post-Nizam Shahi landed elites. The transfer of lands and rights into ʿAdil Shahi or Mughal hands, it seems, was not always translated into a transfer of loyalties. Indeed, the same sources that demonstrate the positive memory of the Nizam Shah suggest the rejection of ʿAdil Shahi authority and their overall presentation in an unfavourable light. Paramananda positions the Nizam Shah and ʿAdil Shah in clear contrast:

> At that time the Nizam Shah
> Was residing at Deogiri (Devgiri) Fort.
> A religious man, he ruled the land
> And was ever served
> By Jadhavrao and the others
> Who ruled as the Deccan rajas.
> At that time, too,
> In the city of Bijapur
> The Adil Shah did rule –
> A Muslim surrounded by Muslims.[138]

Limitations of the Deccani System

Not openly hostile, the verse marks a clear contrast between the religiosity of the Nizam Shah from his abode in Devgiri and support by Marathas, and Bijapur's ᶜAdil Shah, with his Muslim following.

Krishnaji Anant is more concrete in his anti-ᶜAdil Shahi sentiment. He suggests that in the early stage of Afzal Khan's campaign against Shivaji in 1659:

> his forces arrived in Tuljapur, where they encamped. They shattered [the image of] Sri Bhavani, titular deity (*kuladevatā*) of the *mahārāja*'s house (i.e. Bhonsle), threw it into a hand mill (*jātem*), and ground it to dust. Soon after Bhavani was broken, a divine voice came from the heavens (*ākaśvāṇī*), and with no body (*aśraṇī*) said: 'oh, Afzal Khan, you wretched! On the twenty-first day from now, I will decapitate you, destroy your entire army, and will satisfy nine crores (*koṭi*) *ćāmuṃḍā*s (blood sucking goddesses)'. Then the army marched and arrived in Pandharpur (*śrīpaṃdhar*). Descending on the bank of the Bhima River, they attacked the deities, then continued to Wai.[139]

The story marks Afzal Khan, and the monarch who sent him, in a particularly negative way within this context. First, Afzal Khan arrived in Tuljapur, strongly associated with Bhavani. Grinding the goddess' image to dust, a phrase associated with Muslim iconoclasm, the voice of the goddess appears and threatens to release the *ćāmuṃḍā*s, mother goddesses (*mātṛkā*) who are summoned in the battlefield to defeat the demons by sucking their blood. Not only directly through Bahavani, family deity of the Bhonsles, summoning the *ćāmuṃḍā*s links the story to the family through the Saivite connection.[140] A second place that is mentioned as a target of Afzal Khan's campaign is Pandharpur, then already one of the most important pilgrimage sites in Maharashtra.[141] The passage as a whole carefully selected the holiest sites in Maharashtra, in particular, in the Maratha context, in order to depict the sultan as an enemy. By that, the evil ᶜAdil Shah emerges as the complete opposite of the *dharmātma* Nizam Shah. Stewart Gordon suggests that this event 'reflected the sectarian orthodoxy that was growing in the declining state of Bijapur'.[142] This sectarian view is possible; however, if it did indeed happen, Afzal Khan's actions came to be understood along the lines of political rather than religious activity, Bhavani being the Bhonsles' family deity.[143]

Either way, the tone towards Bijapur reflects a rejection of ᶜAdil Shahi sovereignty. This rejection, I argue, derived from questions of relations of rulers with language communities and territories. Similarly to Golkonda, the Nizam Shahs based their legitimacy on regional and possibly also linguistic identity. In contrast, the sultans of Bijapur chose a path that did not rely on any vernacular in particular, nor with the territories subsumed in any vernacular, Maharashtra and the Marathi language included. From its inception, the sultanate lacked the territorial manifestation of any vernacular. Bijapur's expansion after 1636 added to this complexity with the addition of Tamil-speaking lands to the Marathi and Kannada regions. In this case, the sultans did not have much to offer to the Marathas and their nascent regional identities: historical links between the Marathas and Bijapur were superficial as the Maratha heartland was not part of Bijapur until the late 1630s. Even Bijapur's implicit use of Vijayanagara's memory, which may have been effective in the sultanate's core until the 1630s, did not appeal to these newly integrated elites. As a whole, argues Sumit Guha, 'in contrast to the Telugu and Kannada countries, Maratha historical memory was largely impervious to the appeal of Vijayanagara as a repository of ancestral glory'. The lack of Vijayanagara memory is demonstrated in writings related to the Bhonsles.[144] Bijapur's ideology, therefore, did not stand much of a chance of succeeding in the Maratha lands. The Mughals were facing similar difficulties in Maharashtra: lacking sufficient ideological framework to allow Maratha cooperation (and incorporation) on a large scale, the Marathas usually rejected imperial rule in the region.[145]

Instead of accepting either claim of sovereignty, the Bhonsles developed their own ideology. Linking the geographical, historical and linguistic identity of Maharashtra, they provided infrastructure that successfully attracted local landed elites. Marathi narratives place Shivaji as a descendant of north Indian Rajputs, a claim that came to promote the supremacy of the Bhonsles as Kshatriyas and link them to Brahminical networks of sovereignty.[146] Connections to the Yadavas of Devgiri were promoted, and additional claims linked the Bhonsles to *jāgīr*s around Daulatabad/Devgiri.[147] The expansion of Shivaji's domains and the increasing incorporation of landed elites into his endeavour brought new historical writing to support this identity. Guha suggests that with the spread of Shivaji's administration in the 1650s, localised histories in Marathi, written for legal and propriety reasons, expanded in scope. They were used to construct a regional identity among Maratha elites, on whose support Shivaji established his power.[148] The use of Marathi increased as the language became the main medium of administration and correspondence; a conscious attempt was made to promote Marathi and to purge Persio-Arabic words in favour of Sanskritic titles, terms and vocabulary.[149] By that, the Bhonsles defined an identity that seems more in line with the previous Nizam Shahi rulers, and as an alternative to the non-specific localisation promoted by the ᶜAdil Shah.

The public identity and political idiom developed by the mid-seventeenth century placed Shivaji in direct competition with the ᶜAdil

Limitations of the Deccani System

Shah. If the latter saw himself as 'King of the Deccan', so did Shivaji. Such claims were made explicit: *Sivabharata* names him 'King of the Deccan' (*dākṣiṇātyo mahārāja*),[150] and in his promise that began the career of the Bhonsles, Sri Sambhu Mahadeva promised Maloji to give his scion the kingdom of the Deccan.[151] M. S. Naravane suggests that the very same aspiration stood behind Shivaji's Karnatak campaign in the 1670s.[152] The creation of a new centre of authority in competition with the court of Bijapur, supported by the Bhonsles' decision to remain peripheral to the sultanate in favour of their own interests, was an appealing option for Marathas in Bijapur's service. Not only in former Nizam Shahi territories, but also in Bijapur's core, those identified as Marathas now had a choice. The growing popularity of Shivaji was not merely the result of his military achievements, although such appeal is undeniable. His success depended on his ability to present a viable option within the specific social circumstances and political environment.

* * *

The different ideologies tried by the sultanates in relations to the locality had clear limitations of various kinds. For the Qutb Shahi sultans the main concern was geographical. Their localised, Telugu-infused political language was insufficient to support their expansion to the other Telugu-speaking regions, namely, Andhra and Rayalaseema. The difficulty was linked to the plurality of Telugu affiliations, with other centres, most notably Vijayanagara or the memory thereof, generating competing foci of identity. Golkonda's failure further fits in a wider historical trajectory that did not always encourage unity between the three regions. At the same time, as the case of Muhammad Saʿid reveals, Golkonda's rule in Telangana remained unshaken even when challenged elsewhere, indicating the continuous appeal of the Qutb Shahi political ideology in the core of that sultanate.

The appeal of the Nizam Shahi sultans as kings of Maharashtra seems to have found audiences among local, Marathi-speaking elites, in particular, the Marathas. Many in this group maintained the memory of the dynasty, long after the dynasty itself lost actual power. Even after its annihilation in 1636, the sultans were remembered as the legitimate rulers of the region, a memory that was integrated into Maratha historiography. The Nizam Shahi success highlights the failure of the ʿAdil Shah in the region and in relation to the same groups. Their idea of all-Deccani, non-particular sovereignty failed to find ways into the former Nizam Shahi territories they gained after 1636. Their non-vernacular vision of localisation was likely successful in the core of the sultanate. However, it failed to address the social and cultural diversity away from the centre, thus enhancing the breaking away of crucial elite groups. This, in turn, brought the decline not only of their control in Maharashtra, but of central authority itself. In that sense, Shivaji's role in the decline of Bijapur was not solely linked to his military success, but also to an ideological one. Shaking the very core of the sultanate from the inside, Bijapur could not sustain the growing pressure from the outside.

Notes

1. Rebellions against Qutb Shahi rule were overall rare, but at the height of Rama Raya's rule in the early 1560s, Vijayanagara instigated rebellions among tributary principalities in Panagal and Ghanpur in central Telangana. See Sherwani, *History of the Qutb Shahi*, pp. 132–3 and 225–6, n. 27.
2. The anonymous chronicler identified the political content of this division, marking the Krishna as 'the border between the Kingdom of Telangana and the Land of Vijayanagara', see *Tarikh-i Qutb Shah*, p. 213r.
3. Inscriptions promote them as descendants of the Eastern Chalukyas of Vengi; additional evidence associates them with the region from the twelfth century. The dynasty disappeared with this rebellion around 1599. See Devi, *After the Kakatiyas*, pp. 230–8.
4. *Tarikh-i Qutb Shah*, p. 161r–v. The principality of Gopal is likely to be Gopalpur, a town on the coast of Orissa, not far from the Andhra border.
5. Holding one's relative hostage was a common practice in early modern India. In the Mughal Empire, even royal princes were kept in court as leverage against rebellious relatives. For example, Kamran (d. 1557), brother of Humayun (r. 1530–40 and 1555–6), held the emperor's infant son Akbar as a safeguard against his brother's ambitions; Dara Shukoh (d. 1659) and Aurangzeb (r. 1658–1707), sons of Prince Khurram (later Shah Jahan), were held hostage in the court of their grandfather, Emperor Jahangir (r. 1605–27). See Faruqui, *Princes of the Mughal Empire*, pp. 71–8.
6. *Tarikh-i Qutb Shah*, p. 164r.
7. Subrahmanyam, 'Persians, Pilgrims', pp. 503–7, suggests that the rise of Masulipatnam as a major trading port can be traced to around 1570, enabling the consolidation of Ibrahim's rule in combination with the rise of new networks around the Bay of Bengal.
8. *Tarikh-i Qutb Shah*, pp. 221v–224v.
9. For instance, the rebellion in Bastar, see Sherwani, *History of the Qutb Shahi*, pp. 294–5. Interestingly, the village histories collected around the turn of the nineteenth century in the region do not record any Qutb Shahi presence, indicating how superfluous and unremarkable their rule was in the region.

10. Richards, *Mughal Administration in Golconda*, pp. 92–7, 122–30; Vaikuntham, *Hyderabad State*, p. 35; Raghunadha Rao, *Modern Andhra*, pp. 14–17; Keay, *The Honourable Company*, pp. 290–4, 341–2; Regani, *Nizam–British Relations*, pp. 71–2, 125–44; Narayana Rao et al., *Textures of Time*, pp. 21–92.
11. This marginal role of Hyderabad is reflected in the collection of *kaifiyat*s from locations around the 'Circar of Kalinga' in the Northern Circars. A brief passage mentions a nameless *faujdār* (or *nabob*) sent from Hyderabad, who unsuccessfully tried to stir (named) local magnates against one another to improve his position. See 'The Kyfyet of Sreengavarumcotah of the Calinga Cirkar', Mackenzie unbound, Class VII, No. 29, pp. 57r–59v.
12. Lycett and Morrison, 'The "Fall" of Vijayanagara'.
13. Dates regarding the various rulers of Vijayanagara, in particular, during this troubled period, are problematic to determine, with a variety of versions extant; see list in Bridges White, 'Beyond Empire', pp. 48–52, table 3.1.
14. Rama Sharma, *Vijayanagar, the Last Phase*, vol. 2, pp. 1–7; Heras, *Aravidu Dynasty*, vol. 1, pp. 248–63; Venkataramanayya, *Further Sources*, vol. 1, pp. 291–300; Nilakanta Sastri, *A History of South India*, pp. 191–3.
15. *Tarikh-i Qutb Shah*, pp. 179v–180r.
16. Rama Sharma, *Vijayanagar, the Last Phase*, vol. 2, pp. 14–37; Heras, *Aravidu Dynasty*, vol. 1, pp. 264–79; Venkataramanayya, *Further Sources*, vol. 1, pp. 301–9; Nilakanta Sastri, *A History of South India*, pp. 193–4; Sherwani, *History of the Qutb Shahi*, pp. 170–2; *Tarikh-i Qutb Shah*, pp. 179v–182v.
17. 'Kyfeat of Commamoor', Mackenzie unbound, Class VII, No. 5, p. 45r. As a whole, and more than in the Mughal Empire, it seems that the lower and middle levels of administration were carried on in the vernacular and based on administrative continuities, see Guha, 'Serving the Barbarian', pp. 499–501.
18. Sherwani, *History of the Qutb Shahi*, p. 121.
19. Sherwani, *History of the Qutb Shahi*, pp. 279–90, and see further discussion below.
20. *Tarikh-i Qutb Shah*, pp. 218r–219v.
21. 'Kayfiyat of Condaveed', Mackenzie unbound, Class VII, No. 4, p. 32r; *Tarikh-i Qutb Shah*, pp. 197v–200r.
22. *Tarikh-i Qutb Shah*, pp. 209v–210v. Needless to say, it is highly unlikely that any court became a Muslim place of worship, in particular, in cases of voluntary cooperation of this kind. The Persian chronicles are dotted with such *topoi* and conventions, stressing political rather than confessional superiority.
23. *Tarikh-i Qutb Shah*, pp. 210v–216v.
24. Rama Sharma, *Vijayanagar, the Last Phase*, vol. 2, pp. 38–135; Heras, *Aravidu Dynasty*, vol. 1, pp. 300–40; Venkataramanayya, *Further Sources*, vol. 1, pp. 310–25; Nilakanta Sastri, *A History of South India*, pp. 194–8;

Subrahmanyam and Shulman, 'The Man Who Would be King?', pp. 230–4.
25. *Hadiqat al-Salatin*, p. 192.
26. Sarkar, *The Life of Mir Jumla*, pp. 27–72, and see discussion later in this chapter.
27. Sherwani, *History of the Qutb Shahi*, pp. 121, 172–3.
28. Bhukya, *Modern Telangana*, pp. 197–207. While the history of the complex relationship between Andhra and Telangan goes back many centuries, some modern writers assume that, like many other issues, the division started only in colonial times: as a difference between the Nizam's autocratic–feudal system and the more advanced coast and Rayalaseema, which were under direct colonial rule. See Forrester, 'Subregionalism in India'.
29. Raghunadha Rao, *Modern Andhra*, pp. 186–93; Sherwani, *History of the Qutb Shahi*, p. 283.
30. Bridges White, 'Beyond Empire', pp. 92–5; Dirks, *The Hollow Crown*, pp. 43–52; Wagoner, *Tidings*, pp. 23–33.
31. For example, the Mahanavami festival discussed in chapter 4.
32. 'Kayfiyat of Condaveed', Mackenzie unbound, Class VII, No. 4, pp. 31v–34v.
33. Heras, *Aravidu Dynasty*, vol. 1, p. 255 and map opposite p. 334. A similar idea of Vijayanagara's might at the period appears in Venkataramanayya, *Further Sources*, vol. 1, p. 318, who argues that 'Venkata II taught the Muhammadans the much needed lesson that they could not always afford to attack the possessions of the emperor of Vijayanagara with impunity'.
34. Stein, *Vijayanagara*, pp. 120–6.
35. Narayana Rao, 'Coconut and Honey', pp. 24–7.
36. Narayana Rao and Shulman, 'Introduction', in Allasani Peddana, *The Story of Manu*, pp. vii–xliii.
37. *Prabandha* is a Telugu genre often compared with the Sanskrit courtly poetry, *mahākāvya*, see discussion in Loewy Shacham, 'Krsnadevaraya's Amuktamalyada', pp. 1–5.
38. Loewy Shacham, 'Krsnadevaraya's Amuktamalyada', pp. 112–61.
39. Loewy Shacham, 'Krsnadevaraya's Amuktamalyada', p. 10.
40. Talbot, *Precolonial India*, pp. 194–6.
41. *Burhan-i Maʾathir*, pp. 537–51; Shyam, *Ahmadnagar*, pp. 178–84.
42. Shyam, *Ahmadnagar*, pp. 207–17, also see Chapter 2 on the assassination of Husayn II as part of the partisan struggle.
43. *Tarikh-i Firishta*, vol. 2, pp. 309–23; *Burhan-i Maʾathir*, pp. 593–618, 625–32; *Muntakhab al-Lubab*, vol. 3, pp. 248–57, 260–2; *Tadhkirat al-Muluk*, pp. 223–7; *Akbarnama*, vol. 3, pp. 1157–8; Shyam, *Ahmadnagar*, pp. 214–27; Qadri, *Chand Bibi*, pp. 71–4.
44. Shyam, *Malik Ambar*, pp. 38–41.
45. Gordon, *The Marathas*, p. 42; *Futuhat-i ʿAdil Shahi*, pp. 267v–270v.
46. *Futuhat-i ʿAdil Shahi*, pp. 269b–270a, reports that Malik Ambar 'searched

Limitations of the Deccani System

for a prince of the Nizam Shahi dynasty, to place over his head as master, so that the populace might agree to obey him'. See also Sarkar, *House of Shivaji*, p. 9.

47. Shyam, *Ahmadnagar*, p. 261. The Italian traveller Pietro della Valle captured this duality in the relationship between the sultan and his general, saying that the king was 'a Boy of twelve years old, who therefore doth not govern it, but an Abyssine slave ... call'd Melik Amber ... [he] governs not fraudulently and with design to usurp, by keeping the King shut up, as I have sometimes heard; but ... he administers with great fidelity and submission towards the young King'. See della Valle, 146.
48. *Futuhat-i ᶜAdil Shahi*, pp. 287a–292a, Sarkar, *House of Shivaji*, pp. 18–23; Shyam, *Malik Ambar*, pp. 110–11; Kulkarni, *Marathas*, vol. 3, pp. 11–12.
49. *Futuhat-i ᶜAdil Shahi*, pp. 271b–272b, Sarkar, *House of Shivaji*, pp. 11–12.
50. *Burhan-i Maʾathir*, p. 525; *Tarikh-i Qutb Shah*, p. 174v; *Tarikh-i Firishta*, vol. 2, pp. 82–3, 86, 125. In an interesting example, *Burhan-i Maʾathir*, p. 436, describes *bargī*s at the service of Bijapur attacking the royal army tent of Ahmadnagar.
51. Eaton, *Social History*, pp. 122–4; Shyam, *Ahmadnagar*, pp. 239, 249; Gordon, *The Marathas*, pp. 44–5; Kulkarni, *Marathas*, vol. 3, pp. 9–12.
52. *Shah Jahan-nama*, pp. 33v–34r; Shyam, *Ahmadnagar*, pp. 297–8.
53. *Basatin al-Salatin*, p. 286; *Shah Jahan-nama*, p. 37r–v; Shyam, *Ahmadnagar*, pp. 297–302; Sarkar, *House of Shivaji*, pp. 27–9; Grant Duff, *Mahrattas*, vol. 1, pp. 100–2; Sardesai, *New History of the Marathas*, vol. 1, pp. 55–7. Khan Jahan had a long career in the Deccan, going back to the early reign of Jahangir; he emerged as a powerful nobleman in the court, and was reportedly highly regarded by the emperor, who called him 'son' (*farzand*); this may be the background to Shah Jahan's suspicions. See *Maʾathir al-Umara*, vol. 1, pp. 716–32; *Tuzuk*, p. 296.
54. Lakhoji Jadhav Rao joined Mughal service in 1620, but later returned to Nizam Shahi service, although he probably remained undecided. This lack of clarity in Lakhoji's position was related to the complicated political game played by Khan Jahan Lodi, Fath Khan and others, in which personal ambitions and dynastic loyalties were entangled. The murder of Lakhoji and his sons pushed the Jadhavs to the Mughal camp; the Mughal chronicler ᶜInayat Khan reports that the surviving members returned to their ancestral Sindkhed and petitioned for Mughal pardon; Lakhoji's brother Jagadeva Rao joined Mughal service with a respectable *manṣab* of 4,000. See *Shah Jahan-nama*, pp. 39v–40r; Sarkar, *House of Shivaji*, pp. 30–1.
55. Between 1628 and 1636, out of 342 *manṣabdār*s (Mughal rank holders), 48 fell into the category 'Deccani' (including Foreigners in the service of the sultanates), of which 39 were Marathas. The numbers fell sharply after 1636, reflecting the tactical rather than ideological content of Mughal–Maratha cooperation on both sides. See Anwar, *Nobility under the Mughals*, pp. 34–6, 54–5.

56. *Shah Jahan-nama*, pp. 48r–49r, 52r–53v.
57. *Shah Jahan-nama*, pp. 49r–52r, 53v–57v, 60r–64v, 67v–68r, provides a detailed account of the Mughal campaign and the famine in Maharashtra and Gujarat at the time. See also *Basatin al-Salatin*, pp. 286–8; Shyam, *Ahmadnagar*, pp. 302–11; Sarkar, *House of Shivaji*, pp. 31–2; Sardesai, *New History of the Marathas*, vol. 1, pp. 58–9; Kulkarni, *Marathas*, vol. 3, pp. 12–13.
58. The following story, reported by Zubayri, demonstrates Fath Khan's popularity and the generals' concerns: 'Burhan Shah sent Ikhlas Khan, Farhad Khan, and Safdar Khan to bring Fath Khan from prison. When they entered [Daulatabad] fort, they put him in a veiled palanquin, and brought him to a house outside the fort. Fath Khan said: "why is there a need for a veil? Take it down!" Ikhlas Khan and the others considered: "If we avoid this and not listen to his words, he will become an even greater enemy." They ignored [their orders], removed the veil from the palanquin, and marched forth. Then, on both sides of the road, preachers and orators showed their respect and said: "this is the light of Malik Ambar!",' *Basatin al-Salatin*, p. 289.
59. Both poisoning and strangulation enabled Fath Khan to claim he was not responsible, but probably did not convince many; the Jedhe chronicler plainly states that 'Fath Khan killed Burhan Nizam Shah'. See *Jedhe Sakavali*, p. 47.
60. *Shah Jahan-nama*, p. 84r–v; *Basatin al-Salatin*, pp. 288–90, 295–7; Shyam, *Ahmadnagar*, pp. 311–14; Sarkar, *House of Shivaji*, p. 31; Sardesai, *New History of the Marathas*, vol. 1, p. 59; Grant Duff, *Maharattas*, vol. 1, pp. 104–6. The Mughals anyway considered Shahaji's loyalty dubious for some time, see *Shah Jahan-nama*, p. 77r–v.
61. *Shah Jahan-nama*, pp. 84v–105r; *Basatin al-Salatin*, pp. 297–301; Shyam, *Ahmadnagar*, pp. 314–20; Gordon, *The Marathas*, p. 46; Sarkar, *House of Shivaji*, pp. 32–5.
62. *Basatin al-Salatin*, p. 303. 'Good order (*intizām*)' serves as a pun on the name of the dynasty.
63. *Shah Jahan-nama*, pp. 124r–125v; *Basatin al-Salatin*, pp. 303–4; Shyam, *Ahmadnagar*, p. 320; Sarkar, *House of Shivaji*, p. 36.
64. *Basatin al-Salatin*, p. 305.
65. Shyam, *Ahmadnagar*, pp. 320–1; Sarkar, *House of Shivaji*, p. 46.
66. Sardesai, *New History of the Marathas*, vol. 1, p. 60. Previously named Nagargaon, the place came to be known as Tulapur, 'city of weighing'.
67. *Basatin al-Salatin*, pp. 305–6. *Jedhe Sakavali*, p. 47, dates this event to August 1632.
68. A Brahmin informer in Bijapur reported to Conde Linhares, Viceroy of Goa, on 10 May 1634, that while the Mughals, Bijapur and independent generals occupied many forts, Shahaji took over a large portion of the Nizam Shahi domains, including Junnar, Nasik and the Konkan; see Sarkar, *House of Shivaji*, pp. 41–2. *Basatin al-Salatin*, pp. 306–7, provides a series

Limitations of the Deccani System

of cases demonstrating Shahaji's tactics. One was convincing Sidi Saba Sayf Khan to turn his forts in Tal Konkan to Shivaji; later, Shahaji attacked him on the ground of his refusal to acknowledge Murtaza's sovereignty. In another case, Shahaji convinced Sanwas (or Srinivas) Rao, governor of Junnar, to marry his daughter to Shahaji's son, Sambhaji, but then imprisoned Sanwas Rao and took over Junnar, Jivdhan and other forts. Grant Duff suggests that (unspecified) Maratha sources support the narrative of substantial expansion under Shahaji, see Grant Duff, *Maharattas*, vol. 1, pp. 110–11.

69. Shyam, *Ahmadnagar*, pp. 322–3; Sardesai, *New History of the Marathas*, vol. 1, pp. 61–2.
70. *Shah Jahan-nama*, pp. 143r–144r. The fall of the 'War Party' in Bijapur facilitated this change in policy.
71. The agreement on the partition of the Nizam Shahi territories was discussed in Chapter 2.
72. *Basatin al-Salatin*, pp. 314–16; *Shah Jahan-nama*, pp. 170v–174v; Shyam, *Ahmadnagar*, pp. 323–8; Sarkar, *House of Shivaji*, pp. 42–5; Sardesai, *New History of the Marathas*, vol. 1, pp. 63–5. See *Jedhe Sakavali*, pp. 49–51. *Basatin al-Salatin*, pp. 307–14, provides a detailed account of the fall of Khawwas Khan and Murari; see also Sarkar, *House of Shivaji*, pp. 45–7.
73. Sarkar, *House of Shivaji*, p. 55.
74. Grant Duff, *Maharattas*, vol. 1, p. 102, suggests that one of Shahaji's main concerns after Khan Jahan left was that the sultan might confiscate his *jāgīr*. The family chronology of the Jadhavs dates Lakhoji's assassination to 15 Shravan 1551/25 July 1629. See *Jedhe Sakavali*, p. 47.
75. For example, Sarkar, *House of Shivaji*, pp. 39–40, suggests that during the Mughal siege of Parenda in 1634, Maloji and Parsuji Bhonsle fought on the Mughal side; several members of the Ghatge family alongside Ambaji and Vioji Bhonsle were in Bijapur's camp. Krishnaji, a cousin of Shahaji, was described as a rebel; another cousin, Kheloji, abandoned Bijapur's side and joined the Mughals because Shahaji gave a few of his forts to Maloji.
76. Eaton, *Social History*, pp. 112–14; Shyam, *Ahmadnagar*, p. 304.
77. Sarkar, *House of Shivaji*, p. 42.
78. *Shah Jahan-nama*, p. 144r–v.
79. I have discussed the different narratives elsewhere, see Fischel, 'Origin Narratives'. The local, and some say royal, origin of the Nizam Shahi dynasty is reflected in a passage by Thévenot, *Travels of Monsieur de Thévenot*, vol. 3, p. 91, who suggested that the 'Nizam Cha . . . is said to have been an *Indian*, and of the Royal Blood'.
80. Malik Naʾib had a *jāgīr* in Beed, central Maharashtra, extended significantly in the early 1480s towards Daulatabad and Junnar. This region became the core of the sultanate of Ahmad Nizam al-Mulk, see Shyam, *Ahmadnagar*, pp. 26–39.
81. *Burhan-i Maʾathir*, p. 250; *Muntakhab al-Lubab*, vol. 3, p. 160.

82. Beach and Koch, *King of the World*, pp. 80–1.
83. O'Hanlon et al., 'Discourses of caste', p. 107. Dalapati describes himself directly as 'minister and record-keeper of Nijāma Shah, overlord of all Yāvanas', see Pollock, *Bouquet*, p. xxiii; Keune, 'Eknath in Context', p. 77.
84. Benson, 'Samkarabhatta's Family Chronicle', pp. 109–10.
85. Pollock, *Bouquet*, pp. xx–xxiii.
86. The term Bhakti and what it entails produced numerous studies. It is complex and multilayered, and, of course, goes beyond the scope of this study. See discussion in Hawley, *A Storm of Songs*; for the Maharashtrian context, see Novetzke, *Religion and Public Memory*, pp. 7–31.
87. Deák, 'Making Sufism Popular'.
88. Feldhaus, 'Maharashtra as a Holy Land'; Chattopadhyaya, *Making of Early Medieval India*, pp. 29–30.
89. Keune, 'Eknath Remembered', pp. 25–7; Keune, 'Eknath in Context'.
90. In the context of Indic writings, an array of terms are used to discuss Muslims, each bears its own connotations. These include, among others, *yāvana*, *mlećcha* (barbarian), *rakṣasa* (ogre), or *asura* (demon). Sometimes used interchangeably, these terms that originate from ancient period or myth highlight the foreignness of the Muslims, demonises them and turns them into the ultimate 'other' within the Indian political imagination, marked as opposing the order represented by Brahmins. See Talbot, 'Inscribing the Other, Inscribing the Self'; Talbot, *The Last Hindu Emperor*, pp. 41–3; Pollock, 'Ramayana and Political Imagination'. This view of the Muslims as anti-dharmic and the role of Hindu kings to defend against them is reflected in the *Kaifiyat* of Kondavidu above.
91. *Sabhasad Bakhar*, pp. 1–2.
92. The digging of wells for the benefit of pilgrims is described by Paramananda in detail, linking it to the dharmic obligations which Maloji fulfilled. See *Sivabharata*, 1.53–8.
93. Bhavani is the primary goddess of the Marathas and family deity of the Bhonsles, identified with southeastern Maharashtra, in particular Tuljapur. She is mentioned as providing both gifts and prophecies in support of the Bhonsles. Famously, she handed a sword to Shivaji, instructing him to fight the Muslims like Durga fought the demons. According to another version, Shivaji purchased a European sword and named it Bhavani to indicate the need for divine support; this was interpreted by people as a gift from the goddess. See Monaghan, *Goddesses and Heroines*, s.v. 'Bhavani'; Pinney, *Photos of the Gods*, pp. 55–6; Kinsley, *Hindu Goddesses*, pp. 109–10.
94. *91 Kalami*, Nos 1–9, pp. 2–7. Variations on the story appear in other *bakhar*s, see Kincaid and Parasnis, *Maratha People*, pp. 115–16.
95. Sohoni, 'Continuities in the Sacred Landscape'.
96. Patwardhan and Rawlinson, *Source Book of Maratha History*, pp. 2–3.
97. *Sivabharata*, 1.42–5, 1.59–70. A similar reference to the Nizam Shah as

Limitations of the Deccani System

king of Devgiri appears in the writings of the early seventeenth-century commentator Ananta Oandit, who identifies 'Nijāma' as 'King of Devagiri', see Pollock, *Bouquet*, p. xxii.
98. *Sivabharata*, 2.1–44.
99. *Sivabharata*, 3; 5.21–3.
100. *Sivabharata*, 4.6–68.
101. The 'evil adviser' appears later with a reference to Fath Khan.
102. *Sivabharata*, 5.1–20, 8.8–73.
103. 'Ahmadnagar', *EI3*.
104. 'Kayfeyeat of the City of Auhamadanagur', Mackenzie unbound, Class IX, No. 7. Other sources suggest that, indeed, a garden was the first structure to be built in Ahmadnagar already in 1490 to commemorate his victory over the Bahmanis; the city was started four years later, and the garden was finally included in the fort. These stories do not include saints, but astrologers were consulted. See Sohoni, 'Farah Bagh', pp. 64–9.
105. Balasubrahmanyan, 'Hare and Hounds'.
106. *Badshahnama*, vol. 1.ii, 178–80; *ʿAmal-i salih*, vol. 2, pp. 148–50; *Muhtakhab al-Lubab*, vol. 3, pp. 393–4; Sherwani, *History of the Qutb Shahi*, pp. 432–8.
107. *Futuhat-i ʿAdil Shahi*, pp. 347r–351v; *Basatin al-Salatin*, p. 315; *Badshahnama*, vol. 1.ii, 167–74; Verma, *Bijapur*, p. 193, suggests that the downgraded title was used only temporarily as Shah Jahan soon thereafter awarded Muhammad the title ʿAdil Shah. As late as 1681, at the eve of Aurangzeb's invasion to the Deccan, we can see the Mughals using the title ʿAdil Shah when discussing the marriage of Shahar Banu, 'daughter of ʿAdil Shah of Bijapur' (*dukhtar-i ʿādil shāh-i bījāpūrī*), see *Maʾathir-i ʿAlamgiri*, p. 210.
108. Richards, *Mughal Empire*, pp. 114–15.
109. The lack of interest in Bijapur after 1636 on behalf of the Mughal court is attested by the limited space the Mughal historian Khafi Khan gives Muhammad ʿAdil Shah, most of which is dedicated to retelling Bijapur's assistance to the Nizam Shahs against Akbar and Jahangir during the reign of Ibrahim II. See *Muntakhab al-Lubab*, vol. 3, pp. 358–9.
110. Sarkar, *Aurangzib*, vol. 1, pp. 54–6, 174–6. Aurangabad is located just 15 km southeast of Daulatabad, Delhi's secondary capital in the early fourteenth century, suggesting that north Indian rulers found this strategic region, on the road to the Deccan, suitable for their southern endeavours.
111. Stein, *Vijayanagara*, pp. 120–39; Narayana Rao et al., *Symbols of Substance*, pp. 23–44.
112. Rama Sharma, *Vijayanagar, the Last Phase*, vol. 2, pp. 1–135; Heras, *Aravidu Dynasty*, vol. 1, pp. 248–340.
113. Particularly desperate was the Qutb Shah, as reflected in the most common type of coin issued by their mint in Hyderabad. Dated 1068/1657–8, the 'valedictory statement' coin carries the Arabic inscription *khutima b'il-*

khayr wal-saʿāda ('it has come to an end well and auspiciously'), accepting that the end was nigh. See Goron and Goenka, *Coins*, pp. 341–2.

114. *Hadiqat al-Salatin* 167, 190-1; Sherwani, *History of the Qutb Shahi*, pp. 455–9; Verma, *Bijapur*, pp. 139–48; Subrahmanyam, *Political Economy*, pp. 322–6.
115. Joshi, 'The Adil Shahis and the Baridis', vol. 1, p. 362. This was a known practice during expansionist phases; recall the agreement between Bijapur and Ahmadnagar on their respective spheres of influence after Talikota, discussed in Chapter 2.
116. Sherwani, *History of the Qutb Shahi*, pp. 454–5; Joshi, 'The Adil Shahis and the Baridis', vol. 1, pp. 362, 365–9; Nayeem, *External Relations*, pp. 102–6.
117. Bernier, *Travels in the Mogul Empire*, pp. 16–17. In Western imagination, Golkonda became synonymous with great wealth; the *Oxford English Dictionary* defines 'Golconda' (noun): 'a source of wealth, advantages, or happiness', likely to derive from the diamond mines. Europeans were greatly interested in the mines during the seventeenth century, as discussed by the Englishman William Methwold in 1622, and some two decades later by the Frenchman Jean Baptiste Tavernier; see Methwold, 'Relations of the Kingdome of Golchonda', pp. 30–2; Tavernier, *Travels in India*, vol. 2, pp. 53–80.
118. *Muntakhab al-Lubab*, vol. 3, pp. 394–6; Sarkar, *The Life of Mir Jumla*, pp. 66–80.
119. Sarkar, *Aurangzib*, vol. 1, pp. 170–210.
120. There are several versions to the story: Muhammad Saʿid may have first tried to join Bijapur with his possessions, and possibly also appealed to the Safavid Shah ʿAbbas II (r. 1642–66), see Nayeem, *External Relations*, p. 107; Sarkar, *The Life of Mir Jumla*, pp. 65, 72; Sherwani, *History of the Qutb Shahi*, pp. 441–2; Sarkar, *Aurangzib*, vol. 1, p. 221. The Mughals version suggests that Muhammad Saʿid was an innocent victim of jealousy in the court (a repeating theme in Persian chronicles), heightened by the haughtiness of his son, Muhammad Amin, who was then residing in Hyderabad. These events changed the sultan's heart against Muhammad Saʿid, who was forced to ask for Mughal protection, supported by a letter from Shah Jahan to ʿAbdullah Qutb Shah; in response, the sultan arrested Muhammad Amin. See *Maʾathir al-Umara*, vol. 3, pp. 530–2. Bernier, *Travels in the Mogul Empire*, pp. 18–20, agrees with the idea of jealousy, but his reports suggest that this was justified by Muhammad Saʿid's great power. He adds that a conspiracy in the court promoted the idea that he had an affair with the queen-mother, leading to the sultan's resentment. The intent to work against Muhammad Saʿid was leaked, bringing him to appeal to Aurangzeb.
121. For full account on Muhammad Saʿid, see Sarkar, *The Life of Mir Jumla*; Kinra, *Writing Self, Writing Empire*, pp. 78–83; *Maʾathir-i ʿAlamgiri*, pp. 13–16, 30–1, 39–40, 43–4.

Limitations of the Deccani System

122. *Futuhat-i ʿAdil Shahi*, pp. 391v–395v.
123. Joshi, 'The Adil Shahis and the Baridis', vol. 1, pp. 359–66. According to Fuzuni, Shahji was a rather minor character in this campaign, mentioned in passing as he was returning to his *jāgīr* without leave (*bī-rukhṣat*). In response, the sultan ordered an attack on Shahji's possessions, indicating that the tension between the two began early on. Unfortunately, Fuzuni's narrative ends soon after this event. See *Futuhat-i ʿAdil Shahi*, pp. 395v–403v.
124. *Sabhasad Bakhar*, pp. 2–5, discusses the various methods used by Shivaji and Dadoji to expand their territories. See also Grant Duff, *Maharattas*, vol. 1, pp. 128–50; Gordon, *The Marathas*, pp. 60–2; Kincaid and Parasnis, *Maratha People*, pp. 21–32. Krishna, *Shivaji the Great*, pp. 17–27, suggests that Shivaji's administration continued practices from Malik Ambar's times.
125. *Jedhe Sakavali*, p. 61; Grant Duff, *Maharattas*, vol. 1, pp. 119–36; Gordon, *The Marathas*, pp. 56–8; Joshi, 'The Adil Shahis and the Baridis', vol. 1, pp. 359–71; Krishna, *Shivaji the Great*, pp. 27–30. It is not clear whether Shahaji and Shivaji worked in tandem throughout the period.
126. Joshi, 'The Adil Shahis and the Baridis', vol. 1, pp. 371–2; Kulkarni, *Marathas*, vol. 1, pp. 13–17.
127. See detailed description of the affairs in Sarkar, *Aurangzib*, vol. 1, pp. 211–13, 223–45; *Maʾathir al-Umara*, vol. 3, pp. 532–4. See also Sherwani, *History of the Qutb Shahi*, pp. 442–4. *Waqiʿat-i ʿAlamgiri*, pp. 15–20, suggests that the attack started as a stratagem when Aurangzeb sent to ʿAbdullah saying that Sultan Muhammad was passing through to be married to the daughter of his brother Shah Shujaʿ in Orissa.
128. While clearly used as a political weapon against Bijapur, it is not impossible that Aurangzeb was right, see discussion in Kruijtzer, 'Bari Sahib', pp. 231–2.
129. *Maʾathir al-Umara*, vol. 3, pp. 534–7; Nayeem, *External Relations*, pp. 168–70; Sarkar, *Aurangzib*, vol. 1, pp. 259–78.
130. *Maʾathir al-Umara*, vol. 3, p. 534; Verma, *Bijapur*, pp. 195–7; Nayeem, *External Relations*, p. 170; Sarkar, *Aurangzib*, vol. 1, pp. 278–9. However, the issue of the Karnatak has not been resolved. The Mughals demanded the submission of the region conquered by Muhammad Saʿid, see Sarkar, *Aurangzib*, vol. 1, pp. 245–51. Interestingly, when addressing this period, the Mughal historian Ishwar Das Nagar briefly mentions the conquest of Golkonda (i.e., Hyderabad) and Bidar, but does not report any conquests in Bijapur, suggesting that, just as in 1636, Golkonda was hit harder than Bijapur. See *Futuhat-i ʿAlamgiri*, p. 8.
131. Sherwani, *History of the Qutb Shahi*, pp. 459–62.
132. Verma, *Bijapur*, pp. 161–7; Gordon, *The Marathas*, p. 58.
133. Verma, *Bijapur*, pp. 30–2; Joshi, 'The Adil Shahis and the Baridis', vol. 1, pp. 371–94; Devadevan, 'The Ravaging Hand'; Sherwani, *History of the*

Qutb Shahi, pp. 639–40. It goes beyond the scope of this study to analyse Shivaji's policies and relations with Bijapur in detail. For a general overview, see Gordon, *The Marathas*, pp. 63–90.

134. Gordon, *The Marathas*, pp. 62–8; Sarkar, *Shivaji and His Times*, pp. 44–58; Kulkarni, *Explorations*, pp. 36–43. In Persian chronicles he is described as *mardūd, bāghī* (rebellious), *maqhūr* (destined to be vanquished), or *malʿūn* (accursed); his actions were seen as *tamarrud* (rebellion) or *shararat* (wickedness). See *Basatin al-Salatin*, pp. 369–71; *Mirʾat al-ʿAlam*, pp. 215–17; *Tarikh-i ʿAdil Shahi*, p. 73.
135. Gordon, *The Marathas*, pp. 46–9. The *jāgīr* bestowed on the Bhonsles in Pune as hereditary, similar to the Mughal concept of *waṭan jāgīr*: hereditary territory reconfirmed by the ruler to its holder to create the façade of royal appointment; it links hereditary rights to royal favours, see Chandra, *Mughal Religious Policies*, pp. 32–5. Gordon, *The Marathas*, pp. 59–60, suggests that 'the core of the rights [given to Shahji] was the hereditary patil rights (village headman) to three villages in the Pune district and the deshmukh rights of Indapur . . . Shivaji's father also held the mokasa of the Pune region. In Bijapuri parlance of the day this meant a hereditary grant of the government's share of the revenue, whether in cash or kind, for maintenance of troops', similar to the Mughal *waṭan jāgīr*. According to the 1716 manual *Ajnapatra*, landed positions were well acknowledged also in the Maratha state under the general term *waṭandar* (from Persian, *waṭandār*, holder of hereditary land); they were considered 'sharers in the kingdom', see *Ajnapatra*, pp. 214–16.
136. Krishna, *Shivaji the Great*, pp. 31–48; *Ajnapatra*, pp. 86–8; *Jedhe Sakavali*, pp. 53–61, lists Shivaji's conquests in Maharashtra and the *deśmukh*s who supported him between 1571–8 and 1649–56 CE.
137. *Mirʾat al-ʿAlam*, p. 405.
138. *Sivabharata*, 1.59–61.
139. *Sabhasad Bakhar*, p. 6; *91 Kalami*, No. 31, mentions briefly an attack on Sri Bhavani in Tuljapur, but not Pandharpur.
140. I am grateful to Professor Rosalind O'Hanlon for her most insightful interpretation and comments for this passage.
141. Pandharpur was a particularly important site of Maharashtriran devotionalism, a holy city of the Varkari Bhakti tradition, focusing on the god Vitthala or Vitobha. This site is crucial both socially/religiously and culturally, as it was one of the sites in the development of Marathi devotional poetry in the fourteenth–seventeenth centuries. See Vaudeville, 'Pandharpur'; Dhere, *Rise of a Folk God*.
142. Gordon, *The Marathas*, p. 67.
143. See Eaton, 'Temple Desecration', on the idea of the destruction of temples as a political rather than religious act.
144. Guha, 'Frontiers of Memory'. Even more than disregard, a Varkari tradition states that the king of Vijayanagara stole the image of Vitthala from

Limitations of the Deccani System

Pandharpur 'out of greed'; the image was recovered and returned to Pandharpur by Eknath's great-grandfather Bhanudas. See Keune, 'Eknath Remembered', p. 25, esp. n. 13.

145. Between 1627 and 1636, many Marathas joined the Mughal side, probably due to the material advantages such association would bring in contrast to the pitiful conditions in war-torn Maharashtra. However, following the peace, immediate incentives ceased and the number of Marathas in Mughal service dropped dramatically at all levels of service. Furthermore, Firdos Anwar suggests that the Marathas were never seen as 'confidants and dependable servants of the crown'. This evidence suggests, then, that the Mughals did not try to incorporate the Marathas systematically and ideologically as they did with the Rajputs, leaving their position often marginal. See Anwar, *Nobility under the Mughals*, pp. 35–6, 55–8, 88–9, 106–8.
146. Gordon, *The Marathas*, pp. 87–8; Krishna, *Shivaji the Great*, pp. 1–5.
147. Laine, *Shivaji*, p. 5; Krishna, *Shivaji the Great*, pp. 49–50.
148. Guha, 'Speaking Historically', pp. 1093–103. See also Deshpande, *Creative Pasts*, pp. 25–41.
149. Guha, 'Transitions and Translations', pp. 26–30; Guha, '*Margi, Desi,* and *Yavani*', pp. 138–41.
150. *Sivabharata*, 1.24.
151. *Sabhasad Bakhar*, p. 1.
152. Naravane, *Shivaji's Carnatic Expedition*, pp. 6–15.

6

Conclusion: Hoopoes and Falcons

The history of the early modern Deccan reveals parallel trends which were seemingly contradictory. The region was unified in many respects: geographically, politically, historically and culturally. The various factors of unity came together to define the Deccan as a discrete space, distinct from both Vijayanagara to the south and the Mughal Empire to the north. Accordingly, early modern sources, as well as modern historiography, have treated the Deccan as a single, coherent historical and geopolitical entity. This unity, however, was limited to only certain aspects. In other respects, the Deccan has been a composite and diverse space, divided according to numerous lines. The most easily traceable division was along political lines: the region was home to simultaneous dynasties, closely linked to one another yet who perceived themselves as independent. Most prominent of these were the Nizam Shahs, ᶜAdil Shahs and Qutb Shahs, by the side of the significantly weaker ᶜImad Shahs, Baridis and numerous local potentates. While the Deccan sultanates saw prolonged periods of conflict, in particular, in the western Deccan, their core regions remained stable throughout the period, limiting shifts to their border regions only.

Politics was only one aspect of intra-regional divisions. Elite society itself was far from homogeneous. On the contrary, at the very heart of each sultanate stood a complex elite which was diverse in terms of religion, language, class, caste and occupation. Both local and foreign groups took part in various aspects of the political, military, economic and cultural life of the sultanates. Most identified with the local political system were the group known as Deccanis, a term broadly referring to those Muslims who saw the Deccan as their home. The Deccanis hailed from diverse backgrounds: some were local converts, others, the descendants of migrants from north India, yet others were new migrants who struck roots in the region. By their side, in all sultanates, members of trans-regional communities, self-styled Foreigners, became a crucial part of the elites. Organised in locality- or family-based networks, many Foreigners combined personal interests in trade, scholarly pursuits, and administrative and military

Conclusion

positions. Those Muslims from Iran and elsewhere in West and Central Asia presented a rejection of the locality in favour of a continuously itinerant lifestyle. Alongside the Deccanis and the Foreigners, various non-Muslim groups, from Telugu-speaking hereditary landed elites to Marathi-speaking Brahmins, were deeply integrated into the service of the sultanates, gaining increasingly high positions in all courts. The non-Muslim elites brought with them their own spatial sensitivities. Those did not always sit neatly contained within a sultanate, but were related to the space created by various vernaculars, localities or wider networks.

This diverse political setting was accompanied by a variety of languages in practice. The vernaculars of Marathi, Kannada and Telugu were employed in certain administrative and judicial functions, besides serving as markers of identity and as an important means of communication. Persian, the language of upper administration, diplomatic correspondence and certain aspects of courtly life, linked the courts of the Deccan with one another and to wider networks of production beyond the Narmada River and across the Arabian Sea. Dakhani, the language associated with the Deccanis, was an important vehicle of urban life, literature and Sufi worship, however, not so much in day-to-day administration. Other languages, notably Arabic and Sanskrit, were practised and enjoyed patronage in various settings in the courts and elsewhere. While the boundaries between the languages were by no means fixed and impervious to one another, a strong sense of identity has often been attached to language use. Languages were affiliated with certain groups and marked, at times, their identity and territory, even if we cannot assume cohesion among all members of a language community. With this social diversity, and furthermore the significance of language in the formation of identity, the courts were involved with varying circles of language production, use and patronage. No language gained precedence over the others; we cannot mark any one language as the 'state language' in the courts of the Deccan sultanates.

The social and cultural diversity brought to parallel, at times competing, notions of territoriality. Each group had its own concept of the space that they considered their domain, even if not exclusively. Certain elites in all three sultanates shared identities that crossed political boundaries, reached the peripheries or stretched to other regions, creating bonds with peers in the neighbouring courts and beyond. The space that each of these groups perceived as their domain carried its own meaning. For each, it marked who was outside and who was inside. All this created a complicated and conflicted social and political system. The various sultanates captured territories that did not fully align with the territorial sensitivities of any of these groups: the Deccanis were divided between the sultanates; the Foreigners continued to follow their trans-regional networks; and all of the vernacular territories were split between a variety of polities, in the Deccan proper and beyond its boundaries.

Within this environment of multiplicity, the Deccan sultanates were able to survive for a long period and even thrive, as attested by their rich and sophisticated cultural output. This success in a contested environment was closely linked to the political language used by the ruling dynasties, and their ability to convey their message to the various elite groups operating in their domain. The Qutb Shahi sultans successfully attracted both Muslims and non-Muslims to their court by projecting multiple identities both as Muslim rulers and as successors of the pre-Muslim Kakatiya dynasty. The Nizam Shahi rulers of Ahmadnagar, even when in decline, maintained their appeal among diverse elites in Maharashtra, Muslim and non-Muslim alike. For many decades, they kept their unique position as a powerful symbol of local political identity and as the only ones under whose name local elites united to resist the Mughals. The ʿAdil Shahs chose to project an all-Deccani, non-vernacular-specific identity, which drew directly on the cache of non-Muslim political memory, from the Western Chalukyas to Vijayanagara.

Those various strategies, which pulled the sultanates in different directions, were rooted in the varying circumstances in each. Selected for their advantages, each strategy had its evident limitations, presenting the sultans with a constant series of dilemmas. On the one hand, pushing towards identification with vernacular and a certain territory meant that beyond this territory, the appeal of the sultans remained limited, putting clear restrictions on successful expansion. Qutb Shahi identification with the Telugu language, Telangana and the Kakatiya past contributed to the sultans' choice to expand away from the Deccan Plateau and into the Telugu-speaking regions to the east and south. In these regions their success remained limited, as competing frames of identification and sovereignty proved to be resilient. Nevertheless, the challenges the Qutb Shahs encountered in these regions did not shake their firm control over Telangana. On the other hand, non-specific policies may have enabled rulers to more effectively appeal diverse territories and their elites, but had limited attraction to those who themselves developed specific territorial-linguistic identities. The ʿAdil Shahs did not emphasise an attachment to any particular vernacular sensitivities beyond lower levels of administration, probably due to the location of the core of their sultanate in between two vernacular regions. This choice was successful among certain circles, for example, Marathi-speaking Brahmins, but failed to attract certain

Conclusion

elites who were strongly attached to territorial-vernacular identity once those emerged, most significantly the Marathas.

In her work on the literary traditions of north India in the fifteenth century, Francesca Orsini suggests that 'literary histories have come down to us with their own geographies. Spread on the north Indian terrain, these look like a series of overlapping maps based on language and content that bear little or no relations to each other'.[1] I suggest extending this idea from north India to the early modern Deccan with its diverse multilingual environment, and from literature to the political domain. Considering the multi-layered map we have noted thus far, the system as a whole does not follow a clear relationship of inclusion and hierarchy. Instead, spaces were partially overlapping, with varying degrees of cohesion and discreteness, in between creating complex ideas of in–out, core–periphery. The Deccan sultanates, then, were based on interacting with this multiplicity, acknowledging it and responding to it.

The Deccan Sultanates in Early Modern India

The political system of the Deccan in the sixteenth and seventeenth centuries seems to follow the opposite historical trajectories in comparison with north India. Following Timur's invasion in 1398, the north experienced a period of imperial decline, giving rise to multiple regional centres. These centres emerged as new foci of patronage networks and multilingual literary cultures.[2] At the time, the Deccan was at the height of its political unity under the Bahmanis, even if this unity was never to the degree of northern imperial consolidation. In the subsequent centuries, the trend reversed. From the closing decades of the fifteenth century, successive attempts were made to unify the north under Delhi's rule. The Lodis and Suris saw only partial and temporary success, but in the last third of the sixteenth century, the Mughals achieved unification to a much more convincing level. Bringing new methods of expansion, incorporation and centralisation, albeit in an ever-changing, gradual and uneven manner, the Mughals sit comfortably in the model of the early modern empire. The Deccan, once again, went in the opposite direction. Bahmani authority crumbled rapidly from the 1480s, and by the turn of the sixteenth century, the five independent sultanates of Ahmadnagar, Berar, Bidar, Bijapur and Golkonda emerged. In the following two centuries, the political setting continued to change. The collapse of Vijayanagara in 1565 and mounting Mughal pressure from the closing years of the century left a significant impact on the sultanates. Pressed from the north, their main attempt now was to expand southwards, a step that created many opportunities but also jeopardised their stability. Notwithstanding the growing risks, the Deccan remained politically divided: when Ahmadnagar collapsed, the Marathas emerged as a new regional power; Vijayanagara was inherited by multiple local power brokers. Furthermore, none of the Deccani actors attempted to unify the region regardless of many cases of inter-dynastic marriage, nor produced rhetoric that suggests such intentions, indicating that the system as a whole lacked a clear centre of gravity – or the ideal thereof.

The history of the region changed radically in the late seventeenth century, when the Mughal emperor Aurangzeb managed to annex the Deccan, eliminating the ᶜAdil Shahi dynasty (1686), the Qutb Shahi dynasty (1687), and the Bhonsle possession in Maharashtra (1688). The campaign followed two earlier successful imperial encroachments in previous decades: Shah Jahan's campaign in the 1630s, and Aurangzeb's in the mid-1650s. This half-century-long decline has been described as gradual and linear, and led to a depiction of this period, and more broadly the sultanates as a whole, as a mere footnote in the history of India, which was written by the Mughals. In their survey of Mughal historiography, Muzaffar Alam and Sanjay Subrahmanyam discuss the Deccan sultanates only briefly, even within the section dedicated to south India. Stressing the ambiguity in the sultanates' sense of sovereignty, it is only Vijayanagara which possessed a 'sovereign idea' of its own in the south, an idea that eventually 'gave way in south India to the Mughals'. Sandwiched between the approaching Mughals to the north and the cultural-historical realm of Vijayanagara to its south, the Deccan is marginalised. This approach is explained by the (forced) self-declaration of the sultans of Bijapur and Golkonda as subservient to the Mughals, where 'over time the fiscal practice in Golconda tended to gravitate little by little towards a perceived Mughal style'.[3] Ignoring Bijapur and the western Deccan altogether, this vision starts from the end, namely, the elimination of Golkonda in the 1680s, and relies on rhetoric more than practice.

There is no doubt that the power mustered by the Mughals was on a different scale to that of the Deccan sultanates. Furthermore, the rhetoric employed by all parties reflects this difference, as we will see later in this chapter. However, are these factors sufficient to consider the Deccan sultanates as remote subjugate bastions of the Mughal Empire? I suggest that the Mughal claims over the Deccan, including those made after 1636, were not realised in full, leaving the sultanates practically independent. Furthermore, direct Mughal rule, once established five decades later, was brief and turbulent: starting only in the late 1680s, by the 1720s Mughal rule remained all but nominal.[4] In contrast to the troubled and short period of Mughal rule, the Deccan sultanates survived for some two centu-

Conclusion

ries, developing their own sense of identity. This is not only a matter of length, but also the stage of Mughal history in which the territories were introduced into the empire. Take, for example, two important Mughal provinces beyond the core region of the empire: Gujarat and Bengal. Both were conquered in the 1570s, during the early stages of imperial expansion under Akbar. Accordingly, they continued to develop within the empire, even though they maintained strong regional identities and idiosyncrasies, leading to the particular nature of Mughal rule there.[5] At the same time, the Mughal emperor kept his right to nominate his own people to the highest positions; recall, for example, Muhammad Saʿid Mir Jumla and his career as governor of Bengal or Prince Aurangzeb's two terms as governor of the (Mughal) northern Deccan. This was not only on the level of the province; Farhat Hasan demonstrates that in the port city of Surat in Gujarat, many officials were appointed directly by the court, even if later they had to negotiate their position with local potentates.[6]

The Deccan sultanates, in contrast, grew outside the imperial system and amid a struggle against it. When the Mughals successfully imposed their conditions over Bijapur and Golkonda, the region remained largely independent. The treaty of 1636 presented humiliating conditions to the sultanates, including forcing the Mughal *khuṭba* and the payment of hefty tribute. However, it also secured the northern border of both Bijapur and Golkonda, with the former even gaining territories to its north. The gap between the expectations of the opposing sides is particularly striking, showcased by Aurangzeb's campaigns of 1656–7. The Mughal prince's actions followed ideas of Mughal paramountcy evident elsewhere in the empire. The pretext of the invasion of Golkonda was claiming Muhammad Saʿid's *jāgīr* as a Mughal possession, suggesting that in Aurangzeb's view, the Mughals were those who had the right to determine the possession of these lands, not ʿAbdullah Qutb Shah. In Bijapur, Aurangzeb worked against the accession of ʿAli II, whom he claimed not to have been Muhammad ʿAdil Shah's son. Succession issues were raised in Golkonda as well, where Aurangzeb demanded that his son, Muhammad Sultan, should marry ʿAbdullah's daughter, declaring their future son heir apparent of Golkonda. This kind of intervention in succession plays along the lines of the Mughal right to confirm inheritance among other subordinate groups; a mere couple of decades later, such an attempt at intervention in the succession of subordinate Rajputs in Marwar (Rajasthan) famously backfired.[7]

Aurangzeb's actions reflect an overall failure of the empire to make inroads into the Deccan sultanates as their accepted sovereigns. On the contrary, the events demonstrate the resilience of the Deccani system to Mughal intervention. The conditions imposed by Shah Jahan were fulfilled briefly, and there is no reason to assume that they changed the political culture of the sultanates. The Deccani expansion thereafter, which continued well into the 1650s, was enabled only because Mughal pressure had been lifted. This continued in the first half of Aurangzeb's long reign; after he ascended the throne in 1658, he did not initiate any major campaign against Bijapur and Golkonda other than one in 1666.[8] Moreover, Aurangzeb's demands in the 1650s were not followed by the local rulers, with the exception of the payment of tribute. His attempts to manipulate Muhammad Sa'id's *jāgīr* came to naught, and Golkonda's general Neknam Khan recaptured the territories in the 1660s; 'Ali 'Adil Shah II remained on the throne until his death in 1672; and the imprisonment of Aurangzeb's son Muhammad Sultan, who sided with Aurangzeb's brother Shuja' in the war of succession, foiled the plan regarding Golkonda's throne.[9] Even the *khuṭba* may not have been a central issue in the Deccan, as we will discuss momentarily. In short, once we examine the events of the mid-seventeenth century from a Deccani perspective, assuming that the Deccan sultanates were merely Mughal tributaries is first, teleological and, second, unproductive. The Mughal emperors were limited in their ability to intervene in the affairs of the sultanates. They did not have the power of hiring and firing or of introducing changes in sultanate administration. Lastly, the sultans were not obliged to send troops to the imperial army.[10] With the weakness of Mughal rule not only after 1636 but even later in the seventeenth century, Mughal expansion fits the wider historical pattern of the difficulty of north Indian empires to control the south.[11]

The Deccan sultanates, then, do not easily fit in the Mughal-centric paradigm of early modern Indian history. At the same time, we cannot position them as similar to the Mughals, working within the same rules but on a smaller scale. Let us briefly recall the basic characteristics of early modern empires as we have outlined in the Introduction. Operating within a world of increasing connectivity, exchange and circulation, empires grew to have extensive geographical spreads that embraced several cultural domains, ecologies and ethnic groups. Central to their endeavour was a notion of hierarchy, manifested by the concept of suzerainty, the overlordship over other polities, with the emperor as 'king over kings'. The hierarchical principles were extended down to the administrative system, all together combined to create (or aspire to create) centralised and vertical structures of power, increasingly putting pressure on horizontal links. The stability of the hierarchical system relied on its adaptability. It further required the creation of a symbolic language that, typically, relied

Conclusion

on claims of universal dominance and divine mandate, often expressed in links to previous empires.

The Deccan sultanates were well integrated into the global system and into networks of exchange and circulation. They all comprised diverse ethnic and linguistic groups and saw periods of substantial expansion. Yet they did not meet some of the basic criteria that would turn them into empires. First and foremost, the region had no clear centre, but rather competing equal courts in dynamic equilibrium. With no central authority to be found, any idea of imperialism encounters a major unanswerable question: whose empire would it be? This ambiguity continues when examining each sultanate separately, suggesting that we cannot simply see the Deccan sultanates as a collective of neighbouring proto- or simply failing empires. The sultanates remained limited in their geographical extent, and expansion was not translated into actual control. The largest sultanate was probably Bijapur in the 1650s, but by then the centre did not have much control, political or symbolic, over the entire state, in particular, the Maratha north and the newly conquered Karnatak. Furthermore, if empire is characterised by a preference for vertical over the horizontal connections, the Deccan sultanates seem to have relied heavily on the latter. Their structure was based on distinct identity groups operating in circles that often crossed political boundaries. Members of the elites remained permanently itinerant, raising suspicion among rulers and ruled alike. Certain elite groups had ideas of sovereignty and association that were sharply different from those held by the sultans. All these indicate the persistence of horizontal elements within each sultanate. Lacking the mechanism, or simply the power, to break horizontal ties in favour of new vertical hierarchies, the rulers were required to utilise all their skills as negotiators to recruit the various elites and tie them to their rule. In situations where these skills were not utilised effectively, for instance, if the sultan was too weak, actual control of the sultanate weakened accordingly. But as a whole, sultanate sovereignty seems to have been a success story, at least in the core regions of the Deccan: until Shivaji, no internal force tried to challenge it.

The Language of Sovereignty

Practical policies aside, the Deccan sultanates seem different from early modern empires in the way in which they presented themselves as reflected in symbolic aspects and political language. In the early modern world, frames of legitimacy aimed at linking emperors to universal notions of sovereignty. In parallel, they worked to create the conditions to encourage the support of the subjects. These frames provided rulers with tools to present themselves as standing in leading positions vis-à-vis competing rulers and as the legitimate leaders within their own domains. Hakan Karateke suggests that legitimacy relies, on the one hand, on the ruler's claim of the right to rule, and, on the other hand, on the subjects' acceptance of the political order. To support a ruler's legitimacy, both actual policies and symbolic measures were employed. The combination of the two aimed at providing rulers with practical power and linking them to socially accepted notions of legitimacy. The right to rule was promoted as hereditary and deriving from one or more superior source. Accordingly, rulers linked themselves to past imperial figures: Timur or Chinggiz Khan in Muslim Asia or the Roman/Byzantine Empire in Europe as well as the Ottomans. Rulers also presented themselves as possessing a divine right by linking them to past spiritual leadership (for Muslim rulers, commonly, the Prophet Muhammad or the caliphate).[12] In the same vein, Zvi Ben-Dor Benite et al. suggest that central to the formation of royal sovereignty was the representation of authority in aesthetic terms, broadly defined (including 'ritual, symbolism, custom, religious, negotiation and conviction, and exchange') as the scaffold on which sovereignty is established. Sovereignty is both the process that produces power and the infrastructure that represents and disseminates this power.[13]

A crucial tool of legitimacy, then, is the association of emperors with pre-existing frames of authority. Such association was enabled by an intensive use of widely known political language. The Muslim East emerged as a broad space in which political language, cultural practices and ideology mixed religious thought and political theory to create a shared Persianate and Islamic culture and political language.[14] Ali Anooshahr argues that early modern Muslim dynasties worked within this common discursive realm, based on 'a standardized set of tropes, frames of reference, and historical teleology for imperial rule [that] had been consolidated and popularized through major historical productions'. Rulers manipulated these symbols according to circumstances and temporal needs by way of reinventing and rewriting their pasts. Heavily relying on Mongol concepts of universal empire, this political language absorbed tropes that communicated with broad political idioms.[15] This invention of the past was related to the changing political circumstances from the late fifteenth century with the rise of empires and, with them, new concepts of kingship. A. Azfar Moin asserts that these new views were constructed around the idea of sacrality. As an extension of the Sufi concept of holy men as the embodiment of sacrality, rulers, too, came to be seen in sacred terms. This understanding followed the memory of Timur and his astrological–

Conclusion

millennial title 'Lord of the Auspicious Conjunction' (*ṣāḥib-qirān*). The link between conqueror and millennial being later also became associated with ʿAli (cousin and son-in-law of the Prophet Muhammad), demonstrating that instead of replacing Islamic scriptures, these ideas of kingship existed in parallel to, and interaction with, Islamic concepts.[16]

This development was manifest in different ways around the Muslim East. In the Ottoman Empire, new models of kingship and legitimacy were created around the understanding of justice, on the one hand,[17] and the caliphate, on the other. Hüseyin Yılmaz suggests that after the collapse of the Abbasid caliphate in 1258, the very idea of a caliphate has not been frozen in time but continued to evolve. No longer relying on particular institutions, the caliphate began to be perceived as flexible, mystical-inspired and abstract. The new shape of caliphate could now coexist with non-Islamic concepts of kingship, as those circulating in the Muslim East. Caliphate was, accordingly, reworked to allow its convergence with messianic ideas, prevalent in the Muslim world towards the close of the first millennium AH (1591 CE). Claiming spiritual authority enabled the sultans to promote their sovereignty to supersede those of rival dynasties with universal claims, Muslim or European, or other claimants of spiritual powers, from the Shiite Safavids to Sufi saints.[18]

The Mughal emperors employed elements from the same world of reference to create their own political vision. Rejecting the Ottoman claims of caliphate, they used the very same title to promote themselves as leaders.[19] This was not only for the purpose of negating the Ottoman claim, but also suggests that the Mughals were rooted within the Islamic traditions and rhetoric. This language was not meant only for the purpose of advertisement in the Muslim world, it was also widely employed in the construction of imperial ideology in their realm. Muzaffar Alam argued that the political ideology of the empire was firmly tied to Muslim political thought. The Mughals worked within notions of the *sharīʿa* not as a strict theological and judicial concept, but with a flexible and wide meaning. This idea appeared in *akhlāq* (ethics) literature, most importantly the compilation of Nasir al-Din Tusi (d. 1274), whose writings circulated among the Timurids and later the Mughal court. Tusi's *Akhlaq-i Nasiri* emphasises the role of the *sharīʿa* in its wider meaning to serve the purpose of peaceful social conduct. Social cooperation of the subject was perceived as crucial, and was secured by imperial reliance on principles of justice (*ʿadl*) to all subjects, achieved by reason (*ʿaql*). With this ethical approach to their rule, the Mughals promoted a concept of universal peace (*ṣulḥ-i kul*), allowing freedom of religion among all communities in the empire.[20] This approach could strike the right chords among many in South Asia.

C. A. Bayly suggests that concepts of ethical government, fused with ideas of body, land and cosmological principles, were found in many Indian traditions, from the Mughals to Vijayanagara. The ethical literature developed as an amalgamation of principles borrowing from various systems of knowledge, from Greek to Islamic to Hindu, with many overlaps, to create a universalising vision. As part of this vision, rulers were to balance the elements and people in their realm and settle disputes.[21] This ideological framework of empire became part of its culture and etiquette, behaviour and taste. Kumkum Chatterjee suggests that 'Mughal political culture, especially in its courtly aspect, was believed to be a vehicle of civilité'.[22] This engagement crucially focused on the place given to the emperor as the 'Perfect Man', turning him into the centre of the system in an 'ideology of paternalism'.[23]

Central to this project was the Mughals' choice to embrace Persian as the state language for administrative use as well for cultural and symbolic purposes. Alam suggests that not being linked to any region in India in particular, the liberal ethos that exists in Persian (even if never solely) served to promote the ethics of the state with its universal, non-denominational values. For local elites, joining imperial elites with all the opportunities it had to offer required not only working knowledge of the language, but also attachment to Persian literacy and Persinised culture and etiquette; those became the markers of good education and sophistication. Therefore, elite individuals and families who sought to join imperial elites became increasingly involved in using, producing and giving patronage in Persian. These political–cultural processes helped to disseminate Mughal imperial ideology in their realm and to create an imperial class out of the heterogeneous elites.[24]

This is not to say that the Mughal Empire went through a complete process of Persianisation and cultural assimilation. Allison Busch demonstrates that Brajbhasha appealed to the aesthetic sense of the nobility by the side of Persian. Considered suitable for certain subjects, the language was used as a means of circulating Indic topics and ideas. Poets were not ignored by the nobility but became part of courtly circles and enjoyed patronage for panegyric work.[25] Chatterjee argues that in Bengal, Persian remained to a great degree outside the dominant Braminical culture. No clear and explicit connection can be drawn between Mughal rulers at the provincial level and local culture.[26] The existence of parallel local idioms under Mughal rule was not limited to the cultural realm. Ramya Sreenivasan demonstrates that the Kachhwaha Rajput chief Man Singh (d. 1604) asserted his kingship in a variety of genres, languages (Sanskrit, Brajbhasha, Persian) and media. These changed according to the circum-

Conclusion

stances, as Man Singh navigated between accepting Mughal authority and constructing his own claims among different Rajput milieus, with varying degrees of success.[27] These cases reflect the vitality and significance of vernacular cultures in the Mughal Empire. But they also demonstrate the dominance of the imperial Persianate culture and the hierarchy within which all languages were operating. As such, Chatterjee's observation that Persian remained at the core of the culture of the political elites seems viable throughout the empire.[28] In sum, the Mughals created a framework of legitimacy that combined imperial language, state ethics, political legitimacy and universal claims within a clear system of political, social, ideological and cultural hierarchy that remained aloof from any locality in particular.

In the Deccan, the local sultanates were operating within the very same political idiom. Ruled by Muslim sultans, having a share in trans-regional networks that linked them to the Mughal world and to West Asia, and hosting a major Iranian element in their elites, the Persianised world was by no means foreign to them. However, the engagement of the sultanates with it was profoundly different than what was practised by the Mughals. Both the depth of this engagement and the different terms in which it was conducted are evident when we examine the relations of the sultanates with the Mughal Empire. These relations cannot be reduced to questions of power and resistance. A clear boundary is marked by the rhetoric, which reveals substantial ideological differences within the shared political language. The historiography of early modern India is heavily focused on the empire, it therefore disregarded the Deccan sultanates and their particular contexts.[29] Yet the sultanates had their own story to tell. The unique voices from the Deccan came to the surface most clearly in times of conflict, when they had to justify themselves by expressing their ideological justification explicitly.

During the war in the 1630s, when Bijapur was under the influence of the 'War Party' and nobles in its court assisted Shahaji Bhonsle in his attempt to resurrect the Nizam Shahi sultanate, Shah Jahan sent this letter the Muhammad ᶜAdil Shah:[30]

> Praise and glory to the ruler, who was created from one drop of water in the womb to his complete might, and from non-being came into being; [God] made me the emperor of the world (*bādshāh-i jahān*). Therefore, it became my obligation to impose the sermon (*khutba*), coinage (*sikka*), and measurement (*dirᶜa*) of Shah Jahan on all parts of the world, especially on the country (*mulk*) of Bijapur, Golkonda and Hyderabad (*bhāgnagar*) and even [all the way to] Sri Lanka (*lankhā*) and on Sri Lanka [itself]. You, who live in those districts, are like the hoopoe (*hudhud*); each one of you cries 'I am the king!' It is most

advisable and best [for you] to tie the rope of obedience around your necks and perform the sermon, coinage, and measurement of Shah Jahan in those cities. Otherwise, I will draw a falcon (*bāz*) [that] will tear the meat off [your] skin [with] its beak, and I will prey [on you] with the kites (*ghalīwāzhān*) of the world. You should listen and understand these words. Do not enter the negligence of a hare's dream because the eagle (*ʿuqqāb*) is [still] in its cage. Therefore, I am sending the *amīr*, the loyal and pure *nawwāb*, the participant in the royal council, Makramat Khan. You should do whatever you think is for your best interest.[31]

Shah Jahan's letter provides a good example of what constitutes an imperial worldview within the lines we have marked before. Using ornate language and laden with metaphors, the letter outlines his position as an emperor, the place he assigns to the sultanate, and the relations between the two. The letter opens with imperial claims for divine mandate, as the creator himself made him the emperor of the world as was common in the ideology of early modern empires. The universal claim is then translated into practical domains: south India as a whole, all the way to Sri Lanka, and in particular the two surviving Deccan sultanates of Bijapur and Golkonda. The meaning of his claim is set forward firmly as the common formal symbols of Islamic sovereignty, namely, *khuṭba* and *sikka*. He adds a third condition, *dirʿa*. I suggest that this unusual term means 'measurement', reflecting the Mughal demand that the sultanates adhere to imperial administrative practices.[32] The Mughal claim of sovereignty does not remain only theoretical. In addition to its divine mandate, Shah Jahan continues, the empire also possesses the ability to enforce. In short, Shah Jahan presents here the main components of imperial legitimacy as we have discussed above.

To support these claims, the letter turns in the second half to use vivid ornithological imagery. The first, and most compelling image, is likening the Deccan sultanates to the hoopoe (Arabic: *hudhud*, Latin: *Upupa epops*). Common throughout Eurasia, the modest-sized hoopoe is not an impressive bird. Not a commanding predator, its diet is based on insects, seeds and berries. The most distinctive feature of the hoopoe is the crown of feathers on its head. Using the hoopoe, then, Shah Jahan marks the sultans of Bijapur and Golkonda as weak and lacking the ability to enforce their royal claim, making their kingship less than convincing. In contrast, Shah Jahan is likened to three species of birds of prey: falcon, kite and eagle, which are only waiting to feed on the weak hoopoe. On plain level, this image creates a clear hierarchy of power between the birds of prey on the Mughal side and the puny hoopoe. Similar power relations appear in the second pair, the hare and the eagle, reflecting the prey and the hunter.[33]

Conclusion

Beyond this simple analogy, the Mughal side is laden with imperial imagery. First, is the falcon, a bird long used by royalty for hunting purposes,[34] thus reflecting Shah Jahan's royal status. A visual manifestation of this image can be found on an astrolabe, created for Shah Jahan during the latter part of his reign. On the back of the astrolabe an unusual image of a falcon attacking a bird is engraved; on both sides, two smaller birds (one is possibly a hoopoe) are scuttling away in horror.[35] Furthermore, Shah Jahan was not himself the falcon, but the letter reflects that he was the master of the birds of prey. This idea links him to Solomonic traditions, a common feature in the Mughal political idiom.[36]

Facing this threat of imperial fury and its grim outcomes, Muhammad ᶜAdil Shah's response to Shah Jahan's letter is quite intriguing:

> We are grateful to God that does not spare presumption and arrogance in the world; rather He levels [those who boast with] pride to the ground: 'presumption and arrogance are reserved to the one / whose country is eternal, and self needs nothing (i.e., only God himself)'. The letter that was drawn by ignorant scribes and that was sent to me is now clear. It is brighter than the sun that [God] has given the hoopoe the crown of kings and the throne of emperors since the day of creation. Is it not true that Solomon – may peace be upon him – raised the falcon? What is the power that [your] falcon would attack with its claws and demolish the old foundation? This is a heretical innovation! The hare, even if asleep, at the time of emergency, attacks back and brings destruction. The eagle should remain in the cage. Otherwise, it will fall into the trap because it desires the meat of the hare out of its vile nature. You should not utter these words [anymore], nor should they even cross your mind. I will give you the same tribute I had given before, as the [rule] 'reconciliation is good' (Quran 2:128) applies. You too should not turn away from divine command, so that no one turns away from you.[37]

This upfront letter in response to Shah Jahan reflects a bold stand against imperial threats. The language of the response demonstrates awareness of the content and imagery of the letter and responds in the same currency. Using some of Shah Jahan's images against him, it asks to defend the sultan's position as a rightful king, even if not to undermine the Mughals' royal status.

The response contains four elements. First, it denounces the presumption and arrogance of Shah Jahan and the arrogance of his scribes, deeming Shah Jahan's letter as misinformed. The second part provides a justification to the royal position of the sultans of the Deccan, to which we will return later. The letter then turns to warn that the Deccanis are not as defenceless as they may seem, suggesting that the hare itself may still have some tricks up its sleeve. This interesting image, of the hare turning and attacking its assailant, may be related to the common foundation story in which a hare attacks hounds as a sign of the establishment of a new city and political order, discussed in Chapter 5. As such, it may serve here as another claim of Deccani legitimacy.[38] It can further allude to the guerrilla warfare tactics used by the Deccanis (in particular, Marathas) and which the Mughals found difficult to overcome. In the fourth and final part of the letter, Muhammad ᶜAdil Shah offers an olive branch by paying tribute, thus easing the tension, but without mention of any of the symbols of Mughal sovereignty, namely, *khuṭba*, *sikka* and *dirᶜa*.

The most revealing part of Muhammad ᶜAdil Shah's response is his discussion of the hoopoe, alongside the rest of the bird imagery, which occupies the second part of this short letter. The letter turns against Shah Jahan's presumption to control the bird kingdom and to attack the hoopoe, with a reminder that it is God who created them all. As part of God's creation, the hoopoe's crown is seen as godly mandated. Beyond this general statement, the letter addresses particular story, that of King Solomon and the hoopoe. According to Quran 27:16–45, the king summoned the animals. While examining the birds present, he realised that the hoopoe was missing. When the hoopoe finally appeared, Solomon threatened to punish it. The hoopoe then told about the Land of Sheba, ruled by a queen (known in Muslim tradition as Bilqīs) who sits on a magnificent throne. But the queen and her people do not worship God, but rather the sun. The hoopoe incited Solomon to show the Queen of Sheba the true path of God-worship. Solomon then ordered the hoopoe to deliver a letter to the Queen of Sheba, calling her to submit to God. At the end of the affair, the queen visited Solomon's palace and accepted Abrahamic monotheism. Thereafter, the hoopoe became perceived as 'the harbinger of good news'.[39]

With his reference, Muhammad ᶜAdil Shah willingly accepted his role as a hoopoe, but added a layer of Quranic context, of which Shah Jahan's letter was lacking.[40] By comparing himself with the hoopoe, the sultan tried to convey two messages. First, just as the hoopoe had a place in the divine plan, so did Muhammad ᶜAdil Shah have a role to play.[41] Second, the letter mentions that Solomon raised the falcon in preparation to attack the hoopoe. However, as the Quranic story goes, the hoopoe was not chastised but rather praised for his success. What this line implies is that if Shah Jahan went on with his plans to attack Bijapur, he would be daring to do something that even King Solomon avoided, which would mark this as an unwanted innovation (*bidᶜat-i nau*). All combined, by accepting the image of the hoopoe, Muhammad ᶜAdil Shah marked his own importance as an independent and legitimate sovereign in his own right. Yet he

Conclusion

embraced his own weak position, and employed this to stress the divine protection against Mughal aggression.

If Muhammad ᶜAdil Shah's letter acknowledges the disadvantageous position of Bijapur vis-à-vis the Mughals, other writers asked to place the sultans and the emperor on the same level. In late 1631, while Shah Jahan was amid the same campaign that produced the aforementioned correspondence, ᶜAbdullah Qutb Shah of Golkonda delivered the following speech. Carried in front of his court, his court historian, Nizām al-din Ahmad, recorded the following words:

> Our laudable ancestor, king and conqueror of the Kingdoms of Hindustan, Lord of the Auspicious Conjunction (ṣāḥib-qirān) – may Allah enlighten his tomb! – with the assistance of the Prophet's pure soul and of the commander of the believers ᶜAli (ḥaydar), and with the help of the sacred spirits of the twelve Imams – may Allah's prayers be upon them! – that greatest king, struck the heads and necks of the leaders of the vile infidels and lowborn Hindus in this country with his strength and power of bravery and with his sword that is like Dhu al-Fiqar. He kindled a fire like the striking lightning and created a burning like a [spark from a] blood-shedding dagger in a pile of straw and leaves with his people and army; [thus] he conquered his kingdom. He [then] spread the customs of the nation (millat) of Mustafa (the Prophet Muhammad) and the creed (madhhab) of Murtaza (ᶜAli). About a hundred and forty years passed since that day, and this country is defended and guarded from the calamities of time and from the conquest and hostility of enemies (aghyār).[42]

The speech presents a vision of local sovereignty. Emphasising the circumstances that brought about the foundation of the Qutb Shahi dynasty 140 years earlier (c. 1490, around the beginning of Sultan Quli's autonomous policies), the sultan stresses that his ancestor conquered the land from the infidels by sword and spread Islam there. He adds the assistance of both the Prophet and of ᶜAli as signs of divine guidance.

ᶜAbdullah Qutb Shah delivered this speech in Hyderabad, but the intended audience went beyond the confines of his court to reach Shah Jahan's ears. Even though the Mughals are not directly mentioned, the use of certain terms suggests that the sultan tried to establish himself in opposition to the Mughal emperor – and equal to him. First, is the title by which his ancestor, implying to Sultan Quli, is referred to: 'Lord of the Auspicious Conjunction, king and conqueror of the kingdoms of India' (khaqān-i kishwar-sitān-i ṣāḥib-qirān-i mamālīk-i hindūstān). This long title consists of tropes familiar in Persian writings. As we have seen, 'Lord of the Auspicious Conjunction' (ṣāḥib-qirān), an astrological title that refers to a particular constellation, was perceived as a cosmic sign of legitimacy. Within the early modern Perso-Islamic tradition, ṣāḥib-qirān refers first and foremost to Timur, the illustrious ancestor of the Mughal emperors; the Mughals used the term Timurids to refer to their own dynasty. In addition, this title was also related to ᶜAli. Shah Jahan himself used the title the Second *ṣāḥib-qirān*.[43] Attaching the title to Sultan Quli and other sultans in the Deccan,[44] then, marks them within the same symbolic and ideological framework as the Mughals. The imperial, all-India position of Sultan Quli is also implied in the second part of the epithet, 'king and conqueror of the kingdoms of India' (*hindūstān*, usually referring to north India), may also refer to Timur's invasion of Delhi in 1398. While the speech does not mention the Mughals directly, it positions ᶜAbdullah Qutb Shah as a descendant of a Timur-like conqueror, hence, on the same level as Shah Jahan. Implied from this is that the Mughals can make no claim of superiority over the sultan of Golkonda. The Qutb Shahi claim for legitimate position did not derive only from a Timurid comparison, but had a religious component. Sultan Quli's sword is compared with ᶜAli's sword Dhu al-Fiqar, an image we have encountered in a Bijapuri inscription dedicated by a Hindu. Sultan Quli is further said to have been guided by the Twelve (Shiite) Imams, and he is said to have spread the 'sect of Murtaza', namely, Shiism. This strong religious language promotes ᶜAbdullah's claim for religious guidance and divine position similar to Shah Jahan's claim, once again placing the two on the same level.

Situating the Mughals and the sultans on the same level was not conducted only by exalting the sultans, but also by means of downgrading the Mughals to the mere regional kings of their heartlands. Similar to the titles that describe the Qutb Shah as sovereign or command-giver (*farmān-farmā*, *farmān-dih*) of Telangana, the Mughals were associated with north India (Hindustan). Thus, the emperor was king of Hindustan (*pādshāh-i mamālik-i hindūstān*, *khusrau-i hindūstān*) or king of Hind (*khusrau-i mamālik-i hind*).[45] More specifically, the Mughals are identified as kings of Delhi with similar titles and contrasts between *hindūstān* and *dakkan*.[46] A similar association of the Mughals with Delhi appears in Marathi sources. The *Jedha Sakavali* mentions that Sultan Khurram sat on the throne in Delhi with the title Shah Jahan;[47] the *Ajnapatra* identifies Aurangzeb as 'Lord of Delhi';[48] and Krishnaji Anant calls Shah Jahan 'King in Delhi' (*dillīsa pātśāha*).[49] The link created between Mughals in north India and in Delhi as its symbolic centre, even when the actual seat of power was elsewhere, suggests that in Deccani eyes, the Mughals were legitimate rulers – but elsewhere, beyond the Narmada River. Denying the universalist claims of the Mughals to rule over the Deccan and rejecting their imperial aspirations, these narratives reduced the Mughals to mere local kingdoms, hence not legitimate in the south.

Conclusion

Within this sophisticated use of the shared political language between the Deccan and the Mughal Empire, one issue emerges as most significantly different: the source of legitimacy. In Shah Jahan's letter to Muhammad ᶜAdil Shah, the emperor marked three symbolic steps he demanded from the sultan: *khuṭba*, *sikka* and *dirᶜa*, with the former two serving as most common symbols throughout the Muslim world. The sultan of Bijapur ignored the demands, although later he and his peer from Golkonda had to accept the Mughal *khuṭba* (not *sikka*, though, if we recall the 'valedictory statement' coin from late 1650s Golkonda). This does not mean that prior to 1636 the sultans maintained their own *khuṭba*. Consider the following widely cited letter, dated 1623, sent from Ibrahim ᶜAdil Shah II to the Safavid Shah ᶜAbbas I:

> The lands of the Deccan (*wilāyāt-i dakkan*) form as much a part of the Safavid Empire as the provinces of Iraq, Fars, Khurasan, and Azerbaijan. Accordingly, the names of the Safavid monarchs have been recited in the sermon and will continue to be recited in future. Our forefathers were appointed to rule over these territories and protect them by his Majesty's ancestors. So our function is to rule the countries on his Majesty's behalf and defend them against foreign aggression.[50]

The letter states that the (Sunni) sultan of Bijapur was only happy to commit to Safavid sovereignty. Such act was not new in the context of the Deccan. It can be traced to the very early days of the sultanates: reportedly, already in 1518, Sultan Quli Qutb al-Mulk included the name of the Safavid Shah Ismaᶜil I in his sermon.[51] Statements of this kind brought Alam and Subrahmanyam to state that the sovereignty of the Deccan sultanates was ambiguous 'as there is some evidence that they derived legitimacy from Iran – and as is apparent in the form of their diplomatic correspondence with the Ṣafavids'.[52] This kind of statement surely represents the Mughal concept of sovereignty, which was universal and total; there was no place to acknowledge anyone else as superior. However, I suggest that this does not necessarily mean that the Deccan sultanates were in reality tributaries of the Safavid, only to switch to the Mughal sphere of influence in 1636. Elizabeth Lambourn demonstrates that in the early modern Muslim world, there was no consensus regarding the meaning of *khuṭba*, which remained contested between times and places. Competing concepts created tensions between sovereigns, for each of whom the sermon meant something different.[53] More generally, Kołodziejczyk suggests that the question of sovereignty has never been straightforward. Rather, it reflects aspects of control and ideology: the position of local ruler, the ability to assert imperial control or concepts of inside/outside.[54]

Why would the rulers of the Deccan agree to recite someone else's sermon to begin with? This may be indicative of a certain set of priorities. Jan-Peter Hartung argues that the competition between heads of state reflects an elaborate attempt by rulers to reflect that they 'cared most for the Common Good of all subjects within Muslim governed territory'. Such ethical concern, which resonates with political ideas familiar from the Mughal context, was based on the display of military power and the ability to protect their subjects. He continues that 'it was such strength that caused smaller and considerably weaker kingdoms to diplomatically subject themselves to the rule of the more powerful ones'. Based on this, Hartung explains the correspondence between the ʿAdil Shahs (and in passing also the Qutb Shahs) and the Safavids as loyal submission with the expectation of Safavid military protection in return.[55] This analysis is reasonable in part. *Khuṭba* was indeed linked to legitimising the sultans to their subjects by way of security; the issue of protection is embedded in the sultans' presentation as rulers of the 'well-protected domains' (*mamālik-i mahrūsa*).[56] However, as no military assistance ever arrived in the Deccan, I suggest that the Safavid *khuṭba* was not purely a matter of sovereignty in return for material support. Rather, it derived from the desire to emphasise spiritual and symbolic links between the sultanates to the Safavids.

Colin Mitchell suggests that in the first half of the sixteenth century, Nizam Shahi–Safavid relations emphasised the place of spiritual guidance, and not political alliance.[57] A later letter, sent from ʿAbdullah Qutb Shah to Shah ʿAbbas I around 1628–9, states that 'since old times, there was a connection of familiarity and a bond of friendship between the holy and illustrious family of the Moses-like Ismaʿil Safawi and the lofty Qutb Shahi dynasty'. This long-established connection, continues the letter, was severed at the beginning of the tenth century AH (*c.* 1494 CE), as the hemistich states: 'that one in the land of Iran, and this one in the land of India' (*ān yekī dar mulk-i īrān / īn yekī dar mulk-i hind*). From that time, the letter concludes, strong bonds of friendship and affection continued to exist between the descendants of those great sultans.[58] These statements should be read together: not necessarily carrying actual implications, reciting the Safavid *khuṭba* (or at least declaring a willingness to do so) and describing long-lasting bonds reflect Deccani lack of confidence.[59] Under duress of Mughal aggression, the sultans tried to project stability and reliability among their subjects, to follow Hartung's idea. Considering the distance of the Safavids from the Deccan and their inability (or unwillingness) to send material help, this association may be more of a fanciful way of finding help in a highly contested environment while rejecting Mughal designs.[60] Moreover, they reflect a choice of a distant symbol which could

Conclusion

not in reality curtail Deccani independence. Lastly, it has been noted before that legitimacy relied on links to superior authority. For empires, such superiority had to be in their past so as not to jeopardise any current universalist claims. The same justification of legitimacy was required among the sultans of the Deccan, but without the temporal aspect; to them, the sources of legitimacy were contemporary, possibly due to the sultans accepting their non-imperial position.

The act of reciting the Safavid sermon is significant in another way. The Deccan sultanates were very late to mint their own original coins. Pushkar Sohoni suggests that they began doing so c. 1580 as a response to the Mughal conquest of Malwa and Gujarat on the border of the Deccan and the imposition of Mughal currency there. This, he argues, shows that until the Mughals began to challenge the sultanates, *sikka* was a relatively insignificant sovereign symbol in the Deccan.[61] Phillip Wagoner adds that Bahmani and Vijayanagara coins continued to circulate in the Deccan. The latter were so popular that when the sultanates began to issue their own coins, they were minted according to Vijayanagara standards and Bahmani design. The new coins, however, were not widely accepted.[62] The attitude of the sultanates towards minting reinforces our reading into the question of the *khuṭba*. Together, they reflect another kind of understanding of the basic symbols of sovereignty compared to the Mughals, and promote the idea that we should not assume that similar acts always carried the same meaning.

The use all sultanates made of the political language of the Muslim East to legitimise their position reflects an altogether different approach to questions of state and sovereignty. Instead of a remote, unattached, trans-regional empire that worked on principles of imposition and hierarchy, using tools of uniformity within a seemingly homogenised imperial language, the political structure of the Deccan reflects a more dispersed notion of sovereignty. This notion of sovereignty was not a simple mirror image of empire. Some aspects of the political language and ethics that can be found in the Mughal Empire were promoted while using the same Persianate idiom. Ibrahim ʿAdil Shah II's characteristics as a ruler, for example, resonate with those promoted by Akbar: Zuhuri counts justice (*ʿadālat*) as one of Ibrahim's nine virtues, using the familiar image of 'the lion licking the lamb through fondness'.[63] He further depicts Hinduism and Islam under Ibrahim's reign as tied together in a knot that cannot be undone,[64] in a statement that sits well within the Mughal idea of universal peace (*ṣulḥ-i kul*). However, other elements mark him – and all other sultans – as profoundly different. Instead of imperial rigidity of ideology and language under one powerful sovereign, the sultans preferred plurality and flexibility. Without abandoning their attachment to the Persianate world, they introduced the locality and local idioms; recall Ibrahim as *jagat-guru*, a clearly non-royal title. More generally, accepting their weak position and following centuries of competing historical processes and memories, the sultans embraced unprecedented pluralism, expressed in royal engagement with Persian, Dakhani, Sanskrit and the vernaculars and reflected in the absence of narratives of inter-religious violence within the sultanates. Alongside the lack of a clear centralised political idiom, their language does not reflect an ambiguity of sovereignty. Rather, it suggests the rejection of universal claims in favour of an idiom that had been created out of careful and continuous negotiation with, and the incorporation of, diverse groups in their locality. This was without taking them through the homogenising press of empire. In that sense, the Deccan sultanates were not only sultanates, a term that bears clear Islamicate connotations; they were also very much a product of the Deccan.

This reading of the Deccan sultanates as non-imperial states suggests that the early modern period was the arena for the activity of different kinds of state and not only universal empires. Different from empires in their structures and internal logic, non-imperial polities deserve to be studied on their own terms. An analysis of these polities reveals some of the social and political processes that affected all parts of the early modern world, imperial and non-imperial alike. Factors such as localisation, vernacularisation, involvement of transregional networks, the durability of historical memory, and the overall endurance of horizontal identities had an important role in shaping early modern states and societies. As empires took over regions in which similar systems existed, those factors did not simply disappear, but may have been introduced into, and survived within, the empire. Such trajectories were obscured by imperial centralised structures. They may not have been fully reflected in imperial rhetoric as they did not fully fit into the image of empire. Furthermore, plurality was, at times, deemed irrelevant in the historiography that looked at the early modern empire as a precursor of a centralised and bureaucratised modern state. In order to avoid ignoring these important historical factors, an examination of the sultanates in their own terms offers insights not only for our understanding of the early modern Deccan. It also sheds new light on the early modern world as a whole.

Notes

1. Orsini, 'How to do Multilingual Literary History', p. 239.
2. See the various chapters in Orsini and Sheikh, *After Timur Left*.

Conclusion

3. Alam and Subrahmanyam, 'Introduction', in *The Mughal State*, pp. 33–6; see also Sherwani, *History of the Qutb Shahi*, pp. 439–41.
4. Faruqui, 'At Empire's End'; Gordon, *The Marathas*, pp. 91–131.
5. See discussion in Hasan, *State and Locality*; Chatterjee, *Cultures of History*.
6. Hasan, *State and Locality*, pp. 34–40.
7. Chandra, *Mughal Religious Policies*, pp. 85–98.
8. Sarkar, *Aurangzib*, vol. 4, pp. 1–12. This relative calm of the sultanates is mostly absent from Mughal writing at the time. For example, the chronicler Saqi Mustᶜad Khan mentions Bijapur only three times in this period: one Mughal campaign in 1666; a ruby (*laᶜl*) sent as a gift from Bijapur; and the arrival of (daughter of) 'ᶜAdil Khan' of Bijapur to the court (before her marriage to Prince Muhammad Aᶜzam. Golkonda is not mentioned at all during that time. See *Maʾathir-i ᶜAlamgiri*, pp. 58–60, 81–2, 190. See also Joshi, 'ᶜAdil Shahis and Baridis', vol. 1, pp. 372–92; Sherwani, *History of the Qutb Shahi*, pp. 438–48, 638–41.
9. Sherwani, *History of the Qutb Shahi*, p. 601. There is, of course, no way to tell whether this plan would have worked, considering Aurangzeb's failure to intervene in the succession in Bijapur.
10. For example, an imperial demand of this kind arose in 1670, but ᶜAli ᶜAdil Shah II did not send any troops, see Joshi, 'ᶜAdil Shahis', vol. 1, p. 381.
11. Ludden, 'The Process of Empire', p. 142.
12. Karateke, 'Legitimizing the Ottoman Sultanate'.
13. Ben-Dor Benite et al., 'Editors' Introduction'.
14. Yarshater, 'Persian Presence'; for the early modern period, see Robinson, 'Ottomans–Safavids–Mughals'.
15. Anooshahr, *Turekstan*, citation on p. 173.
16. Moin, *The Millennial Sovereign*. Blain Auer has noted the porous boundaries between Sufi and political language already during the Delhi sultanate, see Auer, 'Sufism and Power'.
17. See Ergene, 'On Ottoman Justice'.
18. Yılmaz, *Caliphate Redefined*.
19. Farooqi, *Mughal–Ottoman Relations*, pp. 173–221.
20. Alam, 'Shariᶜa and Governance'; Alam, *The Languages of Political Islam*, pp. 26–80.
21. Bayly, *Origins of Nationality*, pp. 11–19.
22. Chatterjee, *Cultures of History*, pp. 215–23, citation on p. 222.
23. Moin, *The Millennial Sovereign*, pp. 130–61; Mukhia, *The Mughals of India*, pp. 14–71.
24. Alam, 'The Pursuit of Persian'; Chatterjee, *Cultures of History*, pp. 223–32.
25. Busch, 'Hidden in Plain View'. Even the Akbar's son Prince Danyal is reported to have composed verse in 'Hindi', 'and would occasionally compose verses with correct idiom in the language of the people of India, which were not bad'. See *Tuzuk*, vol. 1, p. 36.
26. Chatterjee, *Cultures of History*, pp. 232–8.

Local States in an Imperial World

27. Sreenivasan, 'Rethinking Kingship'.
28. Chatterjee, *Cultures of History*, p. 235.
29. For example, Satish Chandra asserts that Akbar did not plan to annihilate Ahmadnagar, but to secure his possession of Gujarat with its important seaport; Jahangir's war was meant to reconquer territories previously held by Akbar. The Mughal attitude, then, is presented as deriving from lack of motivation, ignoring the serious problems the Mughals were facing. Similarly, M. Siraj Anwar suggests that the Mughal shelter of the future Burhan Nizam Shah II shows that 'he had made up his mind on a policy of obtaining the submission of the Nizam Shahs as well as other rulers of the Deccan', once again without any reference to the changing circumstances in the Deccan, see Chandra, *Mughal Religious Policies*, pp. 111–19; Anwar, *Mughals and the Deccan*, p. 50. This fits a wider context of disregard of the Deccan: in a survey of South Asia and the Indian Ocean within global history, Stephan Conermann dedicates only a brief mention to the Deccan sultanates in two contexts: Aurangzeb's campaigns and within trade networks, told from the European perspective; the Deccan sultanates again were not perceived as having any voice of their own. See Conermann, 'South Asia', pp. 425–5, 535–40.
30. Full copies of these letters were preserved by the early nineteenth-century historian of Bijapur, Muhammad Ibrahim Zubayri, who relied heavily on seventeenth-century histories in his compilation. There is a possibility that these letters do not reflect an actual correspondence as much as Bijapur's perspective on the question of sovereignty; even so, they serve us well in reflecting on the Deccani use of the political language of the early modern Muslim East.
31. *Basatin al-Salatin*, pp. 302–3.
32. See discussion regarding Mughal measurement and assessment (*zabṭ*) in Habib, *Agrarian System of Mughal India*, pp. 236–59.
33. F. Viré suggests that one of the common names for the tawny eagle (*Aquila rapax*) in Arabic is ʿ*uqāb al-arnab*, lit. 'eagle of the hare', suggesting that the eagle has long been associated with the hare, with the former being the hunter and the latter, the hunted. See 'Arnab', *EI2*.
34. Falconry and hawking were common sports among the nobility over large parts of Eurasia. In medieval Europe, for instance, falconry was reserved by law for the elites. Members of the high classes appeared in public with their hunting birds to show their status. In Sufi poetry, the connection between the falcon and the falconer is likened to the soul that can soar high only to return eventually to God. This image was based on the two meanings of the word *bāz* in Persian: the one being falcon, and the other, to return (*bāz āmadan*). See Almond, *Medieval Hunting*, pp. 41–2; Asani, 'Birds in Islamic Mystical Poetry', p. 172.
35. The Nasser D. Khalili Collection of Islamic Art, Accession No. SCI 53, described and interpreted in Sreeramula Rajeswara Sarma, 'A Descriptive

Conclusion

Catalogue of Indian Astronomical Instruments', pp. 1012–14, available at: https://srsarma.in/catalogue.php, last accessed 24 September 2018.
36. Koch, 'The Mughal Emperor as Solomon'; 'Sulayman b. Dawud', *EI2*.
37. *Basatin al-Salatin*, p. 303.
38. The hare commonly appears in relation to sleep, 'which means real or feigned negligence, as the hare keeps one eye open while sleeping', see Schimmel, *A Two-Colored Brocade*, p. 194.
39. Schimmel, *A Two-Colored Brocade*, p. 75.
40. The letter accuses Shah Jahan in ignorance, however, the story of Solomon and the hoopoe is well known and widely circulated so that it is very unlikely that the Mughal scribes did not know it. This might be an indication that the correspondence as a whole represents Bijapur's position.
41. We might even argue that the role was to promote monotheism in the overwhelmingly Hindu Deccan, an issue that appears time and again in Persian chronicles of the time, but as we have seen does not really match the actual policies of the sultans.
42. *Hadiqat al-Salatin*, pp. 128–9. The theme of Shiism as the *raison d'être* of the Qutb Shahi sultanate persisted to the final days of the sultanate. As late as 1685, a letter from Golkonda's last sultan, Abu al-Hasan Tana Shah (r. 1672–87), to the Safavid Shah Suleyman (r. 1666–94), expresses the role of the sultanate in introducing and spreading Shiism in the sultanate. The sultan further claims that sultanate remained safe under the protection of the Safavids. See discussion in Shakeb, *Relations of Golkonda with Iran*, pp. 97–8.
43. Dale, 'The Legacy of the Timurids'; Balabanlilar, 'Lords of the Auspicious Conjunction'.
44. For example, Burhan Nizam Shah II of Ahmadnagar and Ibrahim ᶜAdil Shah II of Bijapur were also mentioned with the title *ṣāḥib-qirān*, see *Burhan-i Maʾathir*, pp. 584–7; *Tarikh-i Firishta*, vol. 2, pp. 153, 166.
45. *Hadiqat al-Salatin*, pp. 92, 156; *Futuhat-i ᶜAdil Shahi*, p. 352v. *Hind* might mean India as a whole, however, in this case it is an idiom that is later contrasted by a reference to the 'land of the Deccan' (*mulk-i dakkan*). In this context, then, *hind is* synonymous with *hindūstān*.
46. We can find titles such as *pādshāh-i dihlī* or *farmān-rawā-i dihlī*. See *Futuhat-i ᶜAdil Shahi*, p. 322v; *Tarikh-i Firishta*, vol. 2, p. 119; *Hadiqat al-Salatin*, p. 92, or the contradiction between *khusrau-i dihlī* and *salāṭīn-i dakkan* (sultans of the Deccan), see *Futuhat-i ᶜAdil Shahi*, p. 345v.
47. *Jedhe Sakavali*, p. 45.
48. *Ajnapatra*, p. 84.
49. *Sabhasad Bakhar*, p. 5.
50. Nazir Ahmad's translation of the letter from *Makātīb-i zamān-i salāṭīn-i ṣafawiyya*, Asafiya Library, Hyderabad, MS 1214, f. 404ff, reprinted in Nayeem, *External Relations*, app. I, pp. 275–6; facsimile in app. VII.
51. Shakeb, *Relations of Golkonda with Iran*, pp. 55–6.

52. Alam and Subrahmanyam, *The Mughal State*, pp. 33–4.
53. Lambourn, '*Khutba* and Muslim Networks'.
54. Kołodziejczyk, 'What is Inside', pp. 430–1. The argument is regarding the Ottoman case, but I think that it can be applied more broadly.
55. Hartung, 'Enacting the Rule of Islam', pp. 312–13.
56. *Tarikh-i Qutb Shah*, p. 220v; *Hadiqat al-Salatin*, p. 156;
57. Mitchell, 'Sister Shi'ite States?' pp. 59–65.
58. *Hadiqat al-Salatin*, pp. 80–1.
59. The message was received in the Safavid court: the chronicler Iskandar Munshi reports that the rulers of Ahmadnagar, Bijapur and Golkonda recited the *khuṭba* in the name of the Twelve Imams and the Safavid king. See *Tarikh-i ʿAlam-ara-i ʿAbbasi*, p. 116. Throughout the text, the chronicler uses the royal title *shāh* to describe the sultans of the Deccan, in contrast to the overall rejection of their royalty by the Mughals, possibly in another affirmation to the not really subjugate position of the sultans.
60. Riyazul Islam, who was uncomfortable with the statement regarding the Safavid *khuṭba* made by Ibrahim II, whom he considered Sunni, states that without clear reference to the Shiite imams, the *khuṭba* should not be regarded as having any Shiite content, but as solely political, see Islam, *Calendar of Documents*, vol. 2, pp. 131–5. Considering the direct connections to Shiism expressed by Firishta and the deeper flirtation with Shiism as described by Zuhuri and Firishta, this letter adds to the evidence as an example of the multiple face of the ʿAdil Shahi political language.
61. Sohoni, 'The Non-Issue of Coinage'.
62. Wagoner, 'Money Use in the Deccan', pp. 476–9.
63. *Gulzar-i Ibrahim*, vol. 3, pp. 356–7, tr. vol. 3, pp. 372–4.
64. *Gulzar-i Ibrahim*, vol. 3, pp. 361–2, tr. vol. 3, p. 366.

Bibliography

Abbreviations

BL	British Library, London
EI2	*Encyclopaedia of Islam,* 2nd edn, Leiden: Brill.
EI3	*Encyclopaedia of Islam,* 3rd edn, Leiden: Brill.
E.Ir.	*Encyclopaedia Iranica,* Costa Mesa, CA: Mazda.
Mackenzie unbound	India Office, BL, Mackenzie Collection (unbound translations).
SJM	Salar Jung Museum, Hyderabad.
TGOML	Telangana (formerly Andhra Pradesh) Oriental Manuscript Library, Hyderabad
TSA	Telangana (formerly Andhra Pradesh) State Archive and Research Institute, Hyderabad

Primary Sources

Anonymous, *Golconda Letters*, BL India Office MS Add.6600.

Anonymous, *Jedhe Śakāvalī-Karīnā*, ed. A. R. Kulkarṇī (Pune: Mansanman Prakasan, 1999).

Anonymous, *Tārīkh-i Mahdawīyān*, TSA, MS Persian 146.

Anonymous, *Tārīkh-i Sulṭān Muḥammad Quṭb Shāh*, BL India Office Islamic 179; also consulted the following additional manuscripts: TSA, Persian MS history 401; SJM Persian MS history 85.

ᶜAbdul Dihlawī, *Ibrāhīmnāma*, ed. Masᶜūd Ḥusayn Khān (Aligarh: Muslim University, 1969).

Abu al-Faẓl, *The Akbarnama of Abu-l-Fazl: History of the Reign of Akbar Including an Account of his Predecessors*, trans. H. Beveridge (Delhi: Rare Books, 1973 [1921]).

ᶜAlī Muḥammad Khān, *Mirāʾat-i Aḥmadī*, ed. Syed Nawab Ali (Baroda: Oriental Institute, 1927–30).

Bābur, Muḥammad Ẓahīr al-Dīn, *The Baburnama: Memoirs of Babur, Prince and Emperor*, trans. Wheeler M. Thackston (Washington, DC: Freer Gallery of Art and New York: Oxford University Press, 1996).

Bakhtāwar Khān, Muḥammad, *Mirʾāt al-ʿĀlam*, ed. Sajida S. Alvi (Lahore: Research Society of Pakistan, 1979).
Bernier, François, *Travels in the Mogul Empire, AD 1656–1668*, trans. and ed. Archibald Constable (London: Humphrey Milford, Oxford University Press, 1916).
Bīdrī, Qādir Khān, *Tārīkh-i Qādirī*, TGOML Persian MS history 409.
Bījāpūrī, Ḥaẓrat Burhān al-Dīn Jānam, *Irshādnāma*, ed. Muhammad Akbar al-Din Siddiqi (Hyderabad: Osmania University, 1971).
Da Orta, Garcia, *Colloquies on the Simples & Drugs of India*, trans. Sir Clements Markham (London: Henry Sotheran, 1913).
Dattājī Trimala, *Śrī Śivachatrapatīṃcī 91 Kalamī Bakhara āṇi Bhosale Gharāṇyācī Ćaritāvalī*, ed. V. S. Vakasakar (Pune: Vhīnas Prakaśan, 1962).
Elliot, H. M. and J. Dowson (eds), *The History of India, as Told by its Own Historians* (London: Trübner, 1867–77).
Firishta, Muḥammad Qāsim b. Hindū Shāh, *Tārīkh-i Firishta: Tārīkh-i Salāṭīn-i Hindūstān*, ed. John Briggs and Mir Khoirat ʿAli Khan (Bombay: Lithographed at the Government College Press, 1831). Translated by John Briggs and publish as *History of the Rise of the Mahomedan Power in India till the Year A.D. 1612: Translated from the Original Persian of Mahomed Kasim Ferishta* (London: Longman, Rees, Orme, Brown & Green, 1829); compared with BL, India Office Persian MS add.18,875.
Fūzūnī Astarābādī, Mīr Muḥammad Hāshim, *Futūḥāt-i ʿĀdil Shāhī*, BL, Persian MS Add. 27,251. Partial translation in Sarkar, Jadunath. 1955, *House of Shivaji: Studies and Documents of Maratha History: Royal Period*, 3rd edn (Calcutta: M. C. Sarkar).
Ḥusayn b. Ghiyāth al-Dīn Maḥmūd, *Khayr al-Bayān*, BM Persian Ms. Or 3397.
ʿInāyat Khān, *Shāh Jahān-nāma*, BL Ms. Or 175.
Iskandar Munshī, *Tārīkh-i ʿĀlam-ārā-i ʿAbbāsī*, ed. Īraj Afshār (Tehran: Muʾassasa-yi Intishārāt-i Amīr-i Kabīr, 1971), 2 vols. Translation in *The History of Shah ʿAbbas the Great: Tārīḵ-e ʿālamārā-ye ʿAbbāsī*, trans. Roger M. Savory (Boulder, CO: Westview Press, 1978).
Ishwar Das Nagar, *Futūḥāt-i ʿĀlamgīrī*, ed. R. Sinh and Q. Karamtullah (Vadodara: Oriental Institute, 1995).
Jahāngīr, *The Tūzuk-i-Jahāngīrī, or, Memoirs of Jahāngīr*, trans. Alexander Rogers, ed. Henry Beveridge (New Delhi: Munshiram Manoharlal, 1978 [1914]).
Khāfī Khān, *The Muntakhab al-Lubāb*, ed. Maulavī Kabīr al-Dīn Aḥmad (Calcutta: Royal Asiatic Society of Bengal, 1869–1925).
Lahawrī, ʿAbd al-Ḥamīd, *Badshāhnāma*, ed. Malawī Kabīr al-Dīn Aḥmad and ʿAbd al-Raḥīm (Calcutta: Colleges Press, 1867).
Major, Richard Henry (ed.), *India in the Fifteenth Century: Being a Collection of Narratives of Voyages to India, in the Century Preceding the Portuguese Discovery of the Cape of Good Hope; from Latin, Persian, Russian, and Italian Sources* (London: Hakluyt Society, 1857).

Bibliography

Methwold, William, 'Relations of the Kingdome of Golchonda, and other Neighbouring Nations within the Gulfe of Bengala, Arreccan, Pegu, Annassery etc. and the English Trade in those Parts', in *Relations of Golconda in the Early Seventeenth Century*, ed. W. H. Moreland (London: Hakluyt Society, 1931).
Muḥammad Ṣāliḥ Kambo, *ᶜAmal-i Ṣāliḥ or Shāh Jahān Nāmah*, ed. Ghullam Yazdani (Calcutta: Asiatic Society of Bengal, 1927).
Nazim, M., *Bijapur Inscriptions: Memoirs of the Archæological Survey of India*, 49 (Delhi: Manager of Publications, 1936).
Oaten, Edward Farley (ed.), *European Travellers in India during the Fifteenth, Sixteenth, and Seventeenth Centuries* (London: Kegan Paul, 1909).
Paes, Domingo and Fernão Nuniz, *The Vijayanagara Empire as seen by Domingo Paes and Fernao Nuniz*, trans. Robert Sewell (New Delhi: National Book Trust, 1977).
Paramānanda, Kavīndra. *The Epic of Shivaji: Kavindra Paramananda's Śivabhārata*, trans. James W. Laine in collaboration with S. S. Bahulka (Hyderabad: Orient Longman, 2001).
Patwardhan, R. P. and H. G. Rawlinson (eds), *Source Book of Maratha History, vol. 1: To the Death of Shivaji* (Bombay: Government Central Press, 1929).
Qazwīnī, Asad Beg, *Kitāb-i Ḥālāt-i Asad Beg Qazwīnī*, BL MS Or 1837.
Ramchandrapant Amatya, 'Ajnapatra', trans. S. V. Puntambekar, in *Journal of Indian History* 8(1) (1929): 81–105 and (2): 207–33.
Rāzī, ᶜĀqil Khān, *Wāqiᶜāt-i ᶜĀlamgīrī*, ed. Khan Bahadur Maulvi Haji Zafar Hasan (Aligarh and Delhi: Aligarh Historical Institute and Mercantile Printing Press, 1946).
Sabhāsad, Kṛṣṇājī Anant, *Śrī Śivaprabhumće Ćaritra (Sabhāsada Bakhara)*, ed. U. M. Paṭhāṇa (Aurangabad: Samartha Prakashana, 1974).
Sayyid Nūr Allāh, *Tārīkh-i ᶜAlī ᶜĀdil shāhī*, ed. Sharīf al-nisā Anṣārī (Hyderabad: Andhra Pradesh Oriental Manuscript Library, 1991).
Shīrāzī, Rafīᶜ al-Dīn Ibrāhīm, *Tadhkirat al-Mulūk*, TGDML, Persian MS history 1081.
Shīrāzī, Niẓām al-Dīn Aḥmad, *Ḥadīqat al-Salāṭīn-i Quṭbshāhī*, ed. ᶜAli Asghar Bilgrami (Hyderabad: Islamic Publications Society, 1961).
Saqi Mustaᶜad Khan, *Maʾāthir-i-ᶜĀlamgīrī*, ed. Maulawi Agha Ahmad Ali (Calcutta: Baptist Mission Press, 1871). Translation into English available as *A History of the Emperor Aurangzib-ᶜĀlamgir (reign 1658–1707 A.D.)*, trans. Jadunath Sarkar (Calcutta: Asiatic Society of Bengal, 1947).
Sarma, Sreeramula Rajeswara, 'A Descriptive Catalogue of Indian Astronomical Instruments', available at: https://srsarma.in/catalogue.php, last accessed 24 September 2018.
Shāh Nawāz Khān, Nawwāb Ṣamṣām al-Daula, *Maʾāthir al-Umarā*, ed. Molvi ᶜAbd al-Rahim (Calcutta: Royal Asiatic Society of Bengal, 1888), 3 vols. Translation into English available as *The Maāthir-ul-umarā: Biographies of Muḥammadan and Hindu Officers of the Timurid Sovereigns of India from*

1500 to about 1780 AD, trans. H. Beveridge, rev. Baini Prashad (Patna: Janaki Prakashan, 1979 [1911]).

Sikandar ibn Muḥammad Manjhū ibn Akbar, *Miraʾāt-i Sikandarī* (Bombay: Maṭbaʿa-i Fatḥ al-Karīm, 1308 [1890]).

Ṭabāṭabāʾī, Sayyid ʿAlī, *Burhān-i Ma'āthir*, ed. S. Hāshimī (Delhi: Delhi University Press, 1936). Translated into English by T. W. Haig, published as 'History of the Nizam Shahi Kings of Ahmadnagar', *The Indian Antiquary* 49–52 (1920–3).

Tavernier, Jean Baptiste, *Travels in India*, trans. V. Ball (London: Macmillan, 1889).

Thévenot, Jean de, *Travels of Monsieur de Thévenot* (London: printed by Henry Clark, for John Taylor, at the Ship in St Paul's Church-Yard, 1687).

Ulughkhānī, ʿAbd Allāh Muḥammad ibn ʿUmar, *An Arabic History of Gujarat: Zafar al-Wālih bi Muzaffar wa Ālih*, ed. E. Denison Ross (London: J. Murray, 1910–28).

Valle, Pietro della, *Travels of Pietro della Valle in India*, trans. G. Havers, ed. Edward Grey (New Delhi: Asian Educational Services, 1991, reprint).

Zayn al-Dīn b. ʿAbd al-ʿAzīz b. Zayn al-Dīn b. ʿAlī b. Aḥmad al-Shāfiʿī, *Tuḥfat al-Mujāhidīn fī baʿẓ Aḥwāl al-Burtukaliyyīn*, ed. S. Muhammad Husain Nainar (Madras: Madras University, 1953).

Al-Zubayrī, Muḥammad Ibrāhīm, *Tārīkh-i Bījāpūr Musamma bi-Basātīn al-Salāṭīn* (Hyderabad: n.p., 1892).

Ẓuhūrī, *'Nauras'*; *Khwān-i khalīl'*, *'Gulzār-i Ibrāhīm'*, in Mauammad ʿAbduʾl Ghani (ed. and trans.), *A History of Persian Language and Literature at the Mughal Court, vol. 3: Akbar* (Allahabad: The Indian Press, 1930).

Secondary Sources

Abu Lughod, Janet L., *Before European Hegemony: the World System, A.D. 1250–1350* (New York: Oxford University Press, 1989).

Adams, Julia, *The Familial State: Ruling Families and the Merchant Capitalism in Early Modern Europe* (Ithaca, NY: Cornell University Press, 2005).

Agnew, John, 'Representing Space: Space, Scale and Culture in Social Science', in James Duncan and David Ley (eds), *Place, Culture, Representation* (London: Routledge, 1993), pp. 251–71.

Ahmad, Aziz, *An Intellectual History of Islam in India* (Edinburgh: Edinburgh University Press, 1969).

Ahmad, Aziz, 'The Sufi and the Sultan in pre-Mughal Muslim India', *Der Islam* 38/39 (1963–4): 142–53.

Aiyangar, S. Krishnaswami, *South India and Her Muhammadan Invaders* (London, Madras printed by Humphrey Milford, 1921).

Alam, Muzaffar, *The Languages of Political Islam in India, c. 1200–1800* (Chicago, IL: University of Chicago Press, 2004).

Alam, Muzaffar, 'The Culture and Politics of Persian in Precolonial Hindustan',

Bibliography

in Sheldon Pollock (ed.), *Literary Cultures in History: Reconstructions from South Asia* (Berkeley, CA: University of California Press, 2003), pp. 131–98.

Alam, Muzaffar, '*Shariᶜa* and Governance in the Indo-Islamic Context', in David Gilmartin and Bruce B. Lawrence (eds), *Beyond Turk and Hindu: Rethinking Religious Identities in Islamicate South Asia* (Gainesville, FL: University Press of Florida, 2000), pp. 216–45.

Alam, Muzaffar, 'The Pursuit of Persian: Language in Mughal Politics', *Modern Asian Studies* 32(2) (1998): 317–49.

Alam, Muzaffar and Sanjay Subrahmanyam, *Indo-Persian Travels in the Age of Discoveries, 1400–1800* (Cambridge: Cambridge University Press, 2007).

Alam, Muzaffar and Sanjay Subrahmanyam, 'The Deccan Frontier and Mughal Expansion, c. 1600: Contemporary Perspectives', *Journal of the Economic and Social History of the Orient* 47(3) (2004): 357–89.

Alam, Muzaffar and Sanjay Subrahmanyam (eds), *The Mughal State, 1526–1750* (New Delhi: Oxford University Press, 1998).

Alam, S. M., 'The Historic Deccan: a Geographical Appraisal', in V. K. Bawa (ed.), *Aspects of Deccan History: Report of a Seminar* (Hyderabad: Institute of Asian Studies, 1975), pp. 16–29.

ᶜĀlamī, Khadīja, *Mulūk-i Bahmanī: Nukhustīn Ḥākimān-i Mustaqill-i Musalmān dar Dakkan, 748–934Q/1347–1528M* (Tehran: Amīr Kabīr, 1393 [2014]).

Alavi, Rafi Ahmad, *Studies in the History of Medieval Deccan* (Delhi: Idarah-i Adabiyat-i Delli, 1977).

Ali, Daud, 'The Historiography of the Medieval in South Asia', *Journal of the Royal Asiatic Society*, series 3, 22(1) (2012): 7–12.

Ali, Daud and Emma J. Flatt (eds), *Garden and Landscape Practices in Pre-Colonial India: Histories from the Deccan* (New Delhi: Routledge India 2011).

Ali, Omar H., *Malik Ambar: Power and Slavery Across the Indian Ocean* (New York: Oxford University Press, 2016).

Almond, Richard, *Medieval Hunting* (Stroud: Sutton, 2003).

Altekar, A. S., 'The Yadavas of Seundesa', in Yazdani, G. (ed.), *The Early History of the Deccan* (London: Oxford University Press, 1960), vol. 2, pp. 570–2.

Amanat, Abbas, 'Iranian Identity Boundaries: a Historical Overview', in Abbas Amanat and Farzin Vejdani (eds), *Iran Facing Others: Identity Boundaries in a Historical Perspective* (New York: Palgrave Macmillan, 2012), pp. 1–14.

Anooshahr, Ali, *Turkestan and the Rise of Eurasian Empires: a Study of Politics and Invented Traditions* (New York: Oxford University Press, 2018).

Anooshahr, Ali, 'On the Imperial Discourse of the Delhi Sultanate and Early Mughal India', *Journal of Persianate Studies* 7 (2014): 157–76.

Anwar, Firdos, *Nobility under the Mughals (1628–1658)* (New Delhi: Manohar, 2001).

Anwar, M. Siraj, *Mughals and the Deccan: Political Relations with Ahmadnagar Kingdom* (Delhi: B. R. Publishing, 2007).

ᶜAqīl, Muᶜīnuddīn, *Dakan aur Īrān: Salṭanat-i Bahmaniyah aur Īrān ke ᶜIlmī va Tamaddunī Ravwābiṭ* (Karachi: Shamīm Buk Ejansī, 1983).

Arasaratnam, S., 'India and the Indian Ocean in the Seventeenth Century', in Ashin Das Gupta and M. N. Person (eds), *India and the Indian Ocean, 1500–1800* (Calcutta: Oxford University Press, 1987), pp. 94–130.

Asad Allāh, Mīr Navvāb, *Mukhtār al-Akhbār wa Tuḥfat al-Akhyār* (Hyderabad: n.p., 1294 [1877]).

Asani, Ali, '"Oh That I Could be a Bird and Fly, I would Rush to the Beloved": Birds in Islamic Mystical Poetry', in Paul Waldau and Kimberley Patton (eds), *A Communion of Subjects: Animals in Religion, Science, and Ethics* (New York: Columbia University Press, 2006), pp. 170–5.

Ash, Eric H., *The Draining of the Fens: Projects, Popular Politics, and State Building in Early Modern England* (Baltimore, MD: Johns Hopkins University Press, 2017).

Asher, Catherine B., 'Mapping Hindu–Muslim Identities through the Architecture of Shahjahanabad and Jaipur', in David Gilmartin and Bruce B. Lawrence (eds), *Beyond Turk and Hindu: Rethinking Religious Identities in Islamicate South Asia* (Gainesville, FL: University Press of Florida, 2000), pp. 121–48.

Asher, Catherine B., 'Islamic Influence and the Architecture of Vijayanagara', in Anna Libera Dallapiccola and Sephanie Zingel-Avé Lallemant (eds), *Vijayanagara – City and Empire: New Currents of Research* (Stuttgart: Steiner, 1985), pp. 189–95.

Aslanian, Sebouh David, *From the Indian Ocean to the Mediterranean: the Global Trade Networks of Armenian Merchants from New Julfa* (London: University of California Press, 2011).

Atçıl, Abdurrahman, *Scholars and Sultans in the Early Modern Ottoman Empire* (Cambridge: Cambridge University Press, 2017).

Athar Ali, M., 'Political Structures of the Islamic Orient in the Sixteenth and Seventeenth Centuries', in Irfan Habib (ed.), *Medieval India, vol. 1: Researches in the History of India 1200–1750* (Delhi: Oxford University Press, 1992), pp. 129–40.

Athar Ali, M., *The Mughal Nobility under Aurangzeb* (London: Asia Publishing House, for the Department of History, Aligarh Muslim University, 1966).

Auer, Blain H., 'Intersections between Sufism and Power: Narrating the Shaykhs and Sultans of Northern India, 1200–1400', in John C. Curry and Erik S. Ohlander (eds), *Sufism and Society: Arrangements of the Mystical in the Muslim World, 1200–1800* (London: Routledge, 2012), pp. 17–33.

Awalikar, Pandit, *The Marathi–Kannada Relationship* (Prasaranga: University of Mysore, 1981).

Ayalon, David, 'Mamlūk Military Aristocracy: a Non-Hereditary Nobility', *Jerusalem Studies in Arabic and Islam* 10 (1987): 205–10.

Ayyangar, S. K., 'Hindu States in Southern India, AD 1000–1565', in Wolseley Haig (ed.), *The Cambridge History of India, vol. 3: Turks and Afghans* (Cambridge: Cambridge University Press, 1928), pp. 467–99.

Bibliography

Babaie, Sussan, *Isfahan and its Palaces: Statecraft, Shi'ism and the Architecture of Conviviality in Early Modern Iran* (Edinburgh: Edinburgh University Press, 2008).

Babayan, Kathryn, *Mystics, Monarchs, and Messiah: Cultural Landscape of Early Modern Iran* (Cambridge, MA: Harvard University Press, 2002).

Bahl, Christopher D., 'Histories of Circulation: Sharing Arabic Manuscripts across the Western Indian Ocean, 1400–1700', PhD dissertation, SOAS University of London, 2018.

Bailey, T. Grahame, *A History of Urdu Literature* (Calcutta and London: Association Press and Oxford University Press, 1932).

Baker, Alan R. H., *Geography and History: Bridging the Divide* (Cambridge: Cambridge University Press, 2003).

Balabanlilar, Lisa, 'Lords of the Auspicious Conjunction: Turco-Mongol Imperial Identity on the Subcontinent', *Journal of World History* 18(1) (2007): 1–39.

Balachandran, G. and Sanjay Subrahmanyam, 'On the History of Globalization and India: Concepts, Measures and Debates', in Jackie Assayag and C. J. Fuller (eds), *Globalizing India: Perspectives from Below* (London: Anthem, 2005), pp. 17–46.

Balasubrahmanyan, Suchitra, 'The Myth of the Hare and Hounds: Making Sense of a Recurring City-Foundation Story', *Nehru Memorial Museum and Library Occasional Paper, History and Society, New Series* 44 (2014).

Bang, Peter Fibiger and Dariusz Kołodziejczyk, '"Elephant of India": Universal Empire through Time and Across Cultures', in P. F. Bang and D. Kołodziejczyk (eds), *Universal Empire: a Comparative Approach to Imperial Culture and Representation in Eurasian History* (Cambridge: Cambridge University Press, 2012), pp. 1–40.

Baptiste, Fitzroy André, John McLeod and Kenneth X. Robbins, 'Africans in the Medieval Deccan', in Kenneth X. Robbins and John McLeod (eds), *African Elites in India: Habshi Amarat* (Ahmadabad and Ocean Township, NJ: Mapin and Grantha, 2006), pp. 31–43.

Bawa, Oudesh Rani, 'The Role of Sufis and Sants in the Development of Deccani Urdu', *Deccan Studies* 7(2) (2009): 69–81.

Bayly, C. A., *Origins of Nationality in South Asia: Patriotism and Ethical Government in the Making of Modern India* (New Delhi: Oxford University Press, 1998).

Beach, Milo Cleveland and Ebba Koch, *King of the World: the Padshahnama, an Imperial Mughal Manuscript from the Royal Library, Windsor Castle* (London: Azimuth, 1997).

Ben-Dor Benite, Zvi, '*Hijra* and Exile: Islam and Dual Sovereignty in Qing China', in Zvi Ben-Dor Benite, Stefanos Geroulanos and Nicole Jerr (eds), *The Scaffolding of Sovereignty: Global and Aesthetic Perspectives on the History of a Concept* (New York: Columbia University Press, 2017), pp. 279–302.

Ben-Dor Benite, Zvi, Stefanos Geroulanos and Nicole Jerr (eds), 'Editors'

Introduction', in *The Scaffolding of Sovereignty: Global and Aesthetic Perspectives on the History of a Concept* (New York: Columbia University Press, 2017), pp. 1–49.

Ben-Herut, Gil, *Śiva's Saints: The Origins of Devotion in Kannada According to Harihara's Ragaḷegaḷu* (New York: Oxford University Press, 2018).

Benson, James, 'Śaṃkarabhaṭṭa's Family Chronicle: the *Gādhivaṃśavarṇana*', in Axel Michaels (ed.), *The Pandit: Traditional Scholarship in India* (New Delhi: Manohar, 2001), pp. 105–18.

Benson, Janet E., 'Politics and Muslim Ethnicity in South India', *Journal of Anthropological Research* 39(1) (1983): 42–59.

Berktay, Halil, 'Three Empires and the Societies they Governed: Iran, India and the Ottoman Empire', in Halil Berktay and Suraiya Faroqhi (eds), *New Approaches to State and Peasant in Ottoman History* (London: Frank Cass, 1992), pp. 242–63.

Bhagwat, Vidyut, 'Hindu–Muslim Dialogue: a Rereading of Sant Eknath and Sant Shaikh Muhammad', in M. Naito, I. Shima and H. Kotani (eds), *Mārga: Ways of Liberation, Empowerment, and Social Change in Maharashtra* (New Delhi: Manohar, 2008), pp. 77–93.

Bhukya, Bhangya, *History of Modern Telangana* (Hyderabad: Orient BlackSwan, 2017).

Bhupala Rao, K. V., *The Illustrious Maha Mantri Maadanna* (Hyderabad: Savitri Sadanamu, 1984).

Biedermann, Zoltán and Alan Strathern (eds), *Sri Lanka at the Crossroads of History* (London: UCL Press, 2017).

Blake, Stephen P., *Time in Early Modern Islam: Calendar, Ceremony and Chronology in the Safavid, Mughal, and Ottoman Empires* (Cambridge: Cambridge University Press, 2013).

Bouchon, Geneviève and Denys Lombard, 'The Indian Ocean in the Fifteenth Century', in Ashin Das Gupta and M. N. Person (eds), *India and the Indian Ocean, 1500–1800* (Calcutta: Oxford University Press, 1987), pp. 46–70.

Brand, Mark, 'Bijapur under the Adil Shahis (1490–1686)', in Helen Philon (ed.), *Silent Splendour: Palaces of the Deccan, 14th–19th Centuries* (Mumbai: Marg, 2010), pp. 66–77.

Brenner, Neil, Bob Jessop, Martin Jones and Gordon Macleod (eds), *State/Space: A Reader* (Malden, MA: Blackwell, 2003).

Bridges White, Elizabeth Jane, 'Beyond Empire: Vijayanagara Imperialism and the Emergence of the Keladi–Ikkeri Nayaka State, 1499–1763 CE', PhD dissertation, University of Michigan, 2015.

Bronner, Yigal, *Extreme Poetry: The South Asian Movement of Simultaneous Narration* (New York: Columbia University Press, 2010).

Bronner, Yigal and David Shulman, '"A Cloud turned Goose": Sanskrit in the Vernacular Millennium', *Indian Economic and Social History Review* 43(1) (2006): 1–30.

Browne, E. G., *A Literary History of Persia, vol. 4: a History of Persian Literature*

in Modern Times, A.D. *1500–1924* (Cambridge: Cambridge University Press, 1924).
Bredi, D., F. Coslovi and B. Scarcia Amoretti, 'Shi'ism in the Deccan: a Hypothetical Study', *Islamic Culture* 42(2/3) (1988): 97–112.
Bukhārī, Suhayl, *Urdū wa Dakkanī Zabān kā Taqābulī Muṭālaᶜa* (Lahore: Azad Book Depot, 1989).
Bulliet, Richard W., *Islam: the View from the Edge* (New York: Columbia University Press, 1994).
Burbank, Jane and Frederick Cooper, *Empires in World History: Power and the Politics of Difference* (Princeton, NJ: Princeton University Press, 2010).
Busch, Allison, *Poetry of Kings: The Classical Hindi Literature of Mughal India* (New York: Oxford University Press, 2011).
Busch, Allison, 'Hidden in Plain View: Brajbhasha Poets at the Mughal Court', *Modern Asian Studies* 44(2) (2010): 267–309.
Butler Schofield, Katherine, 'Music, Art and Power in 'Adil Shahi Bijapur, c. 1570–1630', in Kavita Singh (ed.), *Scent Upon a Southern Breeze: the Synaesthetic Arts of the Deccan* (Mumbai: Marg, 2018), pp. 68–87.
Butler Brown, Katherine, 'Did Aurangzeb Ban Music? Questions for the Historiography of his Reign', *Modern Asian Studies* 41(1) (2007): 77–120.
Butler Schofield, Katherine, 'Learning to Taste the Emotions: the Mughal *Rasika*', in Francesca Orsini and Katherine Butler Schofield (eds), *Tellings and Texts: Music, Literature and Performance in North India* (Cambridge: Open Book, 2015), pp. 407–21.
Calkins, Philip B., 'The Formation of a Regionally Oriented Ruling Group in Bengal, 1700–1740', *Journal of Asian Studies* 29(4) (1970): 799–806.
Casale, Giancarlo, 'The Islamic Empires of the Early Modern World', in Jerry H. Bentley, Sanjay Subrahmanyam and Merry E. Wiesner-Hanks (eds), *The Cambridge World History, vol. 6: The Construction of a Global World, 1400–1800 CE, Part 1: Foundations* (Cambridge: Cambridge University Press, 2015), pp. 323–44.
Chandra, Satish, *Mughal Religious Policies, the Rajputs, and the Deccan* (New Delhi: Vikas, 1993).
Chandra Shobhi, Prithvi Datta, 'Kalyāṇa is Wrecked: the Remaking of a Medieval Capital in Popular Imagination', *South Asian Studies* 32(1) (2016): 90–8.
Chatterjee, Kumkum, *The Cultures of History in Early Modern India: Persianization and Mughal Culture in Bengal* (New Delhi: Oxford University Press, 2009).
Chattopadhyaya, Brajadulal, *The Making of Early Medieval India*, 2nd edn (New Delhi: Oxford University Press, 2012).
Chaube, J., *History of Gujarat Kingdom, 1458–1537* (New Delhi: Munshiram Manoharlal, 1973).
Chowdhuri, Jagindra Nath, *Malik Ambar: a Biography based on Original Sources* (Calcutta: M. C. Sarkar, [1934?]).

Cipolla, Carlo M., *Guns, Sails and Empires: Technological Innovation and the Early Phases of European Expansion, 1400–1700* (New York: Pantheon Books, 1966).
Cole, J. R. I., *Roots of North Indian Shi'ism in Iran and Iraq: Religion and State in Awadh, 1722–1859* (Berkeley, CA: University of California Press, 1988).
Commissariat, M. S., *A History of Gujarat* (Bombay: Longman, 1938).
Conermann, Stephan. 'South Asia and the Indian Ocean', in Wolfgang Reinhard (ed.), *Empire and Encounters 1350–1750* (Cambridge, MA: Belknap Press of Harvard University Press, 2015), pp. 389–552.
Cousens, Henry, *Archaeological Survey of India, 37: Bijapur and its Architectural Remains* (Bombay: Government Central Press, 1916).
Cousens, Henry, *Notes on the Buildings and Other Antiquarian Remains at Bijapur* (Bombay: Government Central Press, 1890).
Cox, Whitney, *Politics, Kingship, and Poetry in Medieval South India: Moonset on Sunrise Mountain* (Cambridge: Cambridge University Press, 2016).
Cox, Whitney, 'Law, Literature, and the Problem of Politics in Medieval India', in Timothy Lubin, Donald R. Davis, Jr and Jayanth K. Krishnan (eds), *Hinduism and Law: an Introduction* (Cambridge: Cambridge University Press, 2010), pp. 167–82.
Curtin, Philip D., *Cross-Cultural Trade in World History* (Cambridge: Cambridge University Press, 1984).
Da Costa, Palmira Fontes (ed.), *Medicine, Trade and Empire: Garcia de Orta's Colloquies on the Simples and Drugs of India (1563) in Context* (Farnham: Ashgate, 2015).
Daftary, Farhad, *The Ismāʿīlīs: Their History and Doctrines*, 2nd edn (New York: Cambridge University Press, 2007).
Dale, Stephen Frederic, *The Muslim Empires of the Ottomans, Safavids, and Mughals* (Cambridge: Cambridge University Press, 2010).
Dale, Stephen Frederic, 'The Legacy of the Timurids', *Journal of the Royal Asiatic Society*, 3rd series, 8(1) (1998): 43–58.
Dale, Stephen Frederic, *Indian Merchants and the Eurasian Trade, 1600–1750* (Cambridge: Cambridge University Press, 1994).
Dale, Stephen Frederic, 'Steppe Humanism: the Autobiographical Writings of Zahir al-Din Muhammad Babur, 1483–1530', *International Journal of Middle East Studies* 22(1) (1990): 37–58.
Dale, Stephen Frederic, *Islamic Society on the South Asian Frontier: the Māppiḷas of Malabar, 1498–1922* (Oxford: Clarendon Press, 1980).
Dallapiccola, Anna Libera, *The Great Platform at Vijayanagara* (New Delhi: Manohar and American Institute of Indian Studies, 2010)
Dallapiccola, Anna Libera and Sephanie Zingel-Avé Lallemant (eds), *Vijayanagara – City and Empire: New Currents of Research* (Stuttgart: Steiner, 1985).
Dalrymple, William and Anita Anand, *Koh-i-Noor: The History of the World's Most Infamous Diamond* (London: Bloomsbury, 2017).

Bibliography

Darwin, John, *After Tamerlane: The Global History of Empire since 1405* (London: Allen Lane, 2015).

Deák, Dušan, 'Making Sufism Popular: a Case from the Marathi Deccan', *Deccan Studies* 9(2) (2013): 5–24.

Derrett, J. Duncan M., *The Hoysaḷas: a Medieval Indian Royal Family* (Oxford: Oxford University Press, 1957).

Desai, P. B., Shrinivas H. Ritti and B. R. Gopal, *A History of Karnataka*, 2nd edn (Dharwad: Karnatak University, 1981).

Deshpande, Kusumawati and M. V. Rajadhyaksha, *A History of Marathi Literature* (New Delhi: Sahitya Akademi, 1988).

Deshpande, Prachi, *Creative Pasts: Historical Memory and Identity in Western India, 1700–1960* (New York: Columbia University Press, 2007).

Deśmukh, Vijay, *Śakakarte Śivarāy* (Nagpur: Chatrapatī Sevā Pratiṣṭhān Prakāśan, 1980–2).

Devadevan, Manu V., 'The Ravaging Hand: Abdul Karim Khan and the Decline of Bijapur', *Deccan Studies* 8(1) (2010): 59–72.

Devare, T. N., *A Short History of Persian Literature at the Bahmani, the Adilshahi, and the Qutbshahi Courts: Deccan* (Pune: S. Devare, 1961).

Devi, V. Yashoda, *After the Kakatiyas* (Hyderabad: Andhra Pradesh Sahitya Akademi, 1975).

Dhere, Ramchandra Chintaman, *The Rise of a Folk God: Viṭṭhal of Pandharpur*, trans. Anne Feldhaus (New York: Oxford University Press, 2011 [1984]).

Diamond, Jared, *Guns, Germs, and Steel: the Fates of Human Societies* (London: Jonathan Cape, 1997).

Digby, Simon, 'Before Timur Came: Provincialization of the Delhi Sultanate through the Fourteenth Century', *Journal of the Economic and Social History of the Orient* 47(3) (2004): 298–356.

Digby, Simon, 'The Sufi Shaykh and the Sultan: a Conflict of Claims to Authority in Medieval India', *Iran* 28 (1990): 71–81.

Dikshit, G. S., *Local Self-Government in Medieval Karnataka* (Dharwar: Karnatak University, 1964).

Dirks, Nicholas B., *The Hollow Crown: Ethnohistory of an Indian Kingdom* (Cambridge: Cambridge University Press, 1987).

Divekar, V. D., *Survey of Material in Marathi on the Economic and Social History of India* (Pune: Bharat Itihas Samshodhak Mandal, 1981).

Donoso, Isaac, 'The Ottoman Caliphate and Muslims of the Philippine Archipelago during the Early Modern Era', *Proceedings of the British Academy* 200 (2015): 121–46.

Doyle, Michael W., *Empires* (Ithaca, NY: Cornell University Press, 1986).

Eaton, Richard M., 'The Rise of Written Vernaculars: The Deccan, 1450–1650', in Francesca Orsini and Samira Sheikh (eds), *After Timur Left: Culture and Circulation in Fifteenth Century North India* (New Delhi: Oxford University Press, 2014), pp. 111–29.

Eaton, Richard M., '"Kiss my Foot", said the King: Firearms, Diplomacy, and the Battle of Raichur, 1520', *Modern Asian Studies* 43(1) (2009): 289–313.

Eaton, Richard M., *A Social History of the Deccan, 1300–1761: Eight Indian Lives* (Cambridge: Cambridge University Press, 2005).

Eaton, Richard M., 'Temple Desecration and Indo-Muslim States', in David Gilmartin and Bruce B. Lawrence (eds), *Beyond Turk and Hindu: Rethinking Religious Identities in Islamicate South Asia* (Gainesville, FL: University Press of Florida, 2000), pp. 246–81.

Eaton, Richard M., 'The Political and Religious Authority of the Shrine of Baba Farid', in *Essays on Islam and Indian History* (New Delhi: Oxford University Press, 2000), pp. 203–24.

Eaton, Richard M., *The Rise of Islam and the Bengal Frontier, 1204–1760* (New Delhi: Oxford University Press, 1993).

Eaton, Richard M., *The Sufis of Bijapur, 1300–1700: Social Roles of Sufis in Medieval India* (Princeton, NJ: Princeton University Press, 1978).

Eaton, Richard M. and Phillip B. Wagoner, *Power, Memory, Architecture: Contested Sites on India's Deccan Plateau, 1300–1600* (New Delhi: Oxford University Press, 2014).

Eaton, Richard M. and Phillip B. Wagoner, 'Warfare on the Deccan Plateau, 1450–1600: a Military Revolution in Early Modern India?' *Journal of World History* 25(1) (2014): 5–50.

Eck, Diana L., *Darśan: Seeing the Divine Image in India*, 2nd edn (Chambersburg, PA: Anima Books, 1985).

Edwin, P. G., 'The Hoysaḷas and the Tamil Kingdoms', in B. Sheik Ali (ed.), *The Hoysaḷa Dynasty* (Mysore: Prasaranga, University of Mysore, 1972), pp. 66–70.

Eisenstadt, S. N., 'Multiple Modernities', *Daedalus* 129 (2000): 1–29.

Emiralioğlu, Pınar, *Geographical Knowledge and Imperial Culture in the Early Modern Ottoman Empire* (Farnham: Ashgate, 2014).

Ergene, Boğaç A., 'On Ottoman Justice: Interpretations in Conflict (1600–1800)', *Islamic Law and Society* 8(1) (2001): 52–87.

Ernst, Carl W., 'Foreword', in ʿAlī al-Hujwīrī, *Kashf al-Maḥjūb*, trans. Reynold A. Nicholson, (New York: Pir Press, 1999, reprint).

Ernst, Carl W., *Sufism: an Introduction to the Mystical Tradition of Islam* (Boston, MA: Shambhala, 1997).

Fakhri, S. M. Abdul Khader, *Dravidian Sahibs and Brahmin Maulanas: the Politics of the Muslims of Tamil Nadu, 1930–1967* (New Delhi: Manohar, 2008).

Farooqi, Naimur Rahman, *Mughal–Ottoman Relations* (Delhi: Idarah-i Adabiyat-i Delli, 1989).

Farooqui, Salma Ahmad, *Multicultural Dimensions of Medieval Deccan* (New Delhi: Sundeep Prakashan, 2008).

Faruqui, Munis D., *Princes of the Mughal Empire, 1504–1719* (New York: Cambridge University Press, 2012).

Bibliography

Faruqui, Munis D., 'At Empire's End: The Nizam, Hyderabad and Eighteenth-Century India', *Modern Asian Studies* 43(1) (2009): 5–43.

Feldhaus, Anne, *Connected Places: Region, Pilgrimage, and Geographical Imagination in India* (New York: Palgrave Macmillan, 2003).

Feldhaus, Anne, 'Maharashtra as a Holy Land: a Sectarian Tradition', *Bulletin of the School of Oriental and African Studies* 49(3) (1986): 532–48.

Ferguson, Heather L., *The Proper Order of Things: Language, Power, and Law in Ottoman Administrative Discourses* (Stanford, CA: Stanford University Press, 2018).

Firouzeh, Peyvand, 'Sacred Kingship in the Garden of Poetry: Aḥmad Shāh Bahmanī's Tomb in Bidar (India)', *South Asian Studies* 31(2) (2015): 187–214.

Fischel, Roy S., 'Origin Narratives, Legitimacy, and the Practice of Cosmopolitan Language in the Early Modern Deccan', *Purusartha* 33 (2015): 71–95.

Fisher, Michael H., *A Short History of the Mughal Empire* (London: I. B. Tauris, 2016).

Flatt, Emma J., 'The Authorship and Significance of the *Nujūm al-ulūm*: a Sixteenth-Century Astrological Encyclopedia from Bijapur', *Journal of the American Oriental Society* 131(2) (2011): 223–44.

Flatt, Emma J., 'Courtly Culture in the Indo-Persian States of the Medieval Deccan: 1450–1600', PhD dissertation, SOAS University of London, 2009.

Fleischer, Cornell H., 'The Lawgiver as Messiah: The Making of the Imperial Image in the Reign of Süleyman', in Gilles Veinstein (ed.), *Soliman le Magnifique et son temps* (Paris: La Documentation Française 1992), pp. 159–77.

Fleischer, Cornell H., *Bureaucrat and Intellectual in the Ottoman Empire: the Historian Mustafa Âli (1541–1600)* (Princeton, NJ: Princeton University Press, 1986).

Flores, Jorge, *Unwanted Neighbours: The Mughals, the Portuguese, and their Frontier Zones* (New Delhi: Oxford University Press, 2018).

Flores, Jorge, *The Mughal Padshah: a Jesuit Treatise on Emperor Jahangir's Court and Household* (Leiden: Brill, 2016).

Forrester, Duncan B., 'Subregionalism in India: the Case of Telangana, *Pacific Affairs* 43(1) (1970): 5–21.

Fritz, John M., George Michell and M. S. Nagaraja Rao, *Where Kings and Gods Meet: the Royal Centre at Vijayanagara, India* (Tucson: University of Arizona Press, 1984).

Fukazawa, Hiroshi, *The Medieval Deccan: Peasants, Social Systems and States, Sixteenth to Eighteenth Centuries* (Delhi: Oxford University Press, 1991).

Gadre, Pramod B., *Cultural Archaeology of Ahmadnagar during Nizam Shahi Period (1494–1632)* (Delhi: B. R. Publishing, 1986).

Ganapathi, Racharla, *Subordinate Rulers in Medieval India* (Delhi: Bharatiya Kala Prakashan, 2000).

George, Alain, 'Direct Sea Trade between Early Islamic Iraq and Tang China: From the Exchange of Goods to the Transmission of Ideas', *Journal of the Royal Asiatic Society*, Series 3, 25(4) (2015): 579–624.

Glassen, Erika, 'Schah Ismāʿīl I. und die Theologen seiner Zeit', *Der Islam* 48 (1972): 254–68.

Golden, Peter B., '"Eternal Stones": Historical Memory and Notions of History among the Early Turkic People', in Ismail K. Poonawala (ed.), *Turks in the Indian Subcontinent, Central and West Asia: the Turkish Presence in the Islamic World* (New Delhi: Oxford University Press, 2017), pp. 3–63.

Goldstone, Jack A., 'The Problem of the "Early Modern" World', *Journal of the Economic and Social History of the Orient* 41(3) (1998): 249–84.

Gordon, Stewart, 'In the Aura of the King: Trans-Asian, Trans-Regional, and Deccani Royal Symbolism', *South Asian Studies* 32(1) (2016): 42–53.

Gordon, Stewart, *When Asia was the World: Traveling Merchants, Scholars, Warriors, and Monks Who Created the 'Riches of the East'* (New Haven, CT: Yale University Press, 2008).

Gordon, Stewart, *Marathas, Marauders, and State Formation in Eighteenth-century India* (Delhi: Oxford University Press, 1994).

Gordon, Stewart, *The Marathas, 1600–1818* (Cambridge: Cambridge University Press, 1993).

Goron, Stan and J. P. Goenka, *The Coins of the Indian Sultanates* (New Delhi: Munshiram Manoharlal, 2001).

Grant Duff, James, *A History of the Mahrattas* (London: Longman, Rees, Orme, Brown & Green, 1826), 3 vols.

Green, Nile, *Indian Sufism since the Seventeenth Century: Saints, Books, and Empires in the Muslim Deccan* (Abingdon: Routledge, 2016).

Green, Nile, *Making Space: Sufis and Settlers in Early Modern India* (New Delhi: Oxford University Press, 2012).

Gribble, J. D. B., *A History of the Deccan* (London: Luzac, 1896).

Guha, Sumit, 'Serving the Barbarian to Preserve the *Dharma*: the Ideology and Training of a Clerical Elite in Peninsular India c. 1300–1800', *Indian Economic and Social History Review* 47(4) (2010): 497–525.

Guha, Sumit, 'The Frontiers of Memory: What the Marathas Remembered of Vijayanagara', *Modern Asian Studies* 43(1) (2009): 269–88.

Guha, Sumit, '*Mārgī, Deśī,* and *Yāvanī*: High Language of Ethnic Speech in Maharashtra', in M. Naito, I. Shima and H. Kotani (eds), *Mārga: Ways of Liberation, Empowerment, and Social Change in Maharashtra* (New Delhi: Manohar, 2008), pp. 129–46.

Guha, Sumit, 'Speaking Historically: the Changing Voices of Historical Narration in Western India, 1400–1900', *American Historical Review* 109(4) (2004): 1084–103.

Guha, Sumit, 'Transitions and Translations: Regional Power and Vernacular Identity in the Dakhan, 1500–1800', *Comparative Studies of South Asia, Africa and the Middle East* 24(2) (2004): 23–31.

Bibliography

Guha, Sumit, *Environment and Ethnicity in India, 1200–1991* (Cambridge: Cambridge University Press, 1999).
Habib, Irfan, *An Atlas of the Mughal Empire* (Aligarh and Delhi: Centre of Advanced Study in History, Aligarh Muslim University and Oxford University Press, 1982).
Habib, Irfan, *The Agrarian System of Mughal India, 1556–1707* (London: Asia Publishing House, 1963).
Haidar, Mansura, *Indo-Central Asian Relations: From Early Times to Medieval Period* (New Delhi: Manohar, 2004).
Haidar, Navina Najat, 'The *Kitāb-i Nauras*: Key to Bijapur's Golden Age', in Navina Najat Haidar and Marika Sardar (eds), *Sultan of the South: Arts of India's Deccan Courts, 1323–1687* (New Haven, CT: Metropolitan Museum of Art, 2011), pp. 26–43.
Haidar, Navina Najat and Marika Sardar (eds), *Sultans of Deccan India, 1500–1700: Opulence and Fantasy* (New York: Metropolitan Museum of Art, 2015).
Haidar, Navina Najat and Marika Sardar (eds), *Sultan of the South: Arts of India's Deccan Courts, 1323–1687* (New Haven, CT: Metropolitan Museum of Art, 2011).
Haig, Wolseley, 'The Kingdom of the Deccan, AD 1347–1436', in W. Haig (ed.), *The Cambridge History of India, vol. 3: Turks and Afghans* (Cambridge: Cambridge University Press, 1922), pp. 372–404.
Hall, Kenneth R., 'Ports-of-Trade, Maritime Diasporas, and Networks of Trade and Cultural Integration in the Bay of Bengal Region of the Indian Ocean: c. 1300–1500', *Journal of the Economic and Social History of the Orient* 53 (2010): 109–45.
Haravī, Najīb Māyil, *Naqd va Taṣḥīḥ-i Mutūn: Marāḥil-i Nuskha Shināsī va Shīva-hā-yi Taṣḥīḥ-i Nuskha-hā-yi Khaṭṭ-i Fārsī* (Mashhad: Āstān-i Quds-i Raẓavī, 1369 [1990]).
Hart, Jonathan, *Comparing Empires: European Colonialism from Portuguese Expansion to the Spanish–American War* (New York: Palgrave Macmillan, 2003).
Hartung, Jan-Peter, 'Enacting the Rule of Islam: On Courtly Patronage and Religious Scholars in Pre- and Early Modern Times', in Albrecht Fuess and Jan-Peter Hartung (eds), *Court Cultures in the Muslim World: Seventh to Nineteenth Centuries* (London: Routledge, 2011), pp. 295–325.
Hasan, Farhat, *State and Locality in Mughal India: Power Relations in Western India, c. 1572–1730* (Cambridge: Cambridge University Press, 2004).
Hawley, John Stratton, *A Storm of Songs: India and the Idea of the Bhakti Movement* (Cambridge, MA: Harvard University Press, 2015).
Herwadkar, R. V., 'The Bakhars as a Source of Maratha History', *Journal of the University of Bombay* 39 (1970): 333–42.
Hashabeiky, Forogh, *Persian Orthography: Modification or Changeover? (1850–2000)* (Stockholm: Uppsala Universitet, 2005).

Hayavadana Rao, C., *The Dasara in Mysore: its Origins and Significance* (Bangalore: Bangalore Press, 1936).
Hegewald, Julia A. B., *Water Architecture in South Asia* (Leiden: Brill, 2002).
Heras, Henry, *South India under the Vijayanagar Empire: the Aravidu Dynasty* (New Delhi: Cosmo, 1927, reprint 1980).
Hodgson, Marshall G. S., *The Venture of Islam: Conscience and History in a World Civilization* (Chicago: University of Chicago Press, 1974), 3 vols.
Hosain, Hidayat, 'Shah Tahir of the Deccan', in S. M. Katre and P. K. Gode (eds), *A Volume of Indian and Iranian Studies, Presented to E. Denison Ross* (Bombay: Karnatak, 1939), pp. 147–60.
Husain, Ali Akbar, 'The Courtly Gardens of 'Abdul's *Ibrahim Nama*', in Navina Najat Haidar and Marika Sardar (eds), *Sultan of the South: Arts of India's Deccan Courts, 1323–1687* (New Haven, CT: Metropolitan Museum of Art, 2011), pp. 82–9.
Husain, Ali Akbar, *Scent in the Islamic Garden: a Study of Deccani Urdu Literary Sources* (Karachi: Oxford University Press, 2000).
Husain, Mahdi, *Tughluq Dynasty* (Calcutta: Thacker Spink, 1963).
Ḥusayn, Masʿūd, *Muḥammad Qulī Quṭb Shāh* (New Delhi: Sahityah Akadami, 1989).
Hutton, Deborah, *Art of the Court of Bijapur* (Bloomington, IN: Indiana University Press, 2006).
Hutton, Deborah, 'Carved in Stone: The Codification of Visual Identity for the Indo-Islamic Sultanate of Bīdjāpūr', *Archives of Asian Art* 55 (2005): 65–78.
Imaratwale, Abdul Gani, 'Adil Shahi Gardens, Resorts and Tanks of Bijapur: the Sources of Royal Pleasure and Public Utility', in Abdul Gani Imaratwale and Rafiq Ahmad Killedar (eds), *Studies in Medieval Bijapur* (New Delhi: Islamic Wonders Bureau, 2011), pp. 11–27.
Inden, Ronald B., *Imagining India* (Bloomington, IN: Indiana University Press, 1990; reprinted 2000).
Islam, Riyazul, *A Calendar of Documents on Indo-Persian Relations, 1500–1750* (Tehran and Karachi: Iranian Culture Foundation and Institute of Central and West Asian Studies, 1979–82), 2 vols.
Jackson, Peter, *The Delhi Sultanate: a Political and Military History* (Cambridge: Cambridge University Press, 1999).
Jha, Bishwambhar, *The Kākatīyas of Warangal, circa 1000–1323* (Patna: Janaki Prakashan, 1994).
Joshi, P. M., 'Geopolitical and Cultural Relations of Vijayanagar with the Neighbouring Muslim States', in V. K. Bawa (ed.), *Aspects of Deccan History: Report of a Seminar* (Hyderabad: Institute of Asian Studies, 1975), pp. 9–15.
Joshi, P. M., 'Historical Geography of Medieval Deccan', in H. K. Sherwani and P. M. Joshi (eds), *History of Medieval Deccan, 1295–1724* (Hyderabad: Government of Andhra Pradesh, 1973/4), vol. 1, pp. 1–28.
Joshi, P. M., 'The Adil Shahis and the Baridis', in H. K. Sherwani and P. M. Joshi

Bibliography

(eds), *History of Medieval Deccan, 1295–1724* (Hyderabad: Government of Andhra Pradesh, 1973/4), vol. 1, pp. 291–412.

Joshi, P. M., '^cAli ^cAdil Shah I of Bījāpūr (1558–1580) and His Royal Librarian: Two *Ruq^cas*', reprinted from *The Sārdhaśatābdī Commemoration Volume, 1804–1954* (Bombay: Asiatic Society of Bombay, [1954?]).

Joshi, P. M., 'Some Notes on the Textile Industry and Trade of the Kingdom of Bijapur', *Proceedings of the Indian History Congress, seventh session* (1944), pp. 262–5.

Joshi, P. M., and M. Husain, 'Khaljis and Tughluqs', in H. K. Sherwani and P. M. Joshi (eds), *History of Medieval Deccan, 1295–1724* (Hyderabad: Government of Andhra Pradesh, 1973/4), vol. 1, pp. 31–42.

Kafadar, Cemal, *Between Two Worlds: the Construction of the Ottoman State* (Berkeley, CA: University of California Press, 1995).

Karateke, Hakan T., 'Legitimizing the Ottoman Sultanate: a Framework for Historical Analysis', in H. T. Karateke and M. Reinkowski (eds), *Legitimizing the Order: the Ottoman Rhetoric of State Power* (Leiden: Brill, 2005), pp. 13–52.

Keay, John, *The Honourable Company: a History of the English East India Company* (London: HarperCollins, 1991).

Keune, Jon, 'Eknāth in Context: the Literary, Social, and Political Milieus of an Early Modern Saint-Poet', *South Asian History and Culture* 6(1) (2015): 70–86.

Keune, Jon Milton, 'Eknāth Remembered and Reformed: Bhakti, Brahmans, and Untouchables in Marathi Historiography', PhD dissertation, Columbia University, 2011.

Khalidi, Omar, 'Konkani Muslims: an Introduction', *Islamic Culture* 74(1) (2000): 127–53.

Khalidi, Omar, 'The Arabs of Hadramawt in Hyderabad: Mystics, Mercenaries and Moneylenders', in A. R. Kulkarni, M. A. Nayeem and T. R. de Souza (eds), *Medieval Deccan History: Commemoration Volume in Honour of Purshottam Mahadeo Joshi* (Bombay: Popular Prakashan, 1996), pp. 52–75.

Khan, M. H., 'Dakhni-Urdu', in H. K. Sherwani and P. M. Joshi (eds), *History of Medieval Deccan, 1295–1724* (Hyderabad: Government of Andhra Pradesh, 1973/4), vol. 2, pp. 17–25.

Khan, M. Ifzal-ur-Rahman, 'The Attitude of the Delhi Sultans towards non-Muslims: Some Observations', *Islamic Culture* 69(2) (1995): 41–56.

Khan, Maksud Ahmad, 'Shaikh Burhanu'd-din Gharib and his Migration to Deccan', *Proceedings of the Indian History Congress* 53 (1993): 236–43.

Khan, Zahoor Ali, 'Roads to the Deccan in Medieval Times', *Proceedings of the Indian History Congress* 54 (1994): 241–5.

Kincaid, C. A. and Rao Bahadur D. B. Parasnis, *A History of the Maratha People* (Delhi: S. Chand, 1931, reprint 1968).

Kinra, Rajiv, *Writing Self, Writing Empire: Chandar Bhan Brahman and the Cultural World of the Indo-Persian State Secretary* (Oakland, CA: University of California Press, 2015).

Kinsley, David, *Hindu Goddesses: Visions of the Divine Feminine in the Hindu Religious Traditions* (Berkeley, CA: University of California Press, 1986).

Knysh, Alexander, *Islamic Mysticism: a Short History* (Leiden: Brill, 2000).

Koch, Ebba, 'The Mughal Emperor as Solomon, Majnun, and Orpheus, or the Album as a Think Tank for Allegory', *Muqarnas* 27 (2010): 277–311.

Koch, Ebba, 'The Hierarchical Principles of Shah-Jahani Painting', in Milo Cleveland Beach and Ebba Koch, *King of the World: the Padshahnama, an Imperial Mughal Manuscript from the Royal Library, Windsor Castle* (London: Azimuth, 1997), pp. 130–43.

Kodad, S. B., *The Deccani Wars (1542–64)* (New Delhi: Sri Ramachandra Publications, 1986).

Kolff, D. H. A., *Naukar, Rajput, and Sepoy: the Ethnohistory of the Military Labour Market in Hindustan, 1450–1850* (Cambridge: Cambridge University Press, 1990).

Kołodziejczyk, Dariusz, 'What is Inside and What is Outside? Tributary States in Ottoman Politics', in Gabor Karman and Lovro Kuncevic (eds), *The European Tributary States of the Ottoman Empire in the Sixteenth and Seventeenth Centuries* (Leiden: Brill, 2013), pp. 421–32.

Kołodziejczyk, Dariusz, 'Between Universalistic Claims and Reality: Ottoman Frontiers in the Early Modern Period', in Christine Woodhead (ed.), *The Ottoman World* (London: Routledge, 2012), pp. 205–19.

Kozlowski, Gregory C., 'Private Lives and Public Piety: Women and the Practice of Islam in Mughal India', in Gavin R. G. Hambly (ed.), *Women in the Medieval Islamic World: Power, Patronage, Piety* (Basingstoke: Macmillan, 1998), pp. 469–88.

Krishna, Bal, *Shivaji the Great* (Bombay: D. B. Taraporevala, 1932).

Krishnaswamiengar, B. S., 'Origin of the Hoysaḷas', in B. Sheik Ali (ed.), *The Hoysaḷa Dynasty* (Mysore: Prasaranga, University of Mysore, 1972), pp. 38–43.

Kruijtzer, Gijs, 'Barī Ṣāḥib bint Muḥammad Quṭb Shāh', in David Thomas and John Chesworth (eds), *Christian–Muslim Relations: a Biographical History* (Leiden: Brill, 2017), vol. 2, pp. 231–7.

Kruijtzer, Gijs, *Xenophobia in Seventeenth-Century India* (Leiden: Leiden University Press, 2009).

Kruijtzer, Gijs, 'Madanna, Akkanna and the Brahmin Revolution: a Study of Mentality, Group Behaviour and Personality in Seventeenth-Century India', *Journal of the Economic and Social History of the Orient* 45(2) (2002): 231–67.

Kulkarni, A. R., *Madhyayugīna Mahārāṣṭra* (Pune: Ḍāyamaṇḍa Pablikeśansa, 2007).

Kulkarni, A. R., *Explorations in the Deccan History* (New Delhi: Pragati Publications and Indian Council of Historical Research, 2006).

Kulkarni, A. R., *Marathas and the Marathas Country* (New Delhi: Books & Books, 1996), 3 vols.

Kuḷkarṇī, Śrīdhar Raṅganāth, *Śivakālīn Rājanītī āṇi Raṇanītī: Ājñāpatrācyā saṃhitesah* (Mumbai: Popular Prakāśan, 1994).

Bibliography

Kulke, Hermann, 'Mahārājas, Mahants and Historians. Reflections on the Historiography of Early Vijayanagara and Sringeri', in Anna L. Dallapiccola and Stephanie Zingel-Avé Lallemant (eds), *Vijayanagara – City and Empire: New Currents of Research* (Stuttgart: Steiner, 1985), pp. 120–43.

Kumar, Noopur and D. Ravinder Reddy, *Hyderabad: Portrait of a City* (Hyderabad: Noopur Kumar, 2005).

Kumar, Sunil, 'The Ignored Elites: Turks, Mongols and a Persian Secretarial Class in the Early Delhi Sultanate', *Modern Asian Studies* 43(1) (2009): 45–77.

Kumar, Sunil, *The Emergence of the Delhi Sultanate, 1192–1286* (New Delhi: Permanent Black, 2007).

Laine, James W., *Shivaji: Hindu King in Islamic India* (Oxford: Oxford University Press, 2003).

Laine, James W., 'The *Dharma* of Islam and the *Dīn* of Hinduism: Hindus and Muslims in the Age of Śivājī', *International Journal of Hindu Studies* 3(3) (1999): 299–318.

Lakshmi Ranjanam, K., 'Telugu', in H. K. Sherwani and P. M. Joshi (eds), *History of Medieval Deccan, 1295–1724* (Hyderabad: Government of Andhra Pradesh, 1973/4), vol. 2, pp. 145–72.

Lal, Kishori Saran, *History of the Khaljis, AD 1290–1320* (London: Asia Publishing House, 1963).

Lambourn, Elizabeth, '*Khuṭba* and Muslim Networks in the Indian Ocean (Part II): Timurid and Ottoman Engagements', in Kenneth R. Hall (ed.), *The Growth of non-Western Cities: Primary and Secondary Urban Networking, c. 900–1900* (Lanham, MD: Lexington Books, 2011), pp. 127–54.

Leonard, Karen, 'Reassessing Indirect Rule in Hyderabad: Rule, Ruler, or Sons-in-Law of the State?' *Modern Asian Studies* 37(2) (2003): 363–79.

Loewy Shacham, Ilanit, 'Kṛṣṇadevaraya's Āmuktamālyada and the Narration of a Śrīvaiṣṇava Community', PhD dissertation, University of Chicago, 2015.

Ludden, David, 'The Process of Empire: Frontiers and Borderlands', in Peter Fibiger Bang and C. A. Bayly (eds), *Tributary Empires in Global History* (New York: Palgrave Macmillan, 2011), pp. 132–50.

Luther, Narendra, *Hyderabad: A Biography* (New Delhi: Oxford University Press, 2006).

Luther, Narendra, *Prince, Poet, Lover, Builder: Muhammad Quli Qutb Shah, the Founder of Hyderabad* (New Delhi: Ministry of Information and Broadcasting, Govt. of India, 1991).

Lycett, Mark T. and Kathleen D. Morrison, 'The "Fall" of Vijayanagara Reconsidered: Political Destruction and Historical Construction in South Indian History', *Journal of the Economic and Social History of the Orient* 56 (2013): 433–70.

Mancini-Lander, Derek J., 'Tales Bent Backward: Early Modern Local History in Persianate Transregional Contexts', *Journal of the Royal Asiatic Society*, 3rd series, 28(1) (2018): 23–54.

Massey, Doreen, *For Space* (Los Angeles: Sage, 2005).

Massey, Doreen, 'Places and their Pasts', *History Workshop Journal* 39 (1995): 182–92.

Mate, M. S., *A History of Water Management and Hydraulic Technology in India (1500 BC to 1800 AD)* (Delhi: B. R. Publishing, 1998).

Matthee, Rudi, 'Was Safavid Iran an Empire?' *Journal of the Economic and Social History of the Orient* 53 (2010): 233–65.

Matthews, David J., 'Eighty Years of Dakani Scholarship', *Annual of Urdu Studies* 8 (1993): 82–99.

Matthews, David J., 'Dakani Language and Literature, 1500–1700 AD', PhD dissertation, School of Oriental and African Studies, University of London, 1976.

McNeill, William H., *The Pursuit of Power: Technology, Armed Force and Society since A.D. 1000* (Chicago, IL: University of Chicago Press, 1982).

McNeill, William H., *Rise of the West: a History of the Human Community* (Chicago, IL: University of Chicago Press, 1963).

McPherson, Kenneth, *The Indian Ocean: a History of People and the Sea* (Delhi: Oxford University Press, 1993).

Mears, Barbara, 'Symbols of Coins of the Vijayanagara Empire', *South Asian Studies* 24(1) (2008): 77–83.

Mehta, Shirin, 'Akbar as Reflected in the Contemporary Jain Literature in Gujarat', *Social Scientist* 20(9/10) (1992): 54–60.

Merklinger, Elizabeth Schotten, *Indian Islamic Architecture: the Deccan, 1347–1686* (Warminster: Aris & Phillips, 1981).

Merklinger, Elizabeth Schotten, 'The Madrasa of Maḥmūd Gāwān in Bīdar', *Kunst des Orients* 11(1/2) (1976/7): 145–57.

Michell, George and Richard Eaton, *Firuzabad: Palace City of the Deccan* (Oxford: Oxford University Press on behalf of the Faculty of Oriental Studies, 1991).

Michell, George and Phillip B. Wagoner, *Vijayanagara: Architectural Inventory of the Sacred Centre* (New Delhi: Manohar and American Institute of Indian Studies, 2001).

Michell, George and Mark Zebrowski, *Architecture and Art of the Deccan Sultanates* (Cambridge: Cambridge University Press, 1999).

Mill, James, *The History of British India* (London: n.p., 1817).

Miller, Roland E., *Mappila Muslims of Kerala: a Study in Islamic Trends* (Bombay: Orient Longman, 1976).

Mitchell, Colin Paul, 'Sister Shi'a States? Safavid Iran and the Deccan in the 16th Century', *Deccan Studies* 2(2) (2004): 44–72.

Mitchell, Lisa, 'Knowing the Deccan: Enquiries, Points, and Poets in the Construction of Knowledge and Power in Early-Nineteenth-Century Southern India', in Thomas R. Trautmann (ed.), *The Madras School of Orientalism: Producing Knowledge in Colonial South India* (New Delhi: Oxford University Press, 2009), pp. 151–82.

Mohamed, Sayed, *The Value of Dakhni Language and Literature* (Mysore: University of Mysore, 1968).

Bibliography

Moin, A. Azfar, *The Millennial Sovereign: Sacred Kingship and Sainthood in Islam* (New York: Columbia University Press, 2012).
Monaghan, Patricia, *Encyclopedia of Goddesses and Heroines* (Santa Barbara, CA: Greenwood, 2010), 2 vols.
Moore, R. I., 'The Birth of Europe as a Eurasian Phenomenon', *Modern Asian Studies* 31(3) (1997): 583–601.
Morgan, David, *The Mongols* (Cambridge, MA: Blackwell, 1987).
Morris, Ian, *Why the West Rules for Now: The Patterns of History and What They Reveal about the Future* (London: Profile Books, 2010).
Morrison, Kathleen D., *Fields of Victory: Vijayanagara and the Course of Intensification* (New Delhi: Munshiram Manoharlal, 1995).
Morrison, Kathleen D., 'Supplying the City: the Role of Reservoirs in an Indian Urban Landscape', *Asian Perspectives* 32(2) (1993): 133–51.
Morrison, Kathleen D. and Carla M. Sinopoli, 'Economic Diversity and Integration in a Pre-Colonial Indian Empire', *World Archaeology* 23(3) (1992): 335–52.
Mugali, R. S., *History of Kannada Literature* (New Delhi: Sahitya Akademi, 1975).
Mukherjee, Prabhat, *The History of the Gajapati Kings of Orissa*, 2nd edn (Cuttack: Kitab Mahal, 1981).
Mukhia, Harbans, *The Mughals of India* (Oxford: Blackwell, 2004).
Mukhia, Harbans, *Historians and Historiography during the Reign of Akbar* (New Delhi: Vikas, 1976).
Murthy, A. V., Narasimha, *The Sevunas of Devagiri* (Mysore: Rao & Raghavan, 1971).
Naqvi, Sadiq, *The Iranian Afaquies Contribution to the Qutb Shahi and Adil Shahi Kingdoms* (Hyderabad: n.p., 2003).
Naqvi, Sadiq, *Muslim Religious Institutions and Their Role under the Qutb Shahs* (Hyderabad: Dar-ul-Ilm Society, 1993).
Naravane, M. S., *Shivaji's Carnatic Expedition: a Journey through History* (Pune: M. S. Naravane, 2002).
Narayana Rao, Velcheru, 'Multiple Literary Cultures in Telugu: Court, Temple, and Public', in Sheldon Pollock (ed.), *Literary Cultures in History: Reconstructions from South Asia* (Berkeley, CA: University of California Press, 2003), pp. 383–436.
Narayana Rao, Velcheru, 'Coconut and Honey: Sanskrit and Telugu in Medieval Andhra', *Social Scientist* 23(10/12) (1995): 24–40.
Narayana Rao, Velcheru and David Shulman, 'Introduction', Allasani Peddana, *The Story of Manu* (Cambridge, MA: Murty Classical Library of India and Harvard University Press, 2015).
Narayana Rao, Velcheru and David Shulman, *Srīnātha: The Poet Who Made Gods and Kings* (New York: Oxford University Press, 2012).
Narayana Rao, Velcheru, David Shulman and Sanjay Subrahmanyam, 'A New Imperial Idiom in the Sixteenth Century: Krishnadevaraya and His Political

Theory of Vijayanagara', in Jean-Luc Chevillard and Eva Wilden (eds), *South Indian Horizons: Felicitation Volume for François Gros* (Pondicherry: Institut Français de Pondichery, École Française d'Extrême-Orient, 2004), pp. 597–625.

Narayana Rao, Velcheru, David Shulman and Sanjay Subrahmanyam, *Textures of Time: Writing History in South India, 1600–1800* (Delhi: Permanent Black, 2002).

Narayana Rao, Velcheru, David Shulman and Sanjay Subrahmanyam, *Symbols of Substance: Court and State in Nāyaka Period Tamilnadu* (Delhi: Oxford University Press, 1992).

Nayeem, M. A., *The Heritage of the Adil Shahis of Bijapur* (Hyderabad: Hyderabad Publishers, 2008).

Nayeem, M. A., *The Heritage of the Qutb Shahis of Golconda and Hyderabad* (Hyderabad: Hyderabad Publishers, 2006).

Nayeem, M. A., *External Relations of the Bijapur Kingdom (1489–1686 A.D)* (Hyderabad: Bright Publishers, 1974).

Necipoğlu, Gülru, *Architecture, Ceremonial, and Power: the Topkapı Palace in the Fifteenth and Sixteenth Centuries* (New York and Cambridge, MA: Architectural History Foundation and MIT Press, 1991).

Newman, Andrew J., *Safavid Iran: Rebirth of a Persian Empire* (London: I. B. Tauris, 2006).

Nilakanta Sastri, K. A., *A History of South India: From Prehistoric Times to the Fall of Vijayanagar*, 2nd edn (Madras: Oxford University Press, 1958).

Nilakanta Sastri, K. A., 'The Chalukyas of Kalyani', in G. Yazdani, G. (ed.), *The Early History of the Deccan* (London: Oxford University Press, 1960), vol. 1, pp. 315–468.

Nizami, Khaliq Ahmad, *On History and Historians of Medieval India* (New Delhi: Munshiram Manoharlal, 1983).

Nizami, Khaliq Ahmad, *Some Aspects of Religion and Politics in India during the Thirteenth Century* (Delhi: Idara-i Adabiyat-i Delli, 1974, reprint 1978).

Novetzke, Christian Lee, *Religion and Public Memory: a Cultural History of Saint Namdev in India* (New York: Columbia University Press, 2008).

Obeng, Pashington, 'Religion and Empire: Belief and Identity among African Indians of Karnataka, South India', *Journal of the American Academy of Religion* 71(1) (2003): 99–120.

O'Hanlon, Rosalind, 'Letters Home: Banaras Pandits and the Maratha Regions in Early Modern India', *Modern Asian Studies* 44(2) (2003): 201–40.

O'Hanlon, Rosalind and Christopher Minkowski, 'What Makes People Who they Are? Pandit Networks and the Problem of Livelihoods in Early Modern Western India', *Indian Economic and Social History Review* 45(3) (2008): 381–416.

O'Hanlon, Rosalind, Gergely Hidas and Csaba Kiss, 'Discourses of Caste over the Longue Durée: Gopīnātha and Social Classification in India, ca. 1400–1900' *South Asian History and Culture* 6(1) (2015): 102–29.

Bibliography

Orenstein, Henry, *Gaon: Conflict and Cohesion in an Indian Village* (Princeton, NJ: Princeton University Press, 1965).

Orsini, Francesca, 'The Multilingual Local in World Literature', *Comparative Literature* 67(4) (2015): 345–74.

Orsini, Francesca, 'How to do Multilingual Literary History?' *Indian Economic and Social History Review* 49(2) (2012): 225–46.

Orsini, Francesca and Samira Sheikh (eds), *After Timur Left: Culture and Circulation in Fifteenth-Century North India* (New Delhi: Oxford University Press, 2014).

Overton, Keelan, 'Book Culture, Royal Libraries, and Persianate Painting in Bijapur, circa 1580–1630', *Muqarnas* 33 (2016): 91–154.

Overton, Keelan, 'A Collector and his Portrait: Book Arts and Painting for Ibrahim 'Adil Shah II of Bijapur (r. 1580–1627)', PhD dissertation, University of California–Los Angeles, 2011.

Özel, Oktay, *The Collapse of Rural Order in Ottoman Anatolia: Amasya 1576–1643* (Leiden: Brill, 2016).

Pagden, Anthony, *Lord of All the World: Ideologies of Empire in Spain, Britain and France c.1500–c.1800* (New Haven, CT: Yale University Press, 1995).

Parker, Charles H., *Global Interactions in the Early Modern Age, 1400–1800* (Cambridge: Cambridge University Press, 2010).

Parker, Geoffrey, *The Military Revolution: Military Innovation and the Rise of the West, 1500–1800* (New York: Cambridge University Press, 1988).

Parker, Geoffrey, 'The "Military Revolution", 1560–1660: a Myth?' *Journal of Modern History* 48(2) (1976): 195–214.

Pearson, M. N., *The Portuguese in India* (Cambridge: Cambridge University Press, 1987).

Perdue, Peter C., 'Official Goals and Local Interests: Water Control in the Dongting Lake Region during the Ming and Qing Periods', *Journal of Asian Studies* 41(4) (1982: 747–65.

Pereira, José, *Konkani, a Language: a History of the Konkani Marathi Controversy* (Dharwar: Karnatak University, 1971).

Philon, Helen (ed.), *Silent Splendour: Palaces of the Deccan, 14th–19th Centuries* (Mumbai: Marg, 2010).

Pillai, Narasimhacharya Ramaniyapuram Anandan (ed.), *The Kannadas: The People, Their History, and Culture* (New Delhi: Cosmo Publications, 2002), 4 vols.

Pinney, Christopher, *Photos of the Gods: the Printed Image and Political Struggle in India* (London: Reaktion, 2004).

Pipes, Daniel, *Slave Soldiers in Islam: the Genesis of a Military System* (New Haven, CT: Yale University Press, 1981).

Pollock, Sheldon, 'Introduction', *Bouquet of Rasa and River of Rasa* by Bhanu Dhatta (New York: New York University Press and JJC Foundation, 2009).

Pollock, Sheldon, *The Language of the Gods in the World of Men: Sanskrit,*

Culture, and Power in Premodern India (Berkeley: University of California Press, 2006).
Pollock, Sheldon, 'Cosmopolitan and Vernacular in History', *Public Culture* 12(3) (2000): 591–625.
Pollock, Sheldon, 'Ramayana and Political Imagination in India', *Journal of Asian Studies* 52(2) (1993): 261–97.
Prange, Sebastian R., *Monsoon Islam: Trade and Faith on the Medieval Malabar Coast* (Cambridge: Cambridge University Press, 2018).
Qadri, Sayyid Amad-Ullah, *Memoirs of Chand Bibi: the Princess of Ahmadnagar* (Hyderabad: Tarikh Office, Government of Hyderabad, 1939).
Qādrī, Sayyid Shamsullāh, *Tārīkh-i Zabān-i Urdū, Yaʿnī Urdūʾe Qadīm* (Lucknow: Naval Kishor, 1925).
Qādrī Zor, Muḥī al-Dīn, *Dakkani Adab kī Tārīkh* (Aligarh: Educational Book House, 1958, reprint 1989).
Qadri Zore, S. M. (ed.), *Qutb Shahi Sultans and Andhra Samskriti* (Hyderabad: Idara-e-Adabiyat-e-Urdu, 1962).
Quinn, Sholeh, *Historical Writing during the Reign of Shah 'Abbas* (Salt Lake City, UT: University of Utah Press, 2000).
Qureshi, I. H., *The Muslim Community of the Indo-Pakistan Subcontinent (610–1947)*, 2nd edn (Karachi: Ma'aref, 1977).
Raghunadha Rao, P., *History of Modern Andhra* (New Delhi: Sterling, 1978).
Rahman, Fazlur, *Islam*, 2nd edn (Chicago, IL: University of Chicago Press, 1979).
Rama Rao, M., *Karnataka–Andhra Relations (220–1323)* (Dharwar: Kannada Research Institute, Karnatak University, 1974).
Rama Sarma, P. Sree, *A History of Vijayanagar Empire* (Hyderabad: Prabhakar Publications, 1992).
Rama Sharma, M. H., *The History of the Vijayanagar, the Last Phase: Decline and Disappearance (1569–1679)* (Bombay: Popular Prakashan, 1978–80).
Ramachandra Rao, C. V., *Administration and Society in Medieval Āndhra (AD 1038–1538) Under the Later Eastern Gaṅgas and Sūryavaṁśa Gajapatis* (Nellore: Mānsa Publications, 1976).
Ranga, N. G., *Kākatīya Nayaks: Their Contribution to Dakshinapath's Independence, 1300–1370 AD* (Nidubrolu, Andhra Pradesh: Indian Peasant Institute, 1971).
Rao, Ajay K., *Re-figuring the Rāmāyaṇa as Theology: a History of Reception in Premodern India* (Abingdon: Routledge, 2015).
Raychaudhuri, Hemchandra, 'Geography of the Deccan', in G. Yazdani (ed.), *The Early History of the Deccan* (London: Oxford University Press, 1960), pp. 1–63.
Regani, Sarojini, *Nizam–British Relations, 1724–1857* (Hyderabad: Booklovers, 1963).
Reinhardt, Wolfgang (ed.), *Empire and Encounters 1350–1750* (Cambridge, MA: Belknap Press of Harvard University Press, 2015).
Ricci, Ronit, *Islam Translated: Literature, Conversion, and the Arabic Cosmopolis*

of South and Southeast Asia (Chicago, IL: University of Chicago Press, 2011).
Richards, John F., *The Unending Frontier: An Environmental History of the Early Modern World* (Berkeley, CA: University of California Press, 2003).
Richards, John F., 'Early Modern India and World History', *Journal of World History* 8 (1997): 197–209.
Richards, John F., *The Mughal Empire* (Cambridge: Cambridge University Press, 1993).
Richards, John F., *Mughal Administration in Golconda* (Oxford: Clarendon Press, 1975).
Ritti, Shrinivas, *The Seunas: the Yādavas of Devagiri* (Dharwar: Department of Ancient Indian History and Epigraphy, Karnatak University, 1973).
Rizvi, S. A. A., *Muslim Revivalist Movements in Northern India* (Agra: Agra University, 1965).
Roberts, Michael, *The Military Revolution, 1560–1660* (Belfast: Marjory Boyd, 1956).
Robinson, Francis, 'Ottomans–Safavids–Mughals: Shared Knowledge and Connective Systems', *Journal of Islamic Studies* 8 (1997): 151–84.
Roemer, H. R., 'The Safavid Period', in Peter Jackson and Laurence Lockhart (eds), *The Cambridge History of Iran, vol. 6: the Timurid and Safavid Periods* (Cambridge: Cambridge University Press, 1986), pp. 189–350.
Rötzer, Klaus and Pushkar Sohoni, 'Nature, Dams, Wells, and Gardens: the Route of Water In and Around Bidar', in Daud Ali and Emma J. Flatt (eds), *Garden and Landscape Practices in Pre-Colonial India: Histories from the Deccan* (London: Routledge, 2012), pp. 54–73.
Rubiés, Joan-Pau, *Travel and Ethnology in the Renaissance: South India through European Eyes, 1250–1625* (Cambridge: Cambridge University Press, 2000).
Rubinoff, Arthur G., 'Goa's Attainment of Statehood', *Asian Survey* 32(5) (1992): 471–87.
Runciman, W. G., 'Empire as a Topic in Comparative Sociology', in Peter Fibiger Bang and C. A. Baylay (eds), *Tributary Empires in Global History* (New York: Palgrave Macmillan, 2011), pp. 99–107.
Sadiq, Muhammad, *A History of Urdu Literature* (London: Oxford University Press, 1964).
Safrani, Shebhaz H., 'Golconda Alums: Shimmering Standards', in S. H. Safrani (ed.), *Golconda and Hyderabad* (Bombay: Marg, 1992), pp. 69–80.
Şahin, Kaya, *Empire and Power in the Reign of Süleyman: Narrating the Sixteenth-Century Ottoman World* (Cambridge: Cambridge University Press, 2013).
Sahu, Bhairabi Prasad, 'Brahminical Ideology, Regional Identities and the Construction of Early India', *Social Scientist* 29(7/8) (2001): 3–18.
Saksena, Ram Babu, *A History of Urdu Literature* (Allahabad: Ram Narain Lal, 1940).

Santos Alves, Jorge, 'From Istanbul with Love: Rumours, Conspiracies and Commercial Competition in Aceh–Ottoman Relations, 1550s to 1570s', *Proceedings of the British Academy* 200 (2015): 47–62.

Sardar, Marika, 'Golconda through Time: A Mirror of the Evolving Deccan', PhD dissertation, New York University, 2007.

Sardesai, Govind Sakharam, *New History of the Marathas* (Bombay: Phoenix, 1946), 3 vols.

Sardessai, Manohar L., 'The Portuguese Influence on Konkani', *Journal of South Asian Literature* 18(1) (1983): 155–8.

Sarkar, Bihani, *Heroic Saktism: the Cult of Durga in Ancient Indian Kingship* (Oxford: Oxford University Press, 2017).

Sarkar, Jadunath, *House of Shivaji: Studies and Documents of Maratha History: Royal Period*, 3rd edn (Calcutta: M. C. Sarkar, 1955).

Sarkar, Jadunath, *Shivaji and His Times*, 5th edn (Hyderabad: Orient BlackSwan, 1952, reprint 2011).

Sarkar, Jadunath, *History of Aurangzib* (Calcutta: M. C. Sarkar, 1912), 5 vols.

Sarkar, Jagadish Narayan, *The Life of Mir Jumla, the General of Aurangzeb* (Calcutta: Thacker, Spink, 1951).

Sarkar, Nilanjan, 'Necro-Narratives: Rāmarāya in AD 1565 and History', in Nilanjan Sarkar and Vikas K. Verma (eds), *Streaming the Past: Peninsular India in History* (Delhi: Primus Books, 2019), pp. 255–311.

Sarkar, Sumit, *The Swadeshi Movement in Bengal, 1903–1908* (New Delhi: People's Publishing House, 1973).

Schimmel, Annemarie, *A Two-Colored Brocade: the Imagery of Persian Poetry* (Chapel Hill, NC: University of North Carolina Press, 1992).

Schimmel, Annemarie, *Islamic Names* (Edinburgh: Edinburgh University Press, 1989).

Schimmel, Annemarie, *Islam in the Indian Subcontinent* (Leiden: Brill, 1980).

Seshan, K. S. S. (ed.), *Hyderabad-400: Saga of a City* (Hyderabad: Association of the British Council Scholars, Andhra Pradesh, 1993).

Sewell, R., *A Forgotten Empire (Vijayanagar): a Contribution to the History of India* (London: Swan Sonnenschein, 1900).

Shakeb, M. Z. A., *Relations of Golkonda with Iran: Diplomacy, Ideas, and Commerce 1518–1687*, ed. Subah Dayal (Delhi: Primus, 2017).

Shakeb, Ziauddin A., 'The Map of the Sultanate of Golconda', *Islamic Culture* 76(2) (2002): 1–10.

Sharma, B. N. K., *A History of the Dvaita School of Vedānta and its Literature, vol. 2: From the 15th Century to Our Own Time* (Bombay: Booksellers' Publishing, 1961).

Sharma, S. R., 'A Note on the Cultural Background of Political Struggles in Medieval Deccan', *Proceedings of the Deccan History Conference, Hyderabad, First Session* (1945), pp. 171–7.

Sheikh, Samira, *Forging a Region: Sultans, Traders, and Pilgrims in Gujarat, 1200–1500* (New Delhi: Oxford University Press, 2010).

Bibliography

Sherwani, H. K., *History of the Qutb Shahi Dynasty* (New Delhi: Munshiram Manoharlal, 1974).
Sherwani, H. K., 'The Bahmanis', in H. K. Sherwani and P. M. Joshi (eds), *History of Medieval Deccan, 1295–1724* (Hyderabad: Government of Andhra Pradesh, 1973/4), vol. 1, pp. 143–53.
Sherwani, H. K., *Muhammad-Quli Qutb Shah, Founder of Hyderabad* (Bombay: Asia Publishing House, [1967]).
Sherwani, H. K., *The Bahmanis of the Deccan* (Hyderabad: Saood Manzil, 1953).
Sherwani, H. K., 'The "Independence" of Bahmani Governors', *Proceedings of the Indian History Congress, Seventh Session, Madras* (1944), pp. 256–62.
Sherwani, H. K., *Maḥmūd Gāwān: the Great Bahmani Wazir* (Allahabad: Kitabistan, 1942).
Sherwani, H. K., 'The Council of Regency during the Minority of the Bahmani Ahmad III and Muhammad III (1461–1466)', *Journal of Indian History* 29 (1940): 47–53.
Sherwani, H. K. and P. M. Joshi (eds), *History of Medieval Deccan, 1295–1724* (Hyderabad: Government of Andhra Pradesh, 1973/4), 2 vols.
Shokoohy, Mherdad, 'Sassanian Royal Emblems and Their Reemergence in the Fourteenth-Century Deccan', *Muqarnas* 11 (1994): 65–78.
Shyam, Radhey, *The Kingdom of Khandesh* (Delhi: Idarah-i-Adabiyat-i Delli, 1981).
Shyam, Radhey, '˓Imad Shahis', in H. K. Sherwani and P. M. Joshi (eds), *History of Medieval Deccan, 1295–1724* (Hyderabad: Government of Andhra Pradesh, 1973/4), vol. 1, pp. 277–81.
Shyam, Radhey, *Life and Times of Malik Ambar* (Delhi: Munshiram Manoharlal, 1968).
Shyam, Radhey, *The Kingdom of Ahmadnagar* (Delhi: Motilal Banarsidass, 1966).
Siddiqi, Abdul Majeed, *History of Golcunda* (Hyderabad: Literary Publications, 1956).
Ṣiddīqī, Muḥammad Akbar al-Dīn, 'Muqadamma', *Irshādnāma, Taṣnīf Ḥazrat Burhān al-Dīn Jānam Bījāpūrī* (Hyderabad: Osmania University, 1971).
Siddiqi, Muhammad Suleman, 'The Ethnic Change at Bidar and its Influence (AD 1422–1538)', in A. R. Kulkarni, M. A. Nayeem and T. R. de Souza (eds), *Medieval Deccan History: Commemoration Volume in Honour of Purshottam Mahadeo Joshi* (Bombay: Popular Prakashan, 1996), pp. 33–51.
Siddiqi, Muhammad Suleman, *The Bahmani Ṣūfis* (Delhi: Idarah-i Adabiyat-i Delli, 1989).
Simpkins, Robert Alan, 'The Road to Golconda: European Travelers' Routes, Political Organization and Archaeology in the Golconda Kingdom (1518–1687)', PhD dissertation, University of Wisconsin-Madison, 2011.
Simpkins, Robert Alan, 'The Mysterious Milestones of Andhra Pradesh', *Deccan Studies* 8(1) (2010): 5–32.

Singh, Abha, 'Irrigating Haryana: The pre-Modern History of the Western Yamuna Canal', in Irfan Habib (ed.), *Medieval India, vol. 1: Researches in the History of India 1200–1750* (Delhi: Oxford University Press, 1992), pp. 49–61.

Sinha, S. K., *Mediaeval History of the Deccan, vol. 1: Bahmanids* (Hyderabad: Government of Andhra Pradesh, 1964).

Sinopoli, Carla M., 'From the Lion Throne: Political and Social Dynamics of the Vijayanagara Empire', *Journal of the Economic and Social History of the Orient* 43(3) (2000): 364–98.

Sinopoli, Carla M. and Kathleen D. Morrison, 'The Greater Metropolitan Region', in John M. Fritz and George Michell (eds), *New Light on Hampi: Recent Research at Vijayanagara* (Mumbai: MARG Publications, 2001), pp. 100–11.

Skelton, Robert, 'The Mughal Artist Farrokh Beg', *Ars Orientalis* 2 (1957): 393–411.

Sohoni, Pushkar, *Architecture of a Deccan Sultanate: Courtly Practice and Royal Authority in late Medieval India* (London: I. B. Tauris, 2018).

Sohoni, Pushkar, 'The Non-Issue of Coinage: the Monetary Policies of the post-Bahmani Sultanates', *Journal of the Royal Asiatic Society*, 3rd series, 28(4) (2018): 645–59.

Sohoni, Pushkar, *Aurangabad with Daulatabad, Khuldabad, and Ahmadnagar* (Mumbai: JAICO, 2015).

Sohoni, Pushkar, 'Continuities in the Sacred Landscape: Ellora, Khuldabad and the Temple of Grishneshwara: a Single Social Historical Complex', in Syed Ayub Ali (ed.), *Studies in Medieval Deccan History (14th–17th Century): Dr. M. A. Nayeem festschrift* (Warangal: Deccan History Society, 2015), pp. 156–68.

Sohoni, Pushkar, 'Local Idioms and Global Designs: Architecture of the Nizam Shahs', PhD dissertation, University of Pennsylvania, 2010.

Sohoni, Pushkar, 'Change and Memory in Farah Bagh, Ahmadnagar', *Deccan Studies* 5(2) (2007): 59–77.

Soja, Edward W., *Postmodern Geographies: The Reassertion of Space in Critical Social Theory* (London: Verso, 1989).

Sreenivasan, Ramya, 'Rethinking Kingship and Authority in South Asia: Amber (Rajasthan), ca. 1560–1615', *Journal of the Economic and Social History of the Orient* 57 (2014): 549–86.

Stein, Burton, *Vijayanagara* (Cambridge: Cambridge University Press, 1989).

Stein, Burton, 'Mahanavami: Medieval and Modern Kingly Ritual in South Asia', in Bardwell L. Smith (ed.), *Essays on Gupta Culture* (Delhi: Motilal Banarsidass, 1983), pp. 67–90.

Stein, Burton, *Peasant State and Society in Medieval South India* (Delhi: Oxford University Press, 1980).

Stoker, Valery, *Polemics and Patronage in the City of Victory: Vyasatritha, Hindu Sectarianism, and the Sixteenth-Century Vijayanagara Court* (Oakland, CA: University of California Press, 2016).

Bibliography

Streusand, Douglas E., *Islamic Gunpowder Empires: Ottomans, Safavids, and Mughals* (Boulder, CO: Westview Press, 2010).
Streusand, Douglas E., *The Formation of the Mughal Empire* (Delhi: Oxford University Press, 1999).
Subrahmanian, N., 'The Origin of the Hoysaḷas', in B. Sheik Ali (ed.), *The Hoysaḷa Dynasty* (Mysore: Prasaranga, University of Mysore, 1972), pp. 44–53.
Subrahmanyam, R., *The Sūryavaṁśa Gajapatis of Orissa* (Waltair: Andhra University, 1957).
Subrahmanyam, Sanjay, *Courtly Encounters: Translating Courtliness and Violence in Early Modern Eurasia* (Cambridge, MA: Harvard University Press, 2012).
Subrahmanyam, Sanjay, *The Portuguese Empire in Asia, 1500–1700*, 2nd edn (Chichester: Wiley-Blackwell, 2012).
Subrahmanyam, Sanjay, *Three Ways to be Alien: Travails and Encounters in the Early Modern World* (Waltham, MA: Brandeis University Press, 2011).
Subrahmanyam, Sanjay, 'A Tale of Three Empires: Mughals, Ottomans, and Habsburgs in a Comparative Context', *Common Knowledge* 12(1) (2006): 66–92.
Subrahmanyam, Sanjay, *Explorations in Connected History: Mughals and Franks* (New Delhi: Oxford University Press, 2005).
Subrahmanyam, Sanjay, 'Making Sense of Indian Historiography', *Indian Economic and Social History Review* 39 (2/3) (2002): 121–30.
Subrahmanyam, Sanjay, 'Written on Water: Designs and Dynamics in the Portuguese *Estado da Índia*', in Susan E. Alcock et al. (eds), *Empires: Perspectives from Archaeology and History* (Cambridge: Cambridge University Press, 2001), pp. 42–69.
Subrahmanyam, Sanjay, 'Hearing Voices: Vignettes of Early Modernity in South Asia, 1400–1750', *Daedalus* 127 (1998): 75–104.
Subrahmanyam, Sanjay, 'Connected Histories: Notes towards a Reconfiguration of Early Modern Eurasia', *Modern Asian Studies* 31 (1997): 735–62.
Subrahmanyam, Sanjay, 'Of Imarat and Tijarat: Asian Merchants and State Power in the Western Indian Ocean, 1400 to 1750', *Comparative Studies in Society and History* 37(4) (1995): 750–80.
Subrahmanyam, Sanjay, 'Iranians Abroad: Intra-Asian Elite Migration and Early Modern State Formation', *Journal of Asian Studies* 51(2) (1992): 340–63.
Subrahmanyam, Sanjay, 'The Mughal State: Structure or Process? Reflections on Recent Western Historiography', *Indian Economic and Social History Review* 29(2) (1992): 291–321.
Subrahmanyam, Sanjay, *The Political Economy of Commerce: Southern India 1500–1650* (Cambridge: Cambridge University Press, 1990).
Subrahmanyam, Sanjay, 'Persians, Pilgrims, and Portuguese: the Travails of Masulipatnam Shipping in the Western Indian Ocean, 1590–1665', *Modern Asian Studies* 22(3) (1988): 503–30.

Subrahmanyam, Sanjay and David Shulman, 'The Man Who Would be King? The Politics of Expansion in Early Seventeenth-Century Northern Tamilndau', *Modern Asian Studies* 24(2) (1990): 225–48.

Talbot, Cynthia, *The Last Hindu Emperor: Prithviraj Chauhan and the Indian Past, 1200–2000* (Cambridge: Cambridge University Press, 2016).

Talbot, Cynthia, *Precolonial India in Practice: Society, Region, and Identity in Medieval Andhra* (New York: Oxford University Press, 2001).

Talbot, Cynthia, 'The Story of Prataparudra: Hindu Historiography on the Deccan Frontier', in David Gilmartin and Bruce B. Lawrence (eds), *Beyond Turk and Hindu: Rethinking Religious Identities in Islamicate South Asia* (Gainesville, FL: University Press of Florida, 2000), pp. 282–99.

Talbot, Cynthia, 'Inscribing the Other, Inscribing the Self: Hindu–Muslim Identities in pre-Colonial India', *Comparative Studies in Society and History* 37(4) (1995): 692–722.

Talbot, Cynthia, 'Political Intermediaries in Kakatiya Andhra, 1175–1325', *Indian Economic and Social History Review* 31(3) (1994): 263–89.

Tamaskar, B. G., *The Life and Work of Malik Ambar* (Delhi: Idarah-i Adabiyat-i Delli, 1978).

Taylor, Meadows. *Architecture at Bijapur: An Ancient Mahometan Capital in the Bombay Presidency* (London: John Murray, 1866).

Thapar, Romila, 'Significance of Regional History with Reference to the Konkan', in A. R. Kulkarni, M. A. Nayeem and T. R. de Souza (eds), *Medieval Deccan History: Commemoration Volume in Honour of Purshottam Mahadeo Joshi* (Bombay: Popular Prakashan, 1996), pp. 19–29.

Truschke, Audrey, *Culture of Encounters: Sanskrit at the Mughal Court* (New York: Columbia University Press, 2016).

Tuan, Yi-Fu, *Space and Place: The Perspective of Experience* (Minneapolis, MN: University of Minnesota Press, 1977).

Vaikuntham, Y., *State, Economy and Social Transformation: Hyderabad State (1724–1948)* (New Delhi: Manohar, 2002).

Varlık, Nükhet, *Plague and Empire in the Early Modern Mediterranean World* (Cambridge: Cambridge University Press, 2015).

Vashishṭ, Jāvīd, *Mullā Vajhī* (New Delhi: Sāhityah Akādmī, 1996).

Vasumati, E., 'Ibrahim Qutb Shah and Telugu Poets', in S. M. Qadri Zore (ed.), *Qutb Shahi Sultans and Andhra Samskriti* (Hyderabad: Idara-e-Adabiyat-e-Urdu, 1962), pp. 28–42.

Vasumati, E., *Telugu Literature in the Qutub Shahi Period* (Hyderabad: Abul Kalam Azad Oriental Research Institute, 1960).

Vaudeville, Charlotte, 'Paṇḍharpur, City of Saints', in H. Buck and G. Yocum (eds), *Structural Approaches to South India Studies* (Chambersburg, PA: Wilson Books, 1974), pp. 137–61.

Venkataramanayya, N., 'The Eastern Chalukyas and the Chalukyas of Vemulavada', in G. Yazdani (ed.), *The Early History of the Deccan* (London: Oxford University Press, 1960), vol. 2, pp. 469–512.

Bibliography

Venkataramanayya, N., *Further Sources of Vijayanagara History, vol. 1: Introduction* (Madras: University of Madras, 1946).
Venkataramanayya, N. and M. Sarma, 'The Kakatiyas of Warangal', in G. Yazdani (ed.), *The Early History of the Deccan* (London: Oxford University Press, 1960), vol. 2, pp. 575–713.
Verghese, Anila, *Religious Traditions at Vijayanagara as Revealed Through its Monuments* (New Delhi: Manohar and the American Institute of Indian Studies, 1995).
Verlinden, Charles, *The Beginnings of Modern Colonization*, trans. Yvonne Freccero (Ithaca, NY: Cornell University Press, 1970).
Verma, D. C., *Social, Economic and Cultural History of Bijapur* (Delhi: Idarah-i Adabiyat-i Delli, 1990).
Verma, D. C., *History of Bijapur* (New Delhi: Kumar Brothers, 1974).
Viswanathan Peterson, Indira, 'Multilingual Dramas at the Tanjavur Maratha Court and Literary Cultures in Early Modern South India', *Medieval History Journal* 14(2) (2011): 285–321.
Wagoner, Phillip B., 'Money Use in the Deccan, *c.* 1350–1687: the Role of Vijayanagara Hons in the Bahmani Currency System', *Indian Economic and Social History Review* 51(4) (2014): 457–80.
Wagoner, Phillip B., 'The Multiple Worlds of Amin Khan: Crossing Persianate and Indic Cultural Boundaries in the Qutb Shahi Kingdom', in Navina Najat Haidar and Marika Sardar (eds), *Sultans of the South: Arts of India's Deccan Courts, 1323–1687* (New Haven, CT: Metropolitan Museum of Art, 2011), pp. 90–101.
Wagoner, Phillip B., 'From Manuscript to Archive to Print: the Mackenzie Collection and later Telugu Literary Historiography', in Thomas R. Trautmann (ed.), *The Madras School of Orientalism: Producing Knowledge in Colonial South India* (New Delhi: Oxford University Press, 2009), pp. 183–205.
Wagoner, Phillip B., 'Fortuitous Convergences and Essential Ambiguities: Transcultural Political Elites in the Medieval Deccan', *Journal of Hindu Studies* 3(3) (1999): 241–64.
Wagoner, Phillip B., '"Sultan among Hindu Kings": Dress, Titles, and Islamicization of Hindu Culture at Vijayanagara', *Journal of Asian Studies* 55(4) (1996): 851–80.
Wagoner, Phillip B., *Tidings of the King: a Translation and Ethnohistorical Analysis of the Rayavācakamu* (Honolulu: University of Hawaii Press, 1993).
Wallerstein, Immanuel, *The Modern World-System: Capitalist Agriculture and the Origins of the European World-Economy in the Sixteenth Century* (New York: Academic Press, 1974).
Wentworth, Blake, 'Insiders, Outsiders, and the Tamil Tongue', in Y. Bronner, W. Cox and L. McCrea (eds), *South Asian Texts in History: Critical Engagements with Sheldon Pollock* (Ann Arbor, MI: Association for Asian Studies, 2011), pp. 153–76.

White, Sam, *The Climate of Rebellion in the Early Modern Ottoman Empire* (Cambridge: Cambridge University Press, 2011).

Wherritt, Irene, 'Portuguese Loanwords in Konkani', *Hispania* 72(4) (1989): 873–81.

Wink, André, 'Islamic Society and Culture in the Deccan', in Anna Libera Dallapiccola and Stephanie Zingel-Avé Lallemant (eds), *Islam and Indian Regions* (Stuttgart: Franz Steiner, 1993), vol. 1. pp. 217–27.

Wink, André, *Al-Hind, the Making of the Indo-Islamic World* (New Delhi: Oxford University Press, 1990–).

Wink, André, *Land and Sovereignty in India: Agrarian Society and Politics under the Eighteenth-century Maratha Svārajya* (Cambridge: Cambridge University Press, 1986).

Xavier, Ângela Barreto and Ines G. Županov, *Catholic Orientalism: Portuguese Empire, Indian Knowledge (16th–18th Centuries)* (New Delhi: Oxford University Press, 2015).

Yarshater, Ehsan, 'The Persian Presence in the Islamic World', in Richard G. Hovhannisian and Georges Sabagh (eds), *The Persian Presence in the Islamic World* (Cambridge: Cambridge University Press, 1998), pp. 4–125.

Yazdani, G. (ed.), *The Early History of the Deccan* (London: published under the authority of the Government of Andhra Pradesh by Oxford University Press, 1960).

Yazdani, G., *Bidar: Its History and Monuments* (London: Oxford University Press, 1947).

Yılmaz, Hüseyin, *Caliphate Redefined: the Mystical Turn in Ottoman Political Thought* (Princeton, NJ: Princeton University Press, 2018).

Yun-Casalilla, Bartolomé, Patrick K. O'Brien and Francisco Comín (eds), *The Rise of the Fiscal States: a Global History, 1500–1914* (Cambridge: Cambridge University Press, 2012).

Zebrowski, Mark, *Deccani Painting* (London and Los Angeles: Sotheby's Publications and University of California Press, 1983).

Zolberg, Aristide R., 'Origins of the Modern World System: a Missing Link', *World Politics* 33 (1981): 253–81.

Index

ᶜAbdul Dihlawi, 97n, 99n, 164, 166, 177, 181, 187n
ᶜAbdullah Qutb Shah (r. 1626–72), 71, 104n, 192, 198, 200, 214–18, 232n, 233n, 241, 251–2, 254
Abu al-Hasan Qutb Shah (r. 1672–87), 200, 259n
ᶜAdil Shahi sultanate, 2, 16, 31, 67, 71, 89, 108, 125, 136, 150, 155–62, 166–7, 172, 179–81, 184n, 190n, 191n, 192, 196, 211, 213, 217, 220–3, 231n, 236, 238, 240, 254; *see also* Bijapur
āfāqī, 111; *see also* Foreigners
Afghans, 77, 90, 107, 114, 142n
Ahmad I Bahmani (r. 1422–36), 49–50, 73, 142n, 145n
Ahmad II Bahmani (r. 1436–58), 50, 112, 186n
Ahmad III Bahmani (r. 1461–3), 51
Ahmadnagar
  city, 56, 67, 70, 76–8, 82, 86, 131, 204, 209, 214, 231n
  sultanate, 2, 4–5, 15, 28–9, 31, 56, 66–9, 72–8, 81–8, 90–2, 96n, 97n, 98n, 99n, 102n, 103n, 105n, 112, 116–17, 120–33, 138, 142n, 144n, 146n, 147n, 151, 156, 161, 163, 166, 169, 176, 181, 182n, 192, 204–5, 210, 219, 232n, 239–40, 258n, 260n; *see also* Nizam Shahi sultanate
Ahmad Nizam al-Mulk (Ahmad Bahri, Ahmad Nizam Shah, d. 1510), 67–8, 71, 98n, 103n, 115, 145n, 209–10, 213, 229n
Ahmad Nizam Shah II (r. 1595), 204
Akbar (Mughal), 25n, 88, 120, 125, 130–1, 146n, 167, 174, 176, 204, 224n, 231n, 241, 255, 257n, 258n
ᶜAlaʾ al-Din ᶜImad al-Mulk (r. 1510–30), 68, 86–7
ᶜAli, 114, 159, 178, 245, 251–2
ᶜAli ᶜAdil Shah I (r. 1558–80), 58n, 69, 82, 96n, 103n, 120, 123, 125–9, 133, 145n, 146n, 155, 159–64, 167, 170, 175, 179, 186n, 188–9n, 196, 204
ᶜAli ᶜAdil Shah II (r. 1656–72), 100n, 102n, 155, 217–19, 241–2, 257n
ᶜAli Barid (r. 1543–80), 82, 86
ᶜAli Khan Lar, 79, 197–8
Andhra (region), 35–7, 39, 45, 47, 51–2, 55–6, 65n, 68–9, 82, 133, 193–9, 201–2, 209, 223, 226n
Andhra Pradesh, 4–5, 40, 199
Aqqoyunlu, 78, 108
Arabian Sea, 28, 54, 57n, 100n, 237
Arabic (language), 48, 50, 92, 99n, 112, 177, 222, 231n, 237
Asad Beg Qazwini, 92, 99n–100, 176–7, 190n
Aurangabad, 1, 100n, 124, 215–16, 231n, 241
Aurangzeb-ᶜAlamgir (Mughal), 104n, 195, 215–19, 231n, 232n, 233n, 240–2, 252, 257n, 258n

Bahmanis, 3, 28–9, 32, 47–52, 55–6, 57n, 60n, 64n, 66–8, 70–2, 81, 95n, 96n, 100n, 109–10, 112–13, 115, 120, 139, 153, 157–8, 162, 179, 183n, 186n, 200, 209, 214, 231n, 239, 255
Bankapur, 128, 139, 146n, 161
Baridis *see* Bidar

Bay of Bengal, 28, 45, 57n, 100n, 109, 194, 224n
Bengal, 25n, 33, 63n 151, 195–6, 216, 241, 246
Berar, 31, 44, 67, 130–2, 204
  sultanate, 2, 68, 81–7, 98n, 104n, 122, 126, 130, 151, 161, 182n, 185n, 239
Bhakti, 164, 210, 230n, 234n; *see also* devotionalism
Bhavani, 212, 221, 230n, 234n
Bidyapur *see* Bijapur (city)
Bidar
  city, 14, 45, 49–51, 55–6, 82, 86, 100n, 133, 153, 168, 186n, 218, 233n
  sultanate, 2, 5, 67–8, 83–7, 122, 239
Bijapur
  city, 55–6, 67, 71, 158–9, 162, 164–70, 172–3, 175, 178–9
  sultanate, 2, 4–6, 14, 16, 18, 28, 31, 58n, 66–72, 78, 81–6, 89–93, 95n, 96n, 97n, 99n, 102n, 104n, 108, 112, 116–17, 120–30, 133–4, 138, 146n, 150–1, 155–8, 162–3, 169, 171, 174–6, 179–81, 182n, 184n, 186n, 190n, 193, 196, 203, 205–9, 214–24, 227n, 228n, 229n, 231n, 232n, 233n, 234n, 240–3, 247–8, 250–3, 257n, 258n, 259n, 260n; *see also* ᶜAdil Shahi sultanate
Brahmins, 39, 42–3, 55, 65n, 71–2, 118, 156, 183n, 184n, 200, 211, 222, 228n, 230n, 246
  in sultanate service 3, 48, 52, 79, 89, 94, 98n, 151–2, 154–5, 158, 160, 184n, 210, 237, 239
Brajbhasha, 74, 246–7
Burhan Nizam Shah I (Nizam al-Mulk, r. 1510–53), 68, 75, 82–3, 86–7, 98n, 117, 121–3, 149, 210
Burhan Nizam Shah II (r. 1591–5), 88, 92, 125, 130, 138, 146n, 147n, 204, 258n, 259n
Burhan Nizam Shah III (r. 1610–31), 205–6, 228n

Chand Bibi (d. 1600), 6, 70, 96n, 123, 128–9, 131, 145n, 146n, 163, 204–5

Chaul, 90, 92, 216
Chishtis, 49–50, 64n, 70, 98n; *see also* Sufis
Cholas, 35–6, 55

Dakhani (language), 3, 4, 15–16, 33, 50, 71, 73–4, 79, 94, 97n, 98n, 99n, 100n, 101n, 149, 151–2, 155–6, 161, 163–4, 176, 179–81, 184n, 187n, 237, 255–6, 260n
Darya ᶜImad Shah (r. 1530–61), 82–3, 93, 122
Daulatabad, 46, 49–50, 56, 70, 86, 95n, 112, 153, 206–7, 209–13, 222, 228n, 229n, 231n; *see also* Devgiri
Deccan
  plateau, 1, 26–9, 35, 37, 39–40, 53–4, 65n, 66, 68, 93, 100n, 149–50, 167, 181, 192, 194, 238, 256
  sultanates, 2–4, 6–7, 9, 14–18, 26, 28, 30–2, 34, 47, 52, 56, 66–70, 74, 78–87, 89–91, 93–4, 100n, 106, 113, 119, 126–7, 129, 132–3, 135, 139, 149–50, 180–1, 192–4, 199, 203, 214–15, 218, 223, 227n, 236–43, 247–8, 253–6, 257n, 258n
Deccanis, 3, 17, 29, 46, 51, 66–8, 70–80, 89, 106, 111–13, 117, 135–6, 146n, 151, 158, 163, 175, 180, 204–6, 209, 218, 236–8, 240, 242, 249–50, 252
Delhi
  city, 24n, 45–6, 49, 73, 89–90, 99n, 167, 252
  sultanate, 32, 34, 44–7, 51–2, 56, 70, 82, 107–8, 110, 140n, 153, 200, 231n, 239, 257n
Desh, 44–5
Devgiri, 44–6, 156, 161, 212–13, 220–2, 230n; *see also* Daulatabad
devotionalism, 25n, 40, 72, 94, 164, 210, 234n; *see also* Bhakti
dharma, 38, 81, 201, 211–12, 221, 230n
Dwarasamudra, 45, 55, 156

early modern, 2–3, 9–10, 12–14, 17–18, 21n, 23n, 24n, 31, 113, 137–8, 139n, 167, 170, 236, 239–44, 247–8, 252–3, 256, 258n

Index

Eastern Chalukyas of Vengi, 35–7, 47, 224n
Eknath, 42, 210, 234n
Ellichpur, 5, 14, 56, 68, 131–2, 182n, 204
Ethiopians (ḥabshī, ḥabashī), 3, 16, 72–3, 75–6, 89, 94, 98n, 99n, 112–13, 117, 135–6, 146n, 156, 205, 208–9, 218

Fath Khan (ᶜAziz Malik), 73, 205–7, 209, 216–17
Fathullah ᶜImad al-Mulk (d. 1510), 67–8
Fayzi (Abu al-Fayz), 88, 92, 125
Foreigners, 3, 6, 16–17, 29, 33, 48, 50–1, 67–8, 70, 72–80, 89–90, 94, 97n, 98n, 99n, 106–39, 148n, 151, 155–9, 163, 175–80, 204–5, 218–19, 227n, 236–8

Gajapatis of Orissa, 47, 51, 55, 153, 194, 201
Gisu Daraz *see* Muhammad Husayni
Goa, 68, 90–2, 115–16, 121, 139
Gogi, 100n, 162
Golkonda
  fort, 56, 67, 153, 162, 217
  sultanate, 2, 6, 14, 16, 18, 28, 31, 58n, 66, 69–70, 79, 81–5, 89, 99n, 102n, 115–16, 120, 122–3, 126–9, 133–4, 138, 150–8, 162–3, 179–82, 183n, 186n, 192–203, 206, 208, 214–19, 221, 223, 232n, 233n, 239–42, 247–8, 252–3, 257n, 259n, 260n ; *see also* Qutb Shahi sultanate
Gujarat, 25n, 32, 35, 91, 109, 174, 214, 228n, 241, 255, 258n
  sultanate, 33, 68, 80, 85–8, 90, 93, 120, 122
Gulbarga, 45, 47, 49–50, 55–6, 82, 127, 153, 163–4, 172, 186n

ḥabshī *see* Ethiopians
Hindus, 4, 6–7, 48, 51–2, 60n, 79–81, 90, 93, 102n, 111, 142n, 146n, 159–61, 164, 175, 179–80, 186n, 197, 200, 205, 209–10, 212, 214, 230n, 252, 255, 259n
Hindustan, 110, 135, 142n, 177, 220, 251–2, 259n; *see also* north India

Hoysalas, 35–7, 40–1, 44–6, 52, 55, 62n, 63n, 156, 163
Husayn Nizam Shah I (r. 1553–65), 82, 96n, 104n, 122, 125, 127, 145n
Husayn Nizam Shah II (r. 1588–9), 76, 163, 204, 226n
Husayn Nizam Shah III (r. 1631–3), 206–9
Hyderabad, 1, 5–6, 77–8, 92, 148n, 150–1, 153–4, 167, 179, 199, 217, 231n, 232n, 233n, 247, 251

Ibrahim ᶜAdil Shah I (r. 1534–58), 31, 82–3, 96n, 155–6, 158–60, 162–3, 184n, 187n
Ibrahim ᶜAdil Shah II (r. 1580–1627), 74, 88–91, 97n, 99n–100, 120, 125, 146n, 155, 157, 162–81, 185n, 186n, 188n, 189n, 192, 204–5, 224n, 231n, 253, 255–6, 259n, 260n
Ibrahim Nizam Shah (r. 1595), 204
Ibrahim Qutb Shah (r. 1550–80), 31–2, 58n, 69, 82, 84, 114, 126–9, 133–4, 150–2, 161–2, 182n, 189n, 194–200, 224n
ᶜId-i Nauras, 169–75, 181
ᶜImad Shahi dynasty, 2, 69, 98n, 130, 185n, 236; *see also* Berar
Indian Ocean, 13, 90, 107, 137, 258n
iqṭāᶜ, 31, 46, 58n, 115, 177; *see also jāgīr*
Iran, 48, 107–10, 115–16, 118–21, 123–4, 128, 132, 134–6, 138, 140, 141n, 143n, 144n, 157, 162, 168, 186n, 237, 253–4.
Iranians, 3, 29, 92, 103n, 108–9, 116–18, 124, 134–5, 137–8, 165, 175, 215, 247; *see also* Foreigners
Iraq, 122, 176, 253
Isfahan, 116, 126, 133–5, 183n
Ismaᶜil Adil Khan (r. 1510–34), 68, 87, 96n, 97n, 117, 121, 136, 155, 157–8, 162
Ismaᶜilis, 121–4, 142n, 144n
Ismaᶜil Nizam Shah (1589–91), 76, 204

jagat-guru, 174–5, 256
jāgīr, 50, 58n, 67, 82, 115, 131, 195, 197, 199, 207–9, 217–20, 222, 229n, 233n, 234n, 241–2

295

Jahangir (Mughal), 192, 224n, 227n, 231n, 258n
Jains, 42, 174
Jamshid Qutb Shah (r. 1543–40), 126, 128, 152
jihād, 79, 81
Junnar, 115, 207, 228n, 229n

Kakatiyas, 18, 32, 35–41, 44, 46, 51, 60n, 63n, 152–3, 155, 168, 180, 183n, 194, 199, 202, 238
Kalimullah Bahmani (d. 1538), 68, 158, 185n
Kalyani, 37, 50, 55, 82, 157, 174, 218
Kannada, 2, 4, 29–30, 33, 35–6, 39–41, 48, 53, 55–6, 61n, 85, 94, 99n, 155–6, 158, 180, 184n, 222, 237
Karnatak, 28, 35–6, 40, 51, 55–6, 65n, 69, 84–5, 123, 128–30, 178, 217–19, 223, 233n, 243
Karnataka (state), 1, 2, 4, 85
Khaljis, 44–8, 60n, 70, 73
Khandesh, 5, 31, 59n, 85–6, 103n, 122, 130–1, 204
Khan Jahan Lodi, 206, 209, 227n, 229n
Khawwas Khan, 89, 207, 229n
Khurasan, 109, 123, 125, 172, 176, 253
khuṭba, 23n, 87, 95n, 214, 241–2, 247–8, 250, 253–5, 260n
Khwaja Banda Nawaz *see* Muhammad Husayni
Kishwar Khan Lari, 116, 118, 127–8, 146n
Kitāb-i Nauras, 125, 164–5, 174, 176, 178, 180, 190n
Kondavidu, 51, 196–8, 200–1
Konkan, 44, 51–2, 54–7, 62n, 65n, 67, 115, 128, 207, 216, 219, 228n
Krishnadevaraya, 43, 68, 82, 168–9, 201–2
Krishna River, 6, 28, 30–2, 34–5, 46–7, 51, 53, 55, 58n, 65n, 66, 82–3, 97n, 194, 196, 198–201, 216, 218, 224n

Lakhoji Jadhav Rao 206, 209, 211–13, 220, 227n, 229n

Mahanavami, 171–2, 175
Mahanubhava, 40–2

Maharashtra, 1, 2–5, 16, 18, 19n, 20n, 40–2, 57n, 61n, 65n, 67–8, 71, 89, 98n, 101n, 115, 131, 133, 138, 184n, 193, 205–6, 209–14, 217, 219–24, 228n, 229n, 234n, 235n, 238, 240
Mahdawis, 118, 122, 144n
Mahmud Gawan Gilani, 67, 95n, 115–16, 119, 133–4
Makhduma-i Jahan, 163, 186n, 188n
Malabar, 28, 44, 90, 92–3, 109
Malik Ambar, 5–6, 70, 72–3, 90, 97n, 131, 138, 166, 192, 205–6, 208–9, 213, 215, 217, 226n, 227n, 228n, 233n
Malik Hasan Bahri Nizam al-Mulk (Malik Nā'ib), 51, 67, 71–3, 98n, 115, 209, 229n
Malik Qummi, 125, 138, 176, 190n
Maloji Bhonsle, 72, 211–13, 223, 229n, 230n
Malwa, 32, 51, 59n, 68, 87, 131, 255
manṣab, 131, 177, 206–7, 216, 227n
Marathas, 3–4, 15–16, 18, 32, 64n, 90, 94, 101n, 138, 156, 203, 205–11, 213–14, 219–23, 227n, 230n, 235n, 239–40, 243, 250
Marathi, 2–4, 16–17, 29, 33, 35, 39–42, 48, 53–6, 57n, 65n, 94, 97n, 99n–100, 154–6, 158–9, 175–6, 179–80, 183n, 184n, 190n, 209–11, 213, 222–3, 234n, 237, 239, 252, 260n
marriage, 48, 50, 64n, 65n, 68, 83, 86, 90, 96n, 104n, 123–5, 133–4, 144n, 145n, 147n, 148n, 163, 205, 211–12, 218, 229n, 231n, 233n, 240–1, 257n
Mecca, 71, 123, 127, 154
migration, 3, 12, 35, 44, 46, 48–9, 66, 70, 73, 77, 80, 101n, 107–11, 113, 118–21, 125, 135–9, 140, 143n, 157, 162, 168, 176, 186n, 236
mīr jumla, 77, 114–15, 123, 126, 129, 133, 215
Mir Jumla *see* Muhammad Sa'id Ardistani
Mir Shah Mir Isfahan, 115–16, 133–5, 138, 142n, 145n, 147n
mlećcha, 98n, 211, 230n; *see also yāvana*
Mongols, 11, 23n, 108, 140, 200, 244
Mughal empire, 3–4, 6–7, 11, 13–17, 29, 31, 58n, 59n, 70, 77–8, 80, 87–93,

Index

109, 129–32, 136, 140, 146n, 147n, 170, 176, 184n, 192, 195, 199–200, 204–11, 213–20, 222, 224n, 225n, 227n, 228n, 229n, 231n, 232n, 233n, 234n, 235n, 236, 238–42, 245–55, 257n, 258n, 259n, 260n
Muhammad (Prophet), 77, 114, 123, 176, 178, 244–5, 251
Muhammad ᶜAdil Shah (r. 1627–56), 31, 89, 125, 155, 188n, 192, 211, 214–19, 231n, 247–51, 253
Muhammad Husayni, Khwaja Banda Nawaz Gisu Daraz, 49, 70, 73, 97n, 163, 172
Muhammad Quli Qutb Shah (r. 1580–1611), 6, 74, 77–9, 89, 92, 102n, 116, 133–4, 145n, 147n, 151–3, 163, 167, 179, 182n, 195, 197–200, 216
Muhammad Saᶜid Ardistani (Mir Jumla), 115, 119–20, 143n, 198, 215–20, 223, 232n, 233n, 241–2
Murari Brahmin, 89, 207–8, 229n
Murtaza Nizam Shah I (r. 1565–88), 69–70, 75–6, 96n, 123, 125, 129–30, 146n, 185n, 204
Murtaza Nizam Shah II (r. 1600–10), 205
Murtaza Nizam Shah III (r. 1633–6), 208–9, 229n
music, 161, 164–5, 171–4, 178, 187n
Mustafa Khan Ardistani, 116, 118, 123, 126–30, 132, 139, 145n, 146n

Narmada River, 28, 32, 59n, 237, 252
nauras, 163–6, 190n
Nauraspur, 165–75, 181, 205
nāyaka, 4, 38–9, 47–8, 51–2, 181, 196, 198, 200, 202
nāyakwāṛī, 3, 128, 146n, 151–3, 155, 197–8
Niᶜmatullahis, 50, 145n; *see also* Sufis
Nizam Shah, 2, 5, 15–16, 31, 51, 70–1, 84, 89, 95n, 97n, 98n, 99n, 101n, 122, 125, 130, 192–3, 195–6, 203–14, 216–17, 219–23, 226n, 227n, 229n, 230n, 231n, 236, 238, 247, 254, 258n; *see also* Ahmadnagar

north India, 1–4, 9, 11, 13–15, 24n, 32, 42, 46, 49, 59n, 60n, 64n, 70, 73–4, 86, 94, 100n, 109–11, 135, 195, 236, 239, 252; *see also* Hindustan
Nujūm al-ᶜUlūm, 161, 164, 175, 178, 180

Ottomans, 11, 13–14, 21n, 23n, 24n, 31, 71, 161, 244–5, 260n

Pandyas, 26, 35–6, 42, 45, 62n
Penukonda, 196–8, 201
Persian, 3–4, 15–16, 25n, 33, 48, 50, 66, 72, 74, 79, 107–12, 114, 118–19, 137, 139, 141n, 151, 154–5, 157–61, 163–4, 175–81, 182n, 184n, 190n, 210, 222, 237, 246–7, 251, 255–6, 258n
  historiography, 5, 66, 72, 79, 92–3, 97n, 149–51, 154, 190–1n, 200, 225n, 232n, 234n, 259n
Persianate, 63n, 79, 107–8, 110, 117, 119, 139, 155, 163, 168, 175–80, 244, 247, 255–6
peshwa, 114–15, 123, 128–30; *see also wakīl*
Portuguese, 13, 28, 54, 57n, 65n, 68, 80, 90–3, 96n, 209
Pune, 1, 206–9, 234n

Qadiris, 49, 51, 162; *see also* Sufis
Qaraqoyunlu, 71, 108, 110
Qutb Shahi sultanate, 2, 5–6, 18, 19n, 47, 67, 71, 78, 84, 108, 116, 134, 150–5, 157, 162, 179–81, 182n, 192, 194–201, 211, 216–17, 223, 224n, 236, 238, 240, 251–2; *see also* Golkonda

Raichur *doāb*, 35–6, 48, 52–3, 68, 82, 127, 145n
Rajputs, 90, 101n, 142n, 222, 235n, 241, 246–7
Rama Raya, 69, 82–3, 152, 169, 181, 196, 213, 224n
Rayalaseema, 35, 55–6, 69, 193–4, 196–202, 216, 223, 226n
Ray Rao Brahmin, 69, 197, 200

Safavids, 11, 13–14, 17, 24n, 31, 71, 92, 109, 118, 121–3, 125, 128, 140, 161–2, 167, 183n, 186n, 190–1n, 214, 245, 253–5, 259n, 260n
ṣāḥib-qirān, 175–6, 245, 251–2, 259n
Sahyadri Mountains, 1, 51, 54, 59n, 65n, 93
Saivism, 42, 164, 174, 221
Sanskrit, 16, 26, 38–44, 61n, 62n, 142n, 152, 161, 164–5, 174, 182, 210, 212, 222, 226n, 237, 247, 256
sayyid, 76–7, 92, 114, 123, 127, 133–4, 142n, 147n, 155
Sayyid Murtaza Sabziwari, 29, 115, 129–33, 146n
Shah ʿAbbas I (Safavid), 71, 92, 167, 183n, 186n, 253–4
Shahaji Bhonsle, 70, 72, 102n, 193, 206–9, 211–13, 217–20, 228n, 229n, 233n, 247
Shah Ismaʿil I (Safavid), 121, 144n, 253–4
Shah Jahan (Mughal), 31, 170, 192, 206–8, 214, 216, 218, 224n, 227n, 231n, 232n, 240, 242, 247–53, 259n
Shah Nawaz Khan (Khwaja Saʿd al-Din, ʿInayatullah Shirazi), 165–6, 176–7
Shah Tahir Husayni, 87, 114, 117, 121–4, 144n, 145n
Shiite, 75, 95n, 109, 114, 117, 121–2, 144n, 155, 159, 161–3, 165, 172, 175–80, 185n, 245, 252, 259n, 260n
Shivaji Bhonsle, 16, 208, 211–12, 217–24, 230n, 234n, 243
Sholapur, 82–3, 95n, 96n, 205, 207
Sikandar ʿAdil Shah (r. 1672–86), 155
Solomon (Biblical king), 175, 196, 249–50, 259n
Subhan Quli Qutb Shah (r. 1550), 126, 128
Sufis, 16, 46, 49–50, 51, 63n, 70–4, 97n, 98n, 108, 122, 145n, 155, 159, 161–5, 172, 174–5, 180, 186n, 213–14, 237, 244–5, 257n, 258n; see also Chishtis, Qadiris, Niʿmatullahis
Sultan Muhammad Qutb Shah (r. 1612–26), 192, 233n, 241
Sultan Quli Qutb al-Mulk (d. 1543), 68, 108, 116, 183n, 185n, 196, 251–3

Sunni, 75, 115, 117, 121–2, 144n, 155–6, 162–3, 175, 178–80, 186n, 214, 253, 260n

Talikota (Battle, 1565), 69, 81–5, 91, 126–7, 157, 159, 171, 181, 185n, 194, 196, 200–2, 215, 232n
Tamil
  language, 17, 39–40, 42, 222
  region, 27–8, 35–6, 42, 62n, 63n, 101n, 200
Telangana, 18, 35–9, 46, 48, 51–2, 55–6, 65n, 68, 96n, 102n, 150–6, 168, 180–1, 182n, 183n, 194–9, 201–2, 211, 215, 218, 223, 224n, 226n, 238, 252
  state, 1–2, 4, 19, 199
Telugu, 1–5, 17–18, 29–30, 33, 39–41, 43, 48, 51–3, 55–6, 59n, 61n, 62n, 85, 94, 99n, 142n, 150–2, 154–6, 161, 179–81, 182n, 183n, 193–4, 197, 199, 201–2, 216, 222–3, 226n, 237–8
Timur (Tamerlane), 49, 70, 108–9, 239, 244–5, 252
trade, 4, 10, 36–7, 50, 52, 54, 77–8, 91, 93, 107–10, 116, 119–20, 124, 136–9, 215–16, 236, 258n
Tughluqs, 45–50, 52, 70, 73, 95n
Tungabhadra River, 28, 30, 35, 53, 55, 65n, 85
Turkish (language), 48, 157–8
Turkmans, 71, 112, 114, 141n
Turks, 58n, 90, 107, 114, 118, 136, 142n, 153, 157

ulama, 46, 50, 121

Varanasi, 42, 184n, 210
Venkata (Venkatapati) II, 195, 198–9, 201–2, 226n
vernacular, 3–4, 13, 15, 18, 38–44, 50, 53–6, 57n, 58n, 74, 94, 149–50, 154–8, 162–3, 180–2, 192, 199, 210, 214, 221–3, 225n, 237–9, 247, 255–6
Vijayanagara
  city, 55, 69, 85, 142n, 165, 168, 171–2, 196, 214

Index

empire, 3–4, 6, 15, 17–18, 28, 30–2, 37, 47–8, 51–2, 55, 57n, 63n, 64n, 68–9, 71, 79–85, 87–8, 90–1, 93–4, 114, 126–8, 139n, 149, 151–2, 156–7, 161, 163, 165, 168–9, 171, 174–5, 180–1, 194–202, 213, 215, 217, 222–3, 224n, 225n, 226n, 234n, 236, 238–40, 246, 255
Vindhya Mountains, 28, 32, 59n

wakīl, 76, 98n, 114, 116, 123, 127, 129–30, 143n, 207; *see also peshwa*
Warangal 32, 44–5, 47, 51, 95n, 153–4, 156, 180

Western Chalukyas, 18, 32, 34–9, 46, 50, 55, 62n, 82, 157–9, 161, 163, 174–5, 180–1, 187n, 238
Westerners, 111–12; *see also* Foreigners
Western Ghats *see* Sahyadri Mountains

Yadavas, 32, 35–7, 40–1, 44–6, 55, 60n, 156, 161, 163, 210, 212–13, 222
yāvana, 98n, 212, 230n; *see also mleććha*
Yusuf ᶜAdil Khan (d. 1510), 67–8, 75, 91, 95n, 102n, 108–9, 140, 155, 157, 162, 184n

Zuhuri, Maulana Nur al-Din, 124–5, 138, 166, 176, 187n, 255

EU representative:
Easy Access System Europe
Mustamäe tee 50, 10621 Tallinn, Estonia
Gpsr.requests@easproject.com

www.ingramcontent.com/pod-product-compliance
Lightning Source LLC
Chambersburg PA
CBHW071828230426
43672CB00013B/2791